IN ASSOCIATION WITH THE ALPINE CLUB

Volume 98 No 342
THE ALPINE JOURNAL 1993

Address all editorial communications directly to the Hon Editor:
Mrs J Merz, 14 Whitefield Close, Putney, London SW15 3SS

Address all sales and distribution communications to:
Cordee, 3a De Montfort Street, Leicester LE1 7HD

Back numbers:
apply to the Alpine Club, 55 Charlotte Road, EC2A 3QT

or, for 1969 to date, apply to Cordee, as above.

First published in 1993 by the Ernest Press in association with
the Alpine Club, 55 Charlotte Road, EC2A 3QT

Photoset by Parker Typesetting Service, Leicester
Printed and bound in Great Britain by St Edmundsbury Press

A CIP catalogue record for this book is
available from the British Library

ISBN 0 948153 27 X

THE
ALPINE JOURNAL

1993

1. The Everest massif from Thyangboche meadows.
   (*Malcolm Rutherford*) (p170)

THE
ALPINE JOURNAL

1993

**Incorporating the Journal of the Ladies'
Alpine Club & Alpine Climbing**

A record of mountain adventure and scientific observation

Volume 98 No 342

Edited by Johanna Merz

Assistant Editors:
Roy Ruddle and Geoffrey Templeman

THE ERNEST PRESS

in association with

THE ALPINE CLUB, LONDON

Acknowledgements

I am indebted to the members of the 1953 Everest expedition, who have all generously contributed to this 40th anniversary volume.

In particular, I should like to thank the following: Joy Hunt for permission to publish the letters John wrote to her throughout the expedition; Edmund Hillary and George Lowe for their contribution of previously unpublished letters written from Base Camp; Charles Evans for permission to reproduce drawings from his book *Eye on Everest*; Alfred Gregory for contributing a set of superb Everest photographs; and Charles Wylie for a drawing of Tenzing made in 1953 by Lt Col Gordon Borrowman of the 4th Gurkha Rifles.

My warmest thanks go to Bill Norton, second son of Lt Gen E F Norton, who, with his mother the late Mrs Joyce Norton, arranged for his father's sketches to be photographed and kindly allowed them to be reproduced.

I am grateful to several non-members of the Alpine Club and to the many regular contributors worldwide who, every year, help to make the *Alpine Journal* a comprehensive mountain year-book. My special thanks go to my two hardworking Assistant Editors, Roy Ruddle and Geoffrey Templeman, and to Michael Ward, Lindsay Griffin, Roger Payne and Frank Solari for valuable assistance.

Finally, I thank all the members of the Alpine Club who have enthusiastically contributed to this 98th volume of the *Alpine Journal*.

Johanna Merz

Contents

Contributions from:
*H Adams Carter, Adrian Dragos Defta, Evelio Echevarría,
Lindsay Griffin, Harish Kapadia, Paul Nunn, Józef Nyka,
Bill O'Connor, Doug Scott, David Sharman, Ted Whalley and
Andrew Wielochowski.*

MAPS, TOPOS AND LINE DRAWINGS

Maps 1–5, 7, 10–12 and Topos 3–5
redrawn by Ted Hatch

Illustrations

TONY STREATHER
Valedictory Address

Read before the Alpine Club on 4 December 1992

There have been many changes to the Club during the last few years – the most radical, of course, being our move from South Audley Street. I intend to use this as an excuse to break with tradition and change the format of my talk this evening. I have read through all the Valedictory Addresses of the Presidents since I became a member – all, that is, except that of Eric Shipton who wisely declined to give one and instead spoke of some of his exploratory journeys in the Karakoram and Sinkiang. Many were extremely intellectual, for we have had some very learned Presidents; others were witty and a few were rather pompous and boring. Howard Somervell, in 1965, got it right when he said: 'Once every three years the members of the Alpine Club are condemned to listen to a lecture without pictures, without adventure, without excitement, the apparent function of which is to enable the Club to feel what an old bore the retiring President is and thereby to welcome all the more warmly his probably more exciting successor.' At the end of his address, Howard Somervell said: 'We want more members, especially from the younger generation of mountaineers, the ones who are really doing the stuff that counts.' Claude Elliott had said virtually the same thing in 1953. He quoted John Farrar, from back in 1919, who said: 'We have great traditions, a great past – look to it that we also have a great future and that you cannot have if our candidates are already men of mature age.' Things don't change all that much, do they? I am certainly not capable of giving an intellectual address, nor do I believe you would welcome one. What I intend to do is reminisce a little, say something of the last three years, and then take cover behind some slides and talk about two particular expeditions.

I well remember the time when I joined the Alpine Club. The circumstances were rather unusual, particularly by today's climbing standards. I had just returned home after six years in India and Pakistan. This was at the end of 1950. I had gone out there towards the end of the war to join the Indian Army and had stayed on in Pakistan after Partition. During most of the time that I was on the sub-continent I had lived and served among the mountains of the North West Frontier while being seconded from the Army to the Scouts, the Irregular Forces that policed the tribal territories. My daily duties took me walking or riding through the valleys and over the mountain passes along the border with Afghanistan, in some places separated from Russia only by the narrow strip of the Wakhan Corridor. I suppose that it could just be said, with a little stretch of the imagination, that I was one of the last to be playing the Great Game. It was a grand life for a young officer. I was very lucky.

In those days, when we went on leave from the Scouts, we invariably headed for Kashmir. A fellow officer and I went in the summer of 1947. After the first week or so on a houseboat on one of the lakes and generally living it up in Srinagar, we collected together our caravan – a sirdar, pack ponies and a cook – and set off north to see something of the country. A few days' hard walking and we were at the top of the Tragbal Pass just as the sun came up. We were rewarded by the most incredible sight: just in front of us, looking as though we could almost touch it, was the whole of the SE face of Nanga Parbat. This sight made an enormous impact on me and, without my realising it at the time, could well have been the start of my mountaineering career. When, three years later, I was serving in Chitral and a Norwegian party came out to attempt Tirich Mir, I remembered my first sight of that other great mountain and had no hesitation in trying to work my way onto the team in one capacity or another. I could speak the local language and knew the country well, so I offered to be their Transport Officer.

One thing led to another. One of the climbers was taken ill with what was thought at the time to be pneumonia but which today would have been recognised as pulmonary oedema. This bad luck for him was good luck for me and gave me the chance to join the summit team. And so my first peak became 25,264ft Tirich Mir. I had no idea at the time that I had become the first Englishman to reach the summit of a 25,000ft peak since Odell and Tilman were on Nanda Devi in 1936, fourteen years earlier.

I thought no more about this until I got home from Pakistan a few months later and received a letter from a Colonel Tobin inviting me to visit him at the Alpine Club. He thought I might like to become a member. He would be happy to propose me and I would be seconded by a Dr Longstaff. I said all the wrong things and asked all the wrong questions. What social facilities did the Club offer? I had never heard of the Alpine Club and rather assumed it was an ordinary London club of those times where I would be able to stay when I visited London and where I could entertain my friends! This would be most useful for a keen young officer just starting on his career in the British Army! I had no idea of the honour that was being extended to me nor what a privilege it was that Dr Tom Longstaff, who was the retiring President, should himself be interested in me. I learned later of his long connection with the parts of the world where I had been serving and of his distinguished mountaineering career. He was extremely kind to me and advised me on how to complete my application form. One peak was hardly enough, even though it was a pretty high one. What else had I done so that we could make the form look a little better? We settled, in the end, on several years of scrambling in Baluchistan, Waziristan, Gilgit, Chitral and Kashmir, all areas he knew well. That seemed to be enough for the then Committee and I was elected just 42 years ago.

My introductory remarks have dwelt on the past and this is intentional because the theme of my talk this evening is to be the many changes that have taken place in the general field of mountaineering, as well as within our Club, during the period of my membership. At the same time, I have to admit to a weakness for nostalgia; I am afraid there may be more of it to come.

When you did me the honour of inviting me to become your President my immediate reaction was that I was much too old and that we should find someone younger. This feeling was prompted by my clear memory of the time when I was first invited to address the Club. It was after the American K2 expedition of 1953 and I was still young and impressionable. There, sitting on those leather benches down the side of the lecture hall at South Audley Street, were the great, the good and the elderly. There was a certain amount of snoring and every now and again there would be a grunt of approval or disapproval depending on what I was saying! This was enough to make any young chap wonder just what he had let himself in for and perhaps it was the image that this created that made it difficult to attract young members in those days. Anyway, I was determined that those benches should not be taken to' Charlotte Road!

Having mentioned K2, perhaps I could indulge in a little more nostalgia about how my own part in that expedition came about. The same Colonel Tobin, who had proposed me for membership of the Alpine Club, now wrote again saying that I should think about applying to join the expedition that was being planned to attempt Everest in 1953. I had, after all, proved that I could go high even if I was not much of a climber. It was arranged that I should meet Eric Shipton, who at that time was going to lead. I had in fact met him briefly before, when he passed through Peshawar on his way home from his appointment as our Consul General in Kashgar. He now kindly invited me to lunch at his home in Sussex. When I arrived he was gardening. He was combining this with training for the mountains. He had a large old rucksack which he filled with earth at the bottom of the garden and then carried up the hill to the top of the garden where he was preparing a new flower bed. It would be like him to scorn the use of a simple wheelbarrow. The upshot of this meeting was that I was asked to join four other potential members of the expedition, all of whom were experienced alpinists, for a trip to the Alps. I had only been once before on a brief skiing holiday. I thoroughly enjoyed myself but clearly did not impress the others. There may have been some slight resentment that the altitude seemed to have no effect on me whatsoever, but what really let me down was my inept fumbling when the time came to put on crampons. I had hardly used the things on Tirich Mir and this now became all too obvious. The other four were all to become members or reserves but clearly my lack of Alpine experience had disqualified me. I received a brief note from the Everest Office telling me so, but there was little time for disappointment. Almost by the same post came a letter from a Dr Houston in America inviting me to join his team to K2 as Transport Officer and then to climb with them as high as I wished or was able. I shall say more about that expedition later.

But first I must return to the more traditional part of this address and say something of the Club's activities during the past three years. The period has of course been dominated by the move to our new home but this does not mean that little else has happened. Members have continued to be as active as ever in both the Alps and the Greater Ranges and we have held successful symposia and meets in this country as well as in the Alps. We have had some great lectures. I was fortunate in being able to attend the celebrations in Zermatt of the 125th anniversary of the first ascent of the Matterhorn and, in Chamonix, the 40th anniversary celebrations of the first ascent of Annapurna. All these occasions have kept me in touch with the mountains during my time in office, but my first two years were dominated by the move and I had little peace from the problems this created. I lost quite a few nights' sleep pondering over the decisions that had to be taken at that time. I hope that, in the long term, they will turn out to have been the right ones.

The saga of the move has been well recorded by the previous President, George Band, in his article 'Premises! Premises!' in this year's *Alpine Journal*. I do not intend to go through the story again but I do want to emphasise a few points. First, we must all acknowledge what a debt of gratitude we owe to Emlyn Jones for securing our future, back in 1956, by negotiating such a brilliant deal for the extension of the lease at South Audley Street. Nobody then could have appreciated that this would eventually enable us to buy our first freehold property. Both Emlyn Jones and Sir Alan Pullinger did stirling work negotiating and preparing for our possible move to Exhibition Road; but circumstances changed. George Band had hoped to be able to hand over to me having first completed a firm contract for our new premises. When this did not prove possible he generously agreed to head an Alternative Premises Working Party. He and his hard-working colleagues were responsible for finding 55 Charlotte Road and for preparing it for our occupation. Only when all was ready did they hand over to the new House Committee. There is much for which we have to be grateful to George Band.

During this whole period, finance was a major preoccupation and we were fortunate that the Earl of Limerick agreed to chair a newly formed Finance Sub-Committee to co-ordinate and oversee all the various financial matters of the Club. These needed very careful and strict management if we were to have a sound future, and an appeal was launched to raise capital for the Library. Members responded most generously and the Library will now be able to pay a fair rent to the Club for their part of the building.

There was a mass of work to be done in connection with the move and our temporary stay at the Ski Club. The library and our other possessions had to be moved twice, first into store or to the Ski Club and then to our new home. Gangs of willing volunteers, under the able supervision of the indefatigable Bob Lawford, made this possible, while our hard-working Honorary Secretary, Michael Esten, attempted to keep some sort of order in the day-to-day running of the Club. There are too many people to thank them all personally for their help during this turbulent period and, if I tried, I would almost certainly miss some deserving person out; but our thanks go to them all. Here we are well established in our secure new base. We have room to expand and I look forward to the day when we can afford to have a caretaker's flat and some form of bunk accommodation. A comfortable Reading Room on the top floor, where we would also be able to display more of our pictures and other possessions, is perhaps a pipe-dream – but I hope not!

The President now showed slides of two expeditions: the Third American Karakoram expedition (1953) to K2 and the British Kangchenjunga expedition of 1955. The President said that he had always considered himself lucky to have been a member of these. Both were successful classics in their own way and, because of changing times, there could be nothing like them again. While showing the slides, the President made the following comments:

In 1950, when he was on Tirich Mir with the Norwegians, there had been very few other parties in the whole of the Hindu Kush, the Karakoram and the Himalaya except for the French on Annapurna, Houston and Tilman on the south side of Everest and perhaps one or two others. By contrast, the Services expedition to Everest in spring 1992 had found that they were one of 13 parties at Base Camp and that there was a total of 375 people there! This kind of situation must create all sorts of problems and can certainly do no good to the environment.

While talking about K2 the President mentioned that their leader in 1953, Dr Charles Houston, had led the attempt in 1938 when a route on the Abruzzi Ridge had been established. The key to this route was a chimney in a large rock buttress at about 23,000ft. Bill House had led this and it had been known as House's Chimney ever since. The team had not been using oxygen and when the summit had seemed to be within their grasp they had accepted that they were too exhausted to go on and had had the good sense to turn back. There had been criticism at the time that they had not pushed on hard enough, but they had lived to try again. This had not been the case the following year, 1939, when Wiessner, the leader of an American team, had indeed pushed hard for the summit. One of the team and three Sherpas who tried to rescue him had died. Similarly, in 1986, in the final dash for the summit by various groups, though seven had reached it, only two had survived. In 1953 the Houston party, of which the President was a member, had been stuck by storm in their high camp for several days when Art Gilkey had become seriously ill. In an attempt to carry him down, there had been a dramatic fall when five of the party had been held by a brilliant belay by Pete Schoening. Gilkey, who by now was barely conscious, had been swept away in an avalanche but the rest of the team eventually reached Base Camp and were all still alive and active in the mountains. The President had attended a reunion in Colorado only a few weeks previously. He considered that their survival had been largely due to the fact that they were a very close team.

The President went on to talk about the Kangchenjunga expedition and spoke of the unassuming but brilliant leadership of Dr Charles Evans. Charles had remained in support at the high camp, with sirdar Dawa Tenzing, during both summit bids, foregoing the opportunity of being in a summit party himself. He had, of course, also just missed being the first to the summit of Everest with Tom Bourdillon, when they had reached the South Summit, only a few hundred feet from the top, but were brave enough to turn back when they were doubtful that their oxygen would last out and Charles was having trouble with his set. To have gone on could have led to disaster but by turning back they made ultimate success possible for the team as a whole.

The President emphasised that the members of both the K2 and Kangchen-junga expeditions were all still close friends, as indeed were the surviving members of the Everest 1953 expedition, and that these enduring friendships illustrated the primary object of the Club: 'the promotion of good fellowship among mountaineers'.

The President then continued his Address:

I would now like to make just a few final remarks and leave you with some thoughts for the future. When George Band handed over to me, he mentioned Mike Baker's 1989 Report and hoped that due consideration would be given to its recommendations, especially with regard to membership. I am glad to report that, thanks largely to the efforts of our Honorary Membership Secretary Glyn Hughes, there continues to be a very healthy increase in our membership. Many of our new members are, to quote Somervell again, 'from the younger generation of mountaineers, the ones who are really doing the stuff that counts'. Perhaps we have now managed to shed the reputation for being exclusive in a bad sense that tended to stick to us at 74 South Audley Street. I hope that we can claim that our membership does truly represent the best in British mountaineering today, so that we can continue our leading role in exerting an influence for good on the sport of mountaineering.

Two points that particularly concern me about the future arise from remarks that I made when I was talking about my expeditions. Firstly, what can be done to control the ever increasing numbers that are flocking to the mountains – often, sadly, with no regard whatever to their impact on the environment? We have produced a policy statement about this and we must keep it well in mind in the coming years. My second concern is the modern trend, when climbing, to force on to the summit at all costs. The history of K2 over the years is well imprinted on my mind. The Yorkshire Ramblers kindly invited me recently to their Centenary Dinner. In their brochure was a quotation from an address given to them in 1904 by a distinguished past President of theirs and Vice-President of ours, Cecil Slingsby. He said: 'On the mountains, or in the potholes and caves, let prudent thought and remembrance of those left at home govern your daring. It is always hard to turn back, but if ever to go forward is to court an unjustifiable danger, show that moral courage which is greater than physical.' I hope that this advice might be heeded.

Finally I want to thank all those who have helped and supported me during the past three years – sometimes during difficult periods. I am sure you will give my successor, Michael Westmacott, the same support. I wish him the best of luck. I am confident that the Club is in good hands and will continue to flourish. In the years to come, when I retire to the country, I shall look forward to my visits to the Club in London, when I shall hope to be able to stay in the Bunk House and entertain my friends in the Reading Room!

Everest 1953:
Forty Years On

WALT UNSWORTH
Everest Remembered

It is often said that everyone can remember what they were doing when they heard of the assassination of President Kennedy. Those of us who were around at the time can remember what we were doing when we heard of the ascent of Everest. Despite the best attentions of the *Daily Mail*'s ace foreign correspondent Ralph Izzard (who sadly died this year) young James Morris pulled off one of the scoops of the century in getting news of John Hunt's triumph back to *The Times*, who proudly broke it to the world. Actually the world was a little behind in the news – John's daughter Sally once told me that word was passed to the family late on the previous evening and an almighty party was soon in full swing. Only a bunch of happy Welsh farmers knew Everest had been climbed. The world had to wait till morning.

The ascent of Everest was seen as a glorious portent for the New Elizabethan Age everyone was forecasting – how innocent we all were – and certainly there was a feeling that in mountaineering terms the damned thing was out of the way at last. I don't think the idea that the big Himalayan peaks could actually become playgrounds, like their smaller Alpine counterparts, had ever occurred to anybody. The conquest – and I use the word deliberately – was really all that mattered at the time.

James Morris called it 'the last innocent adventure' and if it wasn't perhaps quite the last, the expedition was based on a tradition that was soon to wither under changing social mores.

The team had none of those little dark men who were crawling out of the Salford terraces and up the most gymnastic bits of gritstone and even my father-in-law, whose only acquaintance with mountains was pace-egg rolling on Rivington Pike, wanted to know why Joe Brown wasn't there. A lot of us did. I pointed out to Dad that Alf Gregory came from Blackpool, hoping to mollify him, but I don't think he believed me – Blackpool was not a place people came *from*. Joe's turn came shortly after on Kangchenjunga.

Apart from the nostalgia perhaps the most instructive thing we can do in looking back over 40 years is to try and assess what impact the ascent of Everest had on climbing in this country. A proper study could earn somebody an interesting PhD, but I don't think Everest *started* anything, except possibly a rash of mediocre expedition books. What it did do was give a rocket booster to a development which was already underway. There had been wartime training in mountain related activities for many men, the pre-war outdoors movement begun by the Youth Hostel Association still flourished and Jerry Wright's Mountaineering Association, begun in 1946, was very active. Although many people outside the sport still believed that climbers swarmed up ropes, and the press always referred to ice axes as ice picks, things were better than they had been. There was a glimmer of understanding amongst the public at large; even appreciation of why some men and women felt compelled to indulge in such an arduous and risky activity. The ascent of Everest acted as a catalyst, bringing the whole thing into focus. After Everest climbing was A Good Thing in the public conscious.

Above all, though, we shared a sense of pride in the team's achievement. It was a milestone the like of which few of us will ever see again. Even my father-in-law, whose basic beliefs were socialism and Manchester cotton, thought the lads had done us reet proud.

JOHN HUNT

Letters from Everest

(Plates 2–12)

These extracts from letters to my wife during the 1953 Everest expedition were written in the context of her own climbing experience, both in the Himalaya and in the Alps. During the three years which ended in May 1940 when I returned from India to rejoin my Regiment, Joy and I were stationed in Bengal, where I was serving with the Indian Police. Darjeeling was only an overnight rail journey: to Siliguri in the Bengal–Nagpur express, and thence in the little cog-driven mountain train which climbs up the steep hillsides to Ghoom, and over a ridge to Darjeeling. We took every opportunity, even during long weekends, to travel that way, and onwards into Sikkim. In those years we walked great distances over the length and breadth of that little mountain kingdom. With C R Cooke and a few of our special Sherpa friends we undertook two lightweight expeditions, to the Zemu and the Talung glaciers beneath Kangchenjunga, in the course of which Joy, with limited climbing experience, had reached 20,000ft. During the period immediately following the War, with the advantage of my posting to Allied Forces, Central Europe, at Fontainebleau, we climbed for a further three years in France and Switzerland.

So I was writing to a seasoned mountaineer and, more importantly, to someone who had travelled through the valleys and villages of the Eastern Himalaya, where we had met with Sikkimese, Lepchas, Tibetans and Sherpas. I was aware of the memories I would stir, without the need to dwell on them: the sights, the smells, the sounds, the voices and the music; the toil of plodding up and down steep mountain tracks.

And beyond all this, I remembered her amazement when first viewing one of the Himalayan giants – Kangchenjunga.

Namche Bazar 25.3.53
... The walk has been quite heavenly, specially since we came down from the final high ridge to the Dudh Kosi, which drains from the Everest massif, and turned North. This is a tremendous gorge, reminiscent of the Teesta[1] – very rugged indeed. We have followed the path up it for 3 days, getting progressively higher – here it is 12,000 feet. It has stayed fine, except for some rain two days ago and yesterday it was cloudy. But for the final walk up here the day has been glorious. We had a fine view of Everest and some fantastic nearer views of peaks the size of Siniolchum,[2] all flaked and jagged – quite unthinkably difficult. Flowers have been wonderful – the rhodies above 7,000 feet are deep or pale pink, and all the magnolias have been at their best – great, heavy white blossoms. Several mauve primulas and other flowering bushes. We have

continued the practice of starting off at 6 a.m. and stopping for breakfast about 8–8.30, usually by a stream. This has given us a chance to get cleaned up and have a dip. On one of these occasions we nearly lost Charles Evans. Ed [Hillary] and Chas[3] and I had gone to bathe in the Likhu Khola, a biggish river – Chas plunged in and was at once swept under. He hit a rock, reappeared and then went under again! However he was luckily unhurt and had not taken a mouthful, so managed to get in to the bank before we went to his rescue; it was a nasty moment!

In this Sherpa country the people are very friendly indeed and greet us as we pass their houses. The latter are strongly built stone buildings, with good timber work – very like Swiss chalets – but you will remember them at Lachen.[4] Potatoes and barley are growing at present in their small, stony and walled-in terraces. On arrival here today we found the wife of one of our Sherpas[5] on the path with a teapot of Tibetan tea – the pot decorated with coloured paper in our honour! We had to drink some tho' it was not very nice. Naturally there has been much interest in our arrival and great welcomes for the Sherpas who live here. Crowds of kids are swarming round the camp, some of them playing with kites. The village headman has been to see me, and also some Indians who are manning a frontier check point – they have a wireless which may be useful in emergency. This camp is on a col just above the village, with views both ways to high and fierce-looking peaks.

Thyangboche   29 March 1953
This is written just before we leave on the first period of acclimatization; Chas Evans' party has already gone, as they are trying out Tom B's Closed Circuit Oxygen[6] as well as the O.C. [Open Circuit] This has been an invaluable 3 days, partly restful, partly pretty busy, with instruction in wireless, oxygen, cookers (I have asked Ed to tell Reggie[7] how pleased he is with the latter), sorting out of loads, issuing of kit (everyone is both impressed and delighted with everything – the NZ pair have asked me to send you their special thanks), making up of accounts, articles for Times etc. etc. This is a simply heavenly spot – I won't repeat what has gone to the Times as you'll see it there. Yesterday we were entertained by the Lamas at the monastery. The head Lama, a very portly and impressive old man in fine red robes, looked after us. We entered the sanctuary – you will remember the Gangtok one – where I laid a scarf on the Lama's chair and on that of the Abbot of Rongbuk (+ some money!); then I presented the expedition flag. After that we sat in an upper room and had a meal, the old Abbot was very interesting about Yetis, leaving no doubt whatever in my mind about their existence.

This a.m. prayers were offered for the expedition most of the morning. 6 of us did a training scramble up to 16,000 feet, and tried out our little wireless sets with great success. We had stupendous views all round, and got our first sight of the South Col.

Training camp (circa 17,500ft)   3 Apr 1953
... Here we are 'acclimatizing' and having a thoroughly wonderful, if fairly strenuous time. George [Lowe], Greg [Alfred Gregory], Tenzing and I have

come two days' journey from Thyangboche, and are camped beside a glacier (we have named it Nuptse glacier) which springs from the foot of that great mountain wall. So far we have climbed an easy rock peak using oxygen, starting from 18,000ft and going up to 19,700. The times have averaged 50 minutes, which is a good proof of the value of the oxygen at present stage. Then yesterday we crossed our glacier and set up a light camp for just the 4 of us, at nearly 19,000ft, beneath a very attractive snow and rock peak (we have called it Chukhung peak, after the top village in the valley below). This morning we climbed it by its very steep North face, which I led. It involved a lot of step-cutting and we are all rather pleased to have done our first peak, and without undue effort. We then came down its South side back to this main camp.

Tomorrow we plan to return by crossing a col into the valley which comes down from the Khumbu glacier; this will take us 3 days and depends a little on the weather, its snowing at present.

Base camp   8 Apr 1953
... It's been a very busy 3 days, so much to arrange and think of for the future.

We are all astonishingly well and all have reached much the same standard after the first week of training – I've actually gained 5lbs!! The best sign is the fact that everyone seems pretty happy – Tom Bourdillon came up to me last evening, after we'd had supper by a camp fire, and said what a success he thought it all was.

The next big job ahead is the icefall reconnaissance, which Ed Hillary is taking on. I am moving up after his party, to see the results and take decisions on the spot. Charles [Wylie] and Greg and Tom B are clearing up here on return from their acclimatization period and will meet Jimmy Roberts[8] with the 2nd oxygen consignment. So all is fairly well in hand.

We are feeding well; yesterday had the first Ready Mix scones, which were pronounced to be excellent by all. At lunch today George Band brought me a stew made in 5 mins in one of your Pressure Cookers – and sends you his thanks!

Camp beside Imja Glacier beneath Nuptse   12 Apr 1953
This is the 3rd night spent at this camp, on the 3rd acclimatization period. We (Noyce, Ward, Bourdillon and self) are mainly trying out the Closed Circuit oxygen, and this has come through its trials quite well. We are in quite wonderful country, under the very shadow of this fantastic mountain, and across the way from the Nuptse-Lhotse ridge. Yesterday, Tom and I climbed a very nice rock peak of 19,500 feet, and this was today repeated by Mike Ward and Wilf [Noyce]. Tom and I spent today training Sherpas on steep ice and snow. My little caravan had a most interesting outing among seracs beneath a great ice ridge of 20–21,000 feet which divides us from the valley known as the Hongu away to the East. We got to rather over 21,000 feet before turning back. Ed Hillary's party has gone up to reconnoitre and prepare the Icefall, and tomorrow my party is starting on its way to join them – three days' journey. Meanwhile, Chas Evans has been training a select few of our Sherpas

in using oxygen. I gather from a scribbled note that this has been a great success. Weather has turned nasty on us, and we came up here through 3–4 inches of new snow. Yesterday was fairly nasty too, but today has been glorious again.

13/4   [13 April 1953]

We've come down to the valley (Chukhung) from our training camp, and are now half way up on the other side – in a lovely grassy alp. Tomorrow we hope to cross over to the Khumbu valley on our way to the icefall – and Everest. There is a chance of climbing a peak on the way.

When we get there, it will be the end of one important phase, and the beginning of Everest proper. I think we shall all be very ready in every sense to get on with the real thing at last.

14/4   [14 April 1953]

I'm giving this to Tom Bourdillon, who leaves me tomorrow morning to return to Thyangboche. I've come down beside the Khumbu glacier, and an easy two days' march from the foot of the icefall, after crossing our pass from the Imja valley this morning. For some reason I was going awfully badly, having had a somewhat breathless night, and had to decide to let the others climb a 20,000 feet peak from the pass. I came straight over and have rested up ever since. This was rather tantalizing, as you can imagine, but there could be no doubt I wasn't up to it. Mike has run me over with his stethoscope and given various drugs – he suspects pleurisy but thinks he's checked it. Anyway, I'm feeling much better already!

Tomorrow we go up the glacier and cross it to the foot of Pumori, where there is a frozen lake; this is to be the place where we will rest up for a few days before going up to Base Camp.

Base Camp Khumbu Glacier   21 Apr 1953

I am scribbling this to you in bed before setting out for 2 days' work in the icefall glacier. James Morris, the Times man, is sending a runner back to Kathmandu and its a chance to get letters off. This confounded pen won't write when its cold. You'll have a terrible time trying to read it. We are very nearly all assembled at Base Camp, beneath the icefall and ready for the job. It's been snowing overnight which is a nuisance as we have hundreds of coolies coming up today and tomorrow and there'll be the trouble with snow blindness. We intend to start the loads moving up on 24th, and there's still a good deal to do to make the icefall easily passable for the Sherpas. We shall know the worst by tomorrow about snags high up at the entrance to the Cwm, where there was a huge crevasse last year. So far we've bridged two or three smaller ones lower down, and have a certain amount of beams to put across others.

I am staying tonight at Camp II, half way up, after helping Wilf today, then tomorrow up to Camp III site with Ed Hillary, George Lowe and George Band. Finally, down tomorrow night to launch the Build-up period. The idea is to come right off the mountain half way through – early May – for a rest, while a reconnaissance is made of the Lhotse Face – I shall probably take part in this, so as to make the plan for the assault.

Base Camp Khumbu Glacier   23 Apr 1953
... Well, tomorrow we start the big task of lifting stores into the Cwm. I was up there yesterday, after spending a night at Camp II (half way up) and with Ed and George Band was very much relieved to find only one impassable gap before we could really say we were into the Cwm proper. Tomorrow I am going up there again with Chas Evans and Tenzing.

We have moved the necessary sections of the ladders up to Camp II today, so as to take them on with us tomorrow. Most annoyingly it is snowing hard again and all our hard work on the track will have to be repeated. It's certainly a very serious problem, this icefall, and I only wish I could feel happier about its safety.

Khumbu Glacier   28 Apr 1953
... I came down yesterday from Camp III which is now firmly established at the head of the icefall. Two days ago, Tenzing, Chas Evans, Ed Hillary and self went right up the Cwm, following a reconnaissance the previous evening, and reached the Swiss Camp IV at 22,000ft, where we are going to establish Advanced Base. It was rather a thrill to blaze the trail thus far, and to know that we were, indeed, through. There had been some doubt about getting up the icefall itself, which is exceedingly complicated and difficult – then the big question mark about entering the Cwm, where the Swiss had such trouble last year with monster crevasses – and now, unless there are big changes in the ice which produce fresh problems, we seem to be up to schedule and able to stick to the long-determined programme. The process of ferrying the loads up is well under way. I left Greg and Wilf at Camp III, in charge of moving stores up to Camp IV; others are looking after the ferry service from Base to Camp III, a two day journey. Chas Wylie and George Band are just due back from Camp III, having moved up yesterday afternoon with two Sherpa trains to Camp II. And so it is intended to continue until 2nd May, when we are to have a break of 3 days.

During this break, Chas Evans with Tom B, Chas Wylie and Mike Ward are to carry out a reconnaissance of the Lhotse Face getting as high as they can, the first pair using Tom's Closed Circuit Oxygen, the second pair the Open Circuit. As a result of this reconnaissance I shall decide on what plan to adopt, and we shall be busy between 6th and 10th May preparing for that plan. Time seems to slip away and doubtless before very long we shall be put to the real test.

Camp IV (22,000 feet)[9]   1st May 1953
Chas Evans, Tom Bourdillon and I have arrived up here at the beginning of a reconnaissance of the Lhotse Face. I am spending tomorrow with them and we are going as high as we can, then they are going up to establish our future Camp VI, at about 24,500 feet. It all rather depends on the weather, for hardly had we got in than it started snowing and it's doing so really heavily – all the

track below us must have filled in by now; most disheartening, this regular and heavy new snow.

This recce is a very important affair, for it will show us how to stage the assault. Chas Wylie and Mike Ward are coming up tomorrow using Open Circuit oxygen, while Tom and Chas E are to use Tom's Closed Circuit. We used the latter coming up today, with success, cutting an hour off the time taken last time from III to IV despite the fact we were carrying a good 50lbs. We will eventually make our attempts on the top from here, for it is close enough to the Lhotse Face and quite a comfortable spot.

Base Camp Khumbu Glacier   4 May 1953
... What is there in what we are doing which stirs people so? Letters and telegrams go on coming in full of such fine sentiments.

Chas E, Tom B and I, with the Bourdillon oxygen apparatus [Closed Circuit], went some little way up the Lhotse Face (to 23,500 feet or so), prior to the proper Reconnaissance, and yesterday I had a long day, first going up to Camp V with the Recce party and giving them final instructions and then escorting 3 sick Sherpas down to Camp II en route for Base. It was rather interesting that, whereas I'd used oxygen the day before, I went up to 23,000 again without it, but just as easily as with – in fact, it was altogether a more pleasant experience! I am now worried about the Recce party, as the weather has turned foul just as they are wrestling with the Face. It isn't going to be at all easy, I fear – but then this is no surprise.

Base Camp Khumbu Glacier   7 May 1953
... [This letter will] catch James Morris's runner, with his report on the plan, which resulted from my conference this morning.

Chas Evans' Reconnaissance of the Lhotse Face and the oxygen tests have enabled me to decide on using *both* Closed and Open Circuit equipment, in a double assault on the summit. After lots of thought I've decided on the 'line up' for the assault as follows:

1.	To prepare the Lhotse Face and establish Camp VI (11–15 May)	Lowe Band Westmacott plus 4 Sherpas
2.	To carry to the South Col	Noyce Wylie plus 12 Sherpas
3.	First Assault Party (Closed-Circuit)	Evans Bourdillon
4.	2nd Assault Party (Open Circuit)	Hillary Tenzing
5.	Support Party (to establish Camp VIII on SE Ridge at 27,500 or 28,000ft	Hunt Gregory plus 4 Sherpas
6.	Reserve	Ward

It was tempting to go for the top myself, but I'm sure I've chosen the best men for the job and that my position enables me to control the business and make decisions on the spot. We are now in the final stages of getting stores into the Cwm and, if weather suits, may go straight ahead after the 15th. Equally, we may come down and wait for the weather. At the moment it's pretty ghastly and as you know, so very much depends on this. Ed and I go up to the Cwm again on 9th, to release George Lowe and his team for the Lhotse Face.

Camp III   16 May 1953

... I have come down from Camp VI[10] to arrange the final move to Advanced Base, before we make our bid for the top. The weather has suddenly relented in these last few days and, tho' it has slowed us down, we are now very nearly ready – I've fixed the 20th for the first carry to the South Col (Wilf's) which will be followed by the Assaults if the weather holds – I pray earnestly that it may for the next 10 days at least. At the moment Wilf Noyce and George Lowe are at, or moving up to, Camp VII at 24,000ft,[10] in order to prepare the last bit of the route towards the South Col; Ed Hillary went up there yesterday and set up their tent. Tomorrow stores for Camp VII will be carried up before the assault. All are in fine fettle if a little tensed up – I find the suspense trying too and feel we ought to be 'at it' already in this perfect weather – but there is no speeding up the machine and we must be patient now.

Advanced Base Western Cwm   20th May 1953

... Everything is really in the balance till we see how Wilf fares tomorrow morning. He has the difficult job of preparing a certain critical passage across the Lhotse Face, and taking a string of Sherpas to the South Col. If he succeeds in this, then we shall be half way *set* for the assault in the next few days. The party preparing the route up the Face has unaccountably failed to finish its job – our wireless communications have broken down and we can only watch events from here. They spent all yesterday in Camp; today – as 2 days ago – they started out, only to return. It is tantalizing and desperately disappointing. But we live on, in hopes of success tomorrow – the weather today is glorious and seems fairly set, but how long can it last? You may well imagine just how anxious it all is, for me. All being well, we shall see fairly soon, I hope, but cannot wait indefinitely like this without spirits dropping a bit.

Advanced Base Western Cwm   22nd May 1953

... the first Assault party is just off. Yesterday we watched Wilf Noyce, with Sherpa Annullu, climb to the South Col from Camp VII – a thrilling sight and a very fine effort, for it meant we had conquered the Lhotse Face at long last – after nearly a fortnight's anxiety and struggle. Today Ed Hillary and Tenzing, whom I'd sent up yesterday to 'boost' the morale of the Sherpas, are leading 14 Sherpas to the Col. Chas Wylie is also with them. They are well up in the gully beside the Eperon des Genevois and seem to be going well. Wilf and Annullu have just returned here after their fine and historic effort and their reports are encouraging – little wind and good snow conditions.

Chas E, Tom B and I are going up to Camp V tonight. This means we should be on the Col on the 24th and T and C [Tom Bourdillon and Charles Evans] will try for the top, from the Col, on the next day.

Ed and Tenzing are at the moment on their way to the Col – they are to come down and follow us up as soon as possible – 24 or 48 hours interval.

Adv Base   29th May 1953
This scrap of a letter will go by hand of James Morris, of the Times, who will probably be off to UK with the final news in a day or two. I got down from the South Col with the first Assault Party yesterday – more or less whole – but I fear we are really casualties after our effort on the 26th. You will know the story so I won't go over it all. It was funny to look westwards from 27,500 feet on the SE Ridge (my limit) to Kangch [Kangchenjunga] – all our old friends of 1937 – just the reverse view I'd had from Nepal Peak.[11]

At this moment we are anxiously waiting for news of Ed Hillary's bid for the top – they are at it now, and I've sent Wilf Noyce with 3 Sherpas up to the Col to help get them down. Wilf was splendid in helping us, for we reached Camp VII in a state of very near exhaustion – in fact I only came down here because we feared Tom Bourdillon might not get down alive.

Some terribly difficult decisions had to be made, but somehow they have easily and all turned out aright. I so felt very sure of the rightness of each one, as of the final outcome, all along, as though guided along a pre destined track a curious sensation of confidence amounting to faith and that big imponderable, the weather has been with us just enough to see us through

Base Camp   1.6.53
... I don't remember when I last sent you a letter; was it before I went up to the South Col? That was the start of the assault and from then until the evening of the 30th, when we knew the outcome of Hillary's and Tenzing's attempt, there has really been no respite at all – some terribly difficult

decisions had to be made, but somehow they have each and all turned out aright. I've felt very sure of the rightness of each one, as of the final outcome, all along, as though guided along a pre-destined track, a curious sensation of confidence answering to Faith. And that big imponderable, the weather, has been with us just enough to see us through.

It started on 21st, when I had sent up Ed and Tenzing to intervene in the vital carry to the South Col. Wilf, one of those leading the Sherpas, had made a wonderful change in the stalemate on the Lhotse Face, by going up to the South Col with one Sherpa; but it was by no means sure that the rest would go on up next day (22nd). There were 14 of them up at Camp VII, and on those loads the assault depended. Only Ed and Tenzing could tip the balance, and I sent them up from Adv Base, knowing well the risk of prejudicing their effort in the second assault. But first things first, and it worked. On that day (22nd) we watched no less than 17 little dots emerge from the serac in front of Camp VII and continue steadily, if slowly, up the face and across the traverse. All but one went on without hesitation into the couloir leading to the Col – and that defaulter's load was taken by someone else. With the essential backing thus ensured, I decided that the first assault party should start, the weather had been good for a week, and we must tempt Providence no longer. So off we went – on oxygen – to Camp V that night, Chas E, Tom B, myself and Sherpas Da Namgyal and Balu.

Soon after our arrival, down came Ed, Tenzing, both dreadfully tired, and a few of the stoutest of the Sherpas; the rest stayed up at Camp VII. Among these was Dawa Thondup,[12] well in his 40s, whose medical fitness had been in doubt up to the last minute and addicted to strong drink – a remarkable performance this.

Next day we went up to VII and on 24th evening reached the South Col. It was blowing as only it can on that dread and desolate spot and we will none of us forget the terrible struggle – lasting over an hour, to erect our Pyramid tent. We were so exhausted at the end, when we had put up this tent and the Meade, that it was already out of the question to go for the Summit on the next day, as planned. One day's delay thus resulted, spent at 26,000 feet on the South Col of Everest in fine weather. I even managed to walk – very slowly – to both edges of this curious, stony plateau, and photograph the views both ways. To the east, over the left shoulder of Makalu, was Kangch and its Satellites – I could make out the twins, Nepal Peak and Tent Peak, just as I'd seen Everest and her neighbour from that group in 1937.

We had a good night on oxygen on 25th and got away early on 26th though Tom and Chas had some delay with freezing up of the Closed Circuit valve system. I was with Da Namgyal, our mission [being] to place stores for the Ridge Camp as high as possible – the camp to be finally established by the second support party accompanying Ed's assault party. We were pretty heavily laden, for the other porter, Balu, who should have been in my party, had utterly failed to turn out of his tent.

Well, we made our way (both on oxygen) up to the crest of the SE Ridge by a very steep couloir, following T and C – I can't describe to you the agonies of it – my oxygen wasn't functioning properly and it seemed a struggle for dear

life to make each 5–6 paces upward – a terrible nightmare. We stopped for
some time at the skeleton of the Swiss tent, used by Lambert and Tenzing in
May 1952, then managed by a great effort – laboured step by step, fighting for
breath, to get up another 150–200 feet, with the weather closing in (snow,
wind and mist). Da Namgyal was now at the end of his tether and I had to
urge him on to a convenient-looking ledge, where we could dump the kit[13] – a
Meade tent, assault rations, kerosine, oxygen (we left our own bottles for use
as sleeping oxygen). We actually tried to scrape a platform for the tent, but in
our feeble state it was useless and in any case I wanted it placed higher – at the
top of a shoulder on the Ridge[14] – by the second party. Through the mists I
could still see T and C above us, just getting to the crest of the shoulder. We
started down probably 11.30 a.m. terribly slow and wobbly now without
oxygen. I had left my second bottle by the Swiss tent and for a time tried to use
it on the way down to the couloir – but owing to the defect (in my mask) I
found this worse and decided to carry it down to be used by the 2nd party. We
secured each other, rope length by rope length, in the couloir – Da Namgyal
had one slip, then at last we were on easier ground, and the strength seemed to
leave one like water. I could see the 2nd Assault Party winding up the Lhotse
Face and already two figures at the Col. As we descended they came towards
us – Ed and Tenzing. I collapsed hopelessly into tears and found I'd no more
strength to walk in. Ed was splendid in propping me and eventually bringing
oxygen, which just did the trick. He kept me on it for some time after, in the
little 'Blister' tent.

Later George and Greg arrived, *jubilant*, they'd seen T and C on the South
Pk! For some time we thought they might well have made the summit (they
were seen at 1.15 p.m.) – the Sherpas with the second party thought the South
PK *was* the top. But when they at last came down, at about 4.30 p.m. we
learnt that they had NOT, quite rightly following their briefing and not having
enough oxygen for the double journey; they reported the connecting ridge as
formidable.

Followed a grim night of strong gale, T, C and I crammed in the Meade and
without oxygen, to assist Ed and Tenzing with their support party to get off.
We were in pretty poor shape next day, Tom specially so.

It was blowing a gale anyway and Ed had not started. A 24 hour delay was
decided on, luckily we were sufficiently provisioned in food, fuel and oxygen
to last this out. We sat through the morning in fair misery in the Pyramid,
failing to get the stove to light – outside, all hell was let loose and I began to
feel toward the S. Col as the Swiss had – it had an atmosphere of death. About
midday it was time for Tom and Chas to go down, taking with them yet
another 'failure' from our elite Ridge team – the renowned Ang Temba. They
left; 5 minutes later Chas was back. Tom was in a very bad way – perhaps
dying – on that villainous slope up to the ridge – on his knees and unable to
make it. Another Sahib[15] must join this party to get him down to VII and
below alive. Here was a quandary. I had decided my post was here, to take
decisions on the send-off of the 2nd Assault and to support Ed on return. I
turned to Greg and George, it must be one of them. Then, in their chagrin, I
saw my mistake. I was finished, they were fresh. That Ridge Camp must be

pushed higher and they were already – as I had been – one man short. I must go down. But it was a bitter decision to take. Packed up with help of the others, in haste, while Tom was being given oxygen and physical help to the top of the Eperon [Geneva Spur]. Ed carried my pack and I said farewell to him and George on the top, before joining the other three.

We stumbled and stopped and straggled our way down the endless slopes of the Lhotse Face to VII – Tom improving with his oxygen, I getting more tired. Reached there to find it occupied, to our joy and relief, by Wilf and Mike [Ward] who had anticipated our need. It was as well. Ang Temba fell head first into the crevasse above the camp, and Wilf was able to extricate him. Wilf too, at my bidding, stayed to feed and care for us (Tom, Temba and self) that night, while Mike escorted Chas [Evans] down to IV. We three were helplessly weary, and I had already decided to send Wilf up with 3 fresh Sherpas, to reinforce Ed's party. Chas [Wylie] would be able to send the Sherpas up here to VII.

Next day we plodded on down, reached IV – a veritable haven – about 1 p.m., having passed Chas [Wylie] bringing up the three Sherpas to join Wilf. It was a glorious day and we felt pretty sure the second assault was on.

On 29th, all day, no news. I'd fixed that Wilf should place sleeping bags on the Eperon, arranged so as to indicate 'Summit', 'South Pk', 'Failure'. But we saw nothing despite anxious searching with glasses until dark. We saw Wilf go up with his party and two of them return to Camp VII. We saw three descend from the Col; later, these materialized into Greg and two of the Ridge Sherpas – dead weary but triumphant. Despite yet another 'failure' – Pemba (leaving them, like me, with only *one* useful carrier), Greg, George and Ang Nyima had carried the camp 300 feet higher than my dump (to 28,000 feet) – on the shoulder, thus giving Ed and Tenzing a magnificent send-off to the top.

On 30th came relief to our prolonged tension. First we saw 5 figures crossing the Lhotse Face, down from the Col. This meant that all were *safe* (Ed, Tenzing, Wilf, George and one Sherpa). Then, in early afternoon, three people approached Adv Base – we'd seen them emerge from VII shortly after the 5 had arrived there – I started up to meet them, followed by Mike Westmacott, the strain was at last to be ended one way or another. I realized it was Ed himself, with Tenzing and George Lowe, they made no sign, evidently they'd *not* made it, after all. Then, suddenly, they started gesturing with their axes towards Everest's Summit above us. I couldn't make the mental switch for a second or two, then emotion and joy and wild excitement overwhelmed me utterly and I must have seemed possessed for some time. Weeping foolishly, I embraced Ed and Tenzing in turn.

Shouting to the others, asking questions. Everyone crowded round, everyone was equally mad, the Sherpa team were grasping these two splendid, lucky people by the hand, grinning broadly. Such a scene as I've imagined, but never believed could come true – Everest was climbed yesterday by Ed and Tenzing, at 11.30 a.m. We'd made it, exactly according to plan. We had crowned the efforts of all our illustrious predecessors. We had stood at the apex of this pyramid of hard-won experience and endeavour. What a tale to tell the waiting world!

NOTES

1   The gorge of the Teesta river in Sikkim.

2   Siniolchum, 22,600ft, in Sikkim, described by Douglas Freshfield as 'the most beautiful snow mountain I have ever seen, perhaps the most beautiful in the world', (AJ20, 170, 1900).

3   'Chas' (for Charles Evans and Charles Wylie). My abbreviation, not their nicknames.

4   Lachen, a village in Sikkim, which we passed through on our way to the Zemu glacier.

5   She was the wife of Dawa Tenzing, one of our leading Sherpas (who became famous as sirdar on the first ascent of Kangchenjunga in 1955).

6   Tom Bourdillon and his father helped develop the closed-circuit oxygen system, which reduced the wastage rate and provided a richer supply but was heavier and, being more complicated than the open-circuit system, more liable to breakdown.

7   Reggie Cooke, Indian Posts and Telegraphs, who partnered my wife and myself on expeditions to the Zemu glacier (1937) and Pandim (1940).

8   Lt Col J O M Roberts, 2nd Gurkha Rifles, took part in an ill-fated attempt on Masherbrum in the Karakoram in 1938 with Jimmy Waller, Royal Artillery, one of my companions on Saltoro Kangri in 1935. Jimmy Roberts had a distinguished climbing career and was Deputy Leader to Bonington on the 1972 Everest South West Face expedition.

9   Camp IV (Advanced Base) was, in fact, at 21,200ft.

10 Camp VI was a temporary camp at c. 23,000ft. During the Assault, we went straight from Camp V at 22,000ft to Camp VII at 24,000ft.

11 Nepal Peak, 23,400ft. I made the second ascent of the SW summit, 23,300ft, in November 1937.

12 Dawa Thondup, my oldest Sherpa companion, played a great part on Saltoro Kangri in 1935 with Jimmy Waller and myself. He was with his wife and myself on expeditions and treks in Sikkim in 1937, 1938, 1939 and 1940.

13 In 1976 Captain Henry Day RE, a member of the Joint British Army/ Royal Nepalese Army expedition, brought back my oxygen cylinder from a point which he computed to be between 27,400 and 27,500ft. I am confident that Da Namgyal and I placed the dump (with the oxygen cylinder) between 150 and 200 vertical feet above the height of the Swiss tent, which I believe to have been at about 27,300ft. (The Swiss, in their book *Avant-premières à l'Everest*, gave the location of their tent as 8400m: almost certainly an over estimate.) In my diary, and in letters to my wife and to James Morris, written between 27 and 30 May, I wrote of 27,500ft as the height. I still believe this to be about right.

14 This was where Hillary and Tenzing, supported by Lowe, Gregory and Ang Nyima, pitched the top tent on 28th May 1953 at about 27,900ft.

15 The appellation 'Sahib' was, indeed, an echo of the British rule in India (the 'Raj') which had ended in 1947! It did *not* reflect our relations with the Sherpa team in 1953.

EDMUND HILLARY
A Letter to Jim Rose

(Plates 10–12, 24 and back cover)

This letter was written by Sir Edmund Hillary on 2 June 1953 at Everest Base Camp to his future father-in-law Jim Rose, President of the New Zealand Alpine Club. The letter is unedited.

Base Camp
June 2nd 1953

Dear Jim,

Well all the flurry & bustle is over, all the hard work is finished & at long last we've climbed the jolly mountain. Now Himalayan climbing can settle down into a more normal routine & the 'Everest' sense of values can be put aside. However I must admit that the whole of this expedition has been jolly good fun despite the very real dangers of the icefall & we've had a party that welded into a particularly useful & pleasant team. I think the great feature of the party is how practically every man went high & certainly all did a very useful job. It was far from the case as in previous expeditions, including the Swiss, where a couple of men did all the work.

I must admit that I haven't quite got used to the idea of climbing Everest although I had a couple of wonderful days high on the mountain. After all it is only a couple of years ago that four very ignorant New Zealanders went to Gawhal. We're all back at Base Camp now after some hairraising incidents in our final descent of the icefall & we're very thin & lacking in energy at present as we organise things to start off on our long trek to Katmandu tomorrow. We expect to arrive at the British Embassy by June 20th. John Hunt wants me & Tenzing to fly to England with him & meet our patron the Duke of Edinburgh & attend all the official functions. As they will be paying my fare I was only too willing to agree. I expect to be back in Auckland by the middle of September.

Regarding the climb I'll give you a brief account of the incidents leading up to it & the climb itself.

By May 19th George Lowe, Mike Ward & Da Tenzing were in Camp VII at 24,000' but the Lhotse face attack seemed to have lost its punch & little or no progress was being made towards the traverse to the South Col. However on 20th the first lift of nine Sherpas under Wilf Noyce laden for the South Col went from Camp V to Camp VII & George & his party came down without having made much progress. On the 21st we watched eagerly but only two figures (Wilf Noyce & a Sherpa) left Camp VII & made their way upwards to the South Col. At the same time Charles Wylie & another bunch of Sherpas went from V to VII. This meant that fourteen Sherpas were at Camp VII &

Everest 1953
John Hunt putting on crampons. (*Alfred Gregory*)

3. Entrance to the Western Cwm. Wilfrid Noyce crosses
the bridge over the big crevasse. (*Alfred Gregory*)

Left
4. Nawang Gombu crossi
the big crevasse.
(*Alfred Gregory*)

Facing page, below
6. Tom Bourdillon and
Charles Evans at
the South Col.
(*Alfred Gregory*)

The Lhotse Face Sherpas, standing: Ang Tsering, Ang Norbu, Kancha, Angtharkay, Ang Dawa II; squatting: Annullu, Phu Dorji, Pasang. With Wilfrid Noyce. (*Alfred Gregory*)

Facing page
The first assault. Returning from the first ascent
of the South Summit, Charles Evans and Tom Bourdillon
creep back to camp across the South Col.
(*Alfred Gregory*)

Above
Evans and Bourdillon (L) exhausted after
their summit attempt. (*Alfred Gregory*)

9. The South Summit in cloud, seen from the
Geneva Spur. (*Alfred Gregory*)

Plates 2–12 formed part of an exhibition of photographs by Alfred Gregory
at the Royal Geographical Society in May 1993 to mark the 40th anniversary
of the first ascent of Everest. Many of them are reproduced in his book
Alfred Gregory's Everest published by Constable in 1993.

The summit assault. Hillary and Tenzing on the way
up to the highest camp at 27,900ft. (*Alfred Gregory*)

Right
Edmund Hillary
relaxing after
his return from
the summit.
(*Alfred Gregory*)

Following page
Hillary and Tenzing
after their
successful first
ascent of Everest.
(*Alfred Gregory*)

even though Wilf had made a route to the South Col it was absolutely essential that on the 22nd the whole bunch of Sherpas should go from VII to the South Col or food would run out & the whole attack break down. John decided therefore to reluctantly send Tenzing & me up to ensure that the lift went through according to schedule. Tenzing & I went from IV to VII in 4¼ hours on the 21st & on the next day the 22nd we had our great triumph – we set off with 15 Sherpas & three sahibs & got 14 Sherpas & all the loads to the South Col. Tenzing & I had a strenuous day having to kick & cut a good route the whole way up. Tenzing & I then returned right back to IV. This day was the turning point in the expedition. We now had the South Col stocked.

On May 24th Tom Bourdillon & Charles Evans – the closed circuit team with their support party John Hunt, Da Namgyl & Balu went from Camp VII to the South col in very slow time in bad conditions. The following day they had to rest on the Col while Tenzing & I the open circuit team with our support party George Lowe, Alf Gregory & Pember, AngNima & Angtember went up to Camp VII. We also had five other Sherpas who were carrying loads to the South Col & then descending.

On the 26th we all left Camp VII & set out for the South Col. We soon saw figures on the ridge to the South summit & had a great thrill watching their progress. Tenzing & I were in good form & went on ahead to reach the South Col in 2¾ hours from Camp VII. We were in time to receive an exhausted John Hunt & Da Namgyl who had packed a tent, oxygen, food & fuel to about 27,350ft. Meanwhile Tom & Charles went on & finally reached the South summit at 1 p.m. This was a great triumph. We doctored John Hunt & watched eagerly for the others who finally arrived back at 3.30 completely exhausted. They both had terrible tales of the ridge from the South Summit to the top & even expressed the opinion that it wasn't climbable. This night was a terrible one with very strong wind & great cold. On the 27th there was no hope of us moving upwards & the best we could do was escort a very weak & exhausted party over the Col & down to the long traverse. Both Balu & Angtember had become sick & also went down. Another ghastly windy night followed but the 28th was rather improved. However we had another blow – Pember was sick leaving us only one Sherpa AngNima for the carry up the ridge. We had no alternative but to carry the stuff ourselves. George Lowe, Greg & AngNima left at 8.45 a.m. carrying about 40lbs apiece & working on oxygen at 4 litres. Tenzing & I carrying nearly 50lbs left at 10 a.m. & followed in their tracks. George was going very well indeed & led nearly all the way up to the main ridge & the old Swiss Camp at 27,200. This involved a good deal of stepcutting in firm very steep snow. We caught up to the others on the ridge & we continued up another 150 feet to 27,350 where John had dumped his gear. We still considered this too low for a camp so decided to increase our loads & push on. I added a tent to make my load well over 60 & the others had mostly about 50 lbs. The ridge was steep but the upward sloping rock strata made the climbing reasonably easy. We pushed on & on & couldn't find a spot even the slightest bit flat. After a long pull we followed Tenzing's advice & did a traverse out onto the steep face on the left & finally found a possible spot under a rock bluff. We estimated it was about 27,900 ft

& decided to camp so the others dumped their loads & returned to the South
Col. Tenzing and I spent from 2.30 to 5.30 making a camp site large enough
to pitch the tent & even then it was on two levels. — I spent the whole night
sitting up. Our oxygen due to the reduced lift was very short & I worked out
that if we worked on the reduced flow rate of 3 litres per minute we'd have
sufficient endurance for an attempt but it would be pretty fine. We also had
enough oxygen for four hours sleeping at 1 litre per minute.

At 6.30 a.m. on the 29th we left our tent & set off up the ridge. We were
going well but slowly. It was a magnificent morning with astounding views
everywhere. Taking turns we plugged up the ridge & then reached the enormous 300 ft slope leading to the South summit. This was very steep deep snow
with a light crust on top & made us both very unhappy. However we persisted
& finally reached the South summit at 9 a.m. We were eager for our first view
of the ghastly summit ridge & I was very relieved to see that although it
looked impressive it didn't look by any means impossible. On the right
overhanging the Kangshung great fingers of cornices & then a steep snow
slope running down to the 8,000 ft rock bluffs dropping to the Western Cwm.
I was worried about oxygen endurance so got to work. I cut a trail of steps just
above the rocks & made good progress often dodging larger cornices by
getting onto the rocks themselves. A vertical rock pitch I got up by jamming
between the rock & some vertical snow on the right. A forty foot struggle & I
was on top of it & I was astonished at the energy I had. I hauled Tenzing up —
he wasn't going quite as well but was a good safe & sound companion. I felt
now that it would take a lot to stop me & cut steadily along until a final bump
loomed up & I moved up on a tight rope & was standing on top of the world.
It was quite a moment. Tenzing so far forgot himself as to embrace me & I
banged off a number of photographs. I collected a few stones one of which I'm
keeping for you if you want it.

I was very worried by our oxygen shortage so we wasted no time in
hastening back to the South Summit, down to Camp IX & finally very tired
indeed down to the South Col after a tremendous day. The next day we
descended to the Cwm & so to Base.

Well, this is the bare story, Jim. I must apologise for the dry nature of the
tale but we're all rather anoxic & find it hard to concentrate. We'll have plenty
of opportunity for discussing it in the future around your hospitable fire.

We've just heard by radio that the Queen & Winston Churchill have sent
messages of congratulations to us at Katmandu so we are understandably
excited. Also old Sid Holland [the Prime Minister of New Zealand] has said
some kind words. What a business!

Well, Jim, I must close & send this letter off tonight with the runner. I
would greatly appreciate it if you could give some of these details to my
Mother & to Rex if it's not asking too much. I've written short notes to them
but no climbing details. Our main interest now is to reach Katmandu & hear
what's occurring.

Regards to Mrs. Rose & yourself.

A somewhat confused

Ed.

CHARLES EVANS
From My Everest Sketch Book

(Plates 6–8)

These drawings are from sketches in my diary of the 1953 Everest expedition. Others were made for the adventurers, young and old, to whom I sent illustrated letters and postcards at the time. They were published in *Eye on Everest* in 1955.

In 1952, Eric Shipton, Ed. Hillary, George Lowe, and I visited the Barun Valley and saw this view of Everest's South East ridge.
In the drawing, Lhotse is to the left, the South Col is hidden in the centre and Everest is on the right.

Thyangboche monastery.
The Gompa in the centre, with its
gilded roof, and courtyard, is
surrounded by the small houses of
the lamas and monks.

GEORGE LOWE

1st June 1953: Base Camp

(Plates 6–12)

The following letters were written on Everest to my sister in New Zealand. They have never been published before, nor been seen by others except my family. The letters were written close to the event and show signs of the bias of a New Zealander telling his family what a great job he has done! I hope my companions on Everest will forgive any embarrassment caused by my letters home to the family in New Zealand.

In a day or two the world will know of our success. At present, don't imagine our band of thirteen rolling and rollicking in an ecstasy brought on by victory. If you were at Base Camp now you would see nine climbers and around fifteen Sherpas lying listlessly around the tents with bloodshot and glazed eyes, thin, dirty and bewildered. Ed is now sleeping as he has done for hours and hours; Charles is just smoking and tired; the talk is very desultory and dull; everyone is quite played out. Five of the other lads will be descending from Camp III tomorrow, and they too will come in stiff-legged and flogged after the last two weeks.

Two days ago we were on the South Col urging ourselves to the limit – and now like pricked balloons, all our reserves have gone. Yesterday, we came down to Base Camp. Ed, Charles Evans and I were together on one rope, and it took hours. I have never been so tired, nor had Ed. Now, if you could see us, you would see the most beaten, played out, lustreless team of climbers it is possible to imagine.

I last wrote on 22nd May and since then I have been very high, and the summit has been reached. You will know something of the event from the newspapers, but here, as far as I can recall it, is the day to day happenings from the 22nd.

When the great lift reached the South Col on the 22nd, John Hunt decided to launch the Assault Plan, and accordingly the closed circuit boys went into action. Tom Bourdillon and Charles Evans set off that afternoon with all their bedding tied around their closed circuit apparatus with spare soda-lime canisters and spanners poking out – in all some 50lbs. John Hunt went with them on open circuit as support and possible emergency. Two Sherpas also went, Da Namgyal and Balu, to carry a tent and oxygen above the South Col as a possible emergency ration and shelter in the case of a late descent by Tom and Charles. In the event of this tent and oxygen not being used it was to be added to the second assault party backed by Gregory and three special Sherpas.

It was at this stage that I came into the story. The original plan did not include me, but I was very keen to get to the South Col. Because of Ed and

Tenzing's trip to the South Col with the Sherpa lift, and their consequent
tiredness, they decided to wait a day longer than the original plan. Then it was
discovered, mostly by my propaganda, that a little more oxygen and food
would be advisable.

Accordingly, I was commissioned to escort five Sherpas to South Col along
with Gregory and his three special Ridge Camp boys to back up Ed and
Tenzing. I spent all the 23rd May frantically trying to fix a leak in the oxygen
set I was to use. Finally by cutting and binding one of the rubber feed pipes, I
stopped the hiss. Tom, Charles and John climbed to Camp VII on 23rd.

24th May. Tom, Charles and John with their two Sherpas, crept above
Camp VII and worked slowly to South Col. We watched them through glasses
– in seven hours, they arrived late and very tired. We packed up; Greg and I
with our Sherpas left for Camp V, where we spent the night. A cold night –
our thermometer read −27C at 5a.m.

25th May. Tom and Charles were timed to make an attempt on the South
Peak, and Summit if possible, using closed circuit. Due to wind and their tired
condition from previous day, they stayed on the South Col. Greg and I left for
VI using oxygen (2 litres per minute). We made good time, and at VI changed
to 4 litres and headed up the Lhotse face for VII. You will remember the climb
from V to VII is up the difficult Lhotse face on which nearly 1,000 feet of rope
is fixed. Above VI, I began to falter. I began to pant and weaken, although
Greg was making a slow pace. I began to worry and think I was failing – but it
turned out to be a defect in my oxygen set, which was cutting right out and the
mask was stopping even the outside air getting in. The trip to VII, for me, was
hell and I collapsed on the snow at VII and took a couple of hours to recover.
At VII, I was able to trace the trouble and the set behaved beautifully the next
days. Ed and Tenzing came right through to VII from IV that day, and arrived
fresh and fit.

Although Everest was blowing a cloud plume on these days, the weather
was very settled and the weather reports from Indian radio gave us 'Warm
temperatures, winds 15–20 knots and settled weather. Monsoon still only in
the Andaman Sea'. Camp VII, 24,000 feet approximately, was calm that
night, temperature −28C.

26th May. We left VII at 8.45a.m. and had wonderful conditions for our
climb to South Col. I filmed much of the climb and felt really wonderful. From
the top of the Lhotse face glacier, for perhaps 1,000 feet, is a steady crampon
climb up crevassed slopes and then swings left to traverse above limestone
rock bands and goes diagonally up great snow slopes towards the Col. The
South Col is not reached direct. The rock buttress of 'Eperon de Genevois'
stops this, and our route connected with the very top of the Eperon, over
which we climbed and dropped some 200ft to South Col at 25,850 feet.

About 1p.m. on 26th, we began traversing rock and snow at the top of the
Eperon. The South Peak of Everest was in view looking incredibly steep and
on the final slope I saw two dots, like flies on a wall, about 200 feet below the
cornice of the top. We went mad with excitement as we watched Tom and
Charles go steadily up and over the South Summit, 28,720 feet and, we
thought, off for the main summit. They were higher than anyone ever before,

and apparently going at a very fast rate. They had climbed from the South Col that morning and reached the South Summit in five and a half hours. John, too, had set out with Da Namgyal (both on open circuit) ahead of Tom and Charles, to carry Ridge Camp, but the closed circuit party easily overtook him and far outclassed the open circuit at the highest altitudes. Balu, the other Sherpa, had failed to start – in fact, he refused to go above the South Col.

Greg and I were so excited at seeing Tom and Charles that we ran down to the Col camp to shout the news to Ed and Tenzing. Ed came out of the dome tent with a great whoop and then dived back again. Tenzing, we were hurt to find, lost his smile and did not share our enthusiasm. The idea of team effort seemed not to appeal to him, there seemed no doubt that Tenzing had high hopes of being the first to reach the summit.

Ed's disappearance into the dome I thought strange, and pushed my way in to find John lying quite exhausted with Ed plying him with drinks and oxygen. Ed and Tenzing had arrived on the Col before us and saw John returning with Da Namgyal from his ridge carry. They had carried to 27,350 feet and were returning completely done in. John was staggering and crumpling, and staggering on again, when Ed rushed off to help him. Ed assisted him in on his shoulder and slapped an oxygen mask on him for a good half hour (John's oxygen had run out at 27,350 feet and he came down without). Da Namgyal's hands were frostbitten and he was very tired. John certainly earned our admiration – he's got tremendous guts, and this day he pushed himself to the absolute limit – but this was typical of him all through.

There were three tents on the South Col: a Pyramid, a Dome, and a Meade. They respectively housed four, two and two. The Pyramid had previously been used by Sherpas and was in a disgraceful condition. The floor was in shreds and parting at the stitching of the seams. The windward side had a four-inch tear which later caused great inconvenience by admitting drifting snow and cold wind. The rope guys were far too light and in the tremendous and ceaseless buffeting on the Col they were fraying and broken when we arrived. Ed and I went out in the afternoon into a freezing, roaring wind and began to repair the tent. We found a pile of strong Swiss line and began replacing all the guys and placing rocks around the worst tears in the floor to protect it from the plucking of the wind.

During this time, the South Summit became enveloped in cloud and we began to worry about Tom and Charles. We knew, as they knew, that if their closed circuit sets failed in any way, for they had many gadgets, valves, tubes and canisters susceptible to error, they would not come back. Tom was an exceedingly determined thruster, and we felt his enthusiasm could overcome good sense – but Ed remarked, 'Charles is pretty sensible – I think he'll balance Tom'.

About this time, the three Sherpas who had been chosen to carry with Greg to the Ridge Camp arrived on the Col from VII. They had set out with us and gone slowly and badly. This was disturbing as we had placed high hopes on them. They were Ang Temba, Pemba and Ang Nyima. Ang Temba we thought the best, and were amazed to find when he dumped his load of 30lbs outside the tent he keeled over and for ten minutes did not respond to anything.

Pemba was very tired, while Ang Nyima was quite fresh and unaffected by the altitude.

John, by this time, had recovered and was fretting about Tom and Charles. He kept peering up the ridge looking for their return. The afternoon passed, and we all became more and more worried. As we fixed the last ropes, I saw moving dots at the head of the couloir by which they had reached the ridge. I watched until in the shifting mist I was certain, and shouted the news. Our relief was tremendous.

Their descent of the couloir was frightening to watch. Dog tired, they started down one at a time, each anchoring the other and each falling off as they tried to kick downhill. They slid and fell their rope lengths, each just managing to hold the other. As Tom said, 'We yo-yo'd our way down – it was quite fun!'. Ed and I went out to meet them, and I filmed their arrival. They were still wearing and using their closed circuit and apart from their masks which covered nose, mouth and chin, they were covered in icicles. Ice driblets from the mask outlet had stuck to their windproofs and they were panting and labouring just to move along the flat.

They had not gone far beyond the South Summit – a few yards only – their soda-lime canisters did not leave them with enough time in hand to risk going on. The summit ridge seemed long (Tom judged 2 or 3 hours and Charles thought 4 or more), it was corniced and had a difficult vertical rock step in it. Tom took 18 photographs and they turned to go down. Just below the South Summit they jettisoned two oxygen bottles, having enough left to get to the South Col. These bottles were a vital help in getting Ed and Tenzing to the top two days later.

That night, Ed, Tenzing, Greg and I slept in the Pyramid; John, Tom and Charles squashed into the two-man Meade, while Ang Temba, Pemba and Ang Nyima passed the night in the even smaller Dome. That night for everyone was pure misery. The wind slammed over the Col worrying the tents, whining, roaring and snapping incessantly. It became the curse of the Col, sapping our tempers and eating indelibly into our memories. We will never forget the South Col. We all spent there the most miserable days and nights of our lives.

The temperature dropped until we were all cold, even though fully dressed, (we wore our high altitude boots in the sleeping bags to stop them freezing) with full down clothing in our sleeping bags. I have never been so miserable with freezing feet (they were lightly frostbitten – getting better now) cold knees and back which was rammed hard against the windward side of the tent. My pillow was a kitbag full of frozen snow – hard, cold and unsatisfactory. What a night ! But it was only the first of four which grew increasingly worse.

At 4.30a.m. we began to prepare breakfast in the hope of an early start in carrying Ridge Camp. Our appetites were good – we had carried up some 'luxury food' and ate the lot at breakfast. I remember the menu, vita-wheat biscuits with honey; sardines on biscuit; two tins of pineapple between four; slices of salami; more biscuits and honey and lastly a tin of Australian pears. We ate and spread honey with gloves on and you can imagine what a messy business it was.

Our hopes of starting faded when at 8a.m. the wind velocity increased to over 70 or 80 mph and never looked like decreasing. All day, 27th May, it blew and put the chances of climbing on a ridge out of the question.

Supplies on the Col were limited and Charles and Tom had to go down. Ang Temba was so sick that he too was to go down. John, although he felt as leader he should stay to see and support the main assault, decided to go down and leave me to join the ridge carry. With Ang Temba out of the carry, someone had to replace him, and I was fit. So again, although not supposed in the plan to stay on, I was now in the ridge party.

Ang Temba, Tom, Charles and John left in the howling wind. Their climb to the top of the Eperon (200ft) took nearly two hours. Ed and I assisted them – they were dreadfully weak, but once over the Eperon they were out of the worst wind and going downhill. Their journey to VII was an epic and there they were received by Wilfrid Noyce and Mike Ward. On the 28th they limped to Advanced Base, to good food, attention and rest.

For the remainder of 27th May, we sat out the wind and dreaded the coming night. The night was a repetition of the previous one, in the morning we were stiff, bad tempered, ill-fed, with very frayed morale. The wind mercifully eased, and we stiffly prepared to go. Three hours it took to make a few simple preparations. Then an apparently crippling blow fell. Pemba suddenly spewed over the tent floor and began to groan and said he couldn't go. That left one Sherpa, Ang Nyima, and we needed three. That hour the expedition hopes recorded their lowest reading!

After a discussion we agreed to try and lift the two extra Sherpa loads between us. The weights were about 45lbs each, which seemed Herculean when a good load at this altitude was considered to be 15lbs. Greg, Ang Nyima and I got away at 8.45a.m. Ed and Tenzing decided to delay at least an hour to save their strengths and oxygen while we cut steps up the couloir. We were heavily clothed and with the loads we stomped along like robots. We made a very slow steady pace which we managed to hold to without stopping, and began to make height. The wind dropped to a comparative breeze and we slugged up into the couloir and I began cutting steps. Cutting steps at 27,000 feet is an experience – a study in 'go slow'. It took three hours to get to the ridge at 27,200 feet where we saw the wreckage of the Swiss top camp, one tent with not a vestige of cloth on the aluminium bones. Here we dropped our loads and enjoyed the tremendous view. Lhotse and Makalu were wonderful, Kangchenjunga jutted out above the clouds., Below were the Kangshung and Kharta glaciers with wonderful views of brown Tibet beyond.

Oddly enough I enjoyed and remembered the Couloir climb and the view as if it were at sea-level. I had read that that altitude robbed one of these memories. With me it was not so. Here Ed and Tenzing caught up with us. Greg was going exceedingly well, Ang Nyima the same and we urged him on by saying that if he went a bit higher he would have carried and gone higher than any Sherpa in the world. He was very ambitious and carried magnificently. About 150 feet above we reached John's highest point and found the rolled tent, fuel, and R.A.F. oxygen cylinder and these we added to our loads. Ed took the tent, Greg the R.A.F. cylinder and I took fuel and some of Greg's load. We left there with Ed carrying an estimated 63lbs; Greg and I 50lbs, Ang Nyima and Tenzing with 45lbs. (This of course included the weight of our oxygen sets which, with two bottles up, were about 28lbs.)

From here the ridge is moderately steep – odd broken rock and towers followed by snow ridge. I led and the snow was knee-deep and loose. From then on the upward progress was grim, dead-brained toil. I don't really know how we endured the weight. We pushed up to where we thought a flat spot would be and found it quite untenable. We pushed on again – and again the same thing – and so on. About 2.30p.m. we paused below a snow shoulder and found a tiny ledge where we dumped our loads. Ed and Tenzing began clearing a site which was too small for the tent. Snow flurries were beginning and although very tired we set off within two minutes of arrival, after cheery banter to and from Ed on the chances for the morrow. The height of Camp IX – Ridge Camp – has been estimated at 27,900 feet.

Our return was slow and tough. Greg and Ang Nyima were excessively tired and I recut steps all the way down the couloir. From here Greg was pausing every fifty yards and gasping with exhaustion. I was tired – dreadfully tired – but able to keep moving without pause, and funnily enough with sufficient mentality to appreciate the glorious evening colours over Kangchenjunga and Makalu. I photographed them. Near the tents I unroped and pushed on. Pemba had made a hot drink and I tossed this down, grabbed the movie camera, staggered out, and sitting against a rock filmed the arrival of Greg and Ang Nyima which I hope shows something of the state we were in. We drank hot lemon and tea and crawled into our bags – but not to sleep. The night, the wind and the cold came and we passed another bloody night.

The 29th May finally dawned. On the Col it was windy – it was always windy. The sun hit the top of the tent at about 5a.m. It crept down the walls, releasing the frost of condensed breath in a shower over us, as usual. Greg had decided to go down as he was too weak to be of use to any returning summit party. Ang Nyima and Pemba went down too and left me alone on the Col to receive Ed and Tenzing. At 8a.m. we saw Ed and Tenzing on the way up the final slopes of the South Summit, going slowly but steadily. At 9a.m. they disappeared over the South Summit and somehow then I felt they would reach the top. I boiled soup and lemonade and filled two thermos flasks. I prepared oxygen bottles with all connections and masks ready for instant use and set bedding ready as if to receive casualties. Outside I prepared the spare oxygen frame with two emergency cylinders which I intended to carry up and meet them to assist their descent.

At 1p.m. they appeared again on South Summit and began the descent of the steep loose snow slope. I was wildly excited and leapt into action. I packed the thermos flasks, slung the movie camera in, put on crampons, gloves, vaselined my nose, face and lips against the wind, tied a scarf around my face as extra protection (I was severely wind-burnt and the skin was frost-affected from the previous days and very sore), got into the oxygen carrying frame with two bottles and set off. About 400 yards from camp I began to feel groggy, I was carrying too much, had started too excited and too fast. After the previous day's effort I was not so good as I thought. I looked up and saw they were coming down quite fast and steadily but were so far away that I could be of no immediate help. I tottered back to the tent. There I watched from the tent door. They stopped at Camp IX at 2p.m. and didn't leave there until 3p.m. (they had a boil-up of lemonade and collected their sleeping bags). They came down the ridge and then the couloir going absolutely steadily.

Just before 4p.m. I set out again to meet them, and as I left the tents Wilf Noyce arrived with Passang Phutar. They had been sent by John as a useful support to receive and help the summit party in case of exhaustion. It was good to see them and they began to prepare hot drinks as I left.

I dragged up again and met Ed and Tenzing at the foot of the couloir, some 500 feet above the Col. They were moving fairly rapidly – the only tiredness showed in their slightly stiff-legged walking as they cramponed the last part of the couloir. I crouched, back against the wind, and poured out the thermos contents as they came up. Ed unclipped his mask and grinned a tired greeting, sat on the ice and said in his matter-of-fact way, 'Well, we knocked the bastard off!'.[1] It was not quite matter-of-fact, he was incredulous of what they had done.

Although I had a feeling they had been successful, the statement roused in me a terrific surge of emotion and relief. Tenzing, though tired, was all smiles and I congratulated them both enthusiastically, and Ed's reply was 'It was a wonderful climb, if you had been there you would have done the same'.

We walked down to the tents talking ninety to the dozen.

NOTE

1 To put the record straight, this New Zealand remark, which meant no disparagement to the mountain, was meant for my ears alone. New Zealand slang did and still does take certain swear words and reverses their meaning. Big mountains were referred to with admiration as 'big bastards'. Ed had had to live with the fact that I told the BBC what he said on meeting me, and he has never forgiven me for it!

GRIFFITH PUGH
Everest 1953 Reminiscences

The movement of stores and equipment from our main base at Thyangboche (13,000ft) to the Advanced Base Camp at the foot of the Khumbu Icefall took place in two stages. The first party, led by Ed Hillary, consisted of 38 porters (including some Sherpanis), George Lowe, Mike Westmacott, George Band, Tom Stobart (film cameraman) and myself (physiologist) with our respective Sherpas. Also with us was a 15-year-old boy called Mingma as my assistant.

On our first night out from Thyangboche it snowed heavily; the next day the sky was clear and the glare intense. Few, if any, of the porters had goggles and by evening they were suffering from varying degrees of snow blindness; four had to be paid off as they could not carry their loads. Stobart and I spent the morning improvising goggles using strips of photographic adhesive tape, with small holes for the eyes and enclosing pieces of yellow perspex from panorama goggles. These proved satisfactory and we were able to proceed.

The march lay up the terminal moraine of the Khumbu glacier over rough stony ground. Several porters slipped and fell with their loads. One Sherpani slipped down a slope with the load round her neck. I happened to be by and went to help her. She was not at all pleased. While I was releasing her and fixing her 60lb load, she kept her head turned away so that I could not see who it was. I suppose she was ashamed at having fallen. Another girl, who was almost snow blind, we tried to send back but she refused to accept her money and insisted on going on.

The next camp was at the site of the Swiss Base Camp of the previous spring at 17,000ft. The following day, April 12th, we arrived at the foot of the Icefall and the remains of the Swiss occupation the year before were everywhere, including a large pile of wood which was very welcome. That night it snowed again and the minimum temperature fell to minus 23°C. The second party of porters arrived under Tenzing. Mingma's father Dawa Tenzing who was there said his mother was sending up cold weather equipment from Khumjung so that Mingma could stay.

The Sherpas' comments on the use of oxygen, on which they had been training, were: you don't have to breathe so fast nor so deeply and going uphill is like walking on the level. Dawa Tenzing, on being issued with leather boots, inspected them critically and said 'Well they are cold boots but I expect they will be all right during the warm months of the year'. In fact they were not. There were many complaints about the boots; I think they were probably too tight. It was amusing to watch the faces of the porters at the pay parade – expressions of intense gratification as each received a new ten rupee note and some silver, for carrying from Thyangboche.

On arrival at Base Camp sahibs and Sherpas set about exploring the Icefall. The lower two-thirds were easy but the upper third was extremely broken and dangerous; two log bridges and a ladder were employed. The route was marked with red flags. Meanwhile, a large L-shaped ice cave was being excavated. This was used for cooling respiratory bags during measurement of water loss from the lungs, which turned out to be 3ml per 100 litres of expired gas. The temperature in the cave was constant at minus 7 degrees. There was complete silence in the cave.

At first the party working on the Icefall camped halfway up. This was an eerie experience because of the constant movement of the glacier with creaking and groaning and pistol shot noises. Later on, as acclimatisation improved, climbers preferred to make the whole ascent in a day which took about three hours.

As soon as the route was ready Mingma and Nemi took my equipment to the top of the Icefall where we established a camp on the left of the névé, safe from avalanches. Unfortunately, on opening the ration box containing gas sampling and analysing equipment, what should we find but a load of pickles! I never found out whether this was by accident or deliberate. Anyhow it caused much merriment at the Base Camp; but I was not pleased, to say the least. Mingma turned out to be a valuable asset. He always knew where everything was, especially my spectacles. Unfortunately I lost his services for several days when he became ill with a cold and fever. Was this an infection he contracted from contact with me, similar but opposite to the infections contracted by sahibs on their first contact with Sherpas on earlier expeditions?

Camp 3 was set up near a huge crevasse with the upper wall exposed so that one could see markings on it like the rungs of a tree – I think there were about 46. Climbers staying at Camp 3 were very co-operative in taking part in exercise and other experiments. Moving on to Camp 4 – three hours walk up the glacier – had to be completed early in the morning for fear of avalanches. At Camp 4 I used an Arctic Pyramid tent which was extremely stable against the wind. One morning a Sherpa appeared at the entrance holding a pint mug full of dark red blood. I could not tell whether the blood came from the lungs or the stomach (because blood from the lungs is dark red at this altitude). It seemed important to get the man down to lower altitude as soon as possible, so we started forthwith. In spite of the blood the Sherpa's work capacity seemed unimpaired and we got down to Base Camp four or five hours later.

The work tests I carried out at Camp 3 were repeated at Camp 4 (22,400ft). Some of the subjects who had just returned from ten-day spells laying fixed ropes on the Lhotse Face displayed remarkably high rates of lung ventilation up to 230 litres a minute in one case, compared with 120 litres at sea-level.

One of my non-physiological tasks was conducting James Morris, the *Times* correspondent and a non-mountaineer, up the Icefall. Morris was of slender build and light on his feet and he soon got used to climbing with crampons and was finally able to manage the whole ascent of the Icefall in a day. We were camped to the right of the névé on May 4th when the assault of the Lhotse Face was beginning. We had a good view of the Face and the South Col, but I remember especially the excellent leg of roast lamb we had for supper – a rare treat. The weather had turned unstable at this point and we could not help but admire John Hunt's decision to press on rather than delay the assault. I was at Camp 4 when the party returned from the successful assault on the summit. Hillary and Tenzing arrived first, and I have a picture in my mind of them sitting on packing cases with their legs apart and drinking tea. I examined them briefly; there was no evidence of dehydration and this was confirmed by samples of blood and urine brought back to England for analysis, but their blood pressure was low.

Next day the climbers were in a hurry to get off the mountain and much valuable equipment was left behind. After a day or two of rest at Thyangboche the party set off back to Kathmandu. In the evening of the first day a portly middle-aged Sherpani came to my tent. She was carrying a large basket of eggs carefully packed in grass. She had come to beg me not to take Mingma to Kathmandu where she feared he would be corrupted. She was very upset about this prospect and I had no option but to concede to her request. At the end of the interview she presented me with the eggs.

MICHAEL WARD

The Contribution of Medical Science to the First Ascent of Everest

The Solution of the High-Altitude Problem

(Plates 30–33)

This article should be read in conjunction with 'The Exploration of the Nepalese Side of Everest' by Michael Ward, which appeared in AJ97, 213–221, 1992/93. The two articles, taken together, cover a progression of significant events, both scientific and topographical, which took place between 1945 and the first ascent of Everest in 1953. The linkage is set out in Appendix 3 on pages 50–51.

The opening of Nepal in 1949, and the confirmation of a possible new route up Everest by the 1951 Reconnaissance expedition, gave a powerful impetus to high-altitude studies; for despite the best efforts of medical scientists and mountaineers in the 1920s and 1930s, the final thousand feet of the mountain remained unclimbed. Between 1921 and 1938 about 25 people had reached a height of 27,000ft and above, eight climbing to 28,000ft, both with and without supplementary oxygen. At these heights, ascents without using oxygen are at the limit of what is medically and physiologically possible, yet it was still unclear whether the use of oxygen was as effective as acclimatisation in generating a performance adequate to reach the summit. It was the solution of this problem by Dr Griffith Pugh and his colleagues at the Medical Research Council in London and on the Cho Oyu expedition in 1952 that was to be a key factor in the first ascent of Everest.

The use of supplementary oxygen before the Second World War

Some of the best respiratory physiologists had helped early Everest expeditions. Haldane, Barcroft and others had been adamant that supplementary oxygen should be used for the ascent. Their opinion was influenced by the death of two Frenchmen in 1875 at 28,000ft, an altitude to which they had ascended by balloon without supplementary oxygen. Tissandier, the third member of the party, only just survived. However, in the late 19th century, Conway had climbed to 24,600ft on Pioneer Peak in the Karakoram without the use of oxygen, and Clinton Dent in 1893[1] had stated his conviction that Everest (which he called Gaurisankar) could be climbed without supplementary oxygen and Alexander Kellas in 1920 had reached the same conclusion.[2]

Medical scientists who had underestimated the effects of acclimatisation were amazed when mountaineers on early Everest expeditions in the 1920s and 30s reached heights of 28,000ft without supplementary oxygen. In fact oxygen *was* used on these expeditions, but it did not give as much benefit as it should have done and, confusingly, some mountaineers seemed to climb as fast (or faster) without supplementary oxygen as those who were using it. However, Finch (later Professor at Imperial College, London) reached 27,000ft on Everest in 1922 using supplementary oxygen. He was convinced of its effectiveness and noted that sleeping oxygen combated fatigue and maintained the climber's physical condition. Unfortunately he was not chosen for the 1924 expedition on which four men, climbing without supplementary oxygen, reached 28,000ft; at this height, Mallory and Irvine, using open-circuit oxygen, were last seen by Odell. On this expedition, too, Somervell, a surgeon, was able to measure the amount of oxygen in the depth of the lungs at the highest altitude yet attained.

On expeditions in the 1930s mountaineers and scientists made many contributions. In 1933 Greene developed a very efficient open-circuit apparatus and also advocated the use of oxygen in the treatment of frostbite. This comprised a 500 litre cylinder with a capacity for delivering up to 3 litres per minute and it weighed 12lb 12oz. With hindsight, neither the flow rate nor the amount of oxygen would have been adequate to provide a sufficient boost to performance for long enough. The apparatus was never used on the mountain because, after the two attempts without supplementary oxygen (which had priority) had failed at 28,000ft, the weather became so bad that the party retreated to Base Camp. Unfortunately the slopes of the North Col then became so dangerous from avalanches that no further attempt was possible.[3] Warren, the medical officer in 1935, 1936 and 1938, was initially very keen on the closed-circuit apparatus, and in 1937 he tested it in the European Alps, on the Matterhorn and Wellenkuppe. Because of bad weather the 1936 expedition only reached about 23,000ft, but in 1938 Warren and Lloyd used the closed-circuit apparatus high on the mountain. As a result of technical and practical difficulties in the field, Warren, who had initially been keen on the closed-circuit apparatus, changed his mind and became an advocate of the open circuit,[4] as did Lloyd.

Tilman, who led the 1938 expedition, had little regard for oxygen, nor indeed for any other kinds of scientific investigation on expeditions, since his preference was for keeping things as small and simple as possible. In 1938 he had compromised these principles by taking along, under protest, four sets of oxygen. Oxygen sets for use on Everest, developed in connection with high-altitude flying in the Second World War, were discussed by Roxburgh of the Institute of Aviation Medicine in the 1947 *Geographical Journal*.[5] But there was still, by 1951, no consistent evidence that supplementary oxygen had given a significant boost to performance on the mountain.

Two types of oxygen apparatus had been developed for mountaineers to use at extreme altitude. In the open-circuit apparatus oxygen is added at different flow rates to the air that the mountaineer is breathing. The 'altitude in the depths of the lungs' is determined by the flow rate of the oxygen, enabling the mountaineer to be at a 'lower' altitude than that at which he is actually climbing; this should enable him to climb faster. The exhaled breath is vented to the atmosphere. The apparatus is simple and rugged but a considerable number of oxygen cylinders have to be carried by the climber.

With the closed-circuit apparatus the climber breathes pure oxygen from the cylinder carried on his back, the exhaled air is passed over a soda-lime canister, CO_2 is absorbed and the oxygen is recycled, hence the term 'closed-circuit'. Obviously a lower flow rate of oxygen is used than is necessary in the open-circuit apparatus. The mountaineer is at or near sea-level in the depths of the lungs and this gives him a greater boost, but the apparatus is heavy and, being more complicated than the open-circuit, it is more likely to break down. If it does so, sudden exposure to extreme altitude can cause severe problems, since the mountaineer, at one moment at 'sea-level', is suddenly exposed to the extreme altitude at which he is actually climbing. This occurred to Bourdillon at 26,000ft on the South Col in 1953.

Another important observation at altitude was made by Sir Bryan Mathews FRS (later Director of the Institute of Aviation Medicine at Farnborough and Professor of Physiology at Cambridge) who highlighted the point that heat loss could occur through the lungs as a result of increased respiration, and that this could lead to general body cooling and frostbite.[6] The part played by dehydration in deterioration at extreme altitude was later discussed at an informal meeting at Farnborough in 1947, and the suggestion was made by Rudolf Peters, Professor of Biochemistry at Oxford, that this was due in part to the high rate of breathing.[7]

Throughout the 1920s and 1930s opinion on the use of supplementary oxygen at altitude was divided. In general the doctors and scientists favoured its use, whilst others thought that reliance could be placed on acclimatisation alone. A third group, of which Tilman was one, were the purists who disapproved of the use of supplementary oxygen on principle.

Operation Everest I in the USA (1946)

In 1946 Charles Houston took part in a landmark experiment in high-altitude studies called 'Operation Everest I'.[8,9] A flight surgeon in the US Navy from 1941 to 1946, he had been a member of the successful British-American party that made the first ascent of Nanda Devi in 1936 and had led the 1938 American attempt on K2. With this background he had been working in altitude research and, in 1946, he and the distinguished respiratory physiologist Richard Riley and others conducted 'Operation Everest I' in a decompression chamber at Pensacola Air Base, Florida. In this five-week study, four volunteers were gradually decompressed to a simulated altitude equal to the 'summit of Mount Everest'. However, they used an aneroid barometer calibrated by the International Standard Atmosphere table, and the reading actually corresponded to the barometric pressure found at 30,000ft rather than 29,028ft. Two of the four volunteers managed to exercise on a stationary bicycle ergometer for 20 minutes 'on the summit of Everest' without supplementary oxygen, thus producing the first solid evidence that such efforts were possible at such a height.

On the ground, however, mountaineers without supplementary oxygen at 28,000ft were climbing so slowly that, even from a camp at 27,000ft, it seemed unlikely that they could reach the summit of the mountain and return without an enforced bivouac. Although the technical climbing difficulties of the last 1000ft on Everest did not appear insuperable, the prevailing weather conditions and the lack of modern protective clothing made it a dangerous undertaking. Climbers at this altitude in the pre-war period had suffered from hallucinations, some had died from cold injury, one porter had developed a hemiplegia (stroke), dehydration was marked, fatigue overwhelming and loss of weight extreme. Muscle wasting was so severe that one climber, Smythe, observed that he could almost encircle the muscles of his thigh with the fingers of one hand after a period at extreme altitude.

Medical Research Council in the UK (1951–52)

An event which made a vital contribution to the first ascent of Everest was the involvement of the Medical Research Council in the summer of 1951. At the end of the previous year (1950) a new Department of Human Physiology had been set up for the purpose of carrying out research into all aspects of extreme environments on man. It was here that Michael Ward, an RAMC officer attached to the Brigade of Guards in London while doing his National Service, first met Dr Griffith Pugh, whose research was to play such a vital part on Everest in 1953. Ward, with W H Murray and Tom Bourdillon, was planning an expedition to investigate the Nepalese side of Everest in the autumn of 1951. The introduction to Pugh had come from Tom Bourdillon's father, Dr R B Bourdillon, who had heard about the important new unit through his position as a member of the MRC staff working in the Electro-Medical Unit at Stoke Mandeville Hospital. He rang Ward about it, saw him at the hospital and then Ward went to see Pugh at the MRC laboratories in Hampstead.

Griffith Pugh was a clinical physiologist with an unusual background, ideal for the solution of the high-altitude problem of Everest. An Olympic-class skier and an experienced mountaineer, he had been posted in the Second World War to The Cedars in the Lebanon to join the Mountain Warfare Training Centre. Here he investigated all aspects of the effects of the mountain environment on man, including high altitude, and with A D M Cox, then 'Chief Instructor, Rock', and W J Riddell, 'Chief Instructor, Snow', wrote army manuals on all aspects of mountain warfare. Discharged from the army in 1945, Pugh was taken on the staff of Professor John McMichael's unit at the Postgraduate Medical School, Hammersmith, London, on the strength of his research work in the Lebanon and his wide experience in medicine. This medical school was and has remained one of the powerhouses of British and world medicine.[10]

Pugh was an obvious candidate for the new MRC unit at Hampstead, but as he had never run a department a suitable Director was found in Otto Edholm, at that time Professor of Physiology at the University of Western Ontario.[11] Edholm, with A C Burton, had recently completed a classical monograph on *Man in a Cold Environment*, and work on high altitude was complementary to the department's expertise on cold. Before the departure of the 1951 Everest Reconnaissance expedition, and during its time in Nepal, Pugh's work at the unit gave him ample opportunity to study the problems of high altitude, which became part of the formal programme carried out by this department.

Pugh's methods were similar to those used regularly by physicians and surgeons to investigate and obtain a diagnosis and treat patients; only in this instance the 'diseases' were cold and high altitude. A study was made of the narratives of expeditions from many different countries to the world's highest peaks. Symptoms were identified, together with signs observed by medical officers and fellow climbers. Investigations included noting air temperature, wind speed and climbing rate. To these were added Pugh's own work, both in the laboratory and in the field, to clarify the diagnosis. Finally 'treatment' was suggested, including increased rates of supplementary oxygen, improved insulation for clothing and sleeping-bags, better food and adequate drinking water. At the time, Pugh's approach to the problems of high altitude was innovative, but well tested and successful in the clinical field.

In the summer of 1951 after Eric Shipton returned to the United Kingdom from a diplomatic appointment in Kunming in South-West China, he took over the leadership of the 1951 Mount Everest (autumn) reconnaissance. Edmund Hillary and Earle Riddiford also joined the expedition to Nepal. Before attacking the Khumbu Icefall Shipton and Hillary gained a vantage point at just over 20,000ft on Pumori, from which they were able to see the way clear to the South Col.[12,13] An ascent by this route at last appeared to be a viable possibility, so on his return to the United Kingdom in December 1951 Shipton asked Pugh and the Medical Research Council to help with the scientific problems of an attempt on Everest. In the meantime Swiss mountaineers had obtained permission to attempt Everest from Nepal.

Swiss Everest expeditions in 1952 (spring and autumn)

Most of the Swiss mountaineers who took part in the two 1952 expeditions came from a small but extremely active club in Geneva, L'Androsace.[14] They were an exceptionally strong party, many members having completed routes in the European Alps of far greater difficulty than any that our own 1953 party had done, and requiring more expertise and experience. This was partly because the Swiss had been able to climb during the war, and also because British mountaineering standards in the 1930s had lagged behind those on the Continent.

In sheer mountaineering expertise, therefore, the Swiss group posed the greatest ever challenge to Mount Everest. In the spring of 1952 they easily made the first ascent of the Icefall, made a direct ascent of the South Col by the Geneva Spur and camped on the South Col; but because of a design fault, Lambert and Tenzing could only use supplementary oxygen at rest. As a result there was no boost to performance and they had to stop exhausted at 28,000ft. Another attempt in the autumn failed again, at 26,000ft, as winds of 60mph and temperatures of 50 degrees of frost were encountered on the South Col. This made it impossible to survive for more than a few minutes in the open because the wind chill made the temperature on the exposed skin approach minus 100 degrees C. Even to these experienced Swiss mountaineers 28,000ft seemed to be a physiological barrier.

British research in 1952: the Cho Oyu Expedition

Whilst the Swiss were attempting Everest in the spring of 1952, a British–New Zealand training party went to Cho Oyu, the sixth highest peak in the world and about 20 miles west of Everest. Led by Shipton, its purpose was both to build up a nidus of high-altitude climbers who would eventually go to Everest and to test out oxygen sets, clothing, stoves, tents and all the other equipment to be used in an Everest attempt. Pugh obtained a grant from the Royal Society and insisted that he should go on this expedition in order to complete, at altitude, various experimental procedures that he had started at sea-level. The most important of these was to establish the flow rate of oxygen in the open-circuit sets that would give a boost to mountaineers at extreme altitude by increasing their climbing rate and improving their stamina and physical and mental effectiveness. Despite Houston's work on 'Operation Everest I', of which Pugh was well aware, he believed that the use of adequate supplementary oxygen was absolutely vital if there was to be any hope of climbing the last 1000ft of Everest. For there appeared to be no mountaineer in the UK, or indeed anywhere, whose climbing rate at altitude was fast enough to enable him to get to the summit and descend in a day without the use of supplementary oxygen.

Unfortunately, some members of the party became ill before they reached Cho Oyu. Moreover, the route with the best hope of success lay in Tibet, which carried the risk of a brush with the Chinese communists, and the alternative route from Nepal was obviously too difficult. Shipton now felt that the objective of the expedition, which was to get high-altitude experience, would best be served by the extensive exploration of the then little known Everest region. The attempt on Cho Oyu was therefore abandoned and much valuable exploration carried out.

From the point of view of high-altitude science this expedition was eminently successful. A physiological camp, the first of its type, was set up at 19,000ft on the Menlung La. With Bourdillon, Secord and Colledge to help him, Pugh carried out some of the most important studies in the history of high-altitude research. He showed that a flow rate of four litres of oxygen per minute was essential to counteract the weight of the open-circuit oxygen sets, and also to provide a boost to the climber at great altitude (over 25,000ft). The key effect was that it enabled climbers to ascend continuously rather than intermittently. This was the solution to the high-altitude problem of Everest. The smooth and relatively eventless ascent to the summit by Hillary and Tenzing contrasts dramatically with Norton's agonising description of climbing without supplementary oxygen at 28,000ft: 'Our pace was wretched. My ambition was to do twenty consecutive paces uphill without a pause to rest and pant, elbow on bended knee; yet I never remember achieving it – thirteen was nearer the mark.'

Pre-war Everest expeditions and the spring 1952 Swiss party had only used a flow rate of about two litres per minute and sometimes less – barely enough to counter the weight of the set. This would explain the paradoxical observations of climbers using supplementary oxygen yet getting no boost at extreme altitude on pre-war expeditions. In addition, Pugh confirmed the beneficial effects of using oxygen while asleep, as observed by Finch.[15] Another important finding was the confirmation of the remark made by Professor Peters in 1947 that dehydration at high altitude was severe, loss of water being due to the greatly increased rate of breathing.[7] An intake of about three litres a day was necessary to counter the effects of dehydration. This water intake is rarely if ever accomplished and is one of the reasons for rapid deterioration at great heights. Many other medical and scientific observations were made by Pugh and his team and incorporated in a report to the Medical Research Council.[16, 17]

The Everest 1953 Expedition

In the months following the party's return to the United Kingdom from Cho Oyu, there was controversy as to the leadership of the proposed 1953 expedition and little mountaineering organisation was carried out, but there was no pause in the critical scientific buildup; the decision to use supplementary oxygen in 1953 was taken by the Himalayan Committee of the Alpine Club and the Royal Geographical Society.

While the advantage conferred by the use of supplementary oxygen had not been decisive in the pre-war expeditions, those, like Lloyd, who had used it to 27,000ft on Everest in 1938, were satisfied that it *did* give an increased boost the higher the climber ascended. This was amply confirmed by Pugh's work on Cho Oyu. The increased flow rate that Pugh considered essential would require more oxygen carried at a high pressure, and this could be accommodated in cylinders made of high strength and lighter materials that had been developed during the war. There was obvious scope, too, for reducing the weight of the sets. Finally, both Swiss and French teams were eager to make an attempt on Everest and the oxygen option had to be taken seriously.[18]

In the meantime, Tom Bourdillon and his father and others had been constructing and testing a closed-circuit oxygen set. Though this provided a greater boost than the open-circuit system, its weight was considerable, incorporating as it did the soda-lime canister which absorbed the exhaled carbon dioxide; it was also less reliable. Using closed-circuit oxygen sets, Bourdillon and Evans made the first ascent of the South Summit at 28,250ft from the South Col – but one set then malfunctioned. They very sensibly turned back, as the risks of set failure would involve sudden 'ascent' to 28,250ft from near sea-level in the 'depths of their lungs', and this could cause coma and death. Up to this point their climbing rates had been amazingly fast because, although each carried about 60lbs, in the 'depths of their lungs' they were near sea-level and able therefore to climb at near sea-level rates of ascent.

On Everest in 1953, 198,000 litres of oxygen were taken. Open-circuit oxygen, at a flow rate of four litres per minute, was used from an altitude of

BRITISH HIMALAYAN EXPEDITION

TO CHO OYU, 1952

By Dr L. Griffith C. E. Pugh

PART I.   GENERAL ASPECTS

PART II.   PHYSIOLOGICAL STUDIES

The Index to Griffith Pugh's Report to the Medical Research Council showing the depth and extent of his work on the Menlung La in 1952

26,000ft and above by Hillary and Tenzing and was undoubtedly one of the main reasons why this pair were successful. In fact they used a slightly lower oxygen flow rate of about three litres per minute in their ascent from the last camp, at about 27,900ft, to the summit. The use of adequate supplementary oxygen prevented high-altitude deterioration and contributed to the remarkably good physical and mental condition of the whole party. Pugh's rules on supplementary oxygen were that 4 litres/minute should be used on ascent, 2 litres/minute on descent, and 1 litre/minute when sleeping. These were reinforced by attention to the detail of Pugh's work on dehydration, food, protective clothing and other important factors. There were no accidents and only two cases of mild frostbite on this expedition, and this can be attributed to the physical and mental mobility of the members of the party. Using adequate supplementary oxygen, they were able to adjust to and, when necessary, counter events rapidly and correctly, a dangerous feature of oxygen lack being mental slowness to respond to new and potentially lethal situations.

If all this scientific support and expertise had been available to the Everest expeditions of the 1920s and 1930s, the highest peak in the world would probably have been climbed then. Many factors – good weather, good luck and, in particular, good management – contributed to the successful ascent in 1953, but a critical part was also played by the application of good science to a medical-physiological problem imposed on a mountaineering ascent. Within the next few years every one of the world's ten highest peaks were climbed using these principles.

The ascent of Everest without supplementary oxygen

Man's ability to remain alive depends on the pressure of oxygen in the depths of the lungs (alveolar pressure), which itself is dependent on the barometric pressure, or the weight of the atmosphere on the Earth's surface. At extreme altitude the barometric and therefore oxygen pressure is much lower than at sea-level and at the summit of Everest life can only just be sustained without supplementary oxygen.

When expeditions to the Himalaya were resumed after the Second World War, it gradually became apparent, largely through the work of Pugh in the Everest region in 1952, on Everest in 1953, and on the Silver Hut expedition of 1960–61 in the Everest region, that the barometric pressure on Himalayan peaks was higher than predicted and that it might be possible to climb Everest without supplementary oxygen.

A number of physiological changes contribute to man's ability to acclimatise and function efficiently at high-altitude. In sea-level dwellers it has been shown that some individuals are able to take in more oxygen than others when working maximally during exercise. This was the basis of much of Pugh's work for the selection of ski and mountain troops in the Lebanon in the Second World War, and is now used for the selection of athletes in different disciplines. In some sea-level dwellers the oxygen transport system is more efficient than in others, and some climbers are more efficient in the way that they move, thus not 'wasting' movements and therefore oxygen.

It has been known for many years that stay at great altitude results in both mental and physical deterioration and, as long ago as 1907, Longstaff, with the Gurkha soldier Karbir and the Brocherel brothers, ascended and descended 6000ft in a day on Trisul (23,360ft), thus avoiding both acute mountain sickness and altitude deterioration. A number of rapid ascents and descents of Everest have been made without supplementary oxygen after suitable acclimatisation up to about 17,000ft; but the dangers are considerable, in particular the thickening of the blood due to an increase in the red blood cells may lead to thrombotic or other vascular episodes, and predispose to frostbite as the small peripheral skin vessels tend to get clogged up.

The first ascent of Everest without supplementary oxygen was made in 1978,[19] and by now more than 30 people have climbed to the summit without its use. Each of the world's ten highest peaks have been climbed by at least two mountaineers without supplementary oxygen and one Sherpa has climbed Everest six times.

As the modern mountaineer has the opportunity to ascend to great altitude on many occasions in one season, he is therefore fitter, better acclimatised and more efficient than his forebears. However, if supplementary oxygen is *not* used it is essential that he moves up and down the mountain quickly. At sea-level if an athlete fails to produce an Olympic-class performance he may lose a race or a title; near the summit of Everest he may lose a limb or his life.[20]

(Early experiments in the use of supplementary oxygen on Kamet in 1920 and in Oxford in 1921–22 will be discussed in a further article in the *Alpine Journal 1994*.)

REFERENCES

1   C Dent, 'Physiological Effects of High Altitudes', in *Geographical Journal 1, No 1*, 46–48, 1893.

2   J B West, 'A M Kellas: Pioneer Himalayan Physiologist and Mountaineer', in *AJ94*, 207–213, 1989/90.

3   R Greene, 'The Everest Oxygen Apparatus. 1933' in *Lancet*, 17 November 1934, p.1122.

4   C B M Warren. Personal communication, 1990.

5   H L Roxburgh, 'Oxygen Equipment for Climbing Mount Everest', in *Geographical Journal 109*, 207–216, 1947.

6   B Mathews, 'Loss of Heat at High Altitudes', in *Journal of Physiology 77*, 28–29, 1932.

7   P Lloyd, 'Valedictory Address', in *AJ85*, 3–15, 1980.

8   C S Houston and R L Riley, 'Respiratory and Circulatory Changes during Acclimatisation to High Altitude', in *American Journal of Physiology 149*, 565–588, 1947.

9   C S Houston, A Cymerman, J R Sutton, *Operation Everest II. 1985*, US Army Research Institute of Environmental Medicine, Natick. Mass. 1991.

10 M P Ward, 'Griffith Pugh: An 80th Birthday Tribute', in *AJ95*, 188–190, 1990/91.

11   L G C E Pugh. Personal communication, 1990.

12   M P Ward, 'The Exploration of the Nepalese Side of Everest', in *AJ97*, 213–221, 1992/93.

13   M P Ward, P K Clark, 'Everest 1951: cartographic and photographic evidence of a new route from Nepal', in *Geographical Journal 158 No 1*, 47–56, 1992.

14   E Feuz, 'Events leading up to and preparations for the 1952 Mount Everest Expedition', *The Mountain World* (Ed Marcel Kurz), 39–42, 1953.

15   G I Finch, *The Making of a Mountaineer* with a Memoir by Scott Russell, J W Arrowsmith, 1988.

16   L G C E Pugh, *Report on the Cho Oyu Expedition*. Medical Research Council, London, 1952.

17   L G C E Pugh, 'Scientific Aspects of the Expedition to Mount Everest 1953', in *Geographical Journal 120, Part 2*, 183–192, 1954.

18   P Lloyd. Personal communication, 1991.

19   R Messner, *Everest: Expedition to the Ultimate*. London, Kaye & Ward, 1979.

20   O Oelz, 'Death at Extreme Altitude', in *Journal of Wilderness Medicine* 1, 141–143, 1990.

21   T D Bourdillon, 'Oxygen Apparatus on the Mountain', *AJ59*, 247–263, 1953–54.

APPENDIX 1

MEDICAL SCIENTISTS ON MOUNT EVEREST 1921–1953

(All were from the UK except where indicated)

1921	A M Kellas, A F R Wollaston
1922	T H Somervell, T G Longstaff, A W Wakefield
1924	T H Somervell, R W G Hingston
1933	C R Greene, W McLean
1935	C B M Warren
1936	C B M Warren, G N Humphreys, E H L Wigram
1938	C B M Warren
1950	C S Houston (US)
1951	M P Ward
1952 (Spring)	E Wyss-Dunant (Switzerland)
	G Chevalley (Switzerland)
1952 (Autumn)	G Chevalley (Switzerland)
1952 (Cho Oyu)	R C Evans, L G C E Pugh
1953	R C Evans, L G C E Pugh, M P Ward

APPENDIX 2

PERFORMANCE AT ALTITUDE ON EVEREST WITH AND WITHOUT SUPPLEMENTARY OXYGEN

(See References 15 and 21)

Party	Altitude Difference ft	Load lb	Rate of Climb ft/hr	Oxygen Apparatus
1922	25,000–27,000	–	320	None
	25,500–27,200	40	c400	2.4 l/min. Open
1924	25,300–26,800	–	333	None
1952	25,800–27,200	?	233	O$_2$ at rest
1953	25,800–27,200	40	622	4 l/min. Open
	25,800–27,200	40	494	4 l/min. Open
	25,800–27,200	52	933	Closed
	27,900–29,002	17	210	3 l/min. Open

Note: (1) **Similar climbing rate** when using no supplementary oxygen and when using open circuit oxygen at 2.4 litres/minute.

(2) **Increased climbing rate** when using (a) closed circuit oxygen, and (b) open circuit oxygen at 4 litres/minute.

APPENDIX 3

SIGNIFICANT EVENTS PRECEDING THE FIRST ASCENT OF EVEREST
1945–53

Year	Event	People/ Organisations
1945	First map showing topographical detail and spot heights of Tibetan and Nepalese sides of Everest	Milne/Hinks (London)
	First secret flight over Everest from Nepal	684 Squadron
1946	'First ascent' of Everest in decompression chamber (Florida, USA)	Houston/Riley
1947	Second secret flight over Everest from Nepal	Neame
1949	The opening of Nepal to foreigners	
1950	Tibet occupied by Chinese communists and sealed off to Westerners	
	First reconnaissance expedition to Nepalese side of Everest	Houston/Tilman
1951	**Spring** Cartographic and photographic evidence discovered of a possible route to the summit from Nepal	Ward
	Summer Involvement of the Medical Research Council in solving the high-altitude problem	Ward/Pugh
	Autumn Reconnaissance expedition confirms possible route to the summit of Everest	Shipton/Murray Bourdillon/Ward Hillary/Riddiford

APPENDIX 3 continued

Year	Event	People/Organisations
1952	**Spring** Swiss reach 28,000ft on Everest	Lambert/Tenzing
	Cho Oyu expedition (Nepal)	Shipton (leader)
	Menlung La physiology camp: solution of the high-altitude problem of Everest	Pugh/Bourdillon Secord/Colledge
	Summer Preparations for Everest	Medical Research Council/Institute of Aviation Medicine/Royal Geographical Society/Alpine Club
	Autumn Swiss reach 27,000ft on Everest	Lambert/Reiss/Tenzing/seven Sherpas
	Visit to Zurich for data from Swiss on their two expeditions	Pugh
	Leader of British 1953 expedition appointed	Hunt
1953	**May** First ascent, South Summit (Nepal)	Bourdillon/Evans
	First ascent of Everest	Hillary/Tenzing Hunt (leader)

MICHAEL WESTMACOTT
Because We Were There

A question regularly put to me since 1953 is 'How were you selected for the expedition'? or, from a fellow-climber when his or her companion has been more than usually inept, 'How did *you* get on that expedition?' John Hunt has given his version of events, with typical discretion, in The Book. What follows is a worm's eye view. But don't expect startling revelations. There are no skeletons, no dirty linen, as far as I know.

It began for me with a splendid day traversing the Matterhorn, Zmutt-Hörnli, with Dick Viney, returning to the valley in the late afternoon. It was the fine season of 1952, when the foreign currency allowance was £25; by dint of sleeping always in huts (scarcely any of my contemporaries had tents, sleeping-bags or cars in those days) I managed three weeks in Switzerland and brought home £4. Based on huts, we were taking full advantage of the good weather, did a number of classic routes and saved ourselves hundreds of pounds in guides' fees. As we made for our doss at Stafelalp Dick said 'We've had a marvellous day's climbing, Mike. Nothing like it in the Himalayas – all slog, slog, slog – but wouldn't you give anything to go to Everest next year?'

He was right, but I don't think it had occurred to me before to do anything about it. It was worth a letter when I got home, although I did not think there was much chance. No acknowledgement but, some weeks later, I heard on the PyG grapevine that there was a short list; what names were on it I did not know. Then there was an exciting letter calling me for interview at the RGS. I told my employers I had urgent private business in London on Tuesday and took the day off.

The prospect of being interviewed by an unknown Colonel Hunt, a full colonel no less, was a bit daunting for an ex-lieutenant RE. I need not have worried. This was no brass-hatted inquisitor probing for weak points, but someone who wanted to get to know me. We talked mostly about the climbs I had done and the people I had done them with. I wanted to be selected solely on the basis of my climbing record. Perhaps quixotically, I did not tell him that I spoke some Urdu, which was to come in useful later, because I felt this would hardly be fair to other aspirants, friends of mine, who had not had the luck to serve in India. When with John Hunt, one bends over backwards to be fair. I left the interview with the thought that, if I were to be turned down, I would be happier to accept refusal from John than from most people.

Again a period of waiting; again the grapevine, this time more specific. There were still two places to be filled and I was still in the running. Then there was another letter and next morning the names of the party in *The Times*.

We were all very lucky just to be around at that time, with approximately the right qualifications. Thirty years of expeditions had built up the necessary know-how. Clothing was improving, with the use of synthetics. Oxygen equipment benefited from wartime developments. Griffith Pugh's work on the physiology of high altitude crowned his predecessors' achievements. John was an ideal leader. And, on a more personal note, there was far less competition than there would have been a few years later. Not too many people had managed to get in four good alpine seasons since the war. George Band and I, with no Himalayan experience, were particularly lucky and may well have owed our selection to the good weather in the Alps in 1952.

I suppose that all of us, ever since, have been trying in one way or another to live up to our membership of that unique and very happy expedition.

Tenzing Norgay 1914–1986 and the Sherpa Team

(Plates: front cover, 4, 5, 10, 12, 26)

Forty years ago there were no jumars, no front-pointed crampons and no modern ice tools. 'Alpine-style' climbing, with very few Sherpas or none at all, had not reached the highest mountains of the Himalaya. Light expeditions – the most enjoyable form of mountaineering, many would agree – were arguably not suited to achieving success on 8000m peaks. The experience of Everest expeditions before 1953 had shown that success depended on adequate support high up in the final phases of the climb. This meant a large, well equipped expedition, capable of sustained assault. This, in turn, meant relying heavily on Sherpas.

John Hunt's task was to succeed where seven assault expeditions had failed. He could not afford to ignore the evidence that a large party had more chance of success than a small one. His plan catered for a team of 35 Sherpas to carry 12 tons of stores to the Advanced Base and nearly one third of a ton to the South Col. This allowed for effective support really high up, initially for two attempts on the summit. This was indeed a large party but, put in perspective, nothing like so big as other expeditions which were to follow.

The Sherpa team, some from Darjeeling and some from Khumbu, carried out their part in this plan magnificently. Their contribution to the success of the expedition was absolutely crucial, and it was right and proper that a Sherpa should have been included in the summit attempts. Specifically, one Sherpa reached the summit, another carried to the highest camp at 27,900ft, another to John Hunt's dump at 27,500ft[*], and 19 to the South Col at 26,000ft, seven of them twice. This was a greater quantity of stores than had ever been carried to such heights before. It meant that the summit assault pairs and their support parties could climb in the knowledge that adequate shelter, food and oxygen, should they be needed, were not far below. It also meant that Hillary and Tenzing had everything they needed for their final night before the summit – a tent, warm clothing, a cooker, food and enough oxygen for the night (special sleeping sets had been provided for this particular night) and to get them to the top and back. While this was the result of careful preparation, planning and of the efforts of the whole expedition, final success could not have been achieved without the sterling performance of our Sherpa team.

Forty years on, what has happened to these splendid men? Tenzing, as we all know, achieved world renown and became an international personality. He

[*]See page 21, note 13.

13. International Catalan Expeditions 1991 and 1992: Jordi Magriña
(leader) below ice pinnacles on the Gasherbrum glacier.
(*Kurt Diemberger*) (p88)

14. Broad Peak East Face: trying to find a route to the ramp through the complex icefall. (*Kurt Diemberger*) (p88)

Tenzing Norgay, 1953
A drawing by Lt Col Gordon Borrowman of the 4th Gurkha Rifles

received the George Medal (the highest civilian award for courage after the George Cross) personally from HM the Queen at Buckingham Palace. All of the Sherpa team received the Queen's Coronation Medal and the Himalayan Club gave their Tiger Badge to those who by their performance on the expedition qualified for this coveted award. Some joined Tenzing as instructors at the Himalayan Mountaineering Institute in Darjeeling which was set up in 1954 by Sri Jawaharlal Nehru, Prime Minister of India, to (in his words) 'produce more Tenzings'. All were in demand as porters and some as sirdars on the spate of expeditions which followed. And many, sadly, are dead; the local expectation of life is not high.

It has not been easy to trace everyone. Indeed, after 40 years, it would be almost impossible to find out about all 35 of the Sherpa team. I have therefore confined myself to the 10 Sherpas whose names are most likely to be familiar to readers of this journal.

Tenzing Norgay

By 1953, Tenzing had climbed Nanda Devi East with the French in 1951 and had taken part in five Everest expeditions (three British expeditions, 1935, 1936 and 1938, and the two Swiss expeditions of 1952). He had climbed to over 28,000ft and had far more experience of Everest than any other Sherpa. Moreover, as a person and as a sirdar he was held in considerable respect by the Sherpas themselves. All of us in 1953 were impressed not only by his engaging personality, but also by his energy, good sense and his authority over the Sherpa team.

After the expedition we were equally impressed by the way he reacted to his new role as an international hero. Publicly compared to Buddha in Kathmandu, hosted by Nehru in Delhi, received by the Queen at Buckingham Palace and honoured wherever he went, he retained his inherent modesty and steadfastly refused to let his head be turned.

His life, however, was to be radically changed. A large house was bought for him in Darjeeling with funds raised by public subscription, organised by an Indian newspaper. He was appointed the first field director of the Himalayan Mountaineering Institute (HMI) and, largely through his achievement on Everest, mountaineering gained recognition in India. He received invitations from all over the world and was a frequent visitor to Europe, particularly to Switzerland and Britain where his many friends were delighted to welcome him to their homes and to maintain the happy relationship forged through challenges shared on high mountains. Such friendships are enduring, and have continued since Tenzing's death, with his family.

In 1964 his wife Ang Hlamu, mother of his two elder daughters, died, and Tenzing married Daku, a highly intelligent Sherpani, much younger than he was, who like him had left Khumbu for Darjeeling. She was a considerable help to him in running his large house and establishment. She bore him three sons and a daughter. Sadly, she died in 1992.

After 22 years as Field Director, Tenzing retired from the HMI in 1976, although he maintained his connection as the Institute's Adviser. He continued his trips overseas, however, and was employed by tour promoters, for instance as a guest lecturer on a cruise tour to the Antarctic and as a tour leader to Lhasa.

In 1987 John Hunt wrote: 'Although Tenzing was an immediate friend to everyone, I like to think that his special affections and loyalty were reserved for his companions in 1953. He joined some of our periodic reunions ... and, on each occasion, it was as though the years had rolled back to those unforgettable weeks we spent together on Everest in 1953.'

Tenzing died in 1986, aged 72. He was described as 'A great leader and ambassador of the Sherpas, who brought recognition and fame to his people'. The procession behind the bier at his funeral was over a kilometre long. To the end he maintained his sense of values, modesty, integrity, and devotion and loyalty to his family, his people, his friends, his homeland, his dogs, and to the mountains.

Dawa Tenzing

Dawa Tenzing was the deputy sirdar of the 1953 Sherpa team. He was in many ways a contrast to Tenzing Norgay, to whom he was unrelated. A strong, tall, patriarchal figure from Khumjung village in Khumbu, he was still pigtailed and had a distinct 'presence', together with a good sense of humour. A veteran of many expeditions, including several with Eric Shipton and Charles Evans, he played a significant part on Everest in 1953, carrying loads twice to the South Col and taking charge of the Sherpa team while Tenzing was on the summit assault. He was a very devout man, a quality which commands great respect among Sherpas, and the performance of the whole team was, I believe, influenced by his example, leadership and reliability.

In spite of advancing years, he continued as an active expedition member. In 1954 he was on Makalu with Edmund Hillary and in 1955 he was sirdar to Charles Evans's expedition which made the first ascent of Kangchenjunga, carrying to nearly 27,000ft. The following year he took over from Passang Dawa Lama as sirdar on the Swiss expedition which made the second ascent of Everest and the first of Lhotse. He took part in three further expeditions: Emlyn Jones's attempt on Ama Dablam, James Roberts's first ascent of Annapurna II, and as sirdar to Dorothea Gravina's ladies Jagdula expedition which climbed Kanjiroba Himal, before returning to Everest with the Americans in 1963, when he carried loads twice to the South Col. On all these expeditions he made an outstanding contribution. A great record of a great mountaineer.

Dawa was much loved by British mountaineers. On visits to Britain he was an impressive sight, complete with pigtails and Tibetan dress. At home in Khumbu, however, he suffered a double tragedy when his son Mingma was killed on an expedition, and his wife, on hearing the news, committed suicide. Dawa moved to Thyangboche, living close to the monastery, supported by a pension initiated by Tony Streather and contributed by British climbers.

When, to mark the 25th anniversary of the ascent of Everest, the team members trekked from Darjeeling to Khumbu, they unexpectedly met Dawa Tenzing on the track coming the other way. It was a joyous and emotional reunion with much embracing and back thumping. That alone was worth the two-week walk from Darjeeling, but we were to see him again over the three-day Mani Rimdu festival at Thyangboche, where he enjoyed the position of honour at the side of the High Lama.

We were saddened to hear of his death a few years later. He was one of that small élite band who have made the name of Sherpa known and respected throughout the world.

Annullu

Annullu was Dawa Tenzing's younger brother, and an equally fine Sherpa. An instantly likeable person with a ready smile, his smart turnout contrasted with his elder brother's more rugged appearance. In 1953 it was he who, with Wilfrid Noyce, first reached the South Col and paved the way for the large party of porters which made the vital lift to the Col the next day, to set up the high base from which the assaults were made. Later Annullu carried again to the South Col.

Annullu took part in the successful expedition of 1955 to Kangchenjunga and, in 1956, to Everest with the Swiss, carrying again to the South Col. With his brother, he was on Ama Dablam and Annapurna II before joining Hillary's Makalu expedition of 1961, when he carried a load to Camp 7 at 27,000ft and almost reached the summit. He was then involved in an accident with a number of other Sherpas, helping to rescue them in spite of having broken a rib and being in great pain himself. The following year he was with the Germans on Pumori, and in 1963 again on Everest, this time with the Americans, keeping the Icefall open for eight weeks.

Sadly he was killed in an accident on the relatively easy crossing of the Ambu Lapcha. He was one of the most popular of Sherpas. He was married three times and left seven children.

Ang Nyima

Young, strong and capable, Ang Nyima had been on both the Swiss Everest expeditions of 1952. A chain smoker, he had to be given a special ration of cigarettes in 1953. In spite of this, he carried to Camp 9 at nearly 28,000ft, the only Sherpa, apart from Tenzing, to do so. After Everest he played a leading role in Jimmy Roberts's expeditions to Machapuchare and Annapurna II where he reached the summit (26,041ft). On Machapuchare he proved himself thoroughly safe, unprotected on extremely steep ice, when he had to negotiate the difficult 'Nick' crossing of the N ridge, solo.

Later he was recruited into my regiment, the 10th Gurkha Rifles, and served in Malaya and Borneo, reaching the rank of sergeant. On retirement he returned to his home in Darjeeling, where he died some years later shortly after the death of his son.

Nawang Gombu

Nawang Gombu, Tenzing's nephew, was in 1953 a chubby lad of 17 whose youthful appearance belied his capability. He proved to be an excellent member of the Sherpa team, carrying twice to the South Col. When the HMI was founded he was chosen as one of the original batch of instructors, and when Tenzing retired Nawang Gombu took his place as field director, a post he still holds.

The HMI encourages its instructors to extend their experience, and Nawang Gombu was able to take part in a number of expeditions over the next decade, including those to Saser Kangri, when he reached the summit of Sakang, 24,796ft, and to Nanda Devi, where he had to turn back only 650ft from the summit. He was also a member of expeditions to Garhwal and Kanak, and an observer with Dorothea Gravina's women's party to Cho Oyu.

His triumph came in 1963 when he reached the summit of Everest with Jim Whitaker on the US expedition. Two years later he repeated this success with the Indians, becoming the first man to climb Everest twice. Like his uncle, he became an internationally known mountaineer, and visited many countries, climbing, among other peaks, Mount McKinley and Mont Blanc.

Phu Dorji

Phu Dorji was one of the strongest young Sherpas of our 1953 team. Pigtailed and cheerful, he personified all that was best of the local, Khumbu, Sherpas, carrying his load with apparent ease to the South Col. He was to take part in three further Everest expeditions. With the Americans he carried twice to the South Col, and with the Indian expedition of 1965 he led the support team of Sherpas which carried to the highest camp, estimated at 27,930ft, from which the first party, Nawang Gombu and A S Cheema, reached the summit. While the second and third pairs went to the top, Phu Dorji, resting at Base Camp, received a radio call to tell him that he could be on the fourth summit party provided he could get to the South Col in two days. This he succeeded in doing, and also in reaching the last camp at nearly 28,000ft next day. From here, with Rawat and Ahluwalia, he climbed to the summit on 29 May, 12 years to the day after Hillary and Tenzing. From Base Camp to the summit in four days was a remarkable achievement.

Phu Dorji returned for the fourth and last time to Everest with the Japanese expedition of 1969–70, this time as sirdar. Sadly he was killed in an accident in the Icefall. So ended the life of an outstanding Sherpa, whose record on Everest has, I feel, been insufficiently recognised.

Da Namgyal

Da Namgyal, a somewhat shy and retiring Sherpa, was in 1953 one of only three Sherpas to go beyond the South Col, climbing with John Hunt to 27,500ft with a full load of stores for the high camp. During this vital carry, he was frostbitten in one finger (happily without lasting effect), the only casualty of the expedition.

Unfortunately, little seems to have been recorded about Da Namgyal after 1953. He became an instructor at the HMI where John and Joy Hunt, Alfred Gregory and I had a happy reunion with him in 1973. He died six years later. His son Passang Namgyal is now an instructor at the HMI in his father's place.

Nawang Topke (also spelt Topgay)

Topke was, like Gombu, Tenzing's nephew. Although he looked hardly more than a boy in 1953, he was 22, five years older than his cousin. Like him, he carried loads twice to the South Col. The year before, on the Swiss post-monsoon expedition, he had climbed to 27,000ft.

When the HMI was formed, Topke became an instructor and was able to take advantage of the opportunities for further climbing offered there. After expeditions to Ganesh Himal and Kamet he and Gombu made the first ascent of Sakang, 24,796ft, in the Karakoram. He later reached the summit of Nilgiri Himal in Nepal. This was a winter ascent and his feet were frostbitten.

Wanting a change, Topke left the HMI and at first taught rock climbing to high school students in Kerala. Then when the Nehru Institute of Mountaineering was set up in Uttar Pradesh, he became an instructor there. Again there were opportunities for joining expeditions. On Mrigthuni, he reached the summit; expeditions to Shivling, Banderpunch, Kedar Dome, and Dharmasura followed. He retired in 1987 and returned to his home in Darjeeling. One of his sons is an instructor at the HMI and another is in the army.

Ang Temba

Ang Temba joined the 1953 expedition as an experienced porter. Aged 33, stocky and strong, he had already taken part in five expeditions, including the Swiss post-monsoon Everest attempt of 1952, when he had carried three times to the South Col, on one occasion going even higher. In 1953 he again carried to the South Col and would have gone higher had he not fallen ill.

When the HMI was set up, Ang Temba became an instructor and, in addition to his duties there, took part in a number of expeditions including those to Makalu with the Americans and to Kamet, where he reached the summit, 25,550ft. In 1960 he was again on Everest with the first Indian expedition. He went twice to the South Col and was selected for the second summit attempt which, unfortunately for him, was not made because of bad weather. He retired in 1973.

Dawa Thondup

Dawa Thondup was an old friend. He had been with me on Nilkantha and I knew he had the heart of a lion. He was a young porter on Everest in 1933 and one of the heroic Sherpas who came down from the Silver Saddle on Nanga Parbat in the storm which spelt tragedy to Willi Merkl's 1934 expedition. He was one of two Sherpas who accompanied John Hunt's Peak 36 (later Saltoro Kangri) expedition to the Karakoram in 1935, as well as joining him on two expeditions and several treks in the Sikkim Himalaya. He had later done well with the Swiss on Everest in 1952.

In 1953, John Hunt had specially asked for Dawa to be included in the Sherpa team. At the age of 48, he was by far the oldest member of the 1953 expedition, and the doctor who checked his health before he was selected said he should not go beyond 20,000ft. However, once on the mountain, he soon showed he had no intention of abiding by the doctor's ruling and could carry his load every bit as easily as younger and stronger Sherpas. At his own request, I included him in the party for the first lift of stores to the South Col, but not without some trepidation and only after close consultation with Tenzing. In the event, not only did Dawa Thondup carry to the South Col without any ill effects, but he proved himself an obvious choice for a subsequent lift there. This feat, which he again achieved with apparent ease, must be one of the more remarkable high-altitude performances for one of his age.

John and Joy Hunt, Alfred Gregory and I had the pleasure of his company again when, aged 68, Dawa accompanied us on a trek from Khumbu to Darjeeling for the International Mountaineers Meet of 1973 at the HMI. He was a delightful companion.

These then were some of that happy band which played so significant a part in the success of the 1953 Everest expedition. Their 'co-operation in the essential teamwork of the whole party was beyond praise' (John Hunt's words). This and 'the happy relationship between the Sherpas and the climbing team' (again I quote John Hunt) were, for me, as rewarding as the expedition's achievement in reaching the summit. It was an honour and a privilege to be put in charge of such a splendid group as the 1953 Sherpa team.

ACKNOWLEDGEMENTS

I would like to thank Colonel Dutt and Nawang Gombu of the HMI, Harish Kapadia and his wife Geeta, Trevor Braham, Elizabeth Hawley, Col Alan Jenkins, Lt Col J O M Roberts, and John Sims for their help in preparing this article.

HAMISH NICOL AND MICHAEL WARD
Tom Bourdillon 1924–1956

(*Plates 6–8, 28*)

Hamish Nicol writes:

In 1956 I had not intended to climb in the Alps because it was my final year at medical school, but Tom managed to persuade me. So on 25 July Tom, Dick Viney, Mary my future wife, and I left London by car late in the evening and drove to Lydd airport. In those days it was usual to fly from Lydd to Le Touquet in a box-shaped aeroplane which could carry two cars, thus saving a bit of time on the channel crossing. It was too dark and late to find anywhere to stay at the airport so we simply laid our sleeping-bags and groundsheets on the grass outside the perimeter fence and were soon asleep. The journey across France, which included a stop in Paris, took two days; and the car, a black Ford Consul with a top speed of 65mph, reached Visp on the 27th. En route we had paused at Lausanne to swim in the Lake of Geneva and here Tom had the misfortune to drop his spectacles in the water; they could not be found.

Tom wanted to warm up in the Balschiedertal, at that time a rarely visited valley to the north of Visp, so we stopped in the village of Balschied a few miles from Visp, taking great care to camp at the extremest edge of a hayfield so that no crops could possibly be damaged. The farmer, however, cannot have been very impressed, because we all woke up at 3am in about three inches of water. He had simply gone for a nocturnal ramble, picked up and placed a stone carefully in his irrigation channel in order to flood our part of the field, and he had done this deliberately. The stone was found, removed, the water dispersed and we settled back in our tents for what was left of the night. Roger Chorley and John Tyson had by this time joined us and, on the morning of Saturday 28 July, Tom, Dick, Roger and John left Balschied for the Balschiedertal hut which was reputed to be a five-hour walk. They must have been quite glad to leave the village which had given us such a cold reception. Mary had to catch a train to Milan on Sunday, so it was not until Sunday afternoon that I set off alone up the path to the hut, without a guidebook and without a map. I had no real idea how far it was and when I saw a likely-looking hut far away to the right, I crossed over to it – and was nearly swept away fording a mountain torrent on the way. 'This can't be right,' I thought, but by this time it was too late to go back. I spent an uncomfortable night on the floor of a hay barn and on the morning of Monday 30 July arrived at the hut proper. Four Swiss were in residence. They said that two climbers had failed to return on Sunday night and the other two had gone out to look for them. At 12 noon Roger and John returned. They had searched the west side of the Jagihorn without success. That afternoon, Roger, John and I, with the hut warden and a friend of his, explored the glacier on the east side of the Jagihorn, dreading what we might find there. We found Tom and Dick lying roped together at the foot of their climb. They were dead. They had set off on Sunday to make what they hoped would be a second ascent of the E face of the Jagihorn. I suppose a loose hold gave way and that was it. Tom was never one to choose easy training climbs.

The whole of the next week was a nightmare of grief, interrupted by long-distance telephone calls, visits to the British Consul in Geneva, car journeys to Geneva and back. Alfred Tissiere came over from his home in Lausanne and was a great help. I can remember little of it in sequence or in detail. Like an automaton I did what had to be done. They were buried simply in Visp cemetery after a short service of which I could see and hear nothing because my eyes were tight shut. It seemed to be the only thing to do, the only way I could attempt to blot out the awfulness of that dreadful day. Even now, nearly 40 years later, I am unable to speak about it or confront it without emotion.

The inscription on the tombstone was apt and it read: 'They were most rightly reputed valiant, who, though they perfectly apprehended both what is dangerous and what is easy, are never the more thereby diverted from adventuring.' That was Tom and Dick all over.

I had seen death before, and many times since, but this was utterly different. This was two close admired friends wrenched from life at a very young age. I did not climb again for five years, and came back to it slowly, at a much lower standard, in 1961.

I first met Tom in 1949, at Oxford University. He was already an important man in the Oxford University Mountaineering Club and became its president in 1950. I was a not so young freshman, who had spent two years in the army, and one at Edinburgh University where I learned a lot about mountaineering and little else that was useful. Tom had come up in 1948 and he shook his contemporaries by a daring lead up *Hiatus* on Gimmer crag in December 1948. This was a Very Severe and was finished in darkness, and nothing quite like it had been seen at Oxford since before the war. In September 1949 he had led the *Great Slab* route on Clogwyn du'r Arddu so that, when I first climbed with him in Langdale in 1949, he already had a big reputation. We had left Oxford on 5 December by a train which arrived in Ambleside too late to catch the last bus up to Dungeon Ghyll. So we had to spend the night in the youth hostel in Ambleside and take the first bus the next day. Tom, being the meet leader, had travelled north a day earlier and had spent the first day in the grocer's shop at Chapel Stile laying in provisions for the week. These consisted of oatmeal, bread and jam in roughly equal proportions. Half-way through the week it snowed heavily one night, and next day Tom announced that he and I must have a go at *Gimmer Crack*. The conditions were appalling but Tom was most persuasive. He said it was necessary to 'give the mountain a chance'. There was absolutely no point, he said, in always climbing under ideal conditions of dry rock. We must go out when there was a good chance of failure.

Well we failed all right. The fun did not really start until after Tom had led the first pitch. The second pitch is a very thin traverse across a steep wall, and it was necessary to protect this first with a most complicated running belay using my 12ft sling. The pitch defeated Tom but not without a considerable struggle. It then took him an hour to retrieve my sling, which had cost me 8/6d and was far too expensive to leave behind. After all, eight shillings was two days' pay for an army private in those days.

That summer, the summer of 1950, I was invited to join Tom with his friends in the Alps. This came as a great surprise to me, for I had only had one season in the Alps in 1949 in tricouni-nailed boots and using hemp ropes, and doing very ordinary climbs. In 1950 Viking hawser-laid nylon rope became available in Great Britain for the first time, as did Vibram-soled boots, and this soon led to a rise in expectations and standards. Tom had big ambitions which he kept very much to himself, for he knew that we both needed a lot of practice. At that time nobody in Britain knew anything about 'artificial climbing' which had been practised since the 1930s by Continental climbers in the Dolomites. For some reason the technique had never caught on in the UK, but Tom was soon to change all that. Artificial climbing is the art of using pitons and light aluminium ladders to scale holdless rock and he decided to set up a climbing school in his back garden at Quainton, Bucks. I was his first pupil and our lessons started in June 1950. First he selected a suitable tree with a big strong overhanging branch and into this inserted U-shaped wrought iron bars. If the bars were not quite of the desired shape he simply bent them with his bare hands. Not many people are able to do this, and I was certainly impressed. We used number one nylon and home-made aluminium steps for the ladders or étriers and four of these were produced in Tom's workshop in Quainton. I have a telling picture of Jennifer Bourdillon lying on the grass and surveying our antics. I wonder what she made of it.

Tom was six feet in height and weighed over 14 stone. He had a hesitant but ready smile which played often about his lips. Whenever I go to RLH, the Wayfarers' hut in Langdale, I can see him standing there by the hut door, smiling. He did not lose his temper, was patient and thoughtful for others, yet immensely strong and determined. By profession he was a research physicist, but he was interested in all sorts of things and loved arguing with Dick Viney about politics, philosophy, astronomy or just the weather. He was a passionate family man and worshipped his wife Jennifer and his two children.

On 12 July 1950 Tom and I arrived at Chamonix by train and two days later climbed the W face of the Aiguille Purtscheller. This was a very short *Très Difficile* rock climb and was in fact the first TD climbed by a British party in the Western Alps. Its importance lay in the fact that it allowed British climbers to realise that they too could do climbs of this standard. Two days later Dick Viney and John Saxby joined us at Montenvers and on 22 July the four of us climbed the Ryan-Lochmatter ridge of the Aiguille Plan. Tom allowed the Saxby/Nicol rope to go first, so this was my first big alpine lead. On 25 July Tom and I bivouacked at the foot of the N face of the Aiguille Dru and next day climbed it in 8½ hours. Although a very modest achievement by present-day standards, this was the climb which demonstrated that British climbers had at last recovered from the effects of the war. Chris Bonington, in his recent much acclaimed TV series 'The Climbers', implies that the post-war Golden Age of alpinism began in 1955; but of course it began much earlier than that, and Tom played his part in its earliest beginnings.

We were very much amateurs, rarely bothering to carry a camera or record what we were doing. Later, the great advances were all made by post-war professionals, by Joe Brown and Don Whillans and later still by Chris Bonington and his friends. After one further climb, Tom had to return to England to his job and to his family. I did not climb with him again until 1955 when we did the N ridge of the Peigne, the E ridge of the Crocodile, the first British ascent of the W face of the Aiguille Noire de Peuterey, and, finally, the E face of the Capucin, Bonatti's famous test piece. It was our last climb together. We did set off to attempt the W face of the Dru after a lot more rain and snow had fallen. But the rocks were slippery and covered in verglas and I chickened out. It was perhaps a cowardly decision by me which Tom accepted without argument. He was like that.

What Tom achieved in the great years of 1951, 1952 and 1953 in the Himalaya and, in particular, on Mount Everest I shall leave to others to describe, because they were there.

Michael Ward writes:

In the summer of 1951 when Bill Murray and I were discussing possible members of our Everest reconnaissance party, Tom Bourdillon was one of the first names that came to mind. His simple purpose and passion was to raise the standard of British climbing to that of our European counterparts. The group from Oxford of which he was a member had started the post-war renaissance of British climbing in 1950 by doing routes such as the N face of the Dru and others of similar difficulty. Tom had proposed the formation of a group of British mountaineers similar to the Groupe de Haute Montagne. This was to be called the Alpine Climbing Group in contradistinction to the Alpine Club, most of whose members, in purely climbing terms, seemed an irrelevance to mainstream European mountaineering at that time. I shared his dim view of British post-war achievement, which was reinforced by the patronising and dismissive attitude taken by the Joint Himalayan Committee of the Alpine Club and Royal Geographical Society towards the photographic and cartographic evidence that I had obtained of a route up the unvisited Nepalese side of Everest. When I told Tom about this he, in his rather hesitant manner, said that his father, Dr R B Bourdillon, wished to meet me – and thus the Medical Research Council and Griffith Pugh were involved in the Everest story.

Tom's interest was in climbing hard routes and steep peaks, and his approach to the Khumbu Icefall was that, like all difficult routes, given enough time and effort, it would 'go'. His main regret during the 1951 Reconnaissance expedition was that he did not get enough to eat.

On the 1952 Cho Oyu expedition Tom was a member of Griffith Pugh's physiology party on the Menlung La, which solved the high-altitude problem of Everest by using a high enough flow rate in the open-circuit sets to provide an adequate boost to climbing rate. However, Tom was also impressed by the boost given by using 100% oxygen, as provided by the closed-circuit oxygen apparatus. At the end of the field investigations he and Ray Colledge climbed Pangbuk, c20,000ft, and the view from the top helped sort out the tangled mass of peaks around the Tolam Bau glacier, south of the Menlung La but north of the Tesi Lapcha – an area explored by members of the 1952 Cho Oyu party.

When Shipton was sacked as leader of the proposed 1953 expedition, Tom was incensed and also wished to leave the team. His letter to me about the conduct of the Joint Himalayan Committee was forthright, succinct and uncompromising. It was only Shipton himself who was finally able to per-suade Tom to retract his resignation and join the 1953 party.

During the preparations for Everest Tom was responsible for the oxygen sets. The open-circuit was a modified commercial design, but Tom and his father themselves designed and built the closed-circuit sets. These, though giving a greater boost, were heavier and less reliable. If the set broke down, the climber, at 'sea-level' at one moment, would suddenly become comatose. In fact Tom did collapse dramatically on the South Col when he and Charles Evans, the first assault team, were setting out to descend, the day after their attempt. Tom was naturally extremely disappointed that he had been unable to provide an oxygen set effective enough to get him and Charles to the summit. But, in hindsight, too much was asked of an apparatus known to be experimental.

After 1953, the Joint Himalayan Committee, our *bête noire*, was disbanded and replaced by the Mount Everest Foundation, with Articles of Association drawn up by Lord Tangley, the President of the Alpine Club over this period. This organisation has stood the test of time, and Tom's brainchild, the Alpine Climbing Group, has been a considerable catalyst for British mountaineers.

We owe a lot to Tom Bourdillon.

JOHN HUNT AND DAVID COX

Wilfred Noyce 1917–1962:
Some Personal Memories

(Plates 5 and 29)

The present generation of brilliant young alpinists did not know Wilfrid Noyce, but in our time he was among the foremost climbers of the period just before and following the Second World War. For those who knew him it is difficult to believe that it is 30 years since his tragic death in the Pamirs in 1962: by now he would have been 75. One cannot picture him as ever becoming elderly. His exploits, both in the Alps and in the greater ranges, and indeed on Welsh and Lakeland rock, are well known, and we do not propose to do more than allude to them. 'Exploits' is in fact the last thing Wilf would have called them himself; he did not think in that way. When, for example, he climbed a peak of 7120m, Pauhunri, from Darjeeling and back in just over a fortnight of wartime leave, this was simply because he wanted to make the maximum use of a fleeting opportunity. He took with him just one outstanding Sherpa, Angtharkay – few other people would have been able to keep up with him or would have acclimatised to that height so quickly.

Wilf had an impressive school and university career. A recent letter from Paul Simmonds, a contemporary colleague at Charterhouse, makes it clear that, although in no way assertive, he soon emerged as a natural leader who was the obvious choice to be head of his house and head of the school. He was a fine scholar and a good all round athlete, but the qualities which are particularly emphasised in this letter are 'his austerity towards himself, his moral courage and his lack of fear'. From Charterhouse he won an open scholarship to King's College, Cambridge, where he achieved First Class Honours in both parts of the Cambridge Tripos.

Wilf was a cousin of Colin Kirkus, by whom he was introduced to British rock climbing as a boy. At King's he was exceptionally fortunate in that the generosity of one of its Fellows, A C Pigou, who was a great lover of mountains, made it possible for him to climb for two meteoric seasons with two great guides, Armand Charlet in 1937 and Hans Brantschen in 1938, each of whom must have been delighted to have such a client. At home he was already climbing intensively with Menlove Edwards, the leading British rock climber of the later 1930s. It might be thought that he was extremely lucky to find himself climbing in this sort of company, but the fact was that his talents were altogether exceptional and that other people spotted this very quickly.

What exactly were these talents? Perhaps one would put first his superb sense of balance. Wilf moved easily, and seemingly without effort, when climbing on all but the most difficult rock; it was very rare indeed to see him struggle. He seemed quite unaware of exposure and would stand with his hands in his pockets on narrow, sloping ledges where other people would have been eagerly looking for a handhold, or wanting to drive in a peg for a bit of security. Among memories of his poise and effortless ease, one of us recalls Wilf, in nailed boots, reposing in quiet reflection on small holds halfway up the North West route on Pillar Rock; and, again in boots, moving in smooth and easy rhythm up Eagle Front in Birkness Combe.

But security was a matter to which he appeared to attach too little import-ance. Both of us had occasion to remonstrate at different times about the need to put on the rope on crevassed glaciers. We remember him, too, unaware of the limitations of us lesser mortals, dancing blithely, unroped, across the first of the great avalanche-scoured ice couloirs between the Old Brenva ridge and the foot of the Sentinelle on Mont Blanc one starlight night in 1955, when the security of the other three members of our party was essential. A failure to fix a belay after a long run-out on the East Buttress of Scafell in 1938 may well have been responsible for the seriousness of the accident in which Menlove Edwards saved his life.

Someone who dealt with all normal difficulties so easily was a prime example of the natural climber, as opposed to the sort whose technique is only acquired by conscious effort and through experience. Geoff Sutton, in an obituary notice in the 1963 *Climbers' Club Journal*,[1] made the point that a natural climber loves movement and that Wilf was an outstanding instance of this; also that it was probably for this reason that the more laborious tech-niques of artificial climbing made no appeal to him: they would have 'removed the wings from his heels'. This is perhaps another way of saying that Wilf, however talented he was as a rock climber and mountaineer, was above all a lover of the hills and of movement among them. In Wales, for example, after a full day's climbing, he seldom failed to find time for a considerable evening walk over the tops.

Early in the war he joined one of us as an instructor on a course for officers and troopers of an armoured brigade at Helyg, which in happier times had been Wilf's base for his great climbs with Menlove Edwards. The programme, which included some rock climbing, consisted mainly of exercises which neither of us had associated with Snowdonia. Yet Wilf played his part with great enthusiasm. It was typical of him that at the end of each day during that fortnight he set off, after a strenuous programme of work, to walk and climb on his own.

His resources of stamina were indeed phenomenal. We recall his lead in August 1955 up the seemingly endless steep and exposed face which leads from the Sentinelle ridge to the summit of Mont Blanc, kicking small toeholds for the rest of us, hour after hour. On completing that great route and descending via the Grands Mulets to the Plan de l'Aiguille, his companions were only too glad to complete the descent to Chamonix in the *téléférique*: not so Wilf. Apparently as fresh as when he had left our bivouac some 14 hours earlier, he hastened down on the path.

That double traverse, the Croix du Mont Blanc, had begun at Les Con-tamines several days beforehand with Michael Ward making up the party. We were overtaken by darkness and dense mist during the long climb up to the

Durier hut, groping our way through the enormous crevasses in the Glacier de Miage with visibility only a few yards ahead. It was Wilf, with his uncanny intuitive sense and undiminished stamina, who guided us to the empty, unlit hut that night.

While acknowledging his great successes, it is perhaps as well to recall that, like the rest of us, he also experienced failures on his climbs. There was, for instance, our attempt in 1956 to follow a direct route up the E face of the Requin, an allegedly new climb described by Vallot. We have a telling photo of Wilf standing on a ledge halfway up the face at a point marked by twin pitons, above which even Wilf could discern no prospect of progress. We suspected that the would-be pioneers had retreated from this point, recording a route which at that time was non-existent. For ourselves, we were content to traverse across to the excellent Meyer-Dibona ridge on the right of that face. Incidentally, it was practically dark by the time we got to the top, and the three of us spent a very cold and seemingly endless night standing huddled on a tiny ledge to which we had just had time to abseil before it became totally black.

On another of our encounters with Mont Blanc, in 1954, we were forced to bow to the elements just beneath the summit ridge after climbing the frontier ridge from the refuge on the Col de la Fourche; all hell prevailed on the crest above us, and there was nothing for it but to reverse our route. On both occasions Wilf was totally serene. Before we turned back for the refuge, as we stood in our steps with our noses pressed against the slope, he pronounced that it was time for breakfast.

So far, we have not said much of Wilf as a person, except in the context of mountaineering. After the war, he became a master at Malvern College where he taught modern languages, and then in 1950 he moved to his old school, Charterhouse, for a further ten years. In 1960, two years before he died, he took the bold step of giving up his job in order to write full time. He had already written quite a number of books, mostly about his climbs and the expeditions of which he had been a member. Many passages in these books are vivid and moving, reminding us that there was also a strong streak of the poet in him. But it is clear that he was aiming to move into a wider literary field than was offered simply by descriptive writing about mountaineering. For example, he was becoming more and more interested in analysing the motives, not only for climbing but also for many other kinds of adventurous activities. He was also keenly interested in Italian literature and Italian culture generally.

It was one of the slightly paradoxical things about Wilf that someone so seemingly self-sufficient was such a splendid companion, and, indeed, that he put companionship very high among the things he enjoyed in the mountains. He was an ideal man with whom to share a tent. If one wanted to talk, he was an excellent (and very widely read) conversationalist; if one wanted just to lie in one's sleeping-bag and doze, he was equally happy. He was essentially a gentle, modest person, yet someone whom everyone respected and whose views, always quietly expressed, carried the more weight because of that.

While there were times when he appeared almost absent-minded, preoccupied with his own thoughts, he was also practical and efficient when these qualities were needed. It is hard to imagine him quarrelling with anybody, or ever losing his temper. He was, in fact, one of those rare human beings who, without being in any way aware of it, are a constant influence on other people, and always for the good.

It would be difficult to exaggerate Wilf's contribution to our success on Everest in 1953. There is no doubt that he would have been capable of going to the top. Yet he made no complaint about the supporting role which he was asked to play; he did express the hope that, should the two planned 'assaults' fail, he might be given his chance. He performed his allotted task of escorting some of our high-altitude Sherpas up the Lhotse Face superbly well. None of us, watchers at that anxious time at our camp in the Western Cwm, will ever forget our excitement as he, with Annullu, climbed the upper part of the Geneva Spur on one of those critical days in the second part of May. We raised a cheer as their blue anoraks blended with the sky, framed by the rim of the South Col. It marked a psychological breakthrough. It heartened us all and gave our Sherpas the courage to complete the carry of stores to the camp site on the Col.

Wilf was wearing the same blue anorak as he lay, nine years later, closely bound to Robin Smith in the tight coils of their rope, on a little shelf some 2000ft up the W face of Pik Garmo in the Pamirs, after a fall of 4000ft. For those of us who found them there, it was a moment of indescribable pathos. Yet it seemed to symbolise a new-found friendship between these two men. They were, in age, a generation apart. Each had attained high academic distinction; both were brilliant mountaineers. There they lay, in death united.

From some notes found in his effects at Base Camp, it was clear that Wilf had hesitated about joining the expedition. At that time, when the Cold War still prevailed, what decided him to accept was not only the idea of climbing in the Pamirs, which of course attracted him, but also the idealistic thought that the common ground of mountains and the love of climbing might prove to be 'a bridge perhaps, even in a small way, of the gap separating East and West over all other fields of thought'.

Wilfred Noyce's death was both an immense sadness to his friends and a blow to British mountaineering which will not be forgotten.

REFERENCE

1   Geoff Sutton: Obituary of Wilfrid Noyce, *Climbers' Club Journal*, Vol XIV, No 1, 1963, p 104.

GEORGE LOWE

Some Memories of Tom Stobart
1914–1980

In 1953 there was an unusual duplication of first names: two of each, Charles, Michael, George and Tom. The Toms were both big men but Tom Stobart was the tallest at nearly two metres or 6'6", with straight blond hair and generous big smile. With his photographer's eye, I remember he framed his subjects by making a rectangle with thumbs and forefingers, then moving the frame back and forth in front of his eye.

During the expedition his concentration on filming was total. He was there, bent over his tripod, his right arm and finger angled high above the camera button. We didn't see him as we walked and talked, for he was somewhere getting a long shot or close in on the local colour. At meals on the trek he wasn't eating, he was working. And quickly the pattern was established which accepted that Tom was there but not there. No scenes were directed or planned and no special consideration was given to him. For Tom had developed his expedition filming techniques in a hard school of experience on board an Antarctic voyage, when he found that 'faking was impossible and scientists were not actors'. He accepted that explorers and climbers were not interested in the making of films, at least not until afterwards when they expected the best.

Tom filmed the setting-up of Base Camp and there he asked me to try filming with an unusual camera weighing around four pounds. This camera was designed to take a sealed cassette of 16mm film, driven by a clockwork spring and mounted with a single fixed lens. Each cassette contained only 50ft of film and the clockwork gave eight to ten seconds before rewinding. This small camera, when kept warm inside clothing, produced excellent results up to the South Col. Above that height none of us could find space or energy to carry it.

In the Icefall and up to Camp IV in the Western Cwm, Tom used his big camera and tripod until he became ill with a cough and breathing difficulties. He descended and the doctors confirmed pneumonia. He went down to a yak herder's hut and rested. I think this must have been pulmonary oedema, a condition of which we had little knowledge at that time. He recovered and returned later, to film the memorable scenes of the climbers' return from the summit.

In relaxed mood, he was a skilled raconteur, especially on his youth, his schooling and learning, but especially, for me, on his unconventional decisions to drop everything and chase improbable dreams. After Everest he continued adventure filming which, sadly, ended abruptly in Ethiopia when a guide and interpreter became mentally unstable and shot several of the party with a rifle.

Tom was hit twice in the legs which severed nerves and smashed one knee. This left him partially disabled. He took to cooking and wrote a good book on herbs. There is no doubt that the wounds sustained in Ethiopia had a long-term effect. Sometime in 1980 Tom died suddenly at a rural railway station in England during a visit from his home in Majorca.

JAN MORRIS
The Effect of Everest

Jan Morris, then James Morris, was The Times *correspondent with the expedition – the only correspondent permitted, because* The Times *was a principal financial backer of the enterprise.*

For everyone else the climax of the first successful Everest expedition occurred on May 29, 1953. Not for me. For me it came four days later when, reaching a hand out of my sleeping-bag somewhere west of Namche Bazar, I turned on my radio and learnt that the news of the ascent had reached London, had been published exclusively in *The Times* and had coincided, as it happened, with the coronation of Queen Elizabeth II. As the person responsible for this celebratory conjunction it dawned upon me then, for the first time, that the ascent of Mount Everest might have a lasting effect upon the course of my own life.

In the event it was to influence my affairs, I suspect, more generously than those of most of the climbers. This was very unfair, because until that summer I had been remarkably uninterested in the whole business of Everest expeditions, and I had gone to the mountain more or less as a passenger, courtesy of Hunt and his obliging team. I never got further than the foot of the Lhotse Face, though in anecdote the altitude I reached has grown higher every year. I did nothing whatsoever useful in the way of belaying, step-cutting, putting up tents or contributing to Climbers' Club reminiscence. I ate greedily of the expedition's victuals, presumed shamelessly upon its good nature and secretly sent back to *The Times* obituaries of its members, just in case. In short I was a parasite. Yet nobody was to benefit more from the fame of the Everest achievement, or dine out more often upon the tales of it.

One tale in particular crops up incessantly still, around the world, and I am constantly asked to tell it again. When I first went to America in 1953 I told it in New York, and when I got to San Francisco it was told to me. In Australia earlier this year somebody said: 'Won't you please tell us that Everest story, the one you told at the Foreign Correspondents' Club in Hong Kong in 1974?' Through four decades I have told the story, in after-dinner speech and literary reading, in book and in magazine article.

Unfortunately I am precluded from telling it here, because I recently swore an oath, to somebody absolutely sick to death of the tale, that I would never tell it again as long as I lived. You must simply take my word for it that it was extremely funny. It was also emblematical, as it were, of my connection with the expedition, for it was not a climbing story at all, but concerned the worldly aftermath of the achievement, the gradual metamorphosis of a sporting occasion into a historical footnote.

In those days *The Times*, the pre-eminent newspaper of record, thought of itself as time's own remembrancer, and many of those who worked for it considered themselves more than mere reporters, but instant historians. As a general rule I was of this school myself (though still more I saw myself as a kind of peripatetic *belle-lettrist*), but as it happened on Everest I was excited above all by the technical challenge of getting the news safely back to London out of the Himalaya. We had no radio transmitters, walkie-talkies apart, and it was some 300 miles by difficult wheel-less tracks to the nearest cable office at Kathmandu. Though I was the only correspondent on the mountain, dozens swarmed the foothills or hung about Kathmandu, and the task of defeating the competition, especially with the final news of failure or success, struck me as terrific fun.

I need not bore you with the details of it – the relays of runners I employed, the succession of codes, the hoodwinking of radio operators, the scrambles down the iceflow, the spy-like vigilance of my colleague Arthur Hutchinson in Kathmandu, the skulldug arrangements with Printing House Square. Suffice it to say that when the time came we achieved one of the very last of the old-school scoops – a scoop in the Evelyn Waugh kind, except that the runners carried my dispatches in padlocked bags rather than in forked sticks. In the end *The Times* generously shared the news of the ascent by printing it in its first edition, enabling the rest of Fleet Street to copy it, but still everybody recognised it for what it was, a genuine newspaper coup. *The Times*' own history says that 'seldom had an event brought more credit upon the paper', and it was often coupled, as a dramatic exploit of *Times* newsgathering, with Henri de Blowitz's swashbuckling acquisition of the 1878 Treaty of Berlin, the text of which was published in the paper before Bismarck and Co had even signed it.

The effect upon my ego was disastrous. I was 26, sufficiently pleased with myself already, and the professional kudos that Everest brought me gave me a swollen head which has never quite subsided. I went to Everest an unknown, reported the American magazine *Newsweek*, I came back the trendiest journalist on Fleet Street. Famous hacks breathed alcoholic congratulations at me in El Vino's. I enjoyed my first literary reviews – for had I not, in one of my dispatches, quoted T S Eliot from the Western Cwm? *The Times* gave me a bonus of £200, and when I went with the rest of the team to Buckingham Palace the Queen herself told me how my news had reached her on June 1 (just after dinner, in a red dispatch box). Oh, I was proud as a peacock, that summer of 1953!

But it would have been no more than Andy Warhol's 15 minutes of fame, were it not for the Coronation coincidence. Scoops are not long remembered by the public, and I can see that my association with Everest would not long have affected my life, if it had just been a matter of newspaper hubris. But the fact that the most famous objective of adventure had been reached by a British team at that particular moment, and that my dispatch had been published on the very day of the Coronation – that people did remember, and remember still. At the time it was greeted as an omen of a New Elizabethan Age, to restore the battered and shabby kingdom to its storied splendours. That never happened, alas, but the romance of the affair, the news of Everest reaching the young Queen on the eve of her dedication to the nation, as it might be dispatches from Drake in the Caribbean, struck a chord in the heart of the world that is faintly sounding to this day.

Earlier this year an eminent American historian, knowing nothing of my Everest connection, told me that he was writing a book about the historical consequence of mountains. Did I know, for instance that the news of the first ascent of Everest was deliberately delayed in order to coincide with the coronation of Elizabeth II? Remembering Michael Westmacott's heroic exertions to speed me down the mountain with the news, contemplating the big toe nail which I still lose, every five years or so, as a consequence of that dash into the darkness, recalling the intricate and shady subterfuges by which alone the story got back to London in time, I soon put him right about *that*. What he said, though, demonstrated how closely the two events are associated, and the link between them is what chiefly benefited me.

You would be astonished how often people still say: 'Aren't you the person who got the news home from Everest on Coronation Day – oh! how clearly I remember the excitement of it!' They have generally forgotten, if they ever knew, that it was a *Times* exclusive: very often indeed they quote the headline the *Daily Express* put over its Coronation coverage – ALL THIS AND EVEREST TOO. People far too young to remember the moment have heard of the conjunction of events, and often ask me to tell them how it happened – sometimes adding a request for that terribly funny Everest story they have heard about from Daddy.

The climbers came to glory honestly, by climbing the mountain. My Everest luck has come chiefly from historical romanticism. Almost at once the magic combination of Himalaya and Westminster opened doors for me. I was given a fellowship in America which I would never have won by my own merits, and which was to alter my life for ever after. I was offered a job at the British Embassy in Washington which would, I have little doubt, have given me the entrée to a diplomatic career. For the rest of my ten years in journalism I occupied a special and totally undeserved status as the Coronation Everest correspondent, and ever since, when I see a special light of recognition dawning on strangers' faces, I know it is because they are remembering that drizzly June morning 40 years ago, when the crowds waited in the streets of London to see their young Queen go by, and like wildfire down the streets ran first the rumour, then the hard news, that Everest had been climbed. 'We shall never forget it,' they say. 'To think it was you who sent it!'

Today I recognise my debt to Everest far more clearly than I did 40 years ago. Professional advantage came from it, but there were profounder blessings that I only realise in grateful hindsight – for it does not happen to everyone to play a part, however peripheral, in one of humanity's supreme adventures.

At one level there was the blessing of success. I was never unsure of my abilities, I have to admit, but to have my confidence confirmed in such a spectacular way, and in circumstances so happy and glorious, was a most marvellous gift of my youth. The conceited nature of this very essay, four decades on, proves that after Everest I was never to look back, feeling that in professional matters, at least, destiny had granted me the privilege of permanent good fortune. If Everest made me insufferable in some ways, it gave me a lasting serenity in others.

Serenity of another kind, too, came from the mountain itself. It is not, I think, among the most beautiful of mountains, but it has a charisma of its own. This may be partly a subjective kind of magic – the knowledge that this is the highest of them all, the very apex of our planet – but it is partly what the Chinese would call *feng shui*: the particular balanced shape of the mountain, at least on the southern side, the glacier running away down its flank, its graceful buttresses, and the plume of driven snow that flies like a triumph from its summit. Not having to risk my life by trying to get to the top of it, I was greatly soothed by the benign mass of Everest, and have carried the sensation with me ever since.

And finally there was the happy experience of the expedition itself. I don't want to gush, or be sentimental about acquaintanceships long ago, but I have to say that the British Everest Expedition, 1953, seems to me to have been a very nice group of people. It was a gentlemanly group, in the best classless sense. If there were bitter rivalries among the climbers, they spared me the knowledge of them. If they resented my presence there, so utterly alien to the ethos of Alpinism, they never showed it. I had nothing but kindness from them, and have retained friendships among them ever since. So relaxed and kindly did the whole nature of the enterprise seem to me, in my naivety perhaps, that when Hillary and Tenzing reached the top I did not even think of asking who stepped on the summit first, and don't know to this day.

In short, a delightful euphoria overcomes me still, whenever (which isn't very often) I think these days of my Everest adventure. It was a wonderful experience, and it had altogether enjoyable effects. The coded message by which I reported the ascent of the mountain read like this: SNOW CONDITIONS BAD ADVANCED BASE ABANDONED YESTERDAY AWAITING IMPROVEMENT – which meant, when decoded, SUMMIT OF EVEREST REACHED ON MAY 29 BY HILLARY AND TENZING.

Even as I put the despatch in its bag for the runner, though, I had an afterthought, and added two words *en clair*. ALL WELL, I wrote; and how right I was.

Forerunners to Everest

GEORGE BAND

Mont Aiguille 1492–1992: An 'Everest' in its Day

(Plate 27)

The first ascent of Mont Aiguille in 1492 was possibly the earliest recorded mountaineering challenge – a royal command accepted and triumphantly achieved. This article commemorates its 500th anniversary which by chance falls close to the 40th anniversary of the first ascent of Everest, the ultimate mountaineering challenge.

It was 1987, in the Dauphiné. Mike Banks and I were at the Soreiller hut planning a short route up the impressive spire of the Aiguille Dibona as a final warm-up before, hopefully, traversing the Meije. As we went to bed dark clouds were brewing up uncertain weather and in the morning, when we woke, several inches of snow had fallen, even far below the hut. The high mountains would be out of condition for several days. We thought of driving south towards Nice and the limestone of the Vercors.

Earlier, at La Bérarde, Mike and Sally Westmacott and Natalie Bull had mentioned a possible visit to Mont Aiguille, 2086m, some 40km south of Grenoble. There was talk of an excellent campsite with a warm swimming pool. I had seen the mountain from a distance while driving up from Nice and the Alpes Maritimes some years ago, but had never set foot upon it. With no further information, we approached up winding roads from the north via St Michel les Portes. Suddenly, above the dank pine trees, the huge northern precipice of Mont Aiguille loomed as a ghostly silhouette through the mist. It looked uninviting and repellent. We withdrew and tried again from the southeast, following a *Logis* sign through the meadows of Chichilianne to Richardière and beyond. At the end of the road was the much more comforting Hotel Restaurant au Gai Soleil du Mont Aiguille. As we stepped out of the car a familiar red Nissan drove up and drew in beside us. In it were Mike, Sally and Natalie. Our party was obviously destined to reunite! Within the hour we were sitting down to a huge capon *coq au vin*, with the patron M. Beaume's award-winning *pommes dauphinoises* and two bottles of Côtes du Rhone.

Next day, in the morning sun, we could see the mountain's crenated ramparts towering above the forest. We learnt from the Maison du Parc in Chichilianne that there was no currently available guidebook, but from some topos we were able to supplement our fragmentary knowledge of its climbing history.

Resting on a sloping plinth of shale, the limestone walls of Mont Aiguille stand proud on all sides, a thousand feet high, its summit seemingly remote and inaccessible. Yet it was the scene of the first genuine mountaineering challenge, accepted and achieved. When Charles VIII of France passed by in 1492 he was so struck by its appearance that he ordered his chamberlain, Dompjulian de Beaupré, to make the ascent. He wisely delegated the task to Antoine de Ville, aged 40, Captain of Montelimar, commander of 450 men, and one of the King's most successful campaigners. De Ville chose a team of seven including Noble Raymond Jubie, siege-ladder builder to the King, Pierre Arnaud, master carpenter, and Cathalin Servet, master stone-mason. Spiritual support was provided by Sebastian de Caret, royal master of theology and chaplain to the King, and François de Bosco, de Ville's personal confessor.

On 26 June, after weeks of preparation and with the aid of 'subtle means and engines' and ascending 'half a league of ladders', de Ville successfully led his men to the top. They remained there for several days until the clerk from Grenoble arrived to verify the ascent. It was not repeated until 1834, nearly 350 years later, by a young Frenchman who found blackened rocks and debris from the earlier expedition.

Two other, much more recent, exploits are worth recording. On 27 August 1957 Henri Giraud landed a light aircraft on the summit plateau. Then, on 27 January 1992, 500 years after the first ascent, the extreme skier Pierre Tardivel skied with René Leclerc from the top down through the precipitous series of gullies known as Les Tubulaires, pausing only midway for a short rappel down a vertical section of wall. A little further north, beyond a commemorative plaque placed in 1933, today's normal route of ascent became the world's first via ferrata in 1878 when a steel cable was installed by the Club Alpin Français.

From the hotel, a pleasant hour's walk through alpine pastures followed by pine forest leads to a saddle where there is a good view of routes of all grades up the W face. We followed the voie normale which is still a very worthwhile climb. After the initial fixed cable which traverses up a steep wall, the route dodges behind a detached buttress known as La Vierge. From there a gully system leads onto the plateau. It must have been a revelation to the original pioneers. As Dompjulian relates, 'I have had mass said upon it and have caused three crosses to be set up. It is about a French league in circumference, a quarter of a league in length, and a crossbow shot in width, and is covered with a beautiful meadow, and we have found a beautiful herd of chamois, which will never be able to get away ... It is the most beautiful place that I have ever visited.'[1]

Alas, the chamois are no longer there but the abundant alpine flowers nestling amid the five acres of lush uncropped grass are ample compensation. It slopes up gently towards the north end where Natalie and I lay on our stomachs beside the summit cairn to look over and down the sheer N face.

We spent two more days sampling the few other routes on the mountain which we thought were within our scope. The first day was a mistake. I found myself becoming less and less secure backing up the smooth-flared waterworn runnels of Les Tubulaires. I backed down while I was still in control. Later, we learnt that its chimneys are hardly ever ascended these days but do provide an occasional classic route of descent by rappel. Back at the hotel I must still have

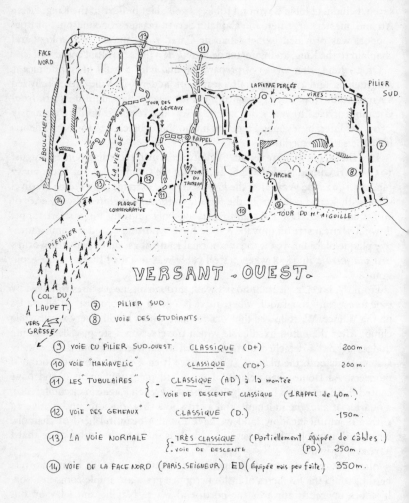

LES PRINCIPALES VOIES DU Mᵗ AIGUILLE

VERSANT - OUEST.

⑦ PILIER SUD.

⑧ VOIE DES ÉTUDIANTS.

⑨ VOIE DU PILIER SUD-OUEST.   CLASSIQUE (D+)   200 m

⑩ VOIE "MAKIAVELIC"   CLASSIQUE (TD+)   200 m.

⑪ LES "TUBULAIRES" { - CLASSIQUE (AD) à la montée
                      { - VOIE DE DESCENTE CLASSIQUE (1 RAPPEL de 40 m.)

⑫ VOIE "DES GEMEAUX"   CLASSIQUE (D.)   -150 m.

⑬ LA VOIE NORMALE   { - TRÈS CLASSIQUE (Partiellement équipée de câbles.)
                     { - VOIE DE DESCENTE   (PD) 250 m.

⑭ VOIE DE LA FACE NORD (PARIS-SEIGNEUR) ED (Équipée mais peu faite.) 350 m.

appeared thoroughly confused, as the response to my fractured French request for tea with lemon was a tray with two Perriers and a crème de menthe!

On our last evening together, two French climbers arrived at the hotel and we were able to seek their advice on a more attractive route. They planned to do the classic *voie Des Gemeaux* next day and were happy to show us the start. If we could manage the initial moves of IVsup/V, where a long reach was helpful, they said we should be able to do the rest and could follow in their tracks. The two Mikes and I resolved to form a mature team: Westmacott in the lead with me in the middle and the veteran Banks, at 63, bringing up the rear; a total of 182 years between us.

It was a superb route. There were six continuous pitches, all around grade IV, steep and exposed, but overly protected with a piton every ten metres and several pitons or a ring bolt at the belay points. The fourth pitch was the crux: a short impending wall where one felt particularly exposed and off balance. Mike led it cleanly but I had few scruples in treating it as an A1. It was followed by a short airy traverse left to an exiguous stance. A strenuous 30m dièdre and a final easier pitch with a small overhang took us to the top of the buttress which was slightly detached from the main cliff. From there a 15m rappel enabled us to traverse into the easier finishing gullies of *Les Tubulaires*.

Our joy on reaching the summit plateau was complete. There we met a father climbing with his teenage son. One of his friends, the father said, had made a first ascent on the E face in 1953 on the very day that Everest had been climbed and, in recognition, had called it the *voie de 29 mai*. I have written this piece nearly 40 years after that historic event, but also in celebration of the 500 years since Antoine de Ville and his seven companions accepted and won the regal challenge of Mont Aiguille. Now that's a real Anniversary!

REFERENCE

1   From 'The Ascent of the Inaccessible' in *Early Mountaineers* by Francis Gribble. T Fisher Unwin, 1899.

MICHAEL WARD

The Everest Sketches of Lt Col E F Norton

(Plates 15–23)

Of all the leaders of British expeditions to Mount Everest, Lt Col (later Lt Gen) E F Norton who led the 1924 expedition was the most talented. He was an excellent climber and organiser, with a great knowledge of natural history, and a gift for writing clear, simple and lucid prose.

When in May 1922, with Somervell and Mallory, he made the first attempt to reach the summit, little was known about the effects of altitude and the highest point previously reached was 24,600ft. They were entering a new and dangerous world. Many scientists believed that it would be impossible to get any higher without supplementary oxygen and, judged by modern standards, their clothing and equipment were primitive – no more than would be sufficient for a normal climbing day in the European Alps.

In 1924, Bruce became ill soon after the party left Darjeeling and Norton took over the leadership. The story of this attempt is one of extraordinary perseverance against misfortune, and of great achievement against heavy odds, of near success and final tragedy. Despite being extremely fatigued from their exertions at lower levels, Norton and Somervell climbed without supplementary oxygen to 28,000ft, when Somervell became ill and had to stop. Norton continued alone to the Great Couloir at 28,100ft and his description of this epic climb is a classic not only for its account of the ascent but also because of its detailed and accurate description of the effects of extreme altitude.

Because he was so modest a man, few outside Norton's family knew that he had a considerable talent for painting and had filled a book with sketches from the 1922 and 1924 expeditions. I found this out quite by chance when talking to Bill Norton, his son, at the Cambridge Alpine Club Dinner at Clare in 1991. Some weeks later, on 11 May, I visited Norton's widow Joyce, who at 90 was extremely spry, active and vigorous. She let me read her husband's diary as well as look at his sketch book. Sadly, she died in October 1992.

On his solo climb to 28,000ft Norton, who had been well schooled in climbing steep, loose and dangerous rock near his family chalet above Sixt, describes in his diary part of the traverse towards the Great Couloir as being so steep that his shoulder almost knocked against the mountain: and here his widow demonstrated by standing in the fireplace with her shoulder brushing the mantelpiece! In some places, too, the rock was overlapping like the tiles of a roof and so loose that the holds had to be replaced after use.

Norton's sketches cover many aspects of the 1922 and 1924 expeditions and 20 have been photographed for the archives of the Alpine Club. The selection reproduced here (Plates 15–23) show their calibre. We are privileged to see them.

ANDRÉ ROCH

Some Words on Everest 1952

An Address given at the Alpine Club Annual Dinner
5 December 1992

Mr President, My Lord, Ladies and Gentlemen,

I am proud and happy to be invited by the Alpine Club, it is a great honour. I will try to talk about our adventure on Everest in 1952.

The first time I met Tenzing, he was one of our porters in 1947 on the attempt on Kedarnath peak in Tehri Garhwal. Trevor Braham, who is here tonight, was our Liaison Officer. Wangdi Norbu, our sirdar, had an accident and fell 300m, taking Alfred Sutter with him. He slid over the bergschrund and landed in deep snow. Sutter fell on him with his crampons. Poor Wangdi was badly wounded. Two days later we dragged him down the mountain and saved his life. As Tenzing was the best and most intelligent of our porters, I promoted him to sirdar to replace Wangdi, and I was glad to pay him more money. Of course it was not my money!

In 1952, thanks to the foundation of Karl Weber, a wealthy man from Zurich, the Swiss got permission from Nepal to try Everest from the south. It was the first time that anyone other than the British could attempt Everest. At the end of April, trying to find the way to Everest Base Camp, Tenzing, Dittert and myself were exploring up a glacier. The sky was overcast. We had no map, only a sketch and Tilman's photos from 1950. We could only see the bottom of the mountains and were comparing their outline with a photo from Tilman's book. Three days later we returned with the whole caravan. Zimmermann the botanist and Lombard the geologist, who were looking at the ground, announced that there were tracks of yeti all over the moraine. We laughed and said it was only Lambert in his bare feet. (Lambert had lost all his toes on the Aiguille du Diable in 1938.) We had not seen these tracks two days earlier as we were looking up at the mountains. This was the same place where Shipton took the best existing photo of yeti tracks the year before, 1951.

The first obstacle on Everest was the Icefall. Dittert, Aubert, Chevalley, Lambert and Tenzing tried to find a way. They came down the same day beaten and very tired. The next day, Flory, Asper, Hofstetter and myself decided to try again. We made camp in the middle of the Icefall. It was a unique experience because the glacier was constantly moving. We could see some ice towers falling on others like bowling balls. It was not reassuring. The next day we came to the last crevasse. It blocked our passage across the whole width of the glacier. Jean-Jacques Asper tried to pendulum across and take a footing on the other side. It did not work. Then he abseiled down and climbed up the other side in an ice chimney. We installed a rope bridge anchored on pieces of wood, which we had brought with us, buried in the snow. The whole caravan went over the rope bridge.

At the foot of the South Col, we tried to go up the Lhotse glacier, but were driven to the left towards a buttress where there was more snow covering the ice slope. The first team, Lambert, Tenzing, Flory, Aubert and some Sherpas tried to climb to the South Col. Unable to do it in a day, they slept in two tents on the snow slope. The next day they reached the plateau of the South Col. Only Tenzing was strong enough to go back to recuperate one of the tents from below.

They had the mission to put a tent as high as possible on the South Ridge and to try for the summit. They pitched a tent at about 8400m. Flory and Aubert returned to the South Col. Lambert and Tenzing decided to stay the night and make a summit attempt the next day. They had not taken sleeping-bags nor stove. They spent the night sitting and melting snow with a candle. The next day Lambert and Tenzing crawled up to the foot of the last steep slope under the South Summit – maybe up to 8600m. That was a good effort but a poor exhibition. Flory and Aubert helped them back down to the South Col.

The next team, Dittert, Chevalley, Asper, Hofstetter and myself, with two Sherpas, went up to the South Col passing the first team coming down. Dittert was very slow, already out of shape. At the South Col the weather was stormy. We were glad to stay in the sleeping-bags coughing and breathing hard. The next day the weather was better. But Dittert, leader of the climbers, gave me the order to go down. For me it was a terrible disappointment to touch Everest and not be allowed to try for the summit. But I knew really that even if I tried, I could not succeed because we had stayed too long too high. We were out of shape.

Hofstetter and myself put on boots and crampons and climbed up the shoulder to reach the top of the slope to go down the buttress. Then Hofstetter said 'It is too late – we have to go back to the South Col'. I was furious. I was desperate and mad at Hofstetter. I wanted to attack him with my ice axe. There was such a rage in me. Why was I so furious? Psychologically I had prepared myself to abandon Everest. And now we were going back again. I was astonished that I could be so angry at 8000 metres. I thought 'I have to quiet down'. I put down my sack and sat on it. After a while we went back to the South Col . . . I had not killed him!

The next day the weather was clear, no wind, great sun. We sat in front of the tent. We could even sunbathe. We put on our boots and crampons without gloves. It would have been the ideal day to go up. But Dittert was worried about the monsoon and afraid of the mountain. He said: 'We don't try, we don't want any accident. We will go down.'

Dittert told me: 'Leave your rucksack, the Sherpa will take it.' How stupid I was to obey. When we were over the bump, going down the buttress, I yelled to Dittert who was higher: 'I can take my rucksack.' The answer came back: 'Shut up!' Something was wrong. He had taken out of my sack the photo and movie cameras and the exposed films and left the sack behind in the tent with my down jacket. Half-way down the buttress, Dittert was so tired that he decided to bivouac on the scree. Bivouac without down jacket, without sleeping-bag, without my rucksack ...! I kept going down with Hofstetter. There was enough stupidity. We arrived down in the dark. The Sherpas saw us coming and brought us tea. We had sleeping-bags in the camp.

Later nobody could understand why I had been so furious. They thought it was just the altitude.

Back down in the valley in Namche Bazar, we were invited by the village chief for a cup of tea. We had lost all our spoons. But there they all were in the chief's house! We left them in his care.

From there the main expedition went directly down south to Jaynagar in India with our equipment. Wyss-Dunant, Dittert and myself walked back to Kathmandu. Why did they choose me to go with them? I was so mad at Dittert that I did not talk to him any more. He asked me, for instance: 'How do you like your eggs?' I answered 'Don't ask me, you know that I don't talk to you'.

Wyss-Dunant had the notion that I was too old at 46 to try for the summit, and Asper at 23 was too young. I did not know it at the time, and learned this only afterwards from the books.

After the monsoon, a second Swiss expedition went to Everest. Weber asked me to lead it. I did not dare to leave my work on avalanches for the state, but I think I should have done it. Chavalley was the leader. Cold and wind beat them above the South Col. Norman Dyhrenfurth was filming. He completed my film from the spring. Ernst Reiss, a very good climber from Davos, took part in this second adventure. On his return home, I went to the station to welcome him. He brought my rucksack back from the South Col. The down jacket had been adopted by some Sherpa. Reiss returned to Nepal in 1956 and made the first ascent of Lhotse.

It had been a wonderful adventure for every one of us. In spite of very good preparation, we behaved like children on the mountain. But it seems that I was the only one to make trouble. A year later the British team succeeded as grown-ups – and deserved the success. We are glad of this and congratulate the British team and the Alpine Club wholeheartedly for their great accomplishment.

And now, Mr President, My Lord, Ladies and Gentlemen, I would like to propose a toast to the health of the Alpine Club.

Cho Traki from just below Jelep La, 2.4.22

Plates 15–23 are sketches by Lt Col E F Norton done on the 1922 and 1924 Everest expeditions. The captions are as they appear in the sketchbooks. (p82)

16. Everest from Rongbuk, 30.4.22

17. Cho Uyo (R) 26,870 feet, Gyachung Kang (L) from Pang La, 28.4.22

Chomolhari from Jelep La, 1.4.24

Mount Everest from above Jikyop (60 miles away), 21.4.24

Geoff Bruce

Noel

Hazard

Mallory,

. Gaurisankar, 26.6.24

. Goodbye to the Plateau (*Primula sikkhimensis* and *Pink polygonum*),
30.6.24

24. Edmund Hillary in 1971 at Manedingma where he had just built a school; with his two remaining children Sarah and Peter (L), and Passang Sherpa (R), the village headman, who now runs the Manedingma medical clinic.

25. Everest reunion at Pen-y-Gwryd, N Wales, 1978. From L: Michael Ward, George Lowe, George Band, Michael Westmacott, Anthony Rawlinson, John Hunt, Griffith Pugh, Alfred Gregory, John Jackson, Edmund Hillary, Charles Wylie, Emlyn Jones, Tom Stobart, Hamish Nicol, Jan Morris.

Tenzing in 1969, with his daughters Nima and Pem Pem.
(*John Hunt*) (p56)

27. Sunrise on Mont Aiguille, 2086m, in 1987. (*George Band*) (p78)

Expeditions

KURT DIEMBERGER

Beyond Broad Peak: A Journey of Discovery

The International Catalan Expeditions 1991-92

Translated from the German by Ernst Sondheimer

(Plates 13, 14, 37-39)

What is a mountain? And how can we really get to know it? Gaston Rébuffat once described the incomparable sweep of the Matterhorn as 'a magnificent heap of stones'. Rising majestically above Zermatt, its strong and simple outline is impressive from every angle. But whilst we toil along a ridge or up a face towards the summit, how can we comprehend its noble form and make it really our own?

It is only when we look at a peak from further away that we can begin to appreciate its varied structure: its corners, ridges, subsidiary summits and rock towers. Perhaps we later return and renew our acquaintance by approaching the mountain from another side. But just as we believe that we are at last penetrating its secrets, once more it eludes our grasp ... 'I have already done over a hundred routes in this massif – I have been climbing here for years – but I am still very far from knowing the mountain.' This was said to me at the foot of Mont Blanc, many years ago, by a famous French mountaineer: it was Lionel Terray.

One thing is certain: those who have simply 'done' the summit may not yet have got to know the mountain. Yes, they will have stood on the top, but really they have only passed by.

Like a moving milestone, Broad Peak has reappeared more than once along the tortuous path of my life – and always in a fresh manifestation. In 1957 it was the realised dream of a 25-year-old: my first Himalayan summit; at the same time it was a gift from the gods: the experience, with Hermann Buhl, of sunset at 8000 metres. The four of us had captured this 'citadel' of rock and ice (or so it appeared from the Baltoro glacier) without help from high-altitude porters or oxygen: the first eight-thousander climbed in 'alpine style'. This ascent in *Westalpenstil*[1] (as Hermann Buhl used to call it) was also a milestone in mountaineering history, for 9 June 1957 marked a turning point. Subsequently, countless numbers of alpinists followed our example.

Twenty-seven years later, on the summit of Broad Peak, past and present combined to form a personal joint high point for Julie Tullis and myself. Just the two of us made the ascent, to the third scale of the 'dragon's back' (that was how it appeared from K2!), carrying rations for a week and a bivouac

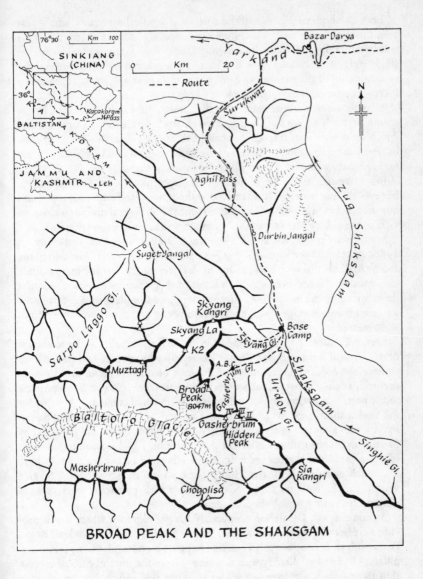

BROAD PEAK AND THE SHAKSGAM

tent. A year earlier we had already glimpsed the Chinese side of Broad Peak together, between the ice pinnacles of the Gasherbrum glacier, and I had recounted to Julie some tales from the mountain's history. But we could only see the three rib-faced summits soaring above the mighty ridge which obscured the lower portion of the mountain, concealing the glacier at its foot. On 18 July 1984 we reached the top, supremely happy, amidst swirling clouds from which thousands of sunlit crystals rained down upon us – a magical moment.

'Let's climb up to the edge of the cornice and look down into China – first you, then me – and well belayed with the rope!' ... The view into the abyss was breathtaking: the marvellous swinging line of the Gasherbrum glacier, the single cleft of the Shaksgam valley in a barren, jagged mountain desert, the endless ocean of the summits of Sinkiang. Only a year ago we had been down there – 3000 metres below the snow at our feet.

'I can recognise the spot reached by the camels,' Julie said. 'Out there, by the dolomitic walls above the Shaksgam river. And the big curve of the glacier, which we couldn't get through because of all the ice pinnacles – it's just below us. How different it looks from how we had imagined it! The glacier extends far behind the summits that we called "the camels"!'

Julie, standing above me at the edge of the cornice, pointed into the deep, her eyes shining with joy. It was a land without name and without people, and our dreams belonged to it. Our yearning for the Shaksgam and for a close-up view of the hidden east face of the mountain was intense beyond measure.

But then we turned towards K2 – it was like a promise. Two years later, in 1986, we reached the summit – but Julie did not return. A day lost during the ascent had, on the way back, made us captives of the terrible high-altitude storm which claimed five victims on K2 at the beginning of August – amongst them my companion. I myself, after seemingly endless days and nights in my icy tent prison, managed with my last reserves of energy to come down from 8000 metres.

Ever since those days my longing for the Shaksgam valley – the mountain desert beyond K2 and Broad Peak – has remained with me. And this wish to explore the hidden glacier valley at the foot of our mountain and to comprehend, at close quarters, the secrets of the east face ... it was like a promise to the past. Eight years elapsed before my dream could come true. I did revisit the Shaksgam in 1988 when I was working with Italian scientists and had to make a film about an enterprise inspired by Professor Desio and launched by the research consortium CNR. On that occasion I had no companions for whom a push into the remote hidden valley beyond Broad Peak would have had much meaning. With two Hunza porters I did in fact reach the Singhié glacier which, with its thousands of gigantic ice pinnacles, bars onward passage upstream through the Shaksgam.

At home again, I searched assiduously for photographs which might provide a clearer picture of the mass of serrated precipices on the E side of Broad Peak, with their continuously changing hanging glaciers, plateaux, ridges and pillars. I had indeed already seen this view – from the summit of Gasherbrum II in 1979 – but it was long ago, under a gloomy sky, and on that occasion my attention was totally absorbed by the enormous Shaksgam valley, flooded with light, and by the sea of summits stretching away to the east and north into Sinkiang. Later, when Julie and I looked down from the Broad Peak cornice, its steepness prevented us from seeing much of the face itself – only ice-clad alcoves and pulpits! But in 1983, when we, as part of an Italian expedition, explored the northern Gasherbrum glacier, both of us had already guessed that there might be a route along a huge ramp leading to a high plateau above the 7000m line attached, like a salver, to the wall of the central summit. Whether and how one could reach this ramp was still unknown and could only be determined by entering the hidden glacier valley itself. However, some Chinese mountaineers who had lately explored the glaciers in the vicinity told me that 'no one has ever reached that place – it is too difficult and the way is endlessly long'.

If I had refused an invitation, in early spring of 1991, to attend the onion feast in Valls near Barcelona, then I would probably, even now, have failed to reach my goal. But I have always loved eating onions; moreover, Jordi Magriña assured me that the 'Calsots', one handbreath in length, are the best onions in the world. With the help of plenty of red wine I managed to consume 35 of them – a respectable total even for a native of Valls. Anyway, I seized this opportunity to talk about Broad Peak and the wild onions which grow on its moraines. Jordi was immediately interested in the mountain and mentioned it to the mayor of Tarragona who was keen to give his town a higher profile – including a satellite radio station which could send reports back home. FEM TARRAGONA ('Let's make Tarragona great!'), as our expedition was called, was born during the onion feast. Four Catalans, one Italian, one Austrian and three Sherpas made up the party. The pesetas from the town hall arrived rather late (the Spanish *mañana* applies also in Catalonia!) but they *did* arrive – and the Chinese readily gave permission for the radio station. The expedition, originally planned for the summer of 1991, was postponed until the autumn, with decreased chances of summit success, but the important thing was: we were going! I was very happy when, at long last, I could be sure of this.

A nasty surprise – does the Gasherbrum glacier 'gallop'?

For the last hour I have felt uneasy: the lofty ice pinnacles stand like close-packed sentinels above the moraine wall. No one shall pass here! That's what they seem to say as we slowly approach with our caravan of 24 camels. All day long we have been moving across scree, over the hundred thousand stones of the kilometre-wide river bed. Today, 24 August 1991, it was only thanks to our strong beasts that we managed to cross the turbulent waters of the Shaksgam to reach the opposite bank. We were dealing with enormous loops, reaching from one side of the valley to the other. Now, after a 40km trek from the last oasis, Durbin Jangal, we are not far from our proposed Base Camp at 4000m. But something seems to have gone wrong with the glacier! I remember it as being entirely different: gentle moraine hills, a dark wall of dolomitic rock on the other side of the valley. That was the picture in 1983 when I made my first reconnaissance here, and in 1982 and 1988 we were still able to pass this spot quite easily. But now the gleaming watchmen seem to be in upheaval, their aspect is wild and threatening, and they have grown higher as if they wanted to leave the edge of the glacier, to climb over it, pushed forward by hundreds more behind them! There is no doubt: the glacier has moved forward – right up to the valley wall on the other side. Soon we know the worst: there is no way forward here! Between the pinnacled glacier and the smooth rock wall there remains only a narrow defile, through which roar the waters of the Shaksgam river. While we try in vain to find a way through the barrier of ice pinnacles two of our best camel drivers attempt, without success, to force a passage through the defile with their strongest animals. Checkmate! We cannot reach our proposed Base Camp site but must stay somewhere around here where Broad Peak is still far away and hidden by massive mountain walls. We are on the 'wrong' bank of the river of ice – on the difficult side where no man has ever forced a way through; the opposite side of the glacier, where the going is relatively easy, is out of reach. It seems, at first sight, as if my 1983 reconnaissance was a total waste of time.

We were all very worried, but Joan Gelabert, the radio operator and technician of our satellite radio station, is the first to regain his composure: 'Perhaps we can still find a way through to Broad Peak and I can manage transmissions from the very top of the moraine!', he suggests. We drag six camels, carrying the 500kg of the radio station, up over a steep scree-slope, while Oscar Cadiach and Alberto Soncini set out for a quick reconnaissance of our 'new' glacier bank. (. . . Is there a walkie-talkie connection 'round the bend', which can penetrate behind the blocking mountain barrier?) Jordi Magriña, Lluis Rafols and I attend to Base Camp – it should be sited as close to the mountain as possible and this is our last day with the camels at our disposal, to bring everything up to the chosen spot! We manage to extort another 40 minutes' worth of footslog from our Chinese–Uigur companions (one liaison officer, one interpreter and several camel drivers) – after that, the terrain becomes too difficult for the animals. But our three Sherpas, Dakipa, Pasang and Pemba Maila, are full of gratitude: this last effort by the camels, which has shifted more than a thousand kilos, will make quite a difference!

Up till now we have managed everything in an incredibly short time: only 12 days from Europe to this spot, via Islamabad, where we met the Sherpas who had flown in from Nepal, and a journey by bus over the Kunjerab Pass towards Kashgar. Joan Gelabert will have to repeat the 40-minute walk at 4200m between radio station and Base Camp many times during the next one and a half months – covering a distance equivalent to a crossing of his entire native Catalonia! And the rest of us? Before we can start climbing the mountain, we have to cover a distance of roughly 20km up the glacier or along its flanks – how many times remains to be seen.

One thing I already know: the Gasherbrum glacier is like a living creature – it moves, it changes, it speaks . . . and now, after all these years, it seems to have started to 'gallop'. Will this continue? If so, what hope is there for future expeditions if they want to establish a Base Camp further upriver? It seems as if the mountain wilderness, all on its own, is barring the way.

For three more days our radio operator looks glum: he can't get through to home! That is worse than merely annoying, since our sponsor, the Mayor of Tarragona, will be eagerly waiting for news. Joan is desperately trying to reconstruct from polystyrene a part of the transmitter which broke when a camel shed its load. At last he succeeds, and as the first sounds from Tarragona emerge from the apparatus, we all breathe deep sighs of relief.

The hidden valley

Ice pinnacles, and yet more ice pinnacles! There must be fifty thousand of them – I try to make an estimate; magical shapes, with blue-green glacier lakes in between them, disappearing in gleaming processions into the distance. Gigantic pillars of rock rear up along the edge of the glacier – my Spanish friends call one of them *Naranjo*, after the orange-coloured rock formation in Picos de Europa. The whole of the southern horizon is filled with the Gasherbrum wall – from Hidden Peak, the eight-thousander, to Gasherbrum III. We shall be gazing at this scene for many days now! Hours of toil up the loose moraine rubble; we are glad to have the Sherpas, but the rest of us, of course, are also carrying heavy loads. At last, whilst we are establishing an intermediate camp, Broad Peak makes its appearance in the glacier's most distant and remote recess! The ramp gleams white, surmounted by the plateau; the mighty ridge appears with its blue shadows – and then the three great summits. Seracs threaten – no, it hasn't become any easier up there since the last time, eight years ago, when I thought I could see a way through at that spot – rather the opposite. Where can we find a passage? 'We won't be able to decide that until we reach it: then all will become clear,' says calm prudent Oscar, a mountaineer with much experience of the Himalaya; usually Jordi is his partner – they have climbed Nanga Parbat together.

The stony track between the long rows of ice pinnacles gradually narrows, until we finally end up in a cul-de-sac; here we manage to find a place, across the glacier stream, where we can squeeze through to the lateral moraine. We scramble up and follow a narrow valley (full of wild onions!) between the moraine and the mountainside; but we constantly have to traverse laboriously across steep, loose scree-slopes. Suddenly, far below, we catch sight of a little duck paddling happily in a glacier lake! It must have lost its way when all the other birds were migrating . . .

On 28 August, at 4850m, we erect the first tents of an Advanced Base Camp (a task which was not completed until 1 September when we brought up the big dome tent). We still cannot look 'round the corner' into the hidden valley, but we can see wild cascades of ice, the summits of the nearby 'camels' towering into the sky, and avalanches whirling down in enormous clouds of spray.

I think of the moment for which Julie and I yearned so much and which is now so near – when the hidden valley under Broad Peak will yield up its secrets. Shall we come again? We shall come again! We were only one day's march away when we had to turn back, but we resolved to return. Now I am here; I have come again – for the two of us.

On a brilliant morning we set out and stumble through a labyrinth of humps, broad pinnacles of rock, white ribs, glacier valleys, trying somehow to find a way between frozen tarns and streamlets . . . but gradually the going improves and we steer towards a dense web of narrow transverse crevasses covering the rising vault of the glacier which rolls down from the valley at the foot of Broad Peak. High above us, gleaming in the morning sun, are its alcoves, bastions and delicately ribbed walls – the mountain looks more beautiful from here than from anywhere else!

Now Gasherbrum IV reveals itself, with its distinctive shape: a trapezium. From this high seven-thousander a diagonal ramp runs down to the end of the valley. Perhaps some complicated passageway to the Baltoro glacier might even be found there – but that does not interest us at present for, while searching for a way up between the pattern of crevasses, we can now also see the regular pyramid of Gasherbrum II (8035m) and, immediately next to it, Gasherbrum III at 7952m. We rest and gaze. Full of emotion we stand in this lonely valley which has remained hidden for so long. We look at the ice cascades of Broad Peak reaching down to the floor of the glacier (not an encouraging sight, but we'll find a way through somewhere!). We walk on, gaze and gaze, and feel that strange tension which grips you when you know that where you are standing no human being has ever set foot before – no one, from the beginning of time – and that you are looking, for the very first time, at one of the most secret corners of the world. Of course it had already been seen from space and from high summits – but to be here yourself is something different. It is a wonderful, indescribable feeling. It is the bliss of discovery.

Kafka's Castle – The eastern precipices of Broad Peak

A shield of rock, probably extending upwards to about 6500m, rises, like the Grandes Jorasses, above a chaos of stacked-up ice blocks, large as houses, with enormous crevasses in between them. The 'small Khumbu icefall' below heaves itself from an invisible plateau at 5500m down to where we are standing, at 5200m, in the bottom of the 'hidden valley'; we are considering where to go next. We have to bend our heads back when we look up at the wide-ribbed face of Broad Peak: dark, verglassed rock, steep and difficult – in fact almost everywhere impossible. The upper edge of this face is at 8000m; the Grandes Jorasses would be a mere alcove in this gigantic structure. Above us, a curved white edge leads up towards a snow summit – surely also a six-thousander; behind it must be the ramp leading to the high plateau beneath the central summit of Broad Peak (also called: Broad Peak Middle, c8000m).

It is confusing terrain and its exploration takes up many days. Three attempts up the icefall lead, each time, to impassable giant crevasses, barring access to the glacier floor above. Quite soon, we consider a completely different possibility: to attack the long SE ridge of Broad Peak, in a wide curve starting from the valley's end under Gasherbrum IV. But the distance is great, the glacier floor is seamed with crevasses, and the ridge, studded with névé towers and cornices, is immensely long. With our three Sherpas and our limited amount of rope we can see no chance of success this autumn; so we turn again towards the central summit.

The steep rock wall at the edge of the icefall is interspersed with icefields. We secure it with rope and thus reach the curved edge which leads up to the nameless six-thousander. An ascent to the col behind it appears possible, indeed tempting, via a vast white bowl ... but then, on 10 September, one of the biggest ice avalanches I have ever seen thunders down from one of the battlements of Broad Peak, engulfing the bowl and the whole glacier floor right down into the 'hidden valley'. Air masses tear at the flapping tent of Camp 1 on the névé edge, 5600m high, and within seconds, as I cling to the fixed rope, I am transformed into a snowman (for days afterwards I have the tiresome sound of water gurgling in my ears). As a result, we all decide that we would rather traverse the nameless six-thousander than venture into this bowl.

But the route over the six-thousander also becomes complicated: '*Un Castello di Kafka, qui al Broad Peak,*' laments Alberto, after our first push towards the summit.' Whilst skirting an ice mushroom, tall as a house, he and Oscar get stuck in a renewed chaos of seracs. Only on 13 September do they reach the double summit of the mountain, c6300m high, which, to recall Tarragona, is baptised 'Tárraco Kangri'. On 16 September Camp 2 is established behind the mountain, at c6200m, and a high-level traverse is found which avoids the up-and-down of the crossing of the two summits.

I myself am no longer a member of the party: I am at Camp 1 waiting for my ankle to improve – I had sprained it in a crevasse during the first summit attempt on the six-thousander. But this takes time. Eventually I descend to Base Camp and, whilst the ankle slowly recovers, I explore the vicinity: I manage to find a passageway between the ice pinnacles to the other side of the glacier; and, once again, I stand on 'Left Ear Peak', a pointed limestone mountain ascended in 1983 by Julie and myself as a film team. Later, carrying a light tent, I advance from Base Camp along the edge of the eastern Skyang glacier to a spot exactly opposite Windy Gap (Skyang La) where it might be possible, with difficulty, to cross to K2. At the same time I discover a nameless col which might well provide a passage to Suget Jangal – a lengthy and certainly not an easy enterprise but one which could provide a link between two Base Camps when the Shaksgam valley is flooded – and without the need to cross the river!

Meanwhile, on Broad Peak, a sudden break in the weather, with enormous falls of new snow, has created a dangerous situation for our lead team – but fortunately they succeed in fighting their way down through the ocean of snow from Camp 2 which had become a trap (in places they managed only 100m per hour!). A brief interval of good weather renews our hope of making a lightning push over the dangerous crux (a huge serac-step) and thus reaching the high plateau under the central summit. But whilst Oscar and Lluis are establishing Camp 3 at 6500m, nearly at the end of the ramp, the weather turns bad again.

And so, in these first days of October, storms and increasing cold draw a line under our enterprise – no summit successes, but a marvellous exploration of the 'no man's land' on the dark side of Broad Peak.

I often recall a small episode: when the approach of winter is in the air, many birds set out on their migration. Some lose their way and perish in the mountains, whilst others fight through to their destination. There was a hoopoe which one day marched in through the door of our Base Camp tent in the most matter-of-fact way. He did not honour us with a single glance, but settled down in a corner and went to sleep. When I tried to capture him next day, in close-up, with my telephoto lens, the fellow flew up and sat on my head – and then transferred to Joan's head, which supports a big mop of hair in which the bird at once began to poke about with its long beak, searching for insects! I remember Joan's look of astonishment and the disbelief on his face when the bird, after a few words of encouragement, returned to my own head: he must have thought that I was a kind of 'St Francis of Assisi'. Our hoopoe stayed for two days; then it flew on.

The Second International Catalan Expedition (1992)

After our first expedition we made every effort to return to Broad Peak as soon as possible. The effort succeeded: the mayor of Tarragona showed understanding, and at the beginning of June 1992 the same basic team set out from Barcelona: Jordi Magriña, Oscar Cadiach, Lluis Rafols, Kurt Diemberger, Alberto Soncini and the radio technician Joan Gelabert. We were joined by two further mountaineers from Catalonia: Enric Dalmau and Jesus Elena. Three high-altitude porters, Tenzing, Nawang and Mingma, completed our new expedition team.

We were greatly helped by the knowledge we had gained on the autumn 1991 expedition – the glacier was quickly mastered and the lower part of the ascent. But during July we had a gruelling battle against unstable weather. Three summit pushes failed because of this, but Camp 3 was finally established at 7350m on the edge of the huge high-level plateau. Below this, the icefall had been conquered and, where necessary, equipped with fixed ropes. Between Camp 1 (c5600m) and Camp 2 (c6300m) the expedition followed a glacier valley which had been avoided on the 1991 reconnaissance because of the danger of ice avalanches. The decision to use this route was not unanimous even though it was considerably shorter than our previous passage over Tárraco Kangri. Kurt Diemberger did ascend to Camp 2 on a single occasion, but he then devoted himself to his own programme of exploration in the region of the Gasherbrum glacier. In spite of the time-saving short cut mentioned above, it seemed, right up until the last moment, as if the weather gods did not wish to grant the summit to our expedition!

On 4 August the summit of Broad Peak was finally reached by Oscar Cadiach, Alberto Soncini, Lluis Rafols and Enric Dalmau. The camels for the return march through the Shaksgam valley were already approaching when these four seized the only chance offered by the weather before the arrival of the next weather front. Snow was already falling above 7000m during the descent! After two expeditions, this was a hard-won success which was made still harder by a forced bivouac at 8000m not far from the summit. Fortunately, only Enric Dalmau suffered slight frostbite to his toes; but he thought this a small price to pay for his first eight-thousander: the central summit of Broad Peak (8016m).

This ascent of the E (and partially NE) face was the first major new climb for 10 years (since the ascent of K2 from the north by the Japanese in 1982) to have succeeded in the region between Hidden Peak and K2, on the Chinese side.

Summary: In autumn 1991 the International Catalan Expedition 'FEM Tarragona', led by Jordi Magriña, explored and made the first attempt on the E face of Broad Peak, reaching 6500m; also, they made the first exploration of the glacier basin below Broad Peak, reaching the base of Gasherbrum IV. Kurt Diemberger explored the eastern Skyang glacier as far as a nameless saddle, opposite Windy Gap (Skyang La), where it might be possible, with difficulty, to cross to K2. In summer 1992 Kurt Diemberger returned to the Shaksgam with the Catalans, four of whom reached the central summit of Broad Peak (8016m) via the E face by the route explored in autumn 1991. The summit was reached on 4 August by Oscar Cadiach, Alberto Soncini, Lluis Rafols and Enric Dalmau.

REFERENCE

1   '*Westalpenstil* was a new way of climbing an 8000-metre peak without the help of high-altitude porters and without using oxygen apparatus, which Hermann Buhl devised in 1957. Fixed camps and a limited number of fixed ropes were permissible. Broad Peak became the first 8000-metre peak to be climbed in this 'alpine style', which was a true pioneering achievement. Today what climbers call alpine style implies also a refusal to use fixed camps and ropes. In fact, Buhl and Diemberger climbed Chogolisa in modern alpine style, and Wintersteller and Schmuck climbed Skil Brum that way immediately after the first ascent of Broad Peak in 1957 without inventing a separate label for a method which they saw as simply a lightweight version of *Westalpenstil*.'
A quotation from *Summits & Secrets* by Kurt Diemberger; new edition, Hodder & Stoughton, 1991.

CHRIS BONINGTON

Indian British Panch Chuli Expedition 1992

(Plates 53–55)

Historical background

Towering above the little hill station of Munsiary, Panch Chuli has always been worshipped and admired by local people, and by pilgrims and traders on their way to Tibet. Its name signifies the five hearths of the legendary Pandavas who are supposed to have cooked their last meal on the five peaks on their way to heaven. The first mountaineer to explore the approaches of the range from the east was Hugh Ruttledge in 1929. W H Murray's Scottish expedition and K E Snelson, with J de V Graaff, attempted the mountain from the east by the Sonar and Meola glaciers respectively in 1950, but made little progress. In 1951 Heinrich Harrer made an attempt from the west up the Uttari Balati glacier, reaching the foot of the W ridge at 6000m – a very impressive achievement by a two-member team. P N Nikore of India claimed a solo ascent of Panch Chuli II in 1952, but this been discounted. Another attempt was made in 1964 by an expedition led by Squadron Leader A K Chaudhury. They failed on Panch Chuli II, but claimed ascents of Panch Chuli III, IV and V, the two latter on the same day. There seems little doubt that they mistook the three small peaks running down from the end of the SW ridge for Panch Chuli III, IV and V.

Panch Chuli I (6355m) was the first peak of the range to be climbed by an Indo-Tibet Border Police expedition led by Hikam Singh in 1972. The SW ridge of Panch Chuli II, at 6904m the highest peak, was climbed the following year by another large ITBP expedition led by Mahendra Singh, when 18 climbers reached the top after almost the entire route had been fixed with rope. In 1991 two Indian army expeditions climbed the NW ridge and the E ridge.

There can be no doubt that Panch Chuli III (6312m), Panch Chuli IV (6334m) and Panch Chuli V (6437m) had never been attempted. Rajrambha (6537m) was first climbed from the north by another ITBP team in 1976.

An Indian–British joint expedition

Panch Chuli was therefore an attractive proposition when Harish Kapadia approached me to suggest a joint expedition. Editor of the *Himalayan Journal* and a keen Himalayan traveller, Kapadia had initiated two previous joint expeditions, one to Rimo in 1985 and the other to Chong Kumdan in 1991, both in the Eastern Karakoram. He provided a successful formula – more like a climbing meet than an expedition with a single objective – within which everyone could realise his own ambitions. The British contingent numbered six and planned to climb as three pairs. Stephen Venebles with Dick Renshaw and Victor Saunders with Stephen Sustad were long-standing climbing partners, whereas my own partner, Graham Little, and I had only climbed together over several weekends in Scotland. The five-man Indian team were all old friends; they were planning a full-scale assault on Panch Chuli II, utilising the help of a small team of high-altitude porters, camps and some fixed rope, while the British members were planning a series of alpine-style ascents on the peaks in the region.

To the Uttari Balati glacier

The expedition left Bombay on 10 May and travelled via Delhi and Ranikhet to Munsiary and the roadhead at Madkot. The team started the approach on 16 May and reached Base Camp at 3270m below the snout of the Uttari Balati glacier on 18 May. The last village was Ramthing, only three hours walk from Madkot, and the route beyond that was along narrow paths across rocky and heavily forested terrain up the dramatically steep Balati valley. 84 porters were employed to carry the expedition baggage. They were willing, cheerful and honest.

The Uttari Balati glacier flows to a particularly low altitude and has three formidable icefalls which were eventually turned on the true right bank. Glacier Camp was established on 22 May near the centre of the glacier above the first icefall at 3900m. A route was initially fixed on the left edge of the second icefall through a series of tottering seracs. An easier but still frightening alternative was found by Harish Kapadia on the right bank, avoiding the second icefall. This was probably the route chosen by Harrer. Another gully led to the top of the third icefall where Advanced Base was established below a small rock buttress (4840m) on 26 May.

Sahadev East (5750m)

Graham Little and I moved up to Advanced Base on 26 May and, after a day's rest, decided to attempt the magnificent peak, later named Sahadev East and West (after the second youngest brother of the Pandavas), on the other side of the glacier. Sahadev West is marked as Point 5782m on the map. We set out at 1.45am, crossed the glacier and climbed easily to the foot of a snow spur leading to the summit of Sahadev East. A difficult bergschrund covered by unstable snow led to steep soft snow lying on ice that led up to the summit, which we reached at 8am and descended by the E ridge to get back to Advanced Base at 11.45am.

The traverse of Rajrambha (6537m)

The rest of the British members reached Advanced Base that afternoon and decided to attempt a complete traverse of Rajrambha from the head of the

Uttari Balati glacier. They set out on 1 June and that day reached 5800m on the E ridge of Menaka (6000m), a subsidiary peak of Rajrambha. The following day they crossed Menaka to stop at 2pm for the usual afternoon storm. On 3 June they reached the foot of the first gendarme on the summit mass of Rajrambha itself. The following day they tried to reach the summit with difficult climbing on snow, ice and rock. They had reached 6300m when they were hit by an electric storm. Saunders, carrying a broken tent pole which they couldn't dismantle, acted as a mobile lightning conductor and was struck by lightning, though fortunately he was not injured. They left their rope in place to ease their progress next day and retreated to a possible camp site, where Saunders fell about 5m through a cornice, injuring his back. Visibility was nil with high winds and driving snow.

The following morning (5 June) it had cleared and they set out as usual at around 4am. Venables fell through a cornice on the way to the summit which they reached at 7am, enjoying superb views of Panch Chuli II to the east and Nanda Devi and its Sanctuary to the west. They then descended the W ridge to a col and went down the steep snow of the S face to the glacier below. They had to descend the complex glacier in cloud but reached Advanced Base just before dark. The five-day traverse was both long and committing over varied ground and gave some magnificent climbing.

Panch Chuli II – South West Ridge

Meanwhile, the Indian team, on the SW ridge of Panch Chuli II, found a route up a shelf leading from the upper Uttari Balati glacier to the Balati plateau, establishing Camp 1 SW on a shoulder at the start of the plateau at 5750m. On 5 June, the first summit team of Muslim Contractor, Monesh Devjani and Pasang Bodh moved up to Camp 2 SW (6120m) on the SW col. They were supported by Harish Kapadia, Bhupesh Ashar and Yograj. The summit team fixed the lower rock step with 100 metres of rope that day.

On 6 June the summit team established and moved up to Camp 3 SW at 6400m on the SW ridge (the route taken by the ITBP expedition in 1973). The support team occupied Camp 2 SW that day. 7 June was cloudy and windy; however, the summit team left camp at 4.45am, reaching the foot of the upper rock band (6600m) in two hours. It was climbed over steep snow and ice in 45 minutes to 6700m. Battered by strong winds, they climbed 45° ice to the junction of the S ridge and SW ridge (6800m). The route ahead was very exposed with stretches of hard ice and huge cornices to the east overlooking the Meola glacier. Using protection and climbing very slowly they reached the summit at 10.15am in heavy cloud.

They immediately started descending and on the way down Devjani fell through a cornice but arrested his own fall. By 12.15pm they were at the bottom of the rock band with the weather now turning for the worse. It took them two hours to locate and reach the tent in white-out conditions with strong winds. They had frequent sightings, throughout the day, of Graham Little and me on the W ridge. On 8 June the three summiters, now very tired, descended the lower rock step through deep powder snow to be received by the support party. Because of the unsettled weather and poor snow conditions it was decided not to put in a second bid for the summit.

Panch Chuli II (6904m) – West Ridge

After our ascent of Sahadev Graham Little and I made an abortive attempt on Nagalphu (6410m), the only major unclimbed peak to the north of Panch Chuli. We retired to base for a rest and on our return decided to concentrate our efforts on Panch Chuli II, and attempt its unclimbed West Ridge. We accompanied the Indian team as far as Camp 1 SW and then branched left onto the upper Balati plateau through a complex crevasse system to establish Camp 2 W (6120m) at the foot of the W ridge on 5 June. Next morning we left camp, carrying our tent and cooking gear, at 3.30am to climb a steep berg-schrund at the base of the ridge which led to continuous ice; this was made easier at times by a thin but precarious crust of old snow. It was necessary to 'pitch' the entire arête and at c6400m we were forced to traverse onto the W face to avoid a serac barrier. The snow now became very unstable and progress was slow. It was only at 3.30pm, after 12 hours of climbing, that we managed to find a possible tent site below a serac wall on the crest of the ridge at 6610m.

The following day (7 June) we worked our way below a series of serac walls and crevasses towards the upper stretch of the W ridge to camp early in the afternoon at the bergschrund below the summit cone, at a height of 6730m. It had been a short day but we wanted to be in position to be able to leave our sacks behind and to reach the summit in the early morning with a good chance of a view.

It snowed heavily that night but dawned fine, though cold and windy. Setting out at 6am, we joined the SW ridge about 150m below the summit and reached the top at 7am to enjoy a magnificent view of Gurla Mandhata in Tibet, and Api and Nampa in West Nepal, to the east. After half an hour on the summit, we returned to the tent, dismantled it and crossed to the SW ridge to descend to the SW col, where we received a wonderful welcome from the Indian team.

The rescue of Vijay Kothari

On our descent to Glacier Camp the following day we learnt that our support team had had a narrow escape. On 4 June, while descending the steep gully bypassing the second icefall, Vijay slipped and gathered speed falling towards a giant bergschrund at the bottom. With great presence of mind, Sundersinh ran down behind him and at great risk to his own life caught hold of Vijay at the last moment. Suffering a broken ankle, Vijay was carried by Harsinh Jnr and Suratram back to Glacier Camp. Wing Commander Srivastava, the liaison officer, rushed to Munsiary and initiated a helicopter rescue for Vijay from Glacier Camp to Bareilly Hospital where he received treatment, and thence to Bombay.

Panchali Chuli (5220m) and Draupadi (5250m)

As we descended to Base Camp we met the Rajrambha team on their way back up the mountain and we decided to utilise the last ten days or so of the expedition in an effort to penetrate the Pyunshani Gadhera and attempt Panch Chuli III, IV or V. Stephen Venables tells this part of the story, but while we had our thrills and spills on Panch Chuli V, Harish Kapadia, with Muslim Contractor and Monesh Devjani carried out some useful exploration.

Kapadia and Contractor made a reconnaissance up the Panchali glacier on 17 June. This small glacier, situated south of Point 4934m, led up to a high col. Joined by Devjani with Prakash and Khubram, the party climbed on 18 June to the head of the glacier and established a camp at 4220m. In view of the poor weather the camp was shifted to 4860m on the 19th. 20 June dawned fine and they climbed to Bainti col (5100m) which lies at the head of the Panchali glacier. A route descended to the Bainti glacier and Paina Gad and this could be used as the pass between the two valleys.

The team first climbed the peak to the north-east – Panchali Chuli (5220m), and then the peak to the west – Draupadi (5250m). Both peaks gave excellent views of the unseen valleys of Bainti and Rula glaciers, Nagling and a host of other unclimbed peaks to the east. The party returned to Base Camp the same day and leaving three porters and provisions for the British team, as had already been agreed, set out for Munsiary the following day (21 June) to complete the final arrangements of the expedition. They reached Madkot on the evening of 22 June and Munsiary the following morning, where I caught up with them in the late afternoon of the 23rd with the news of Stephen's accident.

The expedition had not only been extremely successful in terms of peaks climbed and area explored, it was also a very happy one in which everyone got on well together and there was not one angry word throughout the period. Old friendships were strengthened, new ones made. We were very fortunate to be sponsored by Godrej, one of India's major companies. It was marred by the two accidents but, thanks to the courage and efficiency of the Indian Air Force and the prompt action by team members themselves, two very dangerous situations were avoided and both Kothari and Venables should soon be back in the hills. In spite of everything it was one of the best and most enjoyable expeditions that the team members have ever taken part in.

Summary: The Indian British Panch Chuli Expedition 1992 visited the Balati and Pyunshani valleys, east of Munsiary in the Pithoragarh District, U.P., from 10 May to 29 June (Bombay and back).

Team members:
Harish Kapadia (co-leader), Muslim Contractor, Monesh Devjani, Bhupesh Ashar, Vijay Kothari and Wing Cdr Anil Srivastava (liaison officer).
Chris Bonington (co-leader), Graham Little, Dick Renshaw, Victor Saunders, Stephen Sustad and Stephen Venables.
Supported by: Pasang Bodh (sirdar), Yograj, Khubram, Prakash Chand, Suratram, Sundersinh, Revatram (cook), Harsinh Snr, and Harsinh Jnr.

Peaks climbed:

28 May	Sahadev East (5750m)	Chris Bonington
	1st ascent, via north snow rib	Graham Little
5 June	Rajrambha (6537m)	Dick Renshaw
	Traversed via E ridge over Menaka	Victor Saunders
	peak – 1st ascent	Stephen Sustad
		Stephen Venables
2 June	Menaka (6000m)	As above
	1st ascent	
	Traversed on way to Rajrambha	
7 June	Panch Chuli II (6904m)	Muslim Contractor
	via SW ridge – 2nd ascent	Monesh Devjani
		Pasang Bodh
8 June	Panch Chuli II (6904m)	Chris Bonington
	via W spur – 1st ascent	Graham Little
20 June	Panchali Chuli (5220m)	Harish Kapadia
	1st ascent	Muslim Contractor
	via Panchali glacier	Monesh Devjani
		Khubram
		Prakash Chand
20 June	Draupadi (5250m)	As above
	1st ascent	
	via Panchali glacier	
20 June	Panch Chuli V (6437m)	Dick Renshaw
	1st ascent	Stephen Sustad
	via S ridge	Victor Saunders
		Stephen Venables

Cols reached:

15 June	Bagarthora Col (3800m)	By entire team
20 June	Bainti Col (5100m)	Harish Kapadia
	1st ascent	Muslim Contractor
		Monesh Devjani
		Khubram
		Prakash Chand

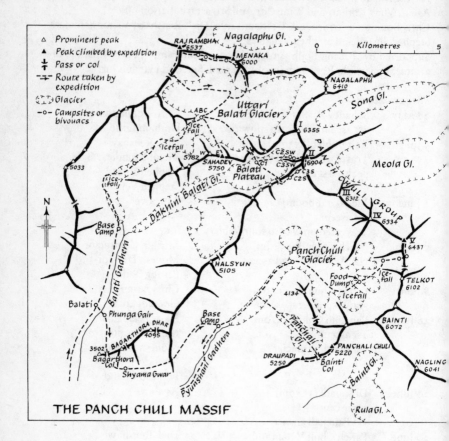

Legend:
- △ Prominent peak
- ▲ Peak climbed by expedition
- ⟊ Pass or col
- ⊤⊤⊤ Route taken by expedition
- Glacier
- –o– Campsites or bivouacs

THE PANCH CHULI MASSIF

Panch Chuli V

(*Plates 56–58*)

After Rajrambha we returned to the valley for a rest and two days later the others came back jubilant from Panch Chuli II. We could have called it a day. We could have spent the remaining time idling in the valley, just 'being'. I could happily have devoted a few days to photographing the flowers on the meadows beside the glacier. Every day the picture changed. While we were on Rajrambha the tiny blades of *Iris kumaonensis* had suddenly sprouted purple flowers, streaked and mottled like the skin of exotic reptiles. My favourite primula *Primula macrophylla* was out, an even deeper vibrant purple. Mysterious grass-like spikes had suddenly materialised into fritillaries, their mottled yellow lanterns echoing the pale trumpets of *Lillium oxypetalum*. Every day brought new delights, new surprises. In 1937 Frank Smythe spent the entire summer, right through the monsoon, exploring, climbing and collecting plants in a valley near here. But just 'being' and looking can feel incomplete, too passive, unless it is earned with the toil of achievement. Although we had all succeeded on respectable objectives and were looking forward excitedly to going home, I needed another project to fill our remaining ten days; even though it meant exposing myself again to risk, I needed another prize to justify my long absence from home. So I was glad when Chris and Harish suggested that we travel round to the Pyunshani valley.

We had hoped all along that there might be a chance to investigate this other western approach to the Panch Chulis. No climber had ever visited the valley, and its cirque of peaks, including Panch Chulis III, IV and V, was untouched. Now we had our chance. It took three days to descend, cross the river, climb through steep forest over a ridge and then traverse down into the parallel Pyunshani valley, where we set up our new Base Camp beside a stream in a glade of birch trees. The convivial glow seduced me, as we relaxed at our new home enveloped in the sweet scent of woodsmoke, enjoying the security of the extended family that had by now become a passable surrogate for the real family waiting at home. I wanted to linger, but we had to leave at dawn. Harish, Monesh and Muslim planned to explore a glacier above the camp. Chris, Stephen, Dick, Victor and I were to take a gamble and travel right up onto the untrodden Panch Chuli glacier and attempt one of the main peaks at the head of the valley. We had five days before the porters would arrive to dismantle Base Camp.

If anyone had a premonition of disaster it was Chris. It was he who commented most darkly on the weather, which was steadily deteriorating as the monsoon approached. It was he who remarked on the second day that if anything were to go wrong we really would be right out on a limb. But Dick, usually a model of caution, was pressing to continue. I was perhaps the most determined to stay in the game, despite the obviously deteriorating weather. After earlier doubts and reservations I now had a totally compelling objective. We had chosen Panch Chuli V because it was the highest and most remote of the unclimbed peaks – a beautiful pyramid rising behind a barrier of icefalls. Now on the second day we discovered just how complex those icefalls were. But I love climbing icefalls, winding and weaving amongst the towers and grottoes, absorbed fully in the fascinating business of finding a route. The complexity and commitment of this approach, where no one had ever trodden before, made the mountain all the more appealing.

On the third day it snowed. We dithered and debated, settling finally on a compromise, stopping early to camp on a col at the foot of the final ridge – the South Ridge of Panch Chuli V. It was a precarious col on a corniced crest, but with three carpenters and an architect in the team the challenge was a pleasure and we constructed a comfortable perch for the tents. To keep the momentum going, Victor and I continued a short way up the ridge, fixing our two ropes ready for a quick getaway should the weather look reasonable in the morning. That evening Chris announced that he would not be coming to the summit. Instead of trying to dissuade us from continuing, he offered generously to sit and wait at the precarious camp, stuck on the ridge with no ropes and virtually no food. Most of the cloud dispersed that night and the rest of us left before dawn, at 3.30am.

Panch Chuli V gave us the best single pitch of climbing on the whole expedition. It was just after dawn and Stephen Sustad was leading, shouting with delight, as he hooked, bridged and laybacked up rocky flakes and ice runnels on the flank of the ridge, completing a magnificent pitch of intricate mixed climbing. It was a beautiful morning and the clouds, for the time being at least, were keeping their distance. As Stephen and Dick led up eight pitches of mixed climbing I dared to hope that we should be allowed to have our summit as a perfect climax to the expedition. Then the angle eased and we moved quickly on firm snow, talking blithely of 'walking' the remaining distance to the top. It was foolish talk for we knew that on Rajrambha and on Panch Chuli II we had all found white snow slopes changing quickly to brittle ice. Here it was the same again. After one ropelength of easy walking, we were back on the points of our crampons, teetering on glass. It meant moving slowly, painfully slowly, stopping to put in ice screws for protection, and we did not reach the summit until mid-afternoon, by which time it was snowing and we were resigned to a long, slow, cold descent dragging on into the night.

We climbed Panch Chuli V at the last moment, by a remote, difficult route, and I was immensely pleased that we had made the effort to see it through. The descent would just be a matter of patient hard work: then we could all go home. We took it in turns to go first, setting up the abseils and traverses, cutting bollards when the ice screws ran out. At nightfall we reached the steep rock buttress. After stopping to fit headtorches we continued down very, very slowly, shivering during the long waits at anchors, cursing dejectedly when the ropes stuck and we had to climb back up to free them. This cold black descent was horrible but it was something we had all done before – just one of those things you had to go through if you want to climb big mountains. Far away in the valley we could see the lights of Munsiari. Then soon after midnight we saw Chris's light at the tent a few hundred feet below and we knew that soon we would be there, drinking hot sweet tea.

At about 2.30am Dick set off down on what would probably be the penultimate rappel. After a long pause he shouted that he had the next anchor organised and Sustad followed. When he joined Dick he realised that the steep rocky section he had just descended was the hard pitch he had led on the way up about 20 hours earlier. One more rappel down steep cliffs would probably get us to the big snowfall level with the ridge camp. Victor went next and, as he neared the bottom, I took out the back-ups to the abseil anchor – a half-inch angle peg, hammered up to the hilt into a horizontal crack. It had been tested thoroughly, not shifting a millimetre during three people's descent. After an hour's shivering wait, it was good to be moving again. I clipped my friction brake into the ropes, checked it carefully, unclipped my safety sling from the anchor, then stepped off the ledge, leaning out to walk backwards down a steep chimney.

I think I had gone about 20ft when the noise started. It was loud, metallic and brutal, but I only realised gradually that it was happening to me. It took me a while to understand that it was *my* body that was being subjected to this vicious battering, punched and pummelled as I swooped, bounced and somersaulted down the mountain. And then I suddenly made the connection: 'Ah yes, of course – I'm on Panch Chuli. The peg came out. What a mean trick.' Looking back now, I still cannot remember the initial swoop – the sudden awful lurch into the void. Nor can I remember the end – only the extended battering in between, when time stopped. It was similar to the incident when, as a small child, I was electrocuted by an overhead cable – the same helpless passive acceptance of hideous violence, distorted outside normal time and space. But this time I realised more precisely what was happening and knew that I was dying.

Victor, Sustad and Dick were waiting, shivering, at the next stance. They were trying to sort out the twisted rope ends and get one threaded through the new anchor when they heard the noise. At first they thought it was rockfall. Then they saw the long dark shape crashing past in a blaze of sparks as crampons and ice axes clashed on the rocks, and someone said, 'The anchor pulled.'. The ropes were whipping past, but through some miracle the kinked ends were twisted around Dick's leg. He and Victor grabbed instinctively, holding tight just as my weight finally came onto the far ends and my body slid on its friction brake to the joining knot, 150ft below them. There was a long, long silence. Then, while they tied the rope ends into the belay, they started to shout down; but there was no reply from the deadweight below.

I awoke to grey silence. I was hanging on a 45 degree snowfield, face pressed against the slope, the ropes twisted tight around my shoulders. I was surprised to be alive, but there was no joy: only a dull self-pity. I thought immediately about Rosie and my baby son Oliver – the two faces waving goodbye six weeks earlier – and realised guiltily that I had almost deserted them. Then I looked up into the first glimmer of dawn. The two ropes stretched up into silence. Where was I? What had held the ropes? What about the others? Had they been pulled off? I moaned, 'Is anyone there?'

There was no answer at first, so I began to organise myself, discovering quickly that my right leg was smashed, with a bloody hole just under the knee. The slightest movement sent spasms of pain through the leg. Then I tried to stand on my left leg but the foot seemed strangely disconnected. The crampon was hanging loose from the boot and later I noticed that the front points were drastically buckled from the force of the fall. I was going to need help. I shouted, louder this time, desperate for reassurance. 'Is anyone there?' This time they answered and torchlight appeared on the cliffs above.

'I've broken my legs.'

'Just wait there and we'll come down as quickly as possible.'

'I'll try and get my weight off the ropes.'

It was more for my own sake than theirs. The harness was burning into my groin and I wanted desperately to sit up. So I fought with my ice axes, pulling them from their holsters, sticking one into the slope, pulling up on battered aching muscles and chopping a seat with the other axe. Then I had to lift myself into it. That meant kicking in my left heel and pushing hard on the broken ankle, dragging the smashed right leg behind and groaning with the pain of it all, terrified of fainting and falling back on the ropes. Then I had to repeat the whole process again, onto a higher seat, where at last I could relax and wait, free from the taut oppression of the ropes.

By the time Victor reached me it was light. We had been on the move for over 24 hours, with no rest and only a litre of liquid between the four of us. We were exhausted and now we were suddenly faced with a long day's hard work. Victor dressed the wound in my right knee, splinted the leg and tied up the bloody mess in a rucksack. Sustad helped Dick organise a safe belay, then set off across the slope to tell Chris what had happened and help him dismantle the camp. It would have been impossible to drag me across to the precarious ridge. Instead, Victor and Dick had to lower me nearly 1000ft down the snowfield to the glacier bowl, where we could camp on less steep ground.

The lower took several hours. I was soaked, shivering and exhausted but slowly realising my incredible luck, surviving a 300ft fall with no spinal or head injuries, then being stopped by Dick's instinctive quick thinking from a further 1000ft slide. It was also wonderful to know that I had four of the world's most competent Himalayan climbers looking after me. Whatever happened, they would see that we escaped. They got on quietly with the job while I concentrated on the bloody lump that had been my right leg. I was too self-obsessed to notice Chris, heavily laden, lose his balance and nosedive 500ft down the slope, shooting across the distant bergschrund onto the glacier. Hours later, when I was finally lowered over the gap onto the glacier, he hardly bothered to mention his own accident. He too had been very lucky, escaping with just some cuts on his face.

They dragged me across the glacier bowl, bumping and twisting over old avalanche debris, screaming with pain, to the tents. Then at last, 36 hours after setting out on our summit climb, we could all rest and relax. Early the next morning Chris and Sustad set off down to get help, leaving Dick and Victor to nurse me in the tent.

We waited four days, in a strange limbo, isolated in the bowl under Panch Chuli V, cut off from the world by a great barrier of tumbling icefalls, yet talking and dreaming of the world below, confident that Chris and Harish, with all their combined prestige and diplomatic skill, would ensure that we eventually returned to that world. On the third afternoon Dick suddenly heard the faint sound of a distant helicopter. But it faded and vanished. We had now run out of food. Even the last tea-bag was finished and we had no idea how much longer we would have to wait; so that night Victor and Dick descended the icefalls to a pre-arranged spot where Sustad had promised to bring up a cache of food. If the cache was not there, they said, they would carry on down, because without food they would be too weak to climb back up to me.

I was woken in the middle of the night by the roar of an avalanche crashing into the bowl. For a moment I was terrified that it was coming for the tent; then I realised it was the huge ice tower that collapsed regularly, sweeping the bowl further down. A few minutes later there was another great crash, then I went back to sleep. Just before dawn I was woken again, this time by Dick and Victor returning.

'What was it like?', I asked.

'Very frightening.'

The icefalls had crumpled and shifted almost out of recognition, but Victor and Dick managed to find a route, successfully reaching the cache which Sustad had carried up after only a short rest at Base Camp. They had eaten a snack and then started back up. Just before they traversed into the upper bowl the first avalanche swept across the route, devastating the whole area with pulverised ice. Only a few moments after they had picked their way through the debris, the second avalanche wiped out their tracks behind them. Our mountain bowl seemed increasingly to be a cruel hostile trap, fulfilling all Chris's premonitions. We had had enough. We wanted to go home.

That fourth morning we heard the helicopter again. Dick and Victor rushed into action, helping me on with my harness and packing up my gear, but after a few moments the sound faded away. Later that morning they cooked a meal – a proper meal with real onions and real potatoes. What a hero Sustad had been to climb all the way back with the cache, only a day after his exhausting descent, bringing us enough food to restore strength and hope. After lunch we were chatting idly when Dick suddenly shouted, 'There it is!' And this time it really was coming closer to fetch us. Within minutes I was sitting outside in the snow, staring happily down the valley. There was a gap in the clouds and climbing up through that gap there was a tiny dark insect. It came steadily closer, zigzagging backwards and forwards, testing the air. Soon we could make out the tricolour of the Indian Airforce, then two masked faces inside the perspex shell, as the helicopter moved in to hover in front of us, shattering the air with its pulsating noise.

We had assumed naively that if a helicopter came it would have a winch and that there would be rescue experts to help pick me up. Now we realised that there was no sophisticated equipment. We could see the faces of the pilot and co-pilot, tense with concentration, fully occupied just keeping their tiny Cheetah craft steady. Afterwards they explained that at that altitude, about 18,500ft, they had to take turns at sucking oxygen, while the other man held the controls. They also had to keep wiping the windows clear of freezing condensation, staring out anxiously at the rotor blades scything within feet of the slope. During my four days in the tent I had forgotten that it was pitched on a ledge, cut from a 30 degree slope. There was no flat landing site, but without a winch the helicopter had somehow to touch down to pick me up.

The pilots spent half an hour experimenting. At one point I thought that they were going to give up and leave us, waiting God knows how many days for a stretcher party to bump my shattered legs all the way down those tortuous icefalls. But then we understood from the pilot's gesticulations that he wanted us to move the tents. Dick held down all the loose objects at a safe distance while Victor dragged me to one end of the ledge and held me there, head down, staring, mesmerised by the giant pulsating insect, so loud and powerful yet so fragile, hanging in the air with its great blades chopping close to our faces. Five times it touched nervously at the ledge, balancing the tip of one skid on the packed surface, before backing off. Then at last it held still, poised precariously while the co-pilot flung open the door and motioned to Victor to get me in.

Victor pushed and I pulled. I stuck, halfway through the door, unable to get any further. I could see the fear in the co-pilot's eyes as he looked sideways, staring at the rotor blades slicing within a foot or two of the slope. At one point I nearly gave up, resigned to taking off draped over the skid, hanging free. But terror forced me to try once more to get into the cockpit. I gesticulated to Victor to lift my better foot onto the footplate, giving me some leverage to push my body back and up into the cockpit. Then I pulled on bruised aching chest muscles, yanking the bad leg behind me like a snapped branch, screaming with the pain as bits of shattered bone grated inside the knee.

I made it. The co-pilot slammed the door shut and with a quick wave we left, escaping down the valley before the clouds cut off our retreat. The co-pilot turned round, smiling with the release of tension. I just said. 'Thank you very much. You are very brave men.'

'No,' he replied, 'it is not us. It is God we must thank.' My eyes prickled with tears of relief as I stared down at the shattered chaos of the icefalls tumbling dizzily beneath us, then back up at the two men in front of me, who had risked their lives, flying this miraculous machine so close to its altitude limit. In a few moments we had left the Panch Chuli glacier behind and the land beneath us was dark green, streaked with pale ribbons of water. We skimmed over the forest, past the valley fork, past the waterfalls where we had camped on the way in all those weeks ago, then over the roofs of Ringo village, across a ridge, over the Goriganga valley and down, slowing gently, to the football pitch in Munsiari where Pasang, Monesh, Muslim, Harish and Chris were waiting to welcome me back to earth.

I wanted to stay with the others and wait till Dick, Sustad and Victor were safely down. Instead of the institutional regime of a military hospital, I wanted to be with my friends, celebrating our successful expedition and my miraculous escape. For it was a double miracle: first that I was not killed or paralysed in the fall and second that within four days of the accident a helicopter arrived at the head of that remote Himalayan glacier to make an extraordinarily dangerous pick-up. But Harish and Chris were adamant. I had to get to hospital immediately and as soon as Harish had finished trying to force food down my throat the helicopter took off again. There was time for a quick last look at the Panch Chulis, just visible amongst the clouds, then we left, descending right over the Himalaya, down, down and down to the immense northern plain of India, where the white egrets flew just below us, skimming the dusty brown fields which would be drenched any day now by the first outburst of the monsoon. For the moment at least I was very glad to leave the mountains far behind.

Summary: In June 1992 Dick Renshaw, Victor Saunders, Stephen Sustad and Stephen Venables made the first ascent of Panch Chuli V (6437m), via the S ridge. During the descent Stephen Venables survived an abseil anchor failure and was helicoptered out with serious injuries in a very difficult rescue operation. The ascent of Panch Chuli V was part of the Indian British Panch Chuli Expedition led by Chris Bonington (who helped with the rescue on the mountain) and Harish Kapadia.

ANDREW POLLARD
'Big Bird Flapping Wings'

The British Chamlang Expedition 1991

(Plates 34–36)

At 12.30pm on 1 August 1990, Andrew Knight and I met in the bar of the Ski Club of Great Britain to plan an expedition. We spent the afternoon reading in the library of the Alpine Club, which had temporary accommodation there, about peaks and valleys in Nepal and realised that we didn't know where to start. By the end of the day we knew where to start. After another week of almost continuous research, one mountain, Chamlang, had caught our imagination.

Chamlang (7319m), which in the Sherpa dialect means 'big bird flapping wings', was first climbed in 1962 by a Japanese team by the S ridge, a route repeated by the Koreans in 1987. The mountain has also been climbed via the W ridge, by the Japanese in 1986 and, more recently, by the Germans in 1990 on a variation of the original W ridge route. Our attempt on the S ridge was to be the first British attempt. Chamlang was surveyed in 1954 by the New Zealand Barun expedition, on which Sir Charles Evans, patron of our trip, was a member. The Japanese ascent (1962) was inspired by the survey in 1955 of Chamlang from the west by Norman Hardie who wrote 'Chamlang has a minor weakness in its line of defence when viewed from the west'.

We arrived in Kathmandu in mid-September 1991, a year after the expedition's conception. The march to Base Camp took two weeks and the variety was tremendous. We began our trek almost at sea-level in the Arun valley, with temperatures in the sun of over 45°C and 100% humidity. These days were sweaty and I remember one evening drinking five litres of tea! During the trek, David Collier, our scientific officer, was conducting experiments in ambulatory blood pressure. The expedition members were enticed into his tent late at night, even invited into his sleeping-bag to be connected up to a selection of gadgets measuring everything from arterial oxygen saturation to blood pressure. Our Nepali staff were fascinated by his flashing lights and rude mechanical noises and sat for hours watching. At least they were impressed, but in true Bart's tradition we were all reluctant subjects, seizing every opportunity to scorn the progress of science. But I believe there is a tremendous amount of data shortly to be released on an unsuspecting Physiological Society. Meanwhile, Richard Hancock, our botanist, collected seeds endlessly – a most curious occupation. For Richard, the pinnacle of the trip was a discovery about the sex life of the gentian.

From Naulekh at the head of the Hinku valley, we headed east, ascending to 5400m and crossing the Mera La below which we made our Base Camp. From the eastern side of the pass we had our first view of Chamlang, an enormous sheer face of snow, ice and rock: the 'big bird'. It was breath-taking and wonderful and I was filled with doubt that we could climb it. Because of a strike by some of our porters it took several days to ferry loads across this glaciated pass and I stayed behind to escort the porters while the rest of the team set up Base.

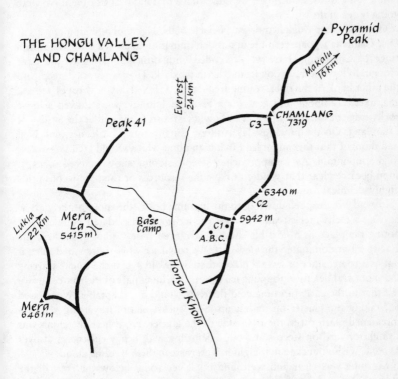

THE HONGU VALLEY
AND CHAMLANG

On 4 October I arrived at a deserted Base Camp; the others, who had gone in two parties to reconnoitre a route to the S ridge of Chamlang, were expected back the next day. Base Camp (4700m) in the early morning sun was glorious. It was a grassy place strewn with large boulders beside a babbling brook from the banks of which hung cold fingers of ice. Before the sun was hot our wigwam-shaped Base Camp tents were covered in frost, and frozen condensation inside the tents fell as snow on our sleeping-bags. The tents were pitched about 100m above the Hongu river, a wild torrent draining innumerable glaciers.

Across the river and now 2.5km straight up above a tremendous face of rock and ice stood the snow-covered summit of Chamlang, golden in the sun. Beautiful and terrifying. Over the previous two days a feat of engineering had been accomplished by various members of the team constructing a rope bridge across the Hongu river, facilitating access to Chamlang. At lunchtime the two parties returned from their reconnaissance. Neither group had found a straightforward way to reach the S ridge of Chamlang and the mood was solemn during the afternoon. In 1962 the Japanese took nearly two weeks to find a route onto the S ridge; we didn't have that amount of time if we were going to reach the top.

On 6 October Angus Andrew, Neil Howells, Ngatemba Sherpa and I left Base Camp at 3.30am resolute in our determination to push a route onto the S ridge of Chamlang. First we descended with difficulty down to the river Hongu, following the brook from Base in the dark. Then we headed steeply up the other bank of the river, resting frequently, weighed down by ropes, stoves, gas, axes, crampons and gear for a bivouac. Initially, we followed a loose rocky ridge to the right of a glacier flowing west from the end of the S ridge of Chamlang. On the previous day Andrew Knight, our joint leader, and Neil had thought that this might lead to a high point which would facilitate access to the mountain. As we approached steeply sloping snow-covered rocks, it soon became clear that we didn't have the resources or the time to push this highly technical route.

Instead, we dropped down onto the moraine below the snout of the glacier, passing a meltwater stream amongst the loose unconsolidated boulders and noting the place as a possible site for Advanced Base Camp. From here the glacier snout dominated the view east. We could see why Andrew had ruled it out as a route, since in several places there were old avalanche tracks scarring the snout and beautiful toppling ice towers overhung part of the route; but we felt that in the early morning cold the risks would be acceptable. We pressed on, taking the glacier on its left up loose rocks, before traversing across a threatened platform to the right side of the glacier. From here the climb was straightforward on steep snow but exhausting with heavy rucksacks at over 5500m. We bivouacked that night in a crevasse in thick freezing cloud.

Morning was clear and we found ourselves 100m below the crest of the glacier. On its right rose the 250m S ridge of Chamlang. Here we chose for Camp 1, launching place for the skies. Later that day, back at Base Camp in the afternoon mist, we reported to the rest of the team with excitement that we had cracked it. Furthermore, this was an original start to the route; the Japanese had started their climb further north and had missed out the first part of the ridge.

On 8 October the arduous task of load carrying began. The fittest of us carried 70lb rucksacks (32kg) and it took all day to reach the site for Advanced Base Camp (5170m). We pressed on to Camp 1 (5740m) the next day and set up siege headquarters – a collection of three tiny tents in a desert of snow. During the next two days two parties investigated the first part of the

S ridge and laid fixed rope down the 250m trade route to its start. We could soon see that the first part of our climb would be to negotiate two rock towers which barred access to the next part of the ridge. Angus and Ngatemba struggled over the first rock tower to be faced by a seemingly impassable wall of rock on the second tower. Back in camp we talked all day about alternative routes, the danger, and giving up. Finally, we decided to push the ridge. However, Andrew who had only been married a few months made the brave decision to turn back. For him the danger was unacceptable. Peter, my elder brother, a man of hidden depth, wild ginger facial hair and enormous appetite, had not acclimatised well and he agreed to support us by carrying loads of food and equipment from Base Camp to Camp 1 alone. This thankless task of support was the key to our success, preserving our strength now that we were reduced to a climbing team of four: Neil, Angus, Ngatemba and myself.

Our next task was to make the first rock tower safe and we spent a day fixing rope in a rising traverse on loose rock. All day our hands and feet dislodged boulders which tumbled down thousands of feet to a distant glacier to the east. After that hard day's climbing Angus and I needed a rest day and we spent the next day at Camp 1 while Neil and Ngatemba pressed on to the second rock tower with more fixed rope, planning to bivouac that evening and go further in the morning. At the same time Dave Gwynne-Jones and Annette Carmichael carried a load of food and gear up the fixed rope to be picked up later. They had a marvellous day and returned buzzing.

The next day we rose early and climbed the fixed rope along the first rock tower. At one point I turned round to see Angus sitting with his head bowed on his chest, emotion hidden behind his reflective goggles. He was clearly quite shaken. Whilst unclipped from the fixed rope, he had stumbled and fallen onto his left shoulder narrowly escaping an enormous fall to his death.

It was nearly midday and we spotted the other two already on the top of the second rock tower some four hours ahead of us but just within earshot. Neil shouted that they were going on. That afternoon was the most glorious climbing for me. We descended from the first rock tower to take a line between the snow plastering the W face of the ridge and the second rock tower above. We were carrying heavy loads of climbing equipment and food to dump in preparation for the summit bid. The climbing was mostly straight-forward on nasty soft snow but with the safety of fixed rope that the other two had left. Every now and then our progress was hampered by a difficult rock pitch, but this was exhilarating in the thin still air, brilliant sunshine and dramatic scenery. Behind we could see Camp 1 and ahead was the summit of Chamlang; in the distance to its left rose the black SW face of Mount Everest looking most unfriendly.

At the end of the fixed ropes we buried our loads in a small cave, blocking the entrance with climbing hardware as protection against theft of food by ravens. These enormous birds had been a repeated problem for us, pecking holes and ripping our tents and then spreading the contents of packets of noodles and cup-a-soups all over the campsite.

Angus and I returned to Camp 1 that night, while Neil and Ngatemba established Camp 2 at 6280m on a thin snow arête on the crest of the S ridge of Chamlang – Base Camp was still visible as a collection of red dots far below. That night I lay awake for a long time. We were almost in a position to go for the summit. We all wanted a rest at Base Camp, some real food and a wash, but this would make us very short on time, and the long walk back to Camp 1 would undo some of the good to be gained by a rest at Base. The next problem was who to send for the summit. Neil and Ngatemba were the strongest. Angus had the most technical expertise and I wanted to go because it was my expedition. Finally, I decided to send the two strongest, realising that this would probably exclude me. Neil and Ngatemba returned the next afternoon and the arrival of Andy and Peter with buffalo fried rice and cooked potatoes decided our fate. We would rest for two days at Camp 1 and then all four go for the top together.

On 18 October we set off for Camp 2, fixing the last 100m of the second rock tower and arriving to pitch tents in the afternoon mist. We ate well on our stocks of food, frozen potatoes reheated in soup, and slept soundly. The morning of 19 October was fine and we set off over the frozen snows northwards at 7.45am. The morning was a long and terrific ridge bash, with incredible exposure and hard work as the sun softened the snow. We climbed as two pairs, Neil and Ngatemba ahead breaking trail. By mid-afternoon we reached the feared rock band which had dominated our conversation as we viewed the mountain from Base Camp. This had been the crux of the climb for the Japanese on the first ascent. Neil led the climbing on the rock band, 50m of technical rock followed by a steep ice slope. Above this, we roped together again as a four, Neil still leading. We were now on steep, unconsolidated snow, 3m deep, and we found ourselves almost swimming to stay on the mountain. Neil fell. Angus shouted, 'He's off!' There was nothing I could do – I was struggling to make any upward progress myself let alone arrest a fall. He whizzed past me and momentarily I realised that we were all about to plummet down the W face, over the rock band, 2300m down, pulled by the rope. Then it was all over, he stopped just past me, incredibly held by Ngatemba, I don't know how. As darkness fell we clambered into a crevasse and dug out places to sleep, brewed and spent a fitful night at 6800m, short of air and desperately cold.

The morning of 20 October was again clear but, as we climbed out of our crevasse leaving behind all of our bivouac equipment, the full force of a high-altitude easterly wind hit us. Painful spindrift struck all exposed flesh and dropped chilling flakes inside our clothing. The slopes were straightforward now and at 10.50am we stood on the summit of Chamlang at 7319m. Unknown and unseen, Peter was watching us through a 1.2m lens from Base Camp as we reached the summit of Chamlang more than 2km above him. From the summit of Mera (6476m), Andy Knight, Annette Carmichael, Carolyn Knight (expedition doctor), David Collier and Dave Gwynne-Jones shared in our success.

Ngatemba took out a Nepali flag and we all posed beside him for photographs. The wind was terrific, burning our faces and taking our breath away. Neil took off his gloves to take some pictures and his fingers were frostbitten within seconds. We hurried down from that unpleasant spot to escape the cruel wind. In no time we reached our bivouac, packed up, had a drink and set off for Camp 2. Just below the bivouac we had to abseil to cross that dangerous unconsolidated snow that had caused us problems on the ascent. We had little climbing hardware left and three 50m abseils to perform. On the first, we placed a snow stake as an anchor and Neil and Angus abseiled down. I followed and as I descended the stake began to pull out of the soft snow, my full weight relying on it. Ngatemba stood on the stake and I thrust my axe into the snow and climbed the rest of the way down. We descended the rock band without problems and Neil and Ngatemba set off for Camp 2 at a terrific pace.

At a rock step some distance further along, Angus made a belay and I descended as he payed out the rope. I followed the footsteps in the ice that the others had made ahead of us, but after a few steps the ice gave way and I was left hanging in my harness over the W face, held by Angus. We could afford no more near misses.

It was dark as we climbed along a knife-edge of snow, following our footsteps of the day before back to Camp 2. The wind was still roaring but with less ferocity than it had seven hours previously when we had stood on the summit where, in the dim moonlight, a plume of snow was blowing unrelentingly east. I was staggering with exhaustion after 10 hours of climbing at high altitude. My mouth was completely dessicated and my lips caked and swollen. I couldn't see Angus but I heard him groan behind and then the rope came tight between us. He had stopped. I turned back to find out what had happened. I found him half buried in a crevasse which split the ridge and into which he had stumbled in the dark. Snow had packed in on top of his legs; he couldn't move. For 15 minutes I lay in the snow vigorously digging him out. I stopped occasionally as waves of nausea brought about by the exertion made me cough and retch down the precipitous W face of the ridge. At last I got him out and at 7pm we collapsed into Camp 2. Neil and Ngatemba Sherpa had been back for an hour and had some hot orange ready; we sat rehydrating in silence and relief.

We spent many hours eating and drinking without conversation. We had done it, but the elation was numbed by exhaustion. Two days later, as the mist swirled up the Hongu valley, we returned to Base Camp to be reunited with our camp staff and the rest of the successful Chamlang expedition team.

Summary: On 20 October 1991 the first British ascent of Chamlang, 7319m, was made by the British Chamlang Expedition. The joint leaders were Andrew Knight and Andrew Pollard. The following members reached the summit by the South Ridge: Angus Andrew, Neil Howells, Andrew Pollard and Ngatemba Sherpa.

HISTORICAL APPENDIX

Survey expeditions

1953 Survey of Inukhu and Hongu valleys by J O M Roberts.

1954 New Zealand Alpine Club Barun expedition. Exploration and survey of the Barun, Iswa and Choyang valleys.

1955 Mt Chamlang survey expedition led by Norman Hardie noted a possible route on the S ridge of Chamlang.

Ascents of Chamlang main summit

1962 1st ascent of Chamlang main summit via S ridge by Japanese Academic Alpine Club of Hokkaido.

1986 2nd ascent by the Japanese via W ridge.

1987 A Korean–Nepalese expedition climbs the S ridge.

1990 A German expedition reaches the summit via the W ridge and W face.

1991 1st British ascent, via S ridge, led by Andrew Knight and Andrew Pollard.

Ascents of other summits of Chamlang

1981 Reinhold Messner and Doug Scott climb to a minor summit of Chamlang at 7010m via N face.

1984 Doug Scott and party climb the east summit of Chamlang (7325m) via NE ridge and N face and then traverse to the central summit (7180m).

1989 A successful ascent of the east summit via the N face by a Netherlands women's expedition.

ACKNOWLEDGEMENTS

We would like to express our gratitude to the many individuals, firms and organisations who contributed to the success of this expedition and, in particular, to Sir Charles Evans, our patron, and to Dr Charles Warren, the Mount Everest Foundation, the British Mountaineering Council, and Himalayan Kingdoms Ltd.

Left
28. Tom Bourdillon talking
into a 'walkie-talkie'
set on Everest in 1953.
The sets were used
between camp and camp
up to 24,000ft.
(*Alfred Gregory*) (p62)

Below Wilfrid Noyce (R) and Robin Smith on the W face of Pik Garmo
in the Pamirs just before their fatal accident on 24 July 1962. (p67)

30. The 1952 Cho Oyu expedition, from L: Secord, Pugh, Colledge, Shipton, Hillary, Evans, Lowe. (p42)

31. Gyachung Kang, 7922m, and Nup La from Nepal. In 1952 Edmund Hillary and George Lowe made the first crossing of Nup La into Tibet. (p42)

Cho Oyu, 8210m, seen from Tibet: the NW face. (p42)

Camp on Nangpa La, looking into Nepal and the N side of Menlungtse.
From near here, in 1951, Murray and Bourdillon saw a possible route up
Cho Oyu via its W face. (p42)

34. Chamlang, 7319m. On the S ridge: Angus Andrew approaching the first rock tower. (*Andrew Pollard*) (p112)

Above
Andrew Pollard (L) and Ngatemba Sherpa on the summit of Chamlang,
Everest behind. (*Neil Howells*) (p112)

Below
The 1st British ascent of Chamlang followed the R skyline up the S ridge,
Makalu behind (L) (*Andrew Knight*) (p112)

The International Catalan Expeditions 1991–92:

Facing page
The enormous flow of the Gasherbrum glacier. Broad Peak is visible in
the far left-hand corner. The route from Base Camp to the real base of
the mountain (about 20km) runs along the opposite rim of the glacier to
that where Joan Gelabert, radio operator, is standing.

Above
Broad Peak East Face: main summit (centre), 8047m. The central
summit (R), 8016m, was reached via the giant ramp (R).

(*Photos: Kurt Diemberger*) (p88)

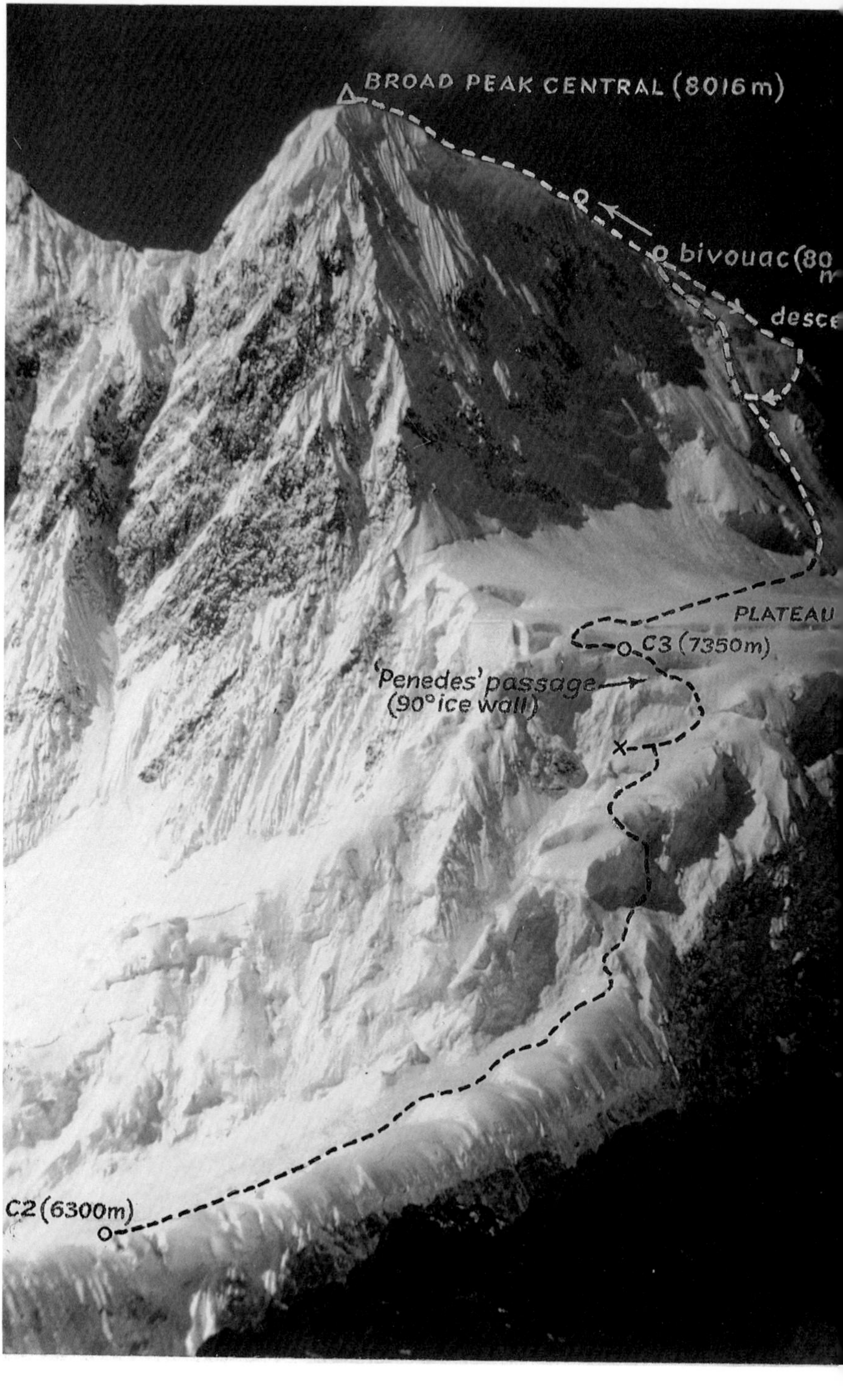
BROAD PEAK CENTRAL (8016m)
bivouac(80
desce
PLATEAU
C3 (7350m)
'Penedes' passage
(90° ice wall)
C2 (6300m)

39. Broad Peak East Face: the central summit, 8016m, was reached on 4 August 1992 by the International Catalan Expedition. (*Kurt Diemberger*) (p88)

KEITH MILNE
Thalay Sagar
(Plates 42, 43)

I first became interested in Thalay Sagar when looking at Pete Thexton's photographs of the unclimbed N face in a *Mountain* magazine article. Several people from the Kunyang Kish trip in 1988 were interested in going to Thalay Sagar and we were fortunate in gaining the 1990 Nick Estcourt Award. I had now seen Rick Allen's spectacular photos of the south side of the mountain, taken when he made the first ascent of Kirti Stambh (6254m) in 1982. It featured a vertical, golden face of granite, accentuated by a tremendous snow cone. It looked like a fairy-tale mountain! I wondered if we could climb it. There was no record of anyone attempting the mountain from the south.

We arrived in India in September 1990. From the road head at Ghuttu, it took four and a half days of walking on good paths through splendid forests to reach an excellent site for Base Camp at about 3700m. The monsoon had just finished so we had not seen Thalay Sagar yet. That evening it cleared and we noticed an orange cliff suspended above the clouds to the north. Mountains always look much higher in the sky than you expect and this was no exception! We suddenly realised how much effort it was going to be to get to the base of the headwall.

Advanced Base Camp was established quickly at the head of the flattish part of the Phating glacier at about 4460m. It was a forbidding place. The regular sound of serac falls echoed around the rock walls, but we seemed to be far enough away from the obvious chutes to avoid the avalanches. There was a choice of routes ahead: looking up from ABC we could see a central rocky buttress flanked by steep crevassed glaciers on both sides. The right-hand glacier looked out of the question, involving 1000m of climbing through a maze of hundreds of crevasses. The glacier on the left was also crevassed and seemed to be threatened by seracs, so we decided to climb the buttress. There was a convenient moraine ridge leading up to where the rock steepened. We had to fix a few ropes on the steeper sections to allow subsequent load carrying. We moved up the ridge until we were surprised to find a camp excavated from the loose rocks. I picked up a remarkably fresh looking packet of Italian biscuits and was even more surprised to find that its sell-by date was August 1990! Had we been beaten to it? In view of the precarious nature of some of the loose rock we had encountered, the Italian team must have used a slightly different line to reach this point. We returned to Base Camp with mixed feelings. Our cook related in broken English that Italian teams had made two previous attempts on the S ridge, but had been forced to retreat.

Above Camp 1 was a steep snow arête which led to a relatively flat glacier with only a few crevasses. From here we became hypnotised by the face above in our search for possible lines up the compact granite. We made a diagonal line to the right to reach the 55 to 65 degree snow and ice slope below the headwall. Our two porta-ledges weighed 7kg each, were unstable to carry and were very cramped for two people. After some deliberation we decided to carry them up, as they might well be essential on the face; but this was an exhausting task and it was all we could do to reach 6100m, making Camp 2 at a small rock band. The next day the weather rapidly deteriorated, but with a tremendous effort we got all the haul bags to the base of the cliff and set up the ledges as it was getting dark. I had mild frostbite on my fingers from handling the tent poles. There followed a terrible night of continuous avalanches down the face. We thought the winter had started and that it might last for days. I knew I could not continue for more than two more days before my finger tips would come up in blisters. The spindrift eased at about 11am the next day and we decided to climb down to the safety of Camp 1.

We discussed the situation: time was running out, we risked missing the porters and the plane if we continued. Annoyingly, the weather was now clear, although it remained windy on the tops, but we were too tired to contemplate another attempt without a rest. It was all we could do to retrieve the equipment from our high point at about 6200m. The mountain had beaten us.

After six months or so, you forget the arduous and uncomfortable times on an expedition and remember only the best moments. We decided to attempt the S face of Thalay Sagar again, but with no porta-ledges (at least for the first attempt) and using minimal fixed rope. We were welcomed at the airport by Gorvind, our liaison officer from 1990, and his boss, Mr C S Pandey, of Trade Wings Ltd. They helped us in many ways and soon we were again walking up the familiar valley. At Kharsoli we discovered that there was a tremendous amount of snow, so it took several extra days of hard work to get all the loads to Base Camp.

It was 12 May and the mountain tops were clear. We spent some time examining the headwall through binoculars and could see small ledges at half height. The plan was to fix ropes to the ledges from a camp at the base of the cliff, pull the ropes and fix them as far as the ridge. We anticipated two main load carries: one to take the equipment and one to take the food. We wanted to reduce the carrying to a minimum, while recognising that it would not be possible to climb such a difficult headwall entirely in alpine style.

The Phating glacier, being covered in snow, was very easy to travel this time and, after establishing ABC, we acclimatised on the snowy peak of Rudugaira (5364m) and other climbs. We had noticed the glacier to the left of the lower buttress, which we had climbed in 1990, now looked a simpler option because it was covered in snow. This would allow us to reach the snow dome at about 5700m without carrying heavy ropes for fixing, and so avoid time-consuming climbing on the lower buttress. Charlie French, Tom Prentice, Julian Fisher and I were keen to try the headwall and we planned to carry all the rock-climbing equipment as high as possible in a two-day push from ABC and then return to Base Camp in a day. We plodded up the steep glacier above ABC until everyone became too tired with the altitude to carry on. It was misty and we decided to camp on a small level area, but we had not reached the safety of the top of the snow dome.

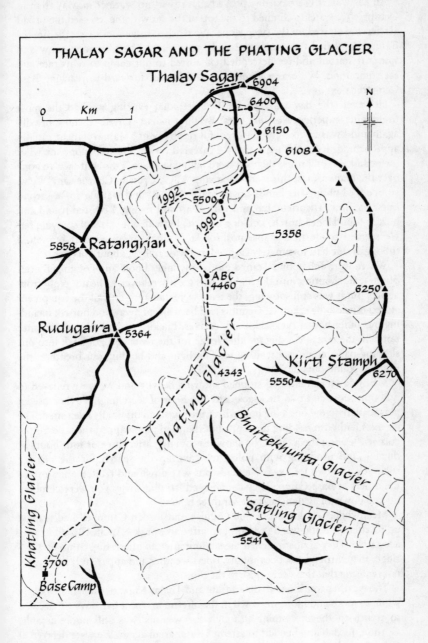

THALAY SAGAR AND THE PHATING GLACIER

An early start the next day proved that it was no warmer in May than in October. We quickly climbed to the top of the snow dome, crossed the broad glacier and started up the steep slope. We reached some rocks near the site for Camp 2 and tied the equipment sacks to a piton. The afternoon snow and spindrift started and we descended exhausted to our camp to rehydrate and eat some food. We crashed out early and looked forward to reaching Base Camp the next day.

However, the day was not finished yet: that evening we had the most frightening experience of our lives. By 8pm it had started to snow heavily again and I was awoken by the dreadful rumbling of a slab avalanche rapidly approaching. It hit the tents and we careered down the steep slope for what seemed like a long time; then we were falling in space. I thought 'We've gone over the main seracs; this is it – next stop ABC'. Crunch. Charlie said 'We've stopped!', holding his hands up to brace the tent and waiting for a second burst of snow. Disorientated and with heart still racing, I twisted round and luckily found a headtorch. Looking outside, I saw that it was still snowing but we seemed to be in a stable position. I gradually realised that our blind toboggan ride had fortunately stopped in a wide trench, about 8m deep.

Where were Julian and Tom? I put on my inner boots and got gingerly out of the tent, shouting into the night. I was greatly relieved to hear a reply from above. But it was still snowing, the tents were damaged and all the equipment stored outside the cramped Geminis had been swept away and buried, including our outer boots, rucksacks and ice axes. Luckily we had all put our inner boots in the tents. We dug another ledge for the tents and got back into our sleeping-bags, anxiously waiting for first light and holding our breath at the slightest sound outside.

When dawn came it had stopped snowing heavily and we were relieved to find our boots and two rucksacks after an hour of searching. We then used a plastic plate to dig out a big hole where the tents had originally been sited. The ice axes had been holding the tents, but they had just snapped the tape off the corners, leaving the axes in the snow. Eventually, after three or four hours of digging and prodding with poles, we gave up the search for the missing rucksack and two ice axes. We made our way down and related our story to the others at Base Camp. They commented 'So that's why you were climbing up and down an avalanche slope for three hours!'

Meanwhile, Gordon Scott, Sue Grimley and Jordan Campbell had teamed up to attempt Ratangrian (5858m), an attractive peak NW of ABC and easily accessible. They almost reached the summit after an interesting climb up the S ridge; they turned back because of suspect weather and apparent lack of time, not realising that they were close to the top.

The weather continued to deteriorate and Thalay Sagar became increasingly white as more and more snow fell in the afternoon. After five days we decided to return to the mountain, although the weather was still unpredictable. Gordon, Jordan and Sue left to attempt Ratangrian again. We were delayed at Camp 1 by bad weather, then moved loads up to Camp 2. The next day we returned to Camp 1 and were pinned down by a storm, worried that we would get struck by lightning. An inter-tent game of battleships kept morale up.

A sudden clearing of the weather and an early start saw the team at Camp 2. The next day the ropes were pulled below Camp 2 and moved up to reach a site for Camp 3, naturally avoiding the site which had been hit by so much spindrift in 1990. Tom and I cut a ledge in the 60 degree slope but hit rock and ice. The afternoon snow soon turned into major spindrift and when Charlie and Julian arrived it was filling in the ledge faster than it could be dug. Things were looking grim. We managed to get a small ledge for the second tent, but Charlie and Julian had little sleep. The Geminis were squashed even smaller than usual by the weight of the snow.

We were now slightly higher than we had been in 1990 and had all the equipment we needed. There seemed to be two lines up the face above. The left line was more broken, but was covered in loose snow. The right-hand line started up steep snow and then onto steep difficult rock. Tom and I started up the right-hand line the next day and fixed two ropes after difficult mixed and aid climbing. Progress was slow; cracks were thin and discontinuous. The afternoon spindrift was a shock, as if things were not difficult enough already. It was all we could manage to abseil off safely.

In a short space of time we had all come to the same conclusion – that the granite headwall was too difficult in the prevailing conditions. We had already been delayed and we did not want to fail to reach the summit a second time. Charlie and Julian decided to go down, partly because they had come on the trip to climb the wall, not snow plod. Charlie also wanted to return to his job in Britain, rather than extend his 'holiday'. Charlie and Julian had a hard time carrying the big wall gear down to the bottom of the slope. Julian fell in a crevasse, but luckily landed on a snow bridge and was rescued by Charlie.

Tom and I spent a day traversing left through deep snow, then ice and up a gully, avalanching with spindrift, to reach a level spot for the tent. A small but frightening avalanche blasted the tent during the evening. The next morning Tom led a difficult icecliff (with only two ice screws) to reach the upper snow slopes which we knew led to the summit rock pyramid. I noticed I had superficial frostbite on my fingers again. I seconded with the pack, struggling to release the haul bag from the overhangs. Next was a deceptively long plod through deepening snow which slowed progress to a snail's pace.

The next day we were very tired and only managed a reconnaissance for the summit push. A 3am start the next morning saw us over the bergschrund at first light and into a difficult chimney. We traversed right, trying to find a route through diagonal snow patches to reach the E ridge. However, the snow was superficial and the rock very poor. Directly above was a vertical face like the Dolomites. Traversing back left I saw a snowy ledge leading left and some abseil pitons.

I followed Tom across the traverse, moved up, and unexpectedly found myself on the arête between the N and S faces, an incredible position, with a new view northwards to Gangotri. We had now joined the line taken on the first ascent in 1979 by Roy Klingfield, John Thackray and Pete Thexton. There was still a long way to go and the climbing looked a lot steeper than I had expected. The rock was loose, but runners could be found after clearing the snow. My frostbite had got worse and was now quite worrying. After four pitches it was mid-afternoon and we knew we were in danger of being caught in the dark. Tom carried on up the arête and I had my cine-camera ready to take some spectacular shots of him climbing up with dry snow blowing from his hands and feet. Luckily the heavy thunder clouds stayed in the valley, only light snow fell and we climbed quickly. I led a short, unexpected traverse on steep ice (with only one ice axe, as the other was rather inconveniently in my pack), followed by an overhanging chimney which turned out to be quite worrying in crampons and badly protected. Tom climbed up the chimney and then led some difficult moves under an overhang on very loose rock and moved up to find a belay. Above was the snowy arête, disappearing into the mist. It looked a long way, but suddenly there we were at the top after only two more pitches. I was incredibly relieved that we had reached the summit after so much hard work on two expeditions. There was hardly any time to take pictures. It was 7pm and time for the radio call!

Abseiling in the dark requires a lot of concentration and I forced myself to go carefully. We then had to reverse the short ice pitch and do some difficult diagonal abseils down the arête, with danger of swinging across the icy N face. A geologist by trade, I was determined to collect some rock samples (later, at ABC, Julian wondered why my pack was so heavy!). We plunged down the final snow gully into our camp at 11pm and found the tent squashed by spindrift avalanches and no energy to dig it out, so it was an uncomfortable night.

The 7am radio call brought us round and forced us to get ready. The descent was like a nightmare, with half the slope awash with deep spindrift and small avalanches. Eventually we staggered into Camp 1, trailing the ropes. The next day we met Gordon and Jordan coming up from ABC and it was handshakes and smiles all round. They continued up to Camp 1 and did a tremendous job clearing the rest of the gear, including empty gas cylinders and snow stakes. Soon everyone was safely back at base celebrating in the big tent.

Julian helped me walk-out and get to hospital in Delhi in only four days; my fingers have since recovered. The main expedition left with only 22 porters and heavy loads, but they still managed to carry 50kg of non-burnable rubbish (by the way, don't tell the porters that they are carrying rubbish!). They arrived in Delhi a few days later to enjoy the luxury of the four star Park Hotel. It had been an immense effort by the whole team and I was glad that everyone had done some significant climbing. Altogether, we had climbed two peaks, two rock routes and had almost reached the top of a third peak. But at the back of our minds we still wondered, could that wall be climbed?

Summary: The British Thalay Sagar Expedition 1990 attempted the unclimbed S face of Thalay Sagar (6904m), Garhwal Himalaya. A high point of 6150m was reached at the base of the headwall before bad weather forced a retreat. During the Thalay Sagar Expedition 1992 Keith Milne and Tom Prentice reached the summit on 6 June by a new route from the south. The snowy peak of Rudugaira (5364m) was climbed on 13 May by Gordon Scott, Susan Grimley and Tom Prentice. The summit of Ratangrian (5858m) was almost reached by Gordon Scott, Jordan Campbell (USA) and Susan Grimley.

LINDSAY GRIFFIN
Mongolian Escape

(Plates 48A, 48B)

It was in 1990 that an exuberant John Blashford-Snell first brought up the prospect of a Raleigh International expedition to North West Mongolia. John, who has all the attributes of the traditional intrepid explorer, not least the characteristic pith helmet which he still insists on wearing to all corners of the globe, seemed to be offering Julian Freeman-Attwood and myself the opportunity to climb in one of the most remote mountain regions of Central Asia. Of course there was a catch! We would spend part of our time acting as guides and instructors to a small group of aspirant mountaineers. 'Well motivated though,' John told us, and then, almost as an afterthought, added that most of the 'students' would be unattached girls in their early twenties! We thought for maybe half a second before giving our answer.

The mystical mountains of the Altai span almost 1500km, yet for most of their length there is little about which to get excited. However, where they pass through the triple border point of Russia, China and Mongolia, only a short distance from the frontiers of Kazakhstan, a compact isolated range rises to over 4000m. This massif – the Tabun Bogdo – lies in the Dead Heart of Asia and was rumoured to hold the most spectacular mountains in the country. Not surprisingly, no information was forthcoming from the Mongolian authorities, and I spent the next two years trying to follow up vague leads in various Eastern Block and Soviet states, always drawing a blank until, two days before our departure, a package arrived from Barcelona containing a sketch map and an incomprehensible report of the 1967 Polish expedition. I packed it in my baggage in the vain hope that we might bump into an itinerant Pole somewhere in Mongolia.

There were to be three 'instructors'. Julian is a wily Shropshire aristocrat with a power-to-weight ratio rivalling an Olympic gymnast. He had come into high standard mountaineering later than most, yet his background, which included almost being blown into several hundred pieces by land mines while making the first crossing of Mauritania's Empty Quarter, stood him in good stead. On the other hand our partner in crime, Ed Webster from Colorado, started climbing when barely out of nappies. This would be his first expedition to the mountains since shortening his digits when climbing to the South Summit of Everest, four years ago.

Now for a few basic statistics: Mongolia has an area equivalent to Denmark, Holland, Belgium, Germany, France, Spain and Portugal all rolled into one – yet with a population of only 2½ million! As half of these are nomads, who live on nothing but mutton and milk and sleep in large circular felt tents called *gers*, the number of permanent settlements is small. Although an independent country for many years, Mongolia had been heavily reliant on the Soviet Union for its basic needs. After 1990 these quickly disappeared. On our arrival in May 1992 the economy had reached rock-bottom; ration books were being issued in the increasingly foodless capital – Ulaan Baatar – and aviation fuel had become very scarce.

We were forced to wait nearly a week in Hovd, the hub of several Raleigh medical and community programmes, but it would be untrue to say that the time was wasted. Across the far side of the river from our camp lay a 200ft high cliff of decomposing granite which sent Ed, and to a lesser extent Julian, into a frenzy of enthusiasm. Although not so sharp on the open walls, where the use of small finger holds is mandatory, Webster is still a demon when it comes to his old speciality – the crack. On our first day he took this esoteric part of Central Asia into modern times by leading us up the awkward *Amarsana* (E2, 5c), named after a popular folk hero.

Our first stroke of luck came the next afternoon. Two of the staff had just returned from *ger* city, as Hovd was becoming affectionately known. To our surprise they had bumped into another foreigner. 'Well, he spoke to us in English but I think he might have said he was Polish,' said the Yorkshire lass. Our eyes widened in disbelief. 'Anyway, we've invited him along for tea.' I raced to my tent and pulled out the Polish article – surely this was a good omen. With the article even vaguely translated, we might gain our first insight into this enigmatic range. When Ryszard Palczewski stepped inside the *ger* an hour later, and announced in perfect English that he ought to make a reasonable translation as it was he who had written the article nearly 25 years ago, we were – well – simply lost for words. More so when he informed us that he had met his future English wife while working in Afghanistan and that he now lived in Brighton, making regular trips three times a year to attend to his farming project in Eastern Mongolia. It's a perverse world that allows you to spend years making unsuccessful enquiries all over Europe, only to find that the best information lay right at your doorstep!

A few more granite gems succumbed to Ed's stumpy hands before we left in a high-wheeled military truck, armed with our newly acquired wealth of knowledge and carrying our imported food, gaz and equipment for the next 1½ months. There are no roads in western Mongolia, only directions, and after three days of travel across a rocky arid wilderness we reached a small Kazakh encampment. A further 20km on foot, with camels carrying the luggage, took us to a base camp site.

During the next five weeks we explored most corners of the range, feeling privileged to be the first western climbers allowed a mountaineering permit. True the scale was not more than the Bernese Oberland, to which there was a close resemblance, but the ambience was distinctly Himalayan! The main peaks had been climbed by their easiest lines, but little, if any, technical climbing had yet been achieved. We were lucky to have students who were talented, and their enthusiasm meant that interesting new routes, rather than straightforward ascents, could be tackled.

Then there were the tracks – snow leopard, bear and ... the other! We were crossing the head of the remote Alexandrov glacier, en route to climb a superb

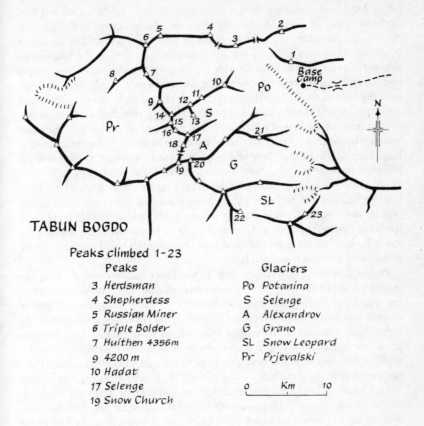

TABUN BOGDO

Peaks climbed 1-23

Peaks		Glaciers	
3	Herdsman	Po	Potanina
4	Shepherdess	S	Selenge
5	Russian Miner	A	Alexandrov
6	Triple Bolder	G	Grano
7	Huithen 4356m	SL	Snow Leopard
9	4200 m	Pr	Prjevalski
10	Hadat		
17	Selenge	0 Km 10	
19	Snow Church		

diamond-shaped face of blue water-ice on a peak that Ryszard had named Snow Church. A set of curious fresh prints crossed the glacier, heading towards China over a high col. They were large, showed a definite toe-shaped formation, and, inexplicably, were in sets of three. We had a choice: should we follow the tracks over the pass in an attempt to discover the origins of this mysterious triped, or should we climb the face? We climbed the face, convinced that the tracks could only have been those of a yeti carrying a snow leopard under one paw!

Towards the end of our stay, after many memorable climbs with our capable students, the main group returned to Hovd, and there was just enough time to attempt Huithen (4356m) Mongolia's highest peak, by the impressive and unclimbed South Face. Unfortunately it meant a tricky two-day crossing of the range via the Alexandrov glacier, 'yeti' pass, and the remote Prjevalski

glacier. Bad weather pinned us down for a day, but by the following evening
the sky was clear and the snow crisp. We reached the summit just after dawn
on 12 July, having climbed the prominent 100m ridge bordering the left side
of the face. To the north lay the vast uninhabited nothingness of the Siberian
Steppe. To the south and west a myriad of unclimbed and mostly unnamed
peaks ran away into China, while the long gentle glaciers on the Mongolian
side of the range flowed towards wide grassy glens reminiscent of the Scottish
highlands. By 2pm we were descending, independently, a vast boulder slope
near the base of the ridge. What happened next has, for better or worse, been
well documented elsewhere, so I offer the following restricted account, with a
certain tinge of regret that it fails to do full justice to all concerned. The slope
was typical of those found all over the lower reaches of Asian mountains –
large angular blocks that, now and again, wobbled underfoot. Only this block
triggered something above! I was knocked rudely forward into a slight hollow,
landing with a large granite boulder across my left leg. Miraculously the
boulder had trapped my leg in a slot just wide enough to stop the full crushing
power, but not, alas, wide enough to prevent a serious double compound
fracture. I passed out for a short while. When I came to I realised that my
lower leg had lost all circulation and knew immediately that I must relieve the
pressure on it before it was too late.

Pushing, heaving or even cursing at the block proved useless. I unsuccessfully tried to cut away the various layers of clothing to reduce the size of
the leg; I tried using the axe and hammer to chisel away at the granite
constriction below; whatever I did seemed futile. Finally I remembered the
rope. After a couple of attempts I managed to lasso another large boulder
above my head and set up a pulley system with a few karabiners. It didn't
work at first, but after increasing to a six to one mechanical advantage I just
succeeded in shifting the block – not enough to withdraw the leg, but enough
so that a minute later a tingling sensation reached my toes. I worked at this for
five hours until located by Julian and Ed, who took a further three hours to
free the leg and construct a makeshift splint. Julian returned to the foot of the
face and collected a tent and sleeping-bag, while Ed helped me bum-shuffle
down for 14 hours to a flat spot on the moraine. Leaving me to practise my
tourniquet techniques, Ed and Julian climbed back over the range (their third
consecutive night out) to reach Base Camp, where they made faint radio
contact with Hovd. With, officially, no aviation fuel now left in the country,
the outlook was bleak.

In the capital, over 1500km distant, the military were unable to help, but
the civilian airline offered a 20-years-old cargo helicopter and a pilot who,
despite having no experience of operating in mountain terrain, was willing to
have a try. After complex negotiations, John Blashford-Snell managed to
obtain sufficient fuel for the helicopter to reach Hovd where the last remains
of emergency fuel hidden in Western Mongolia were released by the state, as a
sort of thank-you for work done by the various Raleigh projects. Unfortunately it was not enough to make the round trip! On the evening of the
fourth day after the accident I heard the sound of rotor blades and, pulling
back the tent door, saw the unwieldy chopper coming over the range from the

north. If it had turned back at this point I would still have felt elated because I now realised that other people knew!

Twice it tried to land but, operating above its ceiling, almost crashed – then disappeared over the moraine. An hour or so later Ed and two other Raleigh staff, including a doctor, arrived carrying an old army stretcher. They were depressed! Having been dumped lower down on the glacier, with no explanation and no gear, not knowing the reliability of the pilot and realising the shortage of fuel, they had then witnessed the chopper depart, possibly for ever. In fact, Jamaldorj, the pilot, had made a bold move. Flying down-valley, he had landed the craft at a suitable altitude and cut the engines to conserve fuel. Restarting the engines an hour or so later he stripped the chopper of all heavy gear, including the starter batteries, and, hoping that he wouldn't stall, flew in for the pick-up.

After a brief stop to collect the batteries, and another at Base Camp, I was flown 150km to a small aerodrome, barely reaching it before the fuel ran out. Here, on the manager's desk in the local 'hospital', the Raleigh doctor cleaned the wound. They didn't have splints but he improvised with long strips of wood, kindly ripped from the surrounding shelves and cupboards by the manager himself! We were now in an area populated solely by Kazakhs – a nomadic people desperately trying to escape from a country rapidly approaching economic collapse. Next day, by another stroke of luck, there was an unscheduled landing by a plane sent on an evacuation mission from Kazakhstan. After five bottles of Vodka changed hands, fuel syphoned from the airliner gave the chopper just enough flying time to reach Hovd, where a Singapore based Lear jet, the first foreign plane ever legally to enter Western Mongolian airspace, was waiting to fly me to Hong Kong. Again, the remaining fuel had to be transferred from chopper to jet, allowing the latter just to make the distance and the Swiss pilot to perform an emergency night landing at Kaitak airport, just one hour before it was closed by an enormous typhoon. A few hours later, and nearly seven days after the accident, I was lying in the operating theatre.

Six months later I am still on crutches, with further operations pending. But I am happy to report that a Queen's Citation has been awarded to Jamaldorj – a spirited pilot who, against all the odds, was prepared to have a go.

Summary: In May–July 1992 a Raleigh International expedition, led by Lindsay Griffin, Julian Freeman-Attwood and Ed Webster, made 23 ascents of peaks and lesser summits in the Tabun Bogdo massif, Mongolian Altai, including the unclimbed S face of Huithen (4356m), Mongolia's highest peak. Several were previously untrodden and more than half were climbed by new routes of varying standard up to alpine TD-/TD. The main ascents were made in the company of Richard Bruton, Vanessa Carter, Bridget Cowen, Claire Gosney, Tom Nichols and Colonel Tsanjid their Mongolian representative. After a serious rockfall accident, Lindsay Griffin was helicoptered out in a difficult and dangerous rescue operation. There is still much scope for ice/mixed routes of great quality in one of the decreasing number of unspoilt wilderness areas left on the planet.

PAUL KNOTT

Mountains of Dagestan

(Plate 47)

We were speeding west in the mist. Suddenly the tarmac ended and we were crossing rough ground. Then the road worsened some more and it turned dark. We were in a kind of tunnel – rough and unlined, wet and bumpy. Lit by a string of light bulbs, it was like some kind of fantasy film set. This was the road to the wilds of Dagestan.

Lying at the Caspian end of the Caucasus, Dagestan contains a number of mountain groups above 4000m. These have always been overlooked in favour of the peaks of the Central Caucasus, and were almost completely neglected during the British exploration of the Caucasus in the late 19th century. In 1890 George Yeld and G P Baker climbed Bazardyuzi (4480m)[1], but these appear to have been the only previous British climbers in Dagestan. The first climber in the Snegovoy and Bogosskiy ranges, which we visited, was the German explorer Gottfried Merzbacher in 1892.[2] Entering from Georgia, he made 9 first ascents in only 38 days. He was followed by another German Moriz von Déchy in 1897.[3] There appear to have been no visits by Western climbers since, but fortunately both explorers published detailed books and maps.

We were travelling with friends from Kiev, Nick Drobotenko, Yuri Cherevko and Mikhail Bogomolov. Even they had found information on the mountains hard to come by, but they had obtained two rather doubtful guidebooks.[4,5] There had never been Mountaineering Camps in Dagestan, so until the collapse of the Soviet Union the area had been extremely difficult to visit. We had travelled together by train to Makhachkala on the Caspian Sea, and were now in a bus heading for the mountains.

After half an hour under the Gimrinskiy ridge we emerged in the setting sun to a moonscape of loose rock. The road wound its way down a steep-sided valley to the village of Gimri, birthplace of the hero of Dagestan, Imam Shamyl. The buildings were roughly built from the local shale, and terraced upon one another's flat roofs. We continued through most of the night along unmade roads with diversions and many hairpins to the junction of the Andiyskoe Koysu (river) and the Gakko river. This was as far as the bus could take us towards out first objective, Diklos (4285m) in the Snegovoy range. We were in a deep, barren valley with turbid water and nowhere to camp, so we spent the day moving to a higher base just below the village of Gakko, using a Lada to transport the gear.

Local children watched us constantly, with a look of wonder on their faces which became even greater when they saw us eating chocolate. The next day we gratefully took up an offer to lock our belongings in a room in the village.

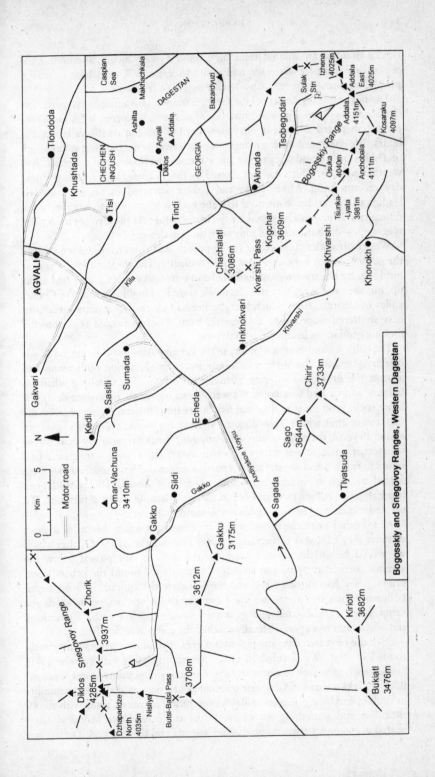

Bogosskiy and Snegovoy Ranges, Western Dagestan

Gakko stood on an isolated lump, high above a river junction and built in the primitive flat-roofed style we had come to expect. Watched by up to 30 people, we pitched the tents on a terrace outside our room.

The next morning we set off for the mountains along a shepherds' path. The landscape was now a pleasant mixture of pasture and forest. With assistance from a shepherd and his donkey, we reached the end of the valley in 2½ hours. We continued up steep grassy slopes towards the hanging valley south of Diklos and found a campsite on a terrace overlooking a waterfall. Bad weather came in, which had not cleared by the morning, so we spent the next day reconnoitring. Mike Doyle and I were attracted by an open couloir leading to the S ridge, convinced that the rock was too poor to have technical difficulties. Everyone else opted for the easiest route via the E ridge; the S ridge was supposedly hard and had only been done in descent.

We set off under clear skies. The approach was soon over and we crossed the glacier and the bergschrund without difficulty. The couloir above was easy but long. By the time we reached the top at around 4000m a mist had come up, but the view west was still clear. We were looking down into the Cheros valley in Georgia, from which Merzbacher had climbed 100 years earlier. An easy shattered ridge led to a forepeak, from which we could see contorted looking gendarmes leading to a final tower.

The ridge looked similar to many in the Pennine Alps but climbing on it was utterly different. The shale was totally insecure, shattering both along and against the grain and offering virtually no belays. The climbing relied on balance and careful footwork. We were knocking down a constant deluge of loose rock. Progress was slow but five hours from the couloir we reached the final tower after which, according to the Russians' book, the going should get easier. Beyond, the ridge continued if anything more precariously than before to another peak. It was barely 50 yards away, but it took a traumatic two hours to reach. I had to retreat off a particularly malicious gendarme; we were forced to turn it on the right with a tentative abseil. The second peak (probably the highest) still did not mark any relenting of the difficulties. We seemed condemned forever to this nerve-shattering game.

At a further peak the crenellations continued yet again, but after a short distance they gave way to a corniced ridge. This was the E summit, after which we would be on the normal route for the descent. We passed below the summit cornice at 7pm, and shortly afterwards we found the others' footprints. They had turned back 200 yards below the summit in a whiteout. Following their footprints, we were established on our descent towards the camp when darkness fell and it started snowing. After endless moraines, snowfields and wet grass we finally reached the camp at midnight.

Over the next two days the mountains remained almost permanently enshrouded in mist. We decided to move to the Bogosskiy range some 40km further east, in search of more attractive routes and possibly better weather. Back at Gakko we found that our belongings had been raided. A large number of roubles had been taken (essential for our return journey), along with all our chocolate and something out of every bag and box. There followed many heated arguments between our Russian friends and the villagers. During one such discussion, Ewan's boots were stolen from outside the flat. This increased the tension still further; some of the villagers started playing with their hunting guns on the balcony outside. We slept inside the room that night to keep close together, and with all our gear.

The next day some of the money and equipment was returned, but even so we did not want to spend another night in the village. We crammed ourselves and our gear into an ancient bus bound for Tindi. As it struggled up the road with a tortured grinding of gears, snowy peaks were visible at the head of the valley. Tindi was perched high above the valley, like Gakko, but it seemed a happier place. Here was a different nationality, one of 40 in Dagestan. One of the village elders found us a campsite and negotiated animals for onward transport. Yuri left next morning with the donkeys. The four English – Adam White, Ewan French, Mike Doyle and myself – set off with light sacks. The walk was pleasant, up a steep-sided valley with several gorges and occasional views of snowy peaks. We were invited into a very primitive peasant woman's house to eat. After another two hours' walk we found Yuri at the hamlet of Tsobegodari, situated in a grassy widening of the valley. We cooked on an open fire as we had no stove between us.

Nick and Mikhail arrived the following day in pouring rain. The day after was wet also, with snow in the mountains – the weather seemed no better than in the Snegovoy range. Then in the afternoon it started to clear so we moved to a higher camp for an attempt on Addalashukhgelmeer (4151m). After the experience of Diklos, we were all agreed on the normal route, the NW ridge first climbed by Merzbacher.

It was a cold, clear night and we set off up frozen scree, making rapid progress. After crossing an old glacier bowl we took a snow slope to the ridge itself. There was much less snow than Merzbacher had found; the ridge was now purely rock. It was loose but easy, particularly since it was frozen together. It steepened to a forepeak, becoming quite delicate in places, then just before the top there were a few moves on good granite – probably the only piece of solid rock in the region. Four hours after leaving camp Adam and I were on the summit; the others followed shortly afterwards. The snow and ice melted to allow a bounding descent on freely running scree.

The following day Adam and Yuri had to leave for home. The rest of us walked up to the Sulak weather station on the north side of Addalashukhgelmeer. It was a low concrete building perched at about 3000m on a shoulder overlooking the North Addala glacier – the ideal alpine hut position. The next afternoon the clouds parted to reveal an impressive cirque. Straight above us was the N face of Addalashukhgelmeer, first climbed in 1984 by Y. Krasnopolskiy at D+, but requiring 50cm pitons for the loose rock. To its left was Addala East (4025m), a beautiful mountain with a snowy spur running up the NE face that was simply waiting to be climbed. There was also an established route up the N ridge at PD+, for the descent. The peaks beyond this, Tunsada (4015m) and Izhena (4025m), were across hard-looking glaciers.

I was ill with some kind of food poisoning, but at 5am the stars were out and I decided to climb anyway. Ewan stayed in his sleeping-bag, conveniently leaving four of us. We went up a grassy spur and onto the dry Addala North glacier, then across and up to a shoulder beneath our route. For once the weather showed no signs of deteriorating. Mikhail sped off, quickly finding a way through the short rocky section and onto snow just left of the crest of the spur. The gradient was easy, so we plodded steadily upwards. We could see straight down to the weather station, and across to Diklos and the Snegovoy range. As we neared the top, the slope steepened and the névé became softer. Mikhail and Nick happily continued, but Mike and I found it insecure. After some less than smooth ropework, we reached the top with the help of the Russians. The summit was a beautiful place to be, in the sunshine for once.

We descended by the same route, using a Russian technique whereby one pair would be roped and moving together at any one time, belayed by the other pair. The position would then be reversed. It was confusing at first, but it was fast as well as safe since three people had a top rope and two also had a handrail. Counting ropelengths, we found it was 500m down to the rocks.

It was time to leave the mountains. It was a week before our flight to London, but we needed all this time and had little room for missed connections. We descended to Tsobegodari to meet the donkeys for the next day. At Tindi we hitched a lift on the back of a truck to Agvali, where we were relieved to find our driver from Makhachkala waiting for us. We continued that evening as far as the bridge over the Andiyskoe Koysu at Ashilta. The next day it would be closed, and the diversion via Chechen-Ingush was unwise with Dagestan number plates. When we reached the bridge it was half dismantled having only about a third of its planks and a four-metre section with no cross-members. After rearranging the planks as best we could, we got across without problems and commandeered the back of a lorry to sleep on at the other side.

We set off as the sun rose, savouring our last hours in the wilds before entering the tunnel to civilisation once more.

Summary: The Snegovoy and Bogosskiy ranges in the west of Dagestan, Eastern Caucasus, received their first visit by British climbers from 11 August to 8 September 1992. A joint British/Ukraine expedition, led by Paul Knott and Nick Drobotenko, made ascents of Diklos (4285m), Addalashukhgelmeer (4151m) and Addala East (4025m). The expedition took place 100 years after the ranges were first climbed on by Gottfried Merzbacher.

REFERENCES

1   G Yeld, 'Dagestan and the ascent of Basardjusi', in *AJ16*, 82–89, 1893
2   G Merzbacher, *Aus den Hochregion des Kaukasus*, 1901. Reviewed *AJ21*, 54–62, 1903.
3   M von Déchy, *Reisen und Forschungen in Kaukasischen Hochgebirge*, 1905. Reviewed *AJ23*, 248–252, 1907.
4   E G Pashuk, P G Leonov, *Alpinizm V Dagestane* (Alpinism in Dagestan), Makhachkala 1986.
5   K Z Akhmedkhanov, *Puteshestvie Po Dagestanu* (Trekking in Dagestan), Moscow 'Fizkultura i Sport', 1988.

Ski Mountaineering
in Greenland

JIM GREGSON

Scenes from the Arctic:
A Greenland Journey

1991 British East Greenland Expedition

(*Plate 59–62*)

The tiny boat slowly chugged its way through the ice floes and disappeared out of sight beyond the snout of the huge glacier pushing straight out into the sea. Somewhere up on the ice, 1000ft above the shore, were our tents, skis and pulks, left for us by our friends now departing on the boat. Twenty miles further inland was our main food and fuel dump, dropped off by helicopter a month earlier. The departure of the boat brought home to us the reality of our situation – isolated in an Arctic wilderness for the next four weeks.

Twenty-four hours earlier we had flown from Reykjavik to the airstrip at Kulusuk, a small island off the east coast of Greenland and just south of the Arctic Circle. Then, in a rainstorm, we had scrambled into the boat for the long evening sailing, through ice-clogged fjords, to Sermiligaq fjord where, in the gloomy dawn light, we stumbled up the moraines to locate the tents and to sleep for a while after our 30-hour journey. The morning brought brighter light and a trip down to the sea and up again to relay the rest of the gear to our first camp, leaving a cache of fuel and foodstuffs for our eventual return. While sorting the equipment and dividing it into four pulk-loads, we were visited by a scavenging Arctic fox, hunger overcoming its natural wariness.

The next day, refreshed by a good sleep, we loaded and harnessed-up to start the glacier trek to Slangen, a gateway pass to the mountains of Schweizerland. As the snow-line was low we could soon step into our skis and haul the pulks more easily, while trying to grasp the scale of the glacier – wider than any in my experience of the European Alps. We worked up through a gentle icefall and gradually rounded a big bend on to the undulating upper glacier stretching for miles in front of us.

After six or seven hours of steady pulling, we stopped to camp and eat, retreating to our sleeping-bags as the temperature fell below freezing point. Another, shorter, day of pulling landed us at Slangen – a broad, level pass with spectacular, enticing vistas of peaks to the north and flanked by interesting mountains on either side. Good weather had now returned and, having pitched the tents, we spread our damp gear to dry quickly in the warm sunshine. As our main food dump was here, we decided to stay a day or two to sort out our supplies and plans, and to climb one of the neighbouring peaks. The food-pile looked huge when we unpacked the boxes but, as on all expeditions, what you've forgotten you can't have; we sorted it into loads for

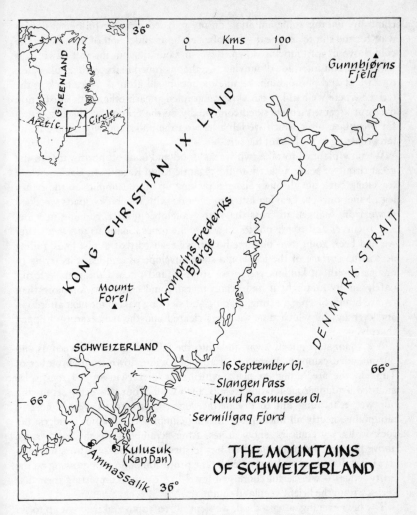

36°

0   Kms   100

GREENLAND

Arctic   Circle

Gunnbjørns
Fjeld

KONG CHRISTIAN IX LAND

Kronprins Frederiks
Bjerge

DENMARK STRAIT

Mount
Forel

SCHWEIZERLAND

16 September Gl.
Slangen Pass
Knud Rasmussen Gl.
Sermiligaq Fjord

66°

66°

Ammassalik   36°

Kulusuk
(Kap Dan)

THE MOUNTAINS
OF SCHWEIZERLAND

outward and return phases of the trip. Obviously our pulk-loads were going to be considerably increased in size and weight for our next move. Slangen, at 1200m, was colder in the shade than the fjords had been, but in the calm of a sunny afternoon it was a pleasant place to sit.

Above our tents rose a fine rock-peak the walls of which were marked by an enormous intrusion or dyke writhing through the cliff like a great fire-breathing dragon. We all felt drawn to this peak and eagerly packed climbing gear for an attempt via a ridge falling to the glacier a couple of miles down from the camp. The ridge gave a mixture of snow and rock climbing on a fine crest, leading us to the summit not long after midnight. Northwards lay hundreds of jagged peaks silhouetted against a purple and pink sky. This deep twilight was as dark as we experienced throughout the expedition – the sun dipped behind the mountains but there was always enough light to travel and climb by. Photographic ambition on my part led to powerful persuasion to wait for the sun to reappear – but after an hour and a half of immobility the cold drove us into moving down. Reversing our ridge in the soft dawn light was a pleasant interlude of moving together as roped pairs, with ample pause to stare at and photograph the fine mountains all around. Once back at the terrace where we had left our skis, we grinned at each other with satisfaction over our ascent; then we skied contentedly up the firm glacier back to camp for breakfast, after which we fell asleep on the pulks and woke some hours later roasting in the heat of the sun.

We now planned to take two weeks' food and haul off northwards to the great cirque of peaks adjacent to the gigantic Knud Rasmussen glacier, before travelling back out through Slangen picking up more summits on the return leg of the journey. Leaving late one evening with our bulky loads we skied down from Slangen to cross the 16th September glacier, running in wide-radius curves and trying not to ski across the ropes linking us together. After we had been going two or three hours, we realised that a mist-bank rolling across the surface of the ice would soon envelope us and leave us trying to navigate without landmarks; so we stopped and pitched the tents – fortunately, as by midnight it had begun to rain, and continued for more than twelve hours. Sleeping, eating, reading and sleeping passed the next afternoon and evening, by which time the skies cleared and the temperature dropped sharply.

A 4.30am start got us away and onto the miles of glacier between us and our intended campsite at the toe of a ridge coming down from an outlier of Tupilak, the area's highest peak, which is a huge twin-topped rock spire guarded by dangerous-looking icefalls. By 9 we had our new camp set up and our wet gear hung out to dry in the sun. All around us were a host of mountains, nearly all unclimbed, offering climbing of all kinds – ridges, big rock walls, icy couloirs, snow arêtes. After scrambling up the rocky ridge above the tents for a few hundred feet to survey some possible lines for us to try, I was distracted and engrossed by the profusion of flowers growing on the gritty ledges – wonderful clumps of jewel-like colour, completing their life-cycles within the brief Greenland summer.

The next evening, after a meal, we slept till 10.30pm and then got up to ski across the glacier ice for an hour towards a fine peak facing our camp. Up a glacier bay, then a gully, before traversing left on ledges to a steep snow arête, we moved continuously together to cross a nice corniced crest just as the sun flooded its flank with golden dawn light. A short rock scramble led to the top, where the view opened out to the north and east across row upon row of pinnacled ridges and massive glaciers and, far beyond, the iceberg-studded seas of the Denmark Strait separating East Greenland from Iceland. To the north-west, the sky was a rich yellow and behind us the mountains glowed in the warm sunrise. We lingered in the calm air, shooting off copious amounts of film, drinking in the expansive panorama and sizing up some of the other neighbouring tops. Eventually we descended without incident and skied happily back to the tents.

The next day we travelled up the 16th September glacier for a few miles to climb through some icefalls to reach the summit of the mountain directly above our camp. This gave interesting route-finding and finished with a rock buttress giving on to a spacious top. From here we could study Tupilak and Rødbjerg, both very fine peaks for strong parties. Fifty miles away lay the bulk of Mount Forel, long thought to be the second highest point in Greenland, and beyond, to the west, the plateau edges of the inland ice, the main ice cap extending across the island for hundreds of miles and up to 10,000ft in thickness.

A few miles to the north lay another peak which attracted us – we studied a possible way of gaining its gleaming snow arêtes by a glacial bay and a steep ice tongue. Part of the latter was hidden by a minor rock buttress, but we felt it was worth having a look at as our next objective. Once through the icefalls we had a wonderful run down firm slopes, refrozen after the sun had left them, onto and down the glacier. After a day and a half of resting, washing, repairing stoves and diary-writing, we decided to make an attempt on the red-rock-walled mountain with the long snow arêtes.

Starting off late in the evening, we went on skis for a couple of hours of uncomfortable travel over ridged and furrowed, hard gritty ice, climbing into the glacier bay that we thought would provide an access-route to the ridge. As the slopes steepened we switched to crampons and moved up to gain a view of the ice tongue we expected to climb, which we had only partially seen from some miles away. When we could see the full extent of the ice slope, even in the midnight twilight, we could grasp what our distant view had not revealed. Instead of the straightforward slope we had hoped for, we were faced with a convoluted, serac-broken sweep of ice hemmed in by rocky spurs. We tried to spy out a possible line, all of us voicing some misgivings, more about the problems of later descent than of going up it. As we deliberated in the half-light, trying to postpone our disappointment at the prospect of giving up, there was a great roar and crashing of blocks as a large serac barrier collapsed and broke loose down our line. That decided it for us; we about-turned and crunched off downwards to retrieve our skis. There were plenty of other mountains.

We decided to make our way back towards Slangen, doing some more climbing as we moved out towards our eventual fjord-head exit point; so we set about dismantling our camp, leaving only footprints and ski-tracks. As we recrossed the wide span of the 16th September glacier, we were overtaken by a creeping fog-bank which disorientated us for a while. When it cleared away after an hour or two, we looked back on our erratically zigzagging trail detouring through ill-seen crevasse zones. Back at Slangen we made two further fine ascents. The first one gave us the steepest ice pitches we had encountered to gain a footing on a corniced ridge leading to a summit pinnacle of rusty-brown but loose rock, with room for only one person at a time. The other peak was climbed via a deeply crevassed icefall and a succession of thin, curling snow ridges high above the glaciers, with a finish on a sharp rock turret. All around lay a vast reservoir of untrodden summits.

Having picked up most of our remaining supplies from our Slangen dump, we eventually set off to descend in the direction of our shore-line rendezvous, hoping to climb another mountain on the way. Benefiting from snow surfaces and increased fitness, we amazed ourselves by skiing rapidly down two-thirds of our glacier descent in a few hours one evening. However, progress was stalled when the weather rapidly changed without warning and we were pinned down in camp by a 24-hour snowstorm with high winds and zero visibility. After a second night we concluded that we had to move on come-what-may, as we needed time in hand to relay loads and get all our gear down to sea-level. The morning was brighter, with breaks in the cloud, so we dug out and packed to go. The next few hours pulling were hard work through the soft new snow, until we had lost enough height to get onto bare glacier ice. Soon after this we could no longer profitably use skis, so we changed to crampons to gain traction over the rough, stony lower reaches of the glacier. Considerable melting had occurred in the weeks since our arrival and the snow cover was much depleted. This led to some manhandling of the heavy pulks to cross belts of moraine on the ice surface. Eventually, a couple of miles from the sea, we had to stop and face up to backpacking everything to the waterside.

Drizzle fell as we stuffed our rucksacks, then strapped more awkward items on the outside. The loads grew to a point where we had to help each other to pick them up. Staggering and bent over, we struggled along the glacier edge and onto the steeply-falling lateral moraine to slip and slide our way down the 2000 feet to the shore – hard, hot, uncomfortable work – until we sank with relief amidst the boulders by the glacier snout. Our first idea was to get the tents up, sleep, and go back up next day for the heavier stuff like ropes, hardware, and the pulks themselves. But after some discussion it was agreed that we would rest briefly and then reascend to collect everything in one more trip. Once it was all down we could relax. Grim-faced, we toiled up the loose slopes once more, realising how tired we were but committed to the labour. The second loads were immense, compounded by the pulks, nearly six feet long, lashed turtle-shell fashion to our sacks. Four very weary climbers tottered down the shifting moraine rubble to camp a few feet above the high tide level, thankful that the worst physical hardship of the expedition was now behind us.

The following day we sorted and packed almost everything into loads for freighting home. The fjord-head was filled with much more floating ice than had been there when we landed, and we paused to consider how our pick-up boat, due the next day, would cope. While waiting for the boat to show up, we could rest and enjoy our surroundings. Three huge glaciers ran down through the mountain into Sermiligaq fjord, making it a beautiful and impressive place. Icebergs calved from the glacier-fronts at all hours of day and night, sometimes in spectacular fashion only yards from our tents; distant booms from across the sea were succeeded many minutes later by surging waves tossing the floating ice hither and thither. We walked along the water's edge and up the adjacent hillsides, absorbed by the colours and shapes of the ice in the sea, the textures of the rocks, and the variety of the flowers still in bloom late in August.

The boat did not arrive on the day we had fixed but the fascinating environs made our extra stay a pleasure. Then the sudden appearance of the red-and-white vessel nudging its way through the ice floes caught us unaware, causing us to scurry around to strike the tents and bundle away the last odds and ends. The *Ulimaut*, a sturdy, converted 36ft fishing-boat, could only get to 30 yards or so from the shore so we and our equipment were ferried aboard by dinghy; the Greenlandic, Inuit people crewing the boat were very welcoming, and soon we were under way bound for Kap Dan, 70 miles distant.

The journey out through the fjords was an eight-hour cruise of delight. The sun shone from a clear blue sky as we sailed past the high icecliffs of the glacier snouts and amongst icebergs huge and small, through narrow channels with mountainsides sweeping straight up out of the water. A moving kaleidoscope of visual experiences lasting all day brought us back to Kulusuk, with a day in hand to visit the Inuit people at Kap Dan village, before flying out to Iceland and home to Britain – with lingering, longing memories of a marvellous expedition to a pristine Arctic wilderness.

Summary: 1991 British East Greenland Expedition to the Schweizerland district, north of Ammassalik, 27 July – 27 August, via Sermiligaq fjord. Participants: Jim Gregson, Simon Molyneux, Brian Povey, Paul H Walker.
Ascents:
Peak 1 (the 'Dragon Peak'), west of Slangen Pass, 66°14'N, 36°40'W, *c*1800m
Peak 2 P1720m, 66°17'N, 36°27'W
Peak 3 66°18'N, 36°27'W, *c*1700m
Peak 4 (Slangen East Peak), 66°13'N, 36°35'W, *c*1900m
Peak 5 66°12'N, 36°40'W, *c*1700m
Also attempted P2070m, 66°20'N, 36°22'W

PHILIP BARTLETT

Undiscovered Mountains of the Kronprins Frederiks Bjerge

The Northern Group Greenland Expedition 1990

When I first visited the Arctic on a University expedition to Baffin Island in 1976 I knew I would want to return. I can remember quite clearly sitting with Steve Parr on the summit of a modest rock peak we had just climbed a few miles from Mt Asgard and gazing eastwards to an indistinct horizon which already seemed magical. It was late afternoon and a typical Arctic landscape of modest snow peaks rose in shades of black and grey from flat colourless glaciers. It shouldn't have been particularly inspiring, but somehow it was. And part of the reason was the knowledge that somewhere beyond that horizon lay Greenland.

The only people I knew who had climbed in Greenland were Lindsay Griffin (but is there anywhere that Lindsay has not climbed?) and Robin Illingworth. Robin had never been to the Himalaya, but had three expeditions to Greenland under his belt and moved within a group who seemed to operate completely outside the relatively well-publicised world of 'big mountains'. The moving force of those Greenland trips was Stan Woolley, a Stowe schoolmaster who, over the years, had led a series of expeditions involving scientific work, exploration and climbing in various combinations, but all of them 'traditional' in style. Arctic expeditions seemed to be like that; gear was decidedly sixties and no one was impressed with news value.

In the autumn of 1989 I was invited along to a discussion of Stan's latest notion – and ended up wondering, not for the first time, why I had not returned to the Arctic before. Projected onto the wall was a slide showing a view north-east into the Kronprins Frederiks Bjerge just north of the 68th parallel on Greenland's E coast. Deer and Fountaine had sledged downhill through the area as part of their circumnavigation of Kangerdlugssuaq fjord in 1936 (*Geographical Journal*, November 1937) but otherwise, so far as we knew, it was unexplored. Most of it looked absolutely flat, but out of those endless glaciers and snowfields the occasional snowy bump was rising. Far away, larger bumps, perhaps large enough to be called mountains, rose against the sky. Some of them had pointed summits and blank rock faces, half hidden. They might prove disappointing of course; then again, they might not. And if they were easy, all the more chance of getting up. I couldn't help reflecting on the amount of time I had spent in the Karakoram attempting ambitious objectives and not getting up them. Like the Karakoram the Arctic is a desert, and even in a photograph you could sense the silence and the emptiness of the place. The only difference seemed to be that there was no altitude problem, no Asian tummy, 24 hours' daylight, and a reputation for stable weather.

The problem with mountaineering in East Greenland has always been access. The peaks rise in a relatively narrow strip between the coast and the inland ice and much of the coastline is not very friendly. Glaciers calve directly into the sea, and sea ice, coming south from the Arctic ocean on the East Greenland current, clogs the fjords and may make the coast totally inaccessible to small vessels. It is possible to sail in, as Robin Knox-Johnston and party demonstrated in the Kangerdlugssuaq area in 1991, but this is an uncertain business. 1991 may have been a good year; 1990 was also fairly ice free. But from what one could see from the air, only a very substantial steel vessel would have made it through to the coast in 1992.

A fundamental change in the situation came in the mid-eighties when a gravel airstrip on the coast just north of Kangerdlugssuaq was opened up for geological purposes. Three years later, and very much at the behest of Stan, the Icelandic aircraft company which serviced the strip agreed to try ski landings. In 1987 Stan and Robin, with Rob Ferguson and Steve McCabe, made the third and what will almost certainly be the last 'traditional' ascent of Gunnbjørns Fjeld, the highest mountain in the Watkins range and thus in Greenland, 60 miles east of Kangerdlugssuaq. They arrived by plane, but only as far as the coast; thereafter it was a question of sledge-hauling for a fortnight, climbing the mountain, and sledge-hauling back again. On the strength of their photographs the pilot Sigurdur Adalsteinsson agreed, the following year, to attempt ski-equipped landings of his de Havilland Twin Otter in the heart of the mountains, and that sort of effort, little changed from the original ascent by Wager's party in 1936, passed into history. During their 1987 expedition Stan's party were tantalised by the sight of the steep granite peaks of the Lemon mountains crowding the E side of Kangerdlugssuaq fjord and of the highest peak in particular, already named by Wager 'The Cathedral'. Stan had known of the Cathedral's existence since 1972 when he led a predominantly scientific expedition to the Lemons and, though there was no time to attempt it either then or in 1987, Stan, Robin and Rob all nursed a strong desire to return; of which more anon.

For 1990, however, Stan's sights were set firmly on the unexplored northern section of the Kronprins Frederiks Bjerge and a circular sledging tour which would return his expedition, after some four weeks, to its landing point on the edge of the ice cap and a pre-arranged pick-up. For this he assembled a team of nine comprising himself, Ted Courtney, Dr Iain Campbell and John Richardson in one group and Rob Ferguson, Jim Lowther, myself, Dave Woolley (no relation) and Mike Parsons in another. The former group, who with the exception of John were old Arctic hands to whom a crossing of the ice cap was a mere nothing, would take a high northerly line close to the nunataks on the edge of the inland ice. The latter would take a southerly line closer to the coast where the mountains would probably be more challenging.

The Northern Group Greenland expedition flew in during unsettled weather in mid-July, with layers of angry cloud covering the Denmark strait both above and below us. I expected Sigurdur to bank the plane and head back for Iceland at any moment, but instead there suddenly appeared, suspended impossibly high in the sky, a vision of bright, almost luminous mountains. And instead of disappearing this extraordinary sight slowly resolved itself into the reality of the Greenland coast, mile upon mile of unknown peaks glinting in the sun. The clouds were left behind as we flew over the coast and ten minutes later we landed on flat snow to a blue sky and hot sun.

There followed 28 days of glorious mountaineering in which the pure joy of being alone in virgin territory overwhelmed all other joys. Jim had put together a master plan for the 'youngsters' team which involved a good deal of sledging in the early stages and then a slow return past the highest peaks in the area, climbing what we could as the fancy took us. The potential hazards became apparent only on the second day when a strong and bitter wind began gusting off the ice cap and Dave developed hypothermia. We got the tents up with difficulty and retired inside. The following day the gale had eased, Dave was fully recovered, and, as we plodded up easy glacier terrain towards Panoramanunatakker, a fine group of bulky, flat-topped mountains, a superb Matterhorn-like peak appeared to the south, dominating the view, and we all agreed that it looked a delectable objective for the return journey.

Pulling one-man sledges, or pulks, was an entirely new experience for some of us; so too was trying to execute turns on cross-country skis. Mike and Jim were the only good skiers and were streets ahead of the rest of us. They spent endless hours discussing the relative merits of different ski waxes – an arcane branch of knowledge entirely lost on Rob, Dave and me who made do with fish scales and skins. Mike and Jim executed perfect telemark turns; we managed half a snow-plough each before falling over, cursing.

So it was a relief sometimes to get off the skis and onto some climbing. The rock was granitic, much of it as good as Chamonix, and there was some superb mixed climbing in ice runnels and along ridges. We climbed something like a dozen peaks; many were minor, but that hardly seemed to detract from the pleasure. Of the better peaks two in particular summed up between them the character of the area and the good fortune we felt in being there. Point 2600m at 67°57′W, 33°57′W was one of the two highest mountains in the range, and as we approached from the north in a cold dawn it presented a formidable 2000ft face of richly striated and coloured rock like something out of a wild west canyon. It was not particularly attractive and it looked very hard. But gradually the glacier fell away in front of us and after negotiating a steep slope and some crevasses, telemark-turning, falling and sliding as appropriate, we found ourselves skiing round the base of those huge cliffs and picking up another glacier on the other side. As we pulled slowly back uphill, now sweating in the morning sun, the south side of the mountain gradually came into view and revealed itself as a long glacier slope apparently without problems and leading straight to the summit. We climbed it easily the next morning. This, I thought, must be what the Alps felt like in the eighteenth century: we were actually living in the pre-Mummery era, when all that was required for total satisfaction was a way to the top. There was no loss because it turned out to be easy. This was exploration, and the easier the better. The mountain's N face fell away vertically at our feet and the view was magnificent. The Matterhorn peak, now only five miles away and rising unmistakably above the intervening ridge, looked superb. Unlike anything else we had done it was pure rock and would clearly involve some hard technical climbing.

Two days later we skied past its W face and climbed to a broad col at the foot of the mountain's SW ridge. The first section of ridge was horizontal and knife-edged and turned out to be classic climbing of astonishing quality. Each side dropped steeply to a glacier system, the granite was perfect, and at a distance the whole thing looked formidable. Watching Rob picking his way methodically along it I just couldn't believe he was making such rapid progress. Yet when you got there the climbing was spectacular but easy, little more than scrambling, with all the blank sections conveniently by-passed by ledges reminiscent of the *vire à bicyclettes* on the Grépon. Above, the ridge steepened and got gradually harder, forcing us onto the face where we eventually fetched up in a little bay, 100ft below the summit. Here Rob pulled out all the stops and led an evil off-width crack which the rest of us struggled to follow on a tight rope. The mountain more or less admitted defeat after that and we clambered, one at a time, onto the summit rock, an airy perch commanding yet another magnificent view. To the north the ice cap formed an unbroken horizon and to the east we could see most of the summits we had climbed. To the south two great glaciers joined and swept down to the sea, where random icebergs broke the dull blue surface.

We returned to base to find that the senior party had also enjoyed a successful trip though, being closer to the ice cap, they had experienced considerably colder conditions. After mutual congratulations there was just time for two more peaks before the clatter of turbo-prop engines broke our isolation and announced the arrival of the Twin Otter, which came down steeply and impossibly slowly a hundred yards from Stan's Union Jack.

When the plane finally got off the ground again two hours later (it was overloaded, the afternoon snow sticky, and it needed several attempts), we followed the coast north-eastwards. It was a beautifully clear day and anonymous mountains stretched in all directions. Finally the unmistakable basalt tiers of the Watkins' mountains reared up ahead. I glued my face to the window and tried to identify the Lemon mountains to their west and the peak which was to have been our objective if a ski landing in the Kronprins Frederiks Bjerge had proved impossible – the Cathedral. It ought to be possible to see it ... but I couldn't pick it out, though the dark trench of Kangerdlugssuaq fjord was there all right. Then, as we turned from the coast and headed out to sea, I saw more mountains high on the horizon – big, snow-covered peaks, glinting in the sun just as they had done when we arrived four weeks before. I asked Ted if he recognised them. He didn't, but thought we were probably looking at the Lindbergs, basalt mountains like the Watkins' and therefore likely to offer only poor climbing, but nevertheless high and unvisited. Full of enthusiasm, I decided there and then to try and organise an expedition to visit both the Lindbergs and the Lemon mountains together and to finish at the coastal airstrip which Stan had used when climbing Gunnbjørns Fjeld in 1987. Stan and Ted would both come; indeed it might be possible to return with exactly the same team. In the event, both Stan and Ted had to decline for health reasons and no one else could make it either. But when the British Expedition to East Greenland flew into the Lindbergs on 18 July 1992 a link with 'the old firm' was there in the form of Robin Illingworth. Robin had not forgotten his appointment with the Cathedral.

Summary: The Northern Group Greenland Expedition 1990 climbed in the Kronprins Frederiks Bjerge and had been preceded first by L R Wager's expedition to the Kangerdlugssuaq region in 1937 and subsequently by a party in 1978 organised by W S L Woolley who also organised the 1990 expedition. Participants in 1990 were W S L Woolley (leader), Philip Bartlett, Dr Iain Campbell, Ted Courtney, Rob Ferguson, Jim Lowther, Mike Parsons, John Richardson and Dave Woolley (no relation). Some 20 peaks were climbed, the area being reached from Iceland by ski-plane.

BIBLIOGRAPHY

L R Wager   'The Kangerdlugssuaq Region of East Greenland',
                     Geographical Journal 90, November 1937.
W S L Woolley *et al*   Report, *Westminster East Greenland Expedition*
                     1972
                     Report, *Northern Group Greenland Expedition* 1987
                     Report, *Northern Group Greenland Expedition* 1990

LUKE HUGHES

Lindbergs and Lemons

The British Mountaineering Expedition to East Greenland 1992

(Plates 44–46)

In old Norse sailing directions it was laid down that to reach the Greenland settlements one must steer from Iceland north-west until a great mountain, Hvitserk, is sighted, then hold this course until the mountain bears north, when the mariner should steer south-west along the edge of the ice to landfall in South Greenland. That mountain landmark, now known as Gunnbjørns Fjeld, was suspected by 'Gino' Watkins, the leader of the Arctic Air Route expedition 1930–31, of being the highest in Greenland; it was certainly the dominant peak amidst the majestic basalt massif which now bears Watkins' name.

From the windows of a Twin Otter more than 60 years later, the geological patterns of the region and the magical light made school-book geology crystal clear; in the north, the lumpen basalt mountains with their horizontal zebra-like patterns of snow and rock; below, rolling bands of sandstone, like huge beached whales lying among the glaciers; to the south, the virgin granite summits of the Lemonbjerge and hundreds of needle-pointed peaks punctur-ing the horizon; most noble of all, the snow-covered summit ridge of the Cathedral.

It was instantly recognisable from the many aerial photographs taken in the thirties by the team of pilots and aerial photographers on Watkins' expedition (many of the archives are now in the Scott Polar Research Institute). Captain Percy Lemon was the first to identify it in 1931 and it has been a treasured, secret, inaccessible prize for Arctic mountaineers over the last 60 years. It is only in exceptional years that the sea is navigable and neither the Inuits nor the Danes had ever bothered to explore most of the east coast.

But in 1931 the Norwegians laid claim to a portion of the east coast and, although the claim was rejected by the International Court at The Hague, the Danes were sufficiently concerned to want the area more thoroughly explored, even by the British. The following year, the Danish Geodetic Institute made a map using a new technique using oblique air photographs (with additional surveying material by Michael Spender). And in 1935, the geologist Lawrence Wager led a year-long survey to further investigate some of his own findings whilst under the auspices of Watkins' expedition some years earlier. He had, in the meantime, taken part in the 1933 British Everest Expedition with Jack Longland, and had acquired both some serious moun-taineering experience and some committed climbing companions.

Now with a team that included Longland and Augustine Courtauld, Wager successfully climbed Gunnbjørns Fjeld and was able to prove (from the summit) Watkins' supposition that it was indeed the highest mountain in Greenland. He then set up field-bases near the coast along with his botanist brother, a meteorologist, two families of Inuits, and other forbearing colleagues. His discovery and investigation of the Skaergaard Intrusion, a geological formation of 'cumulates', dominated the rest of Wager's later life as Professor of Geology at Oxford, and prompted more than 30 articles in learned journals; his subsequent research was to inform the geological experiments conducted during the Apollo space missions to the Moon. Since 1980 annual field expeditions have been sponsored by the University of Toronto and the mining company Platinova Resources Ltd who now claim to have found gold and platinum in minable quantities.

Yet despite all this prospective activity at the coast, the mountainous areas further inland remained unexplored. We aimed to fill in some of the gaps on the map. Our team of nine included Phil Bartlett, myself, Robin Illingworth, Gary Baum, Mike and Jenny Woolridge, Barry Mills, the photographer David Stewart-Smith, and the American climber Bill Pelkey. Few of us could spare more than four weeks and it was going to need bold moves and tight logistics to achieve all the objectives we had set ourselves. We had the advantage of Danish aerial photographs, some of Stan Woolley's notes, and considerable research from the Scott Polar Research Institute. We planned to land on high ground amongst the Lindberg range, to get fit and a feel for the surroundings (the stability of the glaciers, the best times to travel, the optimum gear) and sweep down towards the coast like peak pirates, setting up raiding bases as we went.

On the first night, barely 24 hours from Heathrow, we seized the opportunities offered by nocturnal daylight and climbed four peaks before bedtime, bewitched by the enormity of the ice cap, the dreamy tranquillity of Arctic summer and the knowledge that we could never be benighted. A similarly frantic climbing pattern continued as we moved south (mostly at night when the snow is least sticky) away from the ice-covered basalt lumps towards the granite needles and the first human views that anyone has had of Cathedral from the north-east. We skied across dune-like glaciers in the long, low shadows of evening light and scuttled up peaks from which we could survey potential routes. Intoxicated by the pure aesthetic pleasure of the landscape and the knowledge that no one had ever been here before, we revelled in our very own Playground of the Arctic. No bivouacs, minimum gear, unknown ground, experienced partners, stable rock, sensational views – how the Alps must have seemed to Leslie Stephen.

The important climbs began on Cathedral (2600m), the mountain that was supposedly attempted by the Bonington/Lowther/Knox-Johnston expedition of 1991. There appears to be little doubt, however, that the peak that Wager had in mind is a snow and ice mountain which lies some 6km further into the range than the peak attempted by the Bonington expedition. It has a high roof of snow supported by rock buttresses and is clearly higher than all the

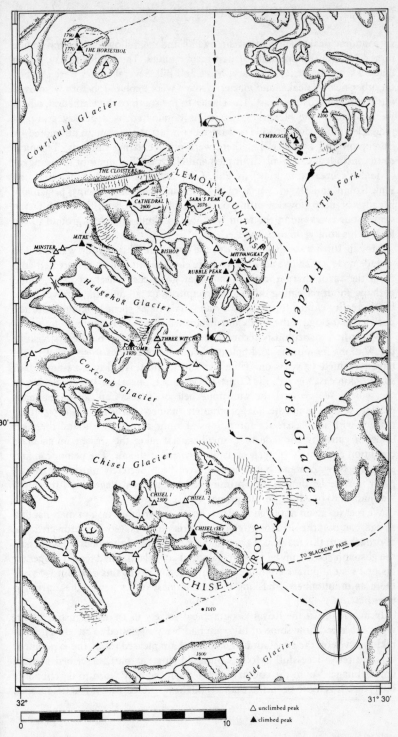

THE HORSESHOE
1790
1770

Courtauld Glacier

CYMBROGI
2200

THE CLOISTERS

LEMON MOUNTAINS

'The Fork'

CATHEDRAL
2600

SARA'S PEAK
2076

MITRE

MINSTER

BISHOP

MITNANGKAT

RUBBLE PEAK

Hedgehog Glacier

Fredericksborg Glacier

THREE WITCHES

COXCOMB
1970

Coxcomb Glacier

30'

Chisel Glacier

CHISEL 1
2300

CHISEL 2

CHISEL GROUP

CHISEL 'SE'

TO 'BLACKCAP' PASS

· 1010

· 1600

Side Glacier

32°   31° 30'

△ unclimbed peak
▲ climbed peak

0   10

Lemon Mountains and Chisel Group - Kangerdlugssuaq
(British Mountaineering Expedition to East Greenland 1992)

surrounding peaks. The first ascent, by Phil and me, followed a fine mixed line up the NE ridge, descending by east-facing gullies. The following day, Robin made a second ascent with Gary, Mike and Bill. Several routes were climbed on other nearby peaks, and glacier systems were explored, before we moved our camp towards the coast. The glacier to the south of the Cathedral, which we nicknamed the Hedgehog glacier, is dominated by a prickly group of pinnacles, since christened 'The Minster' (in fact the mountain attempted by Bonington and Lowther) but there were other enticing summits. Technical routes included 'Coxcomb' by myself and Gary, the E summit of Mitivangkat ('Maiden's breasts' in Inuit) by Phil, Gary and Robin, and 'Mitre Peak' by Phil, Robin and David. Much of the climbing had its problems, principally because of deep powder sitting on steep, black ice on all the north-facing slopes, but everyone in the team was able to climb on virgin ground to the level of his ability, on rock and ice.

Moving further south and towards the coast, the Chisel group was found to include no less than five peaks. Two were climbed but Phil and I retreated 50m from the razor-sharp rocky summit that gives the Chisel its name, timid perhaps about retreating through a precipitous icefall once the sun was on it, but in reality chilled to the bone by an Arctic night spent looking out to the pack ice that clogged the fjords and distant sea. This was isolation.

Wager had meticulously recorded leaving a food dump on the first visit to the Watkins mountains, and half our group were curious to see what might have remained 57 years on. Time was short, and this led to a 24-hour dash some 60km east towards the Christian IV glacier, one of the largest glaciers in the world. We crossed the sandstone belt of 'Black Cap' Pass (abundant marine fossils) and the inappropriately named Sorgenfri ('Sorrow-free') glacier, with its bizarre ice formations. To our surprise we found the food under a cairn by the side of a small glacial lake, the tins in immaculate condition and barely rusty, such is the dryness of the air. The pemmican and even the New Zealand butter would have been perfectly nutritious to any party in trouble, though the Fortnum & Mason Dried Vegetable ('Julienne') was judged to be a little past its prime.

We met up again at the coast. Then began the arduous task of man-hauling sledges across the fearsome glacial debris that has so far protected the approaches to this magical region. In the moraines and riverbeds we witnessed the glistening of the myriad highly-coloured crystals that had teased Wager on his first visit and have continued to tempt geologists to this day. But we were there as mountaineers, basking in the conquest of 17 new routes in virgin territory.

In his lecture at the Royal Geographical Society in 1936, Augustine Courtauld described how some of his team had been interested to see the effect of taking wives on the expedition and added 'I am pleased to say the experiment was entirely successful'. Molly Courtauld, for her part, described a more tender image: 'As to the country itself – well, the only word to describe it is fairyland. It is more beautiful than I thought possible.' And it has left its spell on us.

Above Pumori, 7161m: the route climbed the spur (R) and the right-hand skyline. (*Mal Duff*) (p160)

Below The Japanese Alps: a view along the main ridge. (*Mark Lowe*) (p173)

42. Base Camp for Thalay Sagar, 6904m. The headwall is visible behind
   Rudugaira, 5364m. (*Keith Milne*) (p119)

Climbing the snow ridge on the lower part of Thalay Sagar.
(*Keith Milne*) (p119)

Above
44. East Greenland: the Lemon Mountains. East Peak and West Peak from
    the north. (*Luke Hughes*) (p147)

Below
45. The Three Witches (L) and Coxcomb, 1970m. In the foreground: the
    Hedgehog glacier. (*Luke Hughes*) (p147)

Camp on Fredericksborg glacier. Cathedral (R), 2600m, from the NE.
The first ascent followed the snow ramp onto the ridge, then crossed
mixed ground to the summit. (*Luke Hughes*) (p147)

47. Dagestan: Diklos, 4285m. The first crenellated section of the
South Ridge. (*Paul Knott*) (p130)

A. Lindsay Griffin arranging transport in the Mongolian Altai.
(*Julian Freeman-Attwood*)(p125)

B. Mongolian Altai: the Tabun Bogdo. (*Lindsay Griffin*) (p125)

49. *Above* Jotunheimen: Gravdalen saeter, Hurrungane.
   (*Duncan Mackay*) (p176)

50. *Below* Ålfoten: Derek Smithson on Blånibba with Gjegnalundsbreen in
   the background. (*Kjetil Tveranger*) (p176)

Summary: the nine members of the British Mountaineering Expedition 1992 to East Greenland climbed in the Lindberg and Lemon ranges of the Kangerdlugssuaq basin in July/August. Philip Bartlett and Luke Hughes made the first ascent of Cathedral Peak (2600m). The party explored the Hedgehog glacier, making 16 first ascents including the Minster, Coxcomb, Mitre Peak and the E summit of Mitivangkat (see map). They visited Wager's 1936 food dump and collected plant and lichen samples from the Lindberg and Lemon mountains.

BIBLIOGRAPHY

George Colin Lawder Bertram, 'New light on the fauna of the Arctic', in *Discovery* 1934.

Chris Bonington, 'A Greenland Adventure', in *AJ*97, 27–36, 1992/93.

Chris Bonington & Robin Knox-Johnston, *Sea, Ice and Rock*. Hodder & Stoughton, 1992.

Augustine Courtauld, 'A journey in Rasmussen Land', in *Geographical Journal 88, No 3*, 1936.

Jane Hargreaves, *L R Wager: a life 1904–1965* (privately published).

J Hawksworth, 'Lichens for East Greenland', in *Dryologist Vol 71 No 1*, 1968.

Lewis Jones (ed), report *British Universities East Greenland Expedition 1986*.

Gordon Manley, 'Meteorological observations of the British East Greenland expedition 1935–36', in *Quarterly Journal of the Royal Meteorological Society* 1938.

Vaughan Purvis, 'Safety in Polar Bear Country', in *Arctic Expeditionary Group Blue Book No 1*. Date: mid-eighties.

W G Rigden (ed), report *Durham University Polar East Greenland Expedition 1979*.

Lawrence Wager, 'The form and age of the Greenland Ice Cap', in *Geological Magazine*, April 1933.

Lawrence Wager, *Geological Investigations in East Greenland*, Parts 1–4. Meddelelser on Grønland 1934.

Lawrence Wager, 'The Kangerdslugssuaq Region of East Greenland', in *Geographical Journal 90, No 5*, 1937.

H G Watkins, 'British Arctic Air Route Expedition', in *Geographical Journal 79 and 80*, 1932.

Westminster School, report *Westminster East Greenland Expedition 1972*.

Stan Woolley, *Polar Record Vol 19 No 121*, 1979.

Stan Woolley, report *Northern Group Greenland Expedition 1987*.

Stan Woolley, report *Northern Group Greenland Expedition 1990*.

'A multi-million dollar gold deposit in Greenland?', in *Polar Record*, 1991.

Above and Below
the Snow-line

J G R HARDING

Turkish Ski Traverses II: Kackar Chariot

(*Plates 71, 72*)

In any military mountaineering Pantheon, the Athenian general Xenophon must take pride of place. Not only did his 401 BC expedition to Persia pre-date Hannibal's to Rome by 182 years, but in crossing the Taurus outward bound and then both the Kurdish and Pontic Alps inward en route to the Black Sea he scored a treble. Although it was to this corner of the ancient world that Jason sailed with his Argonauts in 1263 BC to search for the Golden Fleece and open up the Black Sea to Greek commerce, for most 20th-century European travellers, Pontus was as remote as Xanadu and its hinterland *terra incognita*. For me, it was Robin Fedden's 1963 account of these mysterious Pontic Alps that stirred schoolboy memories of Xenophon and sowed the seed of curiosity.

Xenophon's Pontic Alps are now the Kackar Dag, the highest range in NE Turkey. These Little Caucasus, culminating in Kackar Peak (3932m), rise some 100km south-west of their grander namesakes and cover 3600 square kilometres of what was ancient Lazistan. Winds off the Black Sea dump over 100 inches of rain and snow on the mountain wall raised high above the narrow coastal plain to create a botanical mosaic. The littoral's tea plantations and hazelnut groves rapidly revert to forests of chestnut, walnut, alder, hornbeam, oak and spruce – oversized variants of our European familiars. Here, lianas and other parasites trail downwards into a matted undergrowth of blackberry, bay laurel, holly, cotoneaster, privet, ivy, xilax, clematis and fern. Intermingling with the forest and creating impenetrable thickets of its own is the *Rhododendron ponticum*. On Scotland's west coast this exotic grows like a weed: here, in its native habitat, it covers whole mountainsides in livid pink. Above the deciduous tree-line, pine forests compete with swashes of yellow azalea giving way to meadows bejewelled with alpine flowers swept by wave-tossed tracts of the white blossomed *Rhododendron caucasicum*. Up and beyond is the climbers' world of scree and snow, glaciers and granite peaks.

Kackar's modern climbing history dates from three turn of the century visits by the ubiquitous Anglo-German Willi Rickmer Rickmers, a pioneer mountaineer explorer of the Caucasus and Pamirs, twice reinstated to the AC after two world wars, an RGS gold medallist and inaugural honorary member of the Alpine Ski Club. During the 1930s, Austrian and German climbers – Turkey's former wartime allies – mopped up most of the exploratory mountaineering in Turkey. After the Second World War, the first Briton to visit Kackar was the redoubtable traveller Denis Hills whose 1959 and 1963 journeys are elegantly described in *My Travels in Turkey* (Allen & Unwin 1964). Robin Fedden and Basil Goodfellow made first British ascents of

Kackar (3932m) and other peaks in 1963. Sidney Nowill was active in 1976, 1977 and 1980.

It took me 21 years to fulfil the earlier vow to climb in Kackar. In June 1987 my wife and I, with Robert and Susan Sykes, flew to Trabzon, hired a taxi and headed east along the coast. Swinging inland through effulgent green forests emblazoned with rhododendron, we reached Ayder (1250m) after six bumpy hours. From this local resort, famous for its hot springs but with disturbing plans for tourist development, we backpacked south into the hills. We were neither kidnapped, robbed nor molested but climbing was frustrated by the insidious Black Sea mist, lack of a decent map, and compasses which the granitic rock swung unpredictably. The weather too was dreadful – alternate bouts of snow, hail and thunderstorm. But when visible, the country was magnificent and as the snows retreated, alpine meadows became floral tapestries. Then on one fine day, 7 June, all frustration was forgotten when Sykes and I climbed Nanetleme Tepesi (3405m) from the head of the Kaymakcur valley. From this belvedere, the whole range unfolded from the lazy mass of Karchal Dag marking Russia to the east to the unmistakable rock pyramid of Verchenik in the west. This vision spawned the 1991 Kackar ski traverse.

Turkey is, above all, a diverse country. While both the Bolkar and Ala Dag are ranges of Central Asia, Kackar Dag, 650km further east, is alpine in character with the comforting feel of Europe. It is not simply that the Lazes, butts for Turkish wit yet renowned as mariners and pastry-cooks, are an industrious Caucasian remnant. Their migrations from the lower valleys to the summer yailas, with the women dressed like peacocks and the men outlandish in bearskins driving their black bulls before them, have a high drama wholly lacking in Heidi's Swiss cows. But in scale, land forms and architecture, the Kackar seem disconcertingly familiar. The elegant humpbacked pack bridges are unique but the stone-foundationed wooden chalets, eyrie-like on hillsides linked to valleys by primitive *téléfériques*, could be Swiss. Above all, the people are hospitable and friendly.

The 1991 Kackar traverse team comprised David and Anna Williams, David Seddon and Stephen Baker. Like Xenophon, we would enter from the south and exit at Trabzon. I could find no record of a complete Kackar ski traverse but three months before our departure, Ronald Naar, the Flying Dutchman Seven Summiter, wrote to say that he was about to visit the range with a Turkish guide. Naar in the field! We had first met on Mount Olympus in 1985 and our paths had been crossing ever since. His entry to the lists added a *frisson* but when we compared itineraries it looked as if Ronald's, from Yaylalar to Pokut, was more an extended crossing than an east/west traverse.

Of more concern was the Gulf War. Our flights were only confirmed after consulting the Turkish Oracle Sidney Nowill. And it was the memory of the Nowills' hospitality on our first night in Turkey at their flat overlooking the Bosphorus, serenaded by honking foghorns, that sustained us through a lost day in Ankara. From England, it took a three-day journey into winter suspended above the illimitable snow-bound plateau of Eastern Turkey to reach Erzurum and from there, by bus, our roadhead Yusufeli.

As we disembarked, self-conscious with ski and incongruous in garish anoraks on an unseasonably balmy evening, Ozkan attached himself to us. As folk do in Turkey, he had seen us coming. Now, as we wandered with him through the dusty main street in search of taxis for tomorrow, our self-appointed Treking Mauntainer Guy (as his card pronounced) soliloquised about the mountain life. 'There are no bears in Kackar' – Ozkan was doing his best to reassure us – 'and no wolves either – but the butterflies are very beautiful.' Ozkan confided that he guided trekkers during his three month summer season to Kackar, Ararat and the Caucasus. But in winter, he avoided the mountains as 'dangerous with too much snow'.

Ozkan was wrong about bears and wolves, but then he only wanted to please. Over the next fortnight scarcely a day passed without a sighting of bear or wolf spoor. But he was dead right about the snow which proved unpredictable, collapsible to a depth of 4ft and seriously avalanche prone. Monumental, solidified heaps of the stuff filling gullies and valley bottoms were constant reminders of mortality. In the Taurus we had scarcely seen an avalanche. In the Kackar their brooding presence was a feature of everyday life.

On 22 March 1991, blue skies heralded a perfect start to our venture. A 32km competitive slalom between our two taxis on bare treads whisked us up the spectacular Altiparmark valley to the hamlet of Barhal (Altiparmak) at 1200m. From this roadhead, we shouldered sacks. The traverse was to be in three phases: Barhal to Ayder, Ayder to Chat and Chat to Chemlihemshin. This allowed 12 days to take in the four massifs of Altiparmark, Bulut, Kackar and Verchenik. 2392 years before, Xenophon had crossed the Pontic Alps in 10 days.

Eight hours on and 1300m higher, we made our first camp just short of the Kara Gol lake. So far so good but by next morning, barely three hours out, a Black Sea blizzard sent us snow-holing in the lea of a monolithic rock below the black cliffs of Didvake and left us sopping wet. Was this the pattern of things to come? Ski touring blind on sketch maps is bad for the nerves. More of the same next morning set the scene for a 900m thrills and spills descent through the cloud down the Percha valley to Binektashi yaila. At the end of that run we crossed our first bear tracks. But could these monstrous 12" imprints of claws, like splayed crampons, belong to a mere brown bear? More importantly, if confronted, should we stand our ground, go to ground or simply grovel?

A descending traverse across the hillside through forest, cloud and mist brought us gently down to the Kisla valley. Here, the south-facing slopes were wooded with birch and oak as the north were with pine. Passing clusters of deep-eaved, deserted chalets, silent in the snow, we climbed on up beyond the tree-line, to camp early on a rock knoll jutting out above the valley. Snug and secure on this belvedere marked by a solitary pine, our tents were cushioned by a mattress of *Rhododendron caucasicum* while, all around, the sides of the Upper Kisla were seared and scarred by fresh avalanche slides. Plumb 50m below our camp, the gaping gulch of the Ombolat Deresi was buried in 15m of solidified snow blocks.

This ugly passage was best left for an early start and with the dawn came clear skies. Due west the sun had already picked out in luminous pink a snow tooth set between the double col of Kirmizi Gedici (3110m) marking our first watershed. Frozen snow swiftly sped our ski over and past enormous avalanche cones into the maw of the upper Kisla valley which narrowed to a head wall topped by the Kirmizi col. Before us, away in the north-west, invisible beyond serried ridges that peeked out from a cauldron of cumulus cloud, lay the Black Sea. Could this be the mountain Xenophon called 'Thekes' from which his 10,000 first saw the Euxine? Imagination might have caught an echo of 'Thalassa, Thalassa' ('the Sea, the Sea'), but to make this crossing, a Peltast must paraglide or ski like a Williams.

Steeply below, down an icy gully, the undulating snowfields of the upper Avucor valley sparkled reassuringly. On reaching this promised land, by crampon or ski to taste, the pressure lifted. With the sun warming our backs and the snow holding firm, we slalomed downwards past the castellated flanks of Bulut Dag ('the Cloudy One') in snaking turns which desecrated the virgin snow. Racing through, amongst and over the rooftops of chalets snow engulfed to their eaves, this dizzying plunge only stopped at the lip of a waterfall in the bed of the ever-narrowing valley.

The 14km descent from the Kirmizi Gedici to Ayder demolished 1800m of vertical height. But my nostalgic memories of a bustling summer spa soon faded as we trudged down its one street now slushy, grey and deserted. We had banked on reprovisioning at Ayder but the village had been abandoned. Not a shop was open and both electricity and water (save for a single street tap) were cut off. But miraculously, the proprietor of our old haunt the Hilton Oteli was still in situ. This establishment would have nonplussed the chain's founder and its fleas make gnats of their Pyrenean cousins. But its owner gave us olives, cheese, scrambled eggs, bread, butter and rice in his warm kitchen with what remained of the local population. We ate to bust, correctly anticipating some lean days ahead. A more serious preoccupation was David Seddon's knee, injured in descent. This was definitely not a case of 'doctor heal thyself'. The prospect of losing a key player to a quack deputy with only one-third of the traverse completed cast a dark shadow at the close of that otherwise magnificent day.

Next morning, the formal handover of the Kodachrome film canister containing the expedition's pills, potions and placebos confirmed that David was heading for the coast and home. Pensively, the rest of us set off southwards up the Kale Duzu valley into the heart of the range. Bear and wolf spoor preceded us through a pine forest which, at the Asagi Caymakcur yaila, gave way to open snowfields. Here, in June 1987, we had walked through alpine meadows studded with giant yellow peonies and blue gentians. Four years on but three months earlier, the sun seemed warmer as we mounted unstable snow slopes strung out in file and preoccupied with the threat of avalanche. That unsettling 1520m ascent took 9½ hours. Secure beside Kara Deniz Golu (2750m) a snow-covered lake at the foot of the spired Nanetleme Tepesi, I realised belatedly that this had been our summer campsite four years ago.

On 27 March, a 4.30am start took us from shadow to the sunlit Caymakcur col (3210m) marking the Kackar's N/S watershed. We gazed at this new southern horizon before mounting our ski chariots and launching off down the deep-delved Dupeduz valley. Heaving for breath after a lung-blowing descent on perfect snow on a spur just above the Buyuk Chay at Olgunlar, I spotted a tiny figure framed in the valley's narrow shoulders. It was far below but moved purposefully upwards with a skier's gliding stride.

Preoccupied with the loss of Doctor David, we had forgotten Ronald Naar. Coincidence can be taken too far but was this not the day when our paths might again cross? Like raptors we swooped downwards for our preordained tryst past startled shepherdesses raking dung and, at precisely 8am, were a laughing, handshaking and happy snapping group with Ronald, Bas, Henk and Jamal their Turkish guide. They had set out from Yaylalar only the day before. Half an hour on brought another surprise when three local shepherds on primitive skis swept by in straw hats smelling high as badgers. In the heat of the day it took 5½ hours up the airless corridor of the Buyuk Chay to reach the Dilber Duzu (2930m) set in a cirque surrounded by granite peaks. Here we camped opposite the pillared black buttresses of the Devil's Rocks, vaulting 1400m from the valley floor to the summit of Kackar itself. 50m away, the Dutch built a moat and bailey round their tent with food enough for a siege. Next day, 28 March, we all climbed Kackar peak (3932m) in 4½ hours via the frozen Deniz Golu with skins to the summit ridge. Mist obscured the view but we celebrated that evening on the heroic tin of honey humped up by the lion-hearted Jamal, ski-less and goggle-less on the mountain, now eyeless with snow blindness.

Dutch hospitality had significantly extended our range but Good Friday brought the first bad weather in five days and a parting of ways. We were heading west while Ronald and Co were northbound though initially would follow our tracks across the key passage to the Kavron Gap (3270m). A 450m climb via the backwall of Deniz Golu landed us on the first of five cols that link the radiating ridges of Kackar's southern flank. In falling snow and poor visibility the route was uncertain. But on that high trapeze crossing, an avalanche-scoured face, an overcast sky was better than any amount of sun. David was again man of the match – sometimes a mere speck on a baleful wall but always steering a bold, unerring line. We reached the Kavron Gap 4 hours and 20 minutes after leaving camp; dropped 700m into the upper Polovit valley; almost sank without trace through the snow when the sun came out and finally slipped west across yet another ridge down leg-breaking crust to Karam yaila in the upper Kormik valley.

We were now off the sketch map. To reach the Verchenik massif, should we strike due west over the mountains or follow down the Kormik valley via Elévit to Chat? With food and time running out we opted for the 1350m descent to Chat past monstrous avalanche slides through snow so vile that even Williams was spotted doing a sly kick turn. When the snow gave out, we walked through snowdrops, gentians, primulas and clouds of butterflies. Chat itself, set prettily in a confluence of deep valleys, was virtually deserted save for the Oteli Canick's rapacious proprietor Rasim and his monster dog Arslan 'the Lion', Turkey's answer to the Tosa. Health warning: both prey on itinerants. After stuffing ourselves with Rasim's hyperpriced boiled eggs, bread and honey, we decided to carry on to Ortakoy yaila, 800m higher up the Firtina gorge, by way of avalanche debris suspended above a boiling torrent. Kackar's yellow azalea honey, hived in barrels 30m high up in the trees to frustrate the bears, has poisoned over-indulgers from the days of Xenophon and Pompey. We had glutted ourselves on Rasim's, but with no ill effects.

Our last three days in Kackar were a fairy-tale. The saga will oft be retold of how we met Barki Kasholi, the winter guardian of Ortakoy, emerging from the gloom of a Black Sea snowsouper at the close of that endless 12-hour day. How he frustrated his two dogs of their infidel dinner, took us to the bosom of his family to share hearth and home and how, on that stormy night, we slept not in leaky tents in mud and slush but under embroidered sheets scented with lavender in a pine walled dortoir two storeys above Barki's extended family of 150 sheep, 10 cattle and 2 dogs.

On Easter Day 31 March we breakfasted off eggs with golden yolks and bread smothered with orange and raisin jam while the Barkis' daughters suckled their twin pet lambs from a milk-bottle. David gave young Ali a skiing lesson and I gave Barki my Swiss penknife before we skinned on up the Firtina valley towards a pyramidic snow peak emerging through the morning mist. But even as we sighted the fantastic granite spire of Verchenik (3711m), we knew it would remain inviolate. We camped at its feet but our time was up and although, next day, before descending 1900m to Chat, David climbed the pyramid peak Ovit Tepesi (3260m) (the rest of us nearly), the Queen of Kackar remains a vision. That evening in Rasim's rude *hamam*, having emptied a jug of paraffin over my head as water, I remembered All Fools Day.

Marching out of Kackar down the Firtina valley, it struck me that Xenophon might as well have followed this valley down to the coast as any other. His route is still disputed but, though my insight was probably a mere fantasy, in completing the Kackar ski traverse in 12 days it was Xenophon's spirit which had moved us, as ours had been buoyed by the hospitality of others. If you have luck with the weather and rise with the dawn to the four-note reveille of the Caspian Snow Partridge so as to catch the good snow, Kackar will provide unforgettable ski mountaineering.

Summary: *Kackar Dag, Turkey.* First ski traverse from Barhal to Chemlihemshin 22 March–2 April 1991. Party: David Williams, Anna Williams, Stephen Baker and John Harding with David Seddon in part. 22.3.91 Yusufeli to Kara Gol camp. 23.3.91 Kara Gol to Didvake Col. 24.3.91 Didvake Col to Ombolat Deresi. 25.3.91 Ombolot Deresi to Ayder. 26.3.91 Ayder to Kara Deniz Golu (via Caymakcur Deresi). 27.3.91 Kara Deniz Golu to Dibler Duzu via Dupeduz Deresi/Olgunlar and Buyuk Chay. 28.3.91 *Ascend Kackar Dag (3932m).* 29.3.91 Dilber Duzu to Karam Yaylasi (Kormik valley). 30.3.91 Karam Yaylasi camp to Ortakoy via Chat. 31.3.91 Ortakoy to Ovit Yaila. 1.4.91 Ovit Yaila to Chat (*Ascend Ovit Tepesi 3260m DRBW*). 2.4.91 Chat to Trabzon via Chemlihemshin and Firtina valley.

Travels with My Wife

(Plate 40)

During an extended canoe trip down the Alaskan coast I managed to master the US phone system and made an international call to Liz from a decrepit coin box on the pier at Petersburg. I had just been invited to join a small lightweight team to attempt the unclimbed E face of Kedardome in the Indian Himalaya. The route was well known to me as one of *the* targets of modern altitude climbing. In fact several British groups, mostly comprised of enthusiastic rock climbers, had already mounted expeditions to the route without much success.

Petersburg was celebrating Norway's national day. The original founder of the town was an American/Norwegian Peter Buschmann and the Norwegian connection has been jealously fostered for generations. The harbour was bustling with action. A pick-up truck, full of Vikings, stopped on the dockside and the horned occupants clambered into a fishing boat thinly disguised as a longboat. Several young women, very scantily dressed, had been hauled aboard and were being ravished as Liz answered the phone.

Combining climbing on Kedardome with Liz's annual leave seemed a way in which we could be together and both have a good holiday. Liz hadn't been to the East since climbing in Tibet four years previously and jumped at the chance of returning to the Himalaya. Additionally, several years before, she had expressed a desire to climb Pumori, 7165m, on the Nepal/Tibet border. The next time I had been in Nepal I had made a booking for autumn 1991, a date which was now creeping closer. A trip to Kedardome (and a thrash up the easy side) would allow us to judge whether she had a reasonable chance on the much higher and harder Pumori. We were both excited by the prospect and a rough plan had been agreed by the time I hung up.

Despite juggling times and dates, it was quickly apparent that we would have to walk in to Base Camp a few days after the main party. We couldn't afford to skimp on acclimatisation, so I concentrated on planning the fastest turn-round possible between my return from Kenya, where I had guiding commitments, and the start of the walk-in. In the end I flew into Edinburgh one day, changed my equipment and we both flew out the next day en route to Delhi. I had prearranged for a taxi to meet us at the airport. The driver was surprised to learn that our destination was the tiny village of Gangotri at the headwaters of the river Ganga (Ganges), two days' drive away.

After a couple of hours we were travelling sedately north through a rich rural landscape when there was a sudden bang and a slewing stop typical of a bad puncture. The road was absolutely straight and the only visible house, outside which we had skidded to a halt, just happened to be a puncture repair shop. Our driver seemed remarkably calm as the repair man assisted in taking off the damaged tyre, in the process removing a large bent nail which he slipped into his pocket.

Two years later, en route to Pumori, we flew from Kathmandu to Lukla. I had bribed and hassled until we had got our gear on board a grossly over-weight Twin Otter, but in doing so had agreed that the liaison officer would have to be left behind. I was feeling pleased with myself. The pilots always leave the cabin door open so you can see the dials and switches and can watch them pulling levers and twisting things which are presumably vital. You can also see out the front.

I was looking back down the fuselage and grinned at Liz as we approached the Lamjura Pass. I had done the flight several times before and knew that the plane had a height ceiling which allowed clearance of only a few hundred metres. It was amusing to see her look of mild apprehension become more and more pronounced. 'Should we really be this low?' 'Yeah, it always looks pretty dramatic here.'

Then I turned round. Both pilots were straining forward and one was pulling a handle marked 'full throttle'. It looked as if it might detach itself from the ceiling. Two of the dials, rev counters, were vibrating madly but I could see that the indicators were hard against the housing beyond the red. None of this worried me as much as the view, which was of a tree-covered hillside. I could tell that the pilots were mentally flapping, which seemed fair enough as they would hit first. It was a close run thing, we flopped over with ten metres to spare and started the long diving approach to Lukla. In the dry sweat of controlled panic I vowed never to bribe airline porters again.

Whilst watching the repair, Liz got involved in a complicated conversation with a couple of village women who had suddenly appeared. Liz was unfor-tunately sporting a very lurid black eye caused by colliding with a hockey ball, and was not refuting the obvious conclusion that the women had drawn. Sisterly concern was in the air. 'All men are bastards' seemed to be the prevailing opinion. Although innocent, I withered under the dark glances being thrown in my direction.

I had wanted to explore the holy city of Hardwar, but on arrival our taxi driver informed us that, for some reason of protest, the next day had been declared a National Strike and that he would have to stop driving by 8pm otherwise we were likely to be beaten to death. We pressed on. The next town, Rishakeshi, was about an hour further up the west bank of the river. We located the best hotel in town and ordered a pre-dinner drink and buffalo steaks, only to be informed that the whole area, from Hardwar to Gangotri, was not only dry but strictly vegetarian. Exhausted, dusty, hot and hungry, we took solace in a bottle of Muscadet which I had secreted in my rucksack. This was cooled by being wrapped in a wet towel and positioned in front of the air-conditioning unit. It was illegal but delectable.

At dawn, still confused by jet lag, we left to explore the town. It was surprisingly cold, and street children curled tighter in their rags as we passed by. Many people were taking a ritual bath when we arrived at the riverside, totally immersing themselves to be cleansed by Mother Ganga. A fine mist rose from their bodies as they emerged. The strike was total. Apart from a street vendor selling roasted maize nobody was working. He was obviously a simpleton and I suppose no one had told him that he should be on strike. We bought two cobs and ate them for breakfast, huddled over the welcome warmth of his charcoal brazier. Later we found a furtive street trader who sold us a book of postcards. They were, without exception, unimaginably bad. They were so awful that we bought a second set to keep for ourselves.

Before dawn the following morning our taxi driver reappeared and we started north once more. Uttarkashi is a dismal town; an air of putrifaction rose from the gutters. Rotting vegetables and detritus of unidentifiable origin attracted dense clouds of flies. I left Liz to guard our pile of equipment and went in search of somewhere to stay. There appeared to be only one hotel and after an extended period of haggling I procured a room. 'Malcolm, it's disgusting and dirty and there are stains on the sheets,' said Liz miserably. We ate a gloomy meal, sweeping flies from each mouthful before retreating to our room. Liz refused to sleep on the offending sheets and clambered into her sleeping-bag which was designed for high camps on Everest. The ceiling fan pushed humid air, seemingly honey thick, around the room in a dilatory fashion. Mosquitoes whined in the gloom, making diving passes at any exposed skin. It was not going to be a comfortable night.

Two days on from Lukla, across the boiling Dudh Kosi and up an infamous hill, lies Namche Bazar, the Sherpa capital. Nobody in their right mind wants to race up the Namche hill, but all expeditions do so. It's part of the ethos. The Pumori expedition was no exception; everyone shot off at a suicidal pace, except for our sole female member who thought the idea macho and daft. Joe Simpson, with whom I have shared the odd adventure, was still on crutches following an accident in the spring. He won, but was disqualified for using artificial aids.

Namche is a wonderful place to spend an acclimatisation day. PK's Lodge serves yaksteak and chips with imported beer, whilst Ang Phurba, catering for the traditional minded, produces the best daal bhaat *and* chang *in the Khumbu. We ate and drank and told wild stories. We met climbers we hadn't seen for a year or two, and others, new to the Himalaya, who looked self-conscious and serious. Chwang, my sirdar, organised our loads, arranged for the yaks to appear the next morning and joined us for a few pre-dinner beers.*

By noon the next day and after a trying time attempting to slow down our driver, we arrived in Gangotri. We had spotted several wrecks of buses lying at the foot of the gorge through which the track snaked. I pondered out loud that it must be an unnerving experience being in row 18, seat 5, when you go over the edge on such a road. Liz didn't find this at all amusing, whilst I was rocking with laughter. It was then that Liz pointed out that we were both going to travel back care of the local bus company.

'Maybe we won't have to,' I ventured, fishing for a reply. 'Don't be stupid, of course we will.'

'Not if they keep crashing into the gorge like that we won't. There won't be any buses left.'

Above Thyangboche, with Everest directly ahead, I found a memorial, like those that sprout on mountains in the Alps — very dramatic and with ceramic photos of the deceased. Chwang cruised up. 'Swiss expedition, two member dead on Lhotse, leader knocked off trail by yak and fell in gorge this place. Very very danger if not passing yak on inside. Careful Memsahib OK.' He looked meaningful at Liz before turning and striding on up the valley.

I booked us into a small lodge, then immediately found a group of porters who were looking for work and would start in ten minutes. I unbooked the room, paying half-price for the privilege. This undoubtedly reinforced the owner's impression that all Europeans are rich or crazy or, in my case, both. The initial trail out of Gangotri is wide and well marked. It is also oddly lined with street traders selling nothing but polythene waterbottles. I was confused for a while until I realised that all the pilgrims carry some of the river water back to their home villages.

We reached Tatoban in a whirling gale of driven sleet. It was just like a bad day during a Scottish winter. Unfortunately we were dressed for India. By the time we had unearthed and erected a tent we were both pretty cold. Liz clambered into her sleeping-bag, which was designed for high camps on Everest, and looked smug. Mine, now soaked through, was an ultra light-weight. It was not going to be a comfortable night.

Pheriche is a wind-swept Sherpa settlement huddled in the Khumbu valley, hard under Taweche. Sometimes the sun scurries out from behind Ama Dablam to give an illusion of warmth. This is so unnatural that only new-comers to these harsher regions of Nepal are fooled into removing clothing. Pheriche was designed to be wind-swept and cold. It acts as a learning experience for expedition base camps.

Liz was sitting in the courtyard of our lodge, deep in conversation with a small gnarly German guy. The talk went something this: Liz, in excruciating high German, 'What are you going to do when you get to Everest Base Camp?'

'Climb Everest. I hope to do it in three days if the weather looks settled.'

'Oh aye! Have you done any climbing in the Himalaya before?'

'Yes, ten eight-thousand metre peaks.'

'Oh, I see . . . excuse me for a minute.' Liz whizzes inside, interrupting my vital game of Pass the Pigs. 'Malcolm, have you heard of a guy called Michael Dacher?'

Joe and I look up, sigh, sip some more beer, Joe throws a double razorback.

'Liz,' he says, 'you have no sense of history.'

Liz slept and I shivered through the night. I didn't require an alarm clock and had a brew going at the merest hint of dawn. Liz stared miserably into her cup of tea. 'That's it! I'm not going through that again. Last night was horrible. I don't know why I let you talk me into it. I'm not fit enough and my hands get much colder than yours.' She moved into third gear. 'You're just a selfish bastard, dragging me up here, and I'm never doing it again.' A few minutes later she crawled outside to have a pee. 'Mal, quick, come out and look at this – God it's just amazing! What's *that* mountain called – it's like a Tolkienesque fairytale!' She paused, inhaling the crisp pure air. 'It's just fantastic waking up in a place like this, you know.' Thoroughly confused, I took the tent down and we set off on the final day's stage to where we hoped the expedition had established Base Camp.

Above Dugla, in a glorious position within sight of Pumori and Everest, numerous chortens queue along a ridgeline. They give the impression of waiting. Almost alive, they stand and wait and their numbers grow. To visit them on a misty, mysterious day is a powerful experience, for these are the memorials to Sherpas and climbers killed on Everest. Liz shivered a little when I told her what they were, for we have both faced their reality in different ways. Then we set off on the final day's stage to where we hoped to establish Base Camp.

A major part of the interest of climbing expeditions is in the travel to and from base camps. You travel to weird parts of the world and see things denied to most. Once climbing, your focus changes, the challenge takes over and you plan and sweat and get very scared, and hopefully go upwards. I haven't room to write about that here – that's for a different time. It's enough to say that Liz and I, with Mark Warham, reached the summit of Pumori on 9 October 1991. On the 11th an Icelandic friend, Ari Gunnersson, was killed descending from the summit. Kedardome involved hard technical climbing; we just didn't do enough of it to succeed.

HAMISH M BROWN

The Middle Atlas: Jbel bou Iblane and Jbel bou Naceur

(Plates 51, 52)

Mentioning these ranges to even the most experienced guides and climbers based on the Toubkal area will simply draw looks of puzzlement or admissions of ignorance. A few will have heard of them. But the Middle Atlas is all rolling cedar forests surely? Nothing for the mountaineer? Having motored various routes through Ifrane, Azrou, Imouzzer du Kandar and other romantic-sounding places among the forests, cross-country skied at the minute resort of Mischliffen or up Jbel Hebri and bird-watched at the many *dayets* (lochans), this was very much my own feeling about the Middle Atlas.

But a few years ago a friend and I made a sort of far-eastern perimeter tour of Morocco, and from Figuig oasis up to Oudja by bus and from Oudja to Fes by train we were constantly looking leftwards to far and distant snowy mountains. That had to mean big, both in geographical spread and in altitude. The map showed a stippling of 3000m summits and a discouraging lack of roads leading anywhere near them. 'Something lost behind the ranges ... lost and waiting ... Go!', as Kipling's 'Explorer' had it.

The only practical information we gleaned was in Michael Peyron's *Great Atlas Traverse, Morocco*, volume 2. We chose May so that there might still be snow-melt to produce essential water and we took a gifted young Moroccan friend, Ali, from Taroudant (the other end of the country) to be our chief communicator in remote areas where even a knowledge of French would be rare. Both were wise moves. Ali is an aspirant guide and trek organiser of rare talent, his great delight is taking English-speaking groups, he can charm anyone he meets, he is a gifted cook and baker, a fit and cheery lad o' pairts.

The 'normal' approach to the range is from the north-west, probably starting in Fes and from Birtam-tam, 40km on the Oudja road, heading up 32km to Ribat el Kheyr (clearing things with the authorities there) before another 60km of spectacular driving lands one at Taffert forestry hut. The book there showed nothing of mountain doings and few visits of any kind. Yet a tarred road led to its door; that alone was a memorable experience. This entry leads to the Jbel bou Iblane range – a long swoop of crest, streaky-bacon marked with snow in May and having a certain past history of visits by mountain skiers. In fact an incipient ski resort was built under the slopes only there was no water for the hotel and, if there was snow enough for the tows, then the snow blocked all access! Echoes of Mar Lodge. Nomad tents and vast flocks of sheep and goats surround this pink-elephant site now.

Haj Mohammed, the hut guardian, is a tall, imposing figure, his austerity not quite hiding a warm heart. His son gave us a lift out at the end of our wanderings, which was just as well as the 60km to the Ribat was scarcely backpacking country on the minimal rations we had remaining. But we had left this 'more known' entry as our exit for this very reason and chose to go in from the south and tackle Jbel bou Naceur first. Very few people ever made it to bou Naceur from bou Iblane, despite it being the highest spot in all the Middle Atlas (3326m to 3340m or some such: maps and landscape are both confusing to put it mildly).

Aït Idir Mohammed, with whom we base our gangs when in the Toubkal/ Imlil area, fixed up a Land Rover for three days – our major expense – and came with us too for those days. The first day took us from the expedition-popular Hotel Ali in Marrakech to Midelt on the Fes–Tafilelt road that separates High and Middle Atlas. We arrived in early afternoon and for the rest of the day and night the rain poured down. Glen Coe could not have done better. Miraculously the next day was fine for our run down the great Oued Moulouya that moats the Middle Atlas on the south – a big river in a big desert landscape. At Outat Oulad El Haj we took to the *piste* and, with some miscasting, eventually reached the village of Tirnest, its houses on bold prows above green cultivation and backed by raw barren hills. Of bou Naceur we saw nothing. The hills were still steam-drying from the rain. The *piste* was so stony that we had no worries about being bogged down in the Land Rover. Officialdom tried, however.

The headman very grudgingly let us go on but refused to help with mules to carry our gear because we didn't have authorisation from back at El Haj. We were fed and given mint tea, however, and in the afternoon three of us and Ali shouldered heavy rucksacks (a week's food, bivvy gear, ice-axe and crampons) and set off for the invisible mountain. In the blazing heat this was no treat and our crossing of a ridge to gain the long access valley (the Taouchguelt Srhir) was hard graft. Luckily we met a nomad camp and a man with a donkey laden with plastic bottles who led us to the only *source*, a spring where we camped after five hours of steady uphill toil. Bou Naceur only lay a Ben Nevis in height above and holes in the cloud revealed intimidating crags and snowfields.

Jbel bou Naceur has a layered plateau so it is very difficult to tell the bump which is the highest. We were not pleased to wander round finding that each seemed higher than the last (and vice versa!) as, by then, we were desperately dehydrated, having done the equivalent of Fort William to Ben Nevis summit via Tower Gully. One gush of water alone appeared all day, and that low down. Originally we planned to traverse NE to bag another 'Munro', the 3128m Adrar n' Siouane, bivvying at the col between. But the col was obviously waterless and day was vanishing fast as we floundered over the porridge of new snow on the plateau. We had our bivvy at 3100m and ironically watched the sunrise glitter on the distant Oued Moulouya while we melted snow for a freezing breakfast brew. We needed pints not cuppas and Sioune ('bloody slag heap anyway') was abandoned in a desperate downward quest for water.

Snow here just didn't produce melt enough of its own accord – it ablates – and the limestone landscape swallowed all else, only spewing it out in seem-

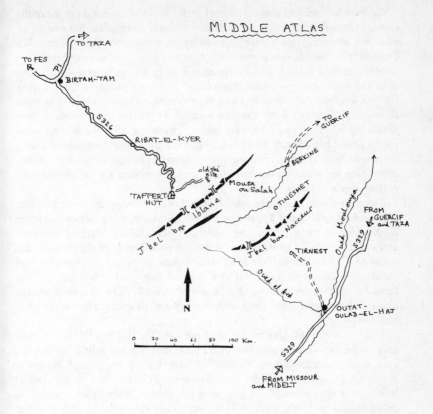

ingly random fashion. The green oasis village of Tinesmet obviously had water
but before then we came on a fine river, a crystal flow suddenly after a dozen
dry gorge river beds. We drank the water, we splashed in the water, we
washed smelly socks in the water, we worshipped the marvellous fluid!

On our way down the gorge to Tinesmet we caught up with an old Berber
leading a donkey laden with firewood. Ali got chatting and soon had the local
situation studied. I wonder what that man thought later? 'Mektoub', no doubt
('it is written'), but this random meeting led to his going with us for the rest of
our route. On entering Tinesmet he whacked his donkey with 'Home, beast!'
and left it in order to take us to the cheik (headman) where we – and he – had
tea and food, as hospitality demands, and he became one of two muleteers to
assist us. No one had taken visitors before, so it was an adventure for them
too. They were great characters; the headman was kindness and hospitality in
genial guise and we stayed in his house overnight. His sons took us on a
ramble to show us their great pride – a triple source, from which they had
year-round drinking water. A three-mile seguia (water channel) from our
picnic gorge/river irrigated the fields.

We were late off and underestimated time and distance so did not make the slopes of bou Iblane as planned. The day was still a long, full, hot one as we swooped westwards on a path dictated by the curvaceous shale stratas. We had an idyllic hour brewing over cedar fires (elevenses) and another brew after climbing up to a pass on 2000m. Another mule caught us up and a gentleman in suit and carrying a briefcase greeted us – an utterly incongruous spectacle. He was a schools' director and had been visiting a remote school. His mule dismissed, he walked down the pass with us. The mules had to make a huge detour on the *piste* to avoid a scarp (miles of towering cliffs like the Ordesa in the Pyrenees) but our city gent bombed down a pedestrian *diretissima*, talking the whole way and then rushing off for home, a village called Beni Smint. Bivvy bags snug among the boxwood, we lay watching the eerie moonlight play on Jbel bou Iblane ahead.

An easier day, made memorable by the flowers growing on the roadside in that verdant valley, and a spring which allowed us to wash (selves and some clothes), led us up to the hanging valley under bou Iblane. Watered meadows and cedar forests faced its barren slopes. A poor house produced mint tea, bread and buttermilk (Ali made his usual contacts!) before we crossed to toil up another 2000ft to a bivouac site. Remarkably quickly the brilliant day turned grey, thunder rolled and it rained periodically. The muleteers erected stone shelters and roofed them with their mules' panniers. They wove grass ropes to order.

At dawn it was still grey but we went anyway. The Jbel bou Iblane is a long, easy range, for all the world like a coal bing (that is being polite), lacking the cliffs and grandeur of bou Naceur but more known because of the easier access on its other, northern, side, where we hoped to end at the Taffert refuge. It is split in two by a gap, with the eastern, higher part bearing the name Mousa ou Salah, 3172m. This gave a huge view after an easy plod but once across the gap, the Tizi n' Tzirouch, 2865m, the weather again began to fail and grey storms trailed across with grumbling thunder. We reached Peyron's 3103m summit and looked along a couple of miles of Grey Corries ridge to the 3081m top which the map gives as its highest. We raced along, expecting to have to bale off at any time, but bou Iblane bore a charmed existence. Storms passed on all sides but we were left untouched. We still baled off as soon as the summit was bagged, losing 2000ft in rapid standing glissades or escalator-smooth scree-runs (remember when Scotland had screes that ran?).

Five miles of valley led to the start of the finest cedar forest I have ever seen. The flowers on the verges were dazzling too. It is this mix of the utterly desolate (vertical and horizontal) and the verdant and habitable that gives the Moroccan mountains much of their attraction. Only the thirsty really appreciate water; only the lonely really lay on such open hospitality. A journey like this has almost a mystical purifying element. It is also a rebuke to our soft, wasteful, selfish western society. The gracious people of the Atlas are the salt of the earth.

Ali had romped off back from ou Salah to our bivvy site to join the muleteers and they had a long tramp along and round a pass at the far end of bou Iblane. Both parties reached the refuge at the same time, which was perhaps symbolic too. In just a few days we had become a good team. Ali had made contacts at every stage and dreams of taking others back to this country lying beyond the plastic world we think of as civilisation. It is too remote and hard ever to be 'popular', as is the soiled 'Toubkal trail', and Ali, as in his own Western Atlas, will guide with respect and understanding. The muleteers rode off, richer, I hope, not just in cash but in meeting us (as we were in having known them). Kipling's poem ends something like 'Lost and waiting. Anyone might have found it. But God's whisper came to me.' In Morocco, everything planned ahead has the words *Insh 'Allah* (God willing) appended. Going into this remarkably unknown range (when one thinks of the Toubkal mobs) we were saying *Insh 'Allah* constantly. But, in the end, it was written, it was done. *Mektoub. Hamadullah.* (Thanks be to God.)

ACKNOWLEDGEMENT

I would like to thank the Mountaineering Council of Scotland who assisted this journey with a grant.

AUTHOR'S NOTE

One of the great snags of wandering in Morocco's remoter areas is the lack of maps. I can perhaps help here – and for most mountain areas of Morocco – and can also put anyone in touch with people like Ali and Mohammed who contribute so much to making Atlas ventures special. Western Atlas, Anti-Atlas, Jbel Sarho, Sirwa, Central Atlas, Middle Atlas, all offer trekking and climbing of the highest calibre, at bargain cheapness, best in the winter, spring and autumn seasons. If interested, send a SAE please to: Atlas Information, 21 Carlin Craig, Kinghorn, Fife KY3 9RX, or contact El Aouad Ali, BP132, Taroudant, Morocco.

MALCOLM RUTHERFORD

A Team Success on Island Peak

(Plates 1, 73)

What are we doing here? The mist is swirling in ominously, the altimeter has just gone round the clock at 6000m and my wife, son and daughter (front-pointing and hard-hatless) are being bombarded by large lumps of ice dislodged with chaotic abandon by frantic Italians. The sirdar has been hit and is in a bemused state. We are on Island Peak and life is exciting – but it all started many weeks before in a grey MoD office.

The Higher Management Committee of the British Services 1992 Everest Expedition (BSEE) decided to take an active part in Nepal during the closing stages of the main expedition. We were hoping, as a long shot, to be at Base Camp during assault bids, and so this aim was a priority. But we also hoped to reach the rock peak Kala Pattar on Pumori's SE ridge and to make an attempt on Island Peak at over 6000m. An assorted 12-strong party gathered at Gatwick on 1 May, with ages ranging from 18 to 58 and experience from nil to considerable. There were two Air Marshals, Dougie Keelan (who led the British Services West Ridge expedition in 1988) and myself, and our respective wives, friends and families. The whole team staggered onto the Royal Nepal Airlines flight for Kathmandu with multi-kiloed 'hand luggage' and anoraks bulging, but were still over allowance. (It subsequently transpired that one of the Air Marshals had packed a portable shower; my daughter Kim had packed a banned 'Snoopy', somewhat lighter, which was later to reach over 6000m – by Sherpa.) However, ground staff were sympathetic, no excess charges were levied, and soon we were slumped in our seats, heading over Hungary to Dubai, gin and tonic in hand, no more planning to do, a great feeling of release.

I can thoroughly recommend the Summit Hotel in Kathmandu. We were looked after very well during a two-day sojourn, sorting out kit and organising trekking and mountaineering permits, and the hotel staff did all our logistic planning for us. Kathmandu was quiet, very quiet, everything shut and a sullen feeling in the air. Four weeks earlier several demonstrators had died in riots and a big protest march was planned during our time there. This was in total contrast to the hustle, bustle, and colours of our visit in 1988 and hammer and sickle banners looked incongruous. In the event the day passed peacefully enough but we were glad to return to the sanctuary of the Summit Hotel whence we should not have strayed.

The flight to the mountain airstrip at Lukla fulfilled our worst expectations. After a five hour wait at Kathmandu airport while rumour and counter rumour abounded (no official information), it transpired that no planes could get in through low cloud and rain. A bad omen: only three weeks before, no planes had got in for 10 days because of smoke haze from forest fires and an angry backlog had built up at Lukla, which has no road out. This included a group who had gone to Thyangboche monastery to find peace, solace, and love for everyone in the world – but five days' wait at Lukla had destroyed their serene state of mind and this flower party were described as murderous. Oh well, back to the Summit pool, more beer, and try again the next day.

Glorious morning on the 5th, looking good, and soon we were approaching the Lukla strip. Angled at 10° upwards, 400m long (at most) and with a sheer cliff instead of run-out, it was pretty committing but exciting, and we disgorged with relief to meet our sirdar, Sonam, and (wait for it) 12 yaks, 18 porters, 6 cook boys! Did we really need all these? It soon turned out that we did, and two hours later, after a lot of shouting, ropework and mud over everything, the motley caravan set off for Phakding in the Dudh Kosi valley.

At this point I will spare the reader the somewhat tedious chronological sequence of events which can stultify expedition reports. Suffice it to say that within the next ten days all but two of the party (one of whom had a mild form of pneumonia) reached Everest Base Camp at 5400m – on different days, since the variation in our ages and fitness resulted in radical discrepancies in 'speed of advance'. I feel the achievement of the Base Camp goal was of great credit to several members of the party, one of whom had never even *camped* before, let alone climbed or trekked. However, one or two had misjudged the Himalayan scale and had a miserable first few days: it pays to get fit in advance.

The days had settled into a loose routine: 'bed tea' at 0530, washing water at 0600, porters shake snow off tents (several inches overnight on occasions), shivering start; massive breakfast three hours down the trail ('do not overtake the cook boys!'), finish walking day between 1400 and 1700, climb quickly into sleeping-bag to thaw out, supper, bed at 1900, bedsores, rock hard ground.

The mornings were generally sunny and pleasant, the afternoons overcast or cloudy, cold, and frankly a bit boring. The lasting memories, though, will be of the superb colouring of hillsides and ravines glowing luscious pink with thousands of rhododendrons and other flowers, multi-tinted and tuneful birds, smiling Nepalis (at last looking a little more prosperous), the bells of hundreds of yaks plodding their stoic way with huge loads, and the Buddhist reveille in the Sherpa capital, Namche Bazar. The latter consisted of an extraordinary cacophony of sound, starting at 0500, which we originally assumed to be from a pneumatic drill or generator with worn bearings. It turned out to emanate from a batch of alpenhorns protruding from the monastery window, at the other end of which could just be discerned inscrutable monks with an interesting sense of humour.

We had two rest days at 4000m and 5000m to acclimatise, but several members of the party went climbing during them. It is very important not to bash straight on up. We saw people suffering badly from altitude sickness, and indeed one American party was down to 50% of starters by its fifth day. Some of us took Diamox to aid acclimatisation. If anything, those not taking it appeared to fare slightly better than those who did, but the sample was too small to be significant. It was, however, useful as an antidote on the few occasions when symptoms of altitude sickness developed.

Base Camp on 12 May was extraordinary. Placed a few metres from the Icefall it was a colourful place with at least twelve expeditions from a variety of countries strewn around the rocky glacier. *Not* as messy as made out; far from it – tidy and cheerful. It was quite a day to be there, too. Somewhere between 36 and 42 people reached the summit that day (queuing at the Hillary Step, and several having paid £20,000 as commercial 'clients'), and all round the camp spontaneous cheering would break out (and in the Russian tents more vodka-slurping) as news came in of recurrent successes. But lest anyone should conclude that Everest had been tamed, it should be mentioned that parties on the South Col had to pass the frozen stiff bodies of two Indian climbers who had recently died of exposure.

At Base Camp we were received by Bronco 'Rottweiler' Lane (who reached the summit in 1976) and BSEE members, and I was able to talk to the Services on the mountain by radio – right into the Hornbein Couloir where good work was being done setting up ropes above Camp 5. (Modern communication methods are undoubtedly useful – but I wonder if they encroach too much on the traditional solitude and independence of mountaineers?) We had to get out of their hair the next day, and yomped down to Gorak Shep and up to Kala Pattar at 5650m, a stupendous viewpoint possibly unmatched anywhere. It was a delight to watch the changing hues and cloud formations on the highest peak in the world.

Our final objective was Island Peak (Imja Tse) at 6189m. This was a mini-expedition in itself: we established our Base Camp in a snowstorm (the traditional site for this has been changed following a tragic accident by a freak avalanche to an RAF party a few years ago – we rebuilt the memorial en route) and pressed on next day to Camp 1 high on the mountain flank. What a plod – 1000m of steep (but easy) ground with the thin air unfriendly to middle-aged lungs! But it was well worth the effort to reach this high camp at over 5800m, since its outstanding position gave glimpses of Ama Dablam (not much higher), Makalu (much higher) and Baruntse (miles of fluted ice).

Easy scrambling on rock following a pre-dawn start saw us onto the glacier by 0700, and soon we had roped up and were negotiating enormous cavernous cravasses before the final 100m ice slope came into view – but so did the Italians, making a noisy and dangerous meal of it. Not technically hard but certainly steep, the ice did not appreciate the flailing Latins. This is where my story started. With less than 80m to the summit a difficult decision had to be made; with some of the party very tired from the climb and altitude and with deteriorating weather, it was clear that to enable a small strong team to make the summit safely some would have to forego the opportunity. Thus it was that four of the party retreated, leaving Dougie Keelan, his son James, and my son Sam (who started his alpine career, aged 10, with a climb of the 4000m Allalinhorn) to climb unroped quickly along the exposed knife-edged ridge to the top in a whiteout. Objective achieved – a team success!

RUPERT HOARE

The Japanese Alps

(Plate 41)

The idea of climbing in Japan came from my friend Mark Lowe who lives in Hong Kong. I was also based in the Far East and we arranged a week's visit in July 1991. Apart from the volcanic cone of Mt Fuji (3776m), the highest peaks in Japan lie in the centre of Honshu province, only about 200km NW of Tokyo, where the most northerly of three mountain ranges, has been designated the Chubu-Sangaku (Japan Alps) National Park. The city of Matsumoto acts as a gateway to the Park, and we arrived there at about midnight having taken an express train from Tokyo's Shinjuku station.

After some difficulty we found a Japanese-style room in a nearby hotel. The door was about 5ft 7in high, a sensible height for me but not for Mark who is nearly six foot! The interior was small with the bedding lying directly on the tatami matted floor and with beautiful, wafer-thin papering on the cupboard doors. Rucksacks and climbing boots do not mix well with Japanese rooms!

Matsumoto is famous for its castle which has a five-tiered donjon built in the 16th century. From the castle there is a fine view of the distant mountains. The rest of the city, like most Japanese towns, is clean and modern but lacking in beauty or historical interest. Above all the streets there are forests of electric wires and advertising signs. Having inspected the castle and town, we took a private railway to Shimashima and then a crowded bus, which climbed steeply up deep valleys through wooded hills and passed through several tunnels to reach the roadhead at Kamicochi at 1500m. This is a popular local destination lying in the Azusa river valley, with mountains all around, and there are hotels, gift shops and a campsite. The 'Kappa Bridge' – a suspension bridge over the crystal-clear waters of the Azusa river – is always thronged with tourists. About 20 minutes' walk downstream there is a memorial to the Rev Walter Weston, an Alpine Club member, who climbed Yari Ga-Dake and other peaks in the Hotaka mountains between 1888 and 1894. The term 'Japanese Alps' was popularised by his celebrated book *Mountaineering and Exploration in the Japanese Alps*.

The following morning we awoke to the sound of steady rain on the tent. After a long and tiring journey, I was quite relieved to have an excuse for a lie-in. Unfortunately, at about 9am, Mark happened to look out and we saw at once that the water level was rising steadily around the tent. We fled to a café! It took most of the rest of the week to dry out the soggy pages of my passport and airline tickets. Even in the rain, the valley around Kamicochi, with its mossy pine, larch and silver birch woods, marshy areas and clear streams, had an exquisite beauty. It was easy to recognise the inspiration for much of Japanese art.

The next day dawned sunny with steam rising from the cold water of the river. We soon dried out the worst of our wet clothes and set off with sleeping-bags, bivvy-bags, stove, and food for four days to make a traverse of the main ridge of the Japanese Alps from Yari Ga-Dake (3180m) to Maehotaka-Dake (3090m). This route is one of the most popular mountain trips in Japan and is equipped with several huts. But as the huts can be crowded and are invariably expensive we chose to be independent. We followed the wide valley bottom with its stony riverbed for several hours and then climbed steeply through the forest beside an attractive torrent. Above, there were lovely grassy slopes with a mass of wildflowers. The mountains and valleys reminded me strongly of the Pyrenees.

After about eight hours of walking we reached a splendid bivouac spot with shelter, water and a fine view over the ridges to the distant cone of Mt Fuji. I was all for stopping, but Mark persuaded me to continue, since the shapely rock peak of Yari Ga-Dake was only about another hour away. It was lucky that he did, for the peak was lost in mist all the next day. We climbed on over scree for about half-an-hour to reach the ridge where we left our packs at a large hut. A further half-hour of scrambling took us to the summit. It was a beautiful viewpoint with lovely mist effects, including a Brocken spectre, in the evening light. We were forced to bivouac near the hut, in order to buy water. Unfortunately our bivvy site on a ridge at over 3000m was quite exposed, and the wind increased steadily until the violent flapping of the bivvy-bags forced us to seek more shelter in the middle of the night.

For the next three days we traversed along the ridge over several 3000m summits. Some of the time we were in thick mist and could easily have been on a ridge in Scotland, but at other times the cloud would suddenly blow away to reveal the deep wooded valleys below. Parts of the ridge had enjoyable scrambling but the more technical sections were all equipped with chains or ladders. We both felt slightly irritated by the abundance of paint marks and ladders, but on the last day, in wild wind and driving rain, we could understand their necessity on such a popular route.

The huts were not unlike Swiss huts, except for the dining-room. Here, one evening, we sat cross-legged on a matted floor eating with chopsticks from a table only a few inches high. The bulk of the meal consisted of sticky white rice and seaweed. The cost of a night, plus evening meal and breakfast, was 7000 yen (about £35!).

The traverse of the main ridge completed our primary objective. Now our plan was to do some rock climbing, but next day we again had heavy rain. Camping below the dripping trees brought back indelible memories of my first alpine season when we camped in the woods at Argentière. Apparently June and July are the rainy season in the Japanese Alps and prospective visitors would do better to choose August or September. Although there is some rock climbing on high crags near the ridge, the best climbing is at Byobu Rock, a large granite crag about 15km up the valley from Kamicochi. Mark had obtained some photocopied topo route descriptions by writing to a local climber he had met on a previous visit to Japan.

Next morning we set out in cloudy weather. The approach to Byobu Rock took 3½ hours and included a knee-deep wade across an icy river. (Prospective climbers would do better to camp nearer the crag.) We scrambled up a long boulder gully leading to a large snow patch; three pitches of V Diff climbing and some scrambling led to a terrace where the routes start. All the climbs on Byobu Rock are artificial, mostly graded IV (A1) or V (A2). Pegs and bolts litter the rock, even where natural protection is available. The crag is several hundred feet high and looked black, wet and daunting, with the mist drifting in and out. Lacking étriers and any experience of artificial climbing (apart from a single pitch on a route called *Benny* at Swanage), I was far from keen to continue.

Mark looked disappointed, but it made no difference since, ten minutes later, the heavens opened and there was torrential rain for the next three hours. We abseiled down with water pouring through our sleeves and made our sodden way back to the campsite at Kamicochi. Next morning we had to leave for Tokyo. It was brilliantly sunny at last, with the valley at its most beautiful. I would like to return.

DEREK A SMITHSON

The Norsk Project

(Plates 49, 50)

'The mountains of Norway – probably the oldest in Europe –
invite us all'[1]
William Cecil Slingsby (1849–1929)

The YRC and William Cecil Slingsby

The Yorkshire Ramblers' Club, which celebrated its centenary in 1992, has always been relatively small, keeping its membership to around 200. The YRC members are mostly Yorkshiremen by birth or adoption, but not all. Most members remain so for life and this has created a club of close friends with a resultant trust, understanding and exceptional selflessness. William Cecil Slingsby, who was one of the finest climbers of his generation, was president of the YRC for ten of its formative years (1893–1903). Geoffrey Winthrop Young described him as 'the first mountaineer to explore the high ranges and glaciers of Norway, and to reveal their possibilities of adventure and beauty to the Norwegians themselves. It was they who named him Father of Norwegian Mountaineering.'[2] Slingsby's book *Norway: the northern playground* is a classic of mountaineering literature.

The origins of the Norsk Project

The idea of the Norsk Project originated in 1988 during informal discussions on how to celebrate the Club's first hundred years. We wanted something that could involve all members, that would relate to Slingsby's activities, and that could involve Norwegians as well. Thus the Norsk Project was born. Our original idea was to repeat all Slingsby's first ascents; but the list of his routes in Norway is formidable and the length of some of his outings intimidating. The number of his first ascents is judged to be 79 and are spread from Lyngsalpene to Jotunheimen. The general view of those visiting Norway (which we did in both the summer and winter of 1990 and 1991) and of the Norwegians who took an interest in the project was that the YRC was unlikely to complete all the first ascents and would therefore be unwise to persist with that ambition. A success/failure attitude might develop which could easily lead to dangerous behaviour; it would also mean leaving out Slingsby's many great routes which did not involve the first ascent of a summit. So our initial plan to try to repeat 'all Slingsby's first ascents' was abandoned.

The Norwegians

We hoped that the project would extend the friendships and understanding between Norwegians and Britons. We found the Norwegians capable of great generosity in response to our enthusiastic interest in their country. We were given introductions to some, others we met in the villages or towns or at the huts. Nearly always we could communicate in English. However, a common language does not ensure understanding, and care was needed to avoid misunderstandings arising from our very different social and mountaineering cultures.

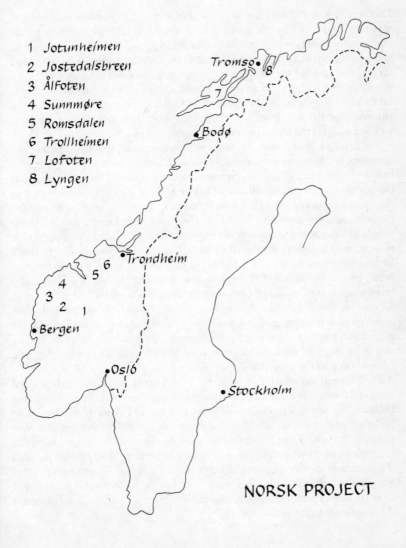

1 Jotunheimen
2 Jostedalsbreen
3 Ålfoten
4 Sunnmøre
5 Romsdalen
6 Trollheimen
7 Lofoten
8 Lyngen

Tromsø
Bodø
Trondheim
Bergen
Oslo
Stockholm

NORSK PROJECT

Reporting the project

Each area to be covered by the project had a co-ordinator and a report was prepared to record the enjoyment, achievements and difficulties that were experienced among these fabulous mountains. Club members were 'spread' from the Jotunheimen to the Lofoten Islands. Two expeditions took place on skis, during March and May, but the main thrust was in the July/August period.

Jotunheimen in winter (March)

This area, which includes the majority of Norwegian mountains over 2000m, was much favoured by Slingsby. He did a notable circumnavigation of the Hurrungane range, which included cutting steps for a horse, using ski and being benighted in Utladalen. Our friends in Norway stocked huts with food for us, they guided us away from danger and provided accommodation in private mountain huts and an elegant hotel. Over and above all this, the local mountaineering clubs, led by Petter Arnt Løvdahl, provided wonderful companions. For the first week our party comprised four Britons and six Norwegians and, for the second week, five Britons and two Norwegians.

The first day, skiing from Tyinosen with heavy packs, tested our fitness and it took us five hours to cover the 20km of undulating country. This brought us to a well equipped private hut, almost perfectly positioned for our purpose, at the northern end of Koldedalsvatnet below Falketind and Hjelledalstind. The next day we enjoyed good clear conditions as we skied up the slope behind the hut and onto Uranosbreen; from here the views were superb, and the sharp profile of Uranostind was especially impressive. We ascended Uranostind and, in worsening weather, continued to Slingsbytind; the intention also to climb Urdaknatten was abandoned. Descending in a near whiteout, with no contrast at all, proved difficult and everyone had at least one tumble. A second and a third attempt was made on Urdaknatten, each thwarted by bad weather, so four of us headed in the opposite direction towards Koldedalstind. This involved us in a long zigzagging ascent on a thin layer of snow on ice up to the ridge and a pleasant snow arête to the summit. The following day, two Britons and a Norwegian made it to the top of Urdaknatten using altimeter and compass to beat the poor visibility.

The planned circumnavigation of the Hurrungane range via Turtagrø and Skogadalsbøen was agreed to be impractical and we decided simply to cross Utladalen to the Årdal Turlag hut at Gravdalen and work from there. The preferred route was in Slingsby's footsteps via Morka-Koldedalen and Vettismorki down to Vetti. However, the risk of avalanche was judged to be too great so we skied up to Smoget and down Fleskedalen. Skiing down through the trees was challenging, and the gymnastics involved in getting up again after you had ended up in a deep snow drift, upside down, unable to get out of your rucksack, were exhausting, especially when they had to be repeated for the umpteenth time!

We stayed in the small but very comfortable DNT hut at Vettismorki, a magical place providing occasional glimpses of Hurrungane and only ptarmigans for company. The next morning we descended to Vetti in Utladalen and down the path towards Hjelle. The signs of spring were in the valley but we turned up to Avdalen. The farmstead at Avdalen was being renovated and we paused there before continuing up, struggling with the deep snow and birch trees on the way to Gravdalen. Another early start in good weather found us using skins up onto Gravdalsryggen heading for the Hurrungane. We followed an undulating ridge for hours but did not reach the main mountains. However, we did have breathtaking views in all directions and then a swift descent down Slufsedalen on near perfect snow. For the final night we descended to Avdalen where kind Norwegians provided a feast of fresh food and champagne. During the weeks following the departure of the Britons several of the routes planned to be done were completed by Norwegians.

Ålfoten in spring (May)

This area was traversed by Slingsby shortly after it was first mapped. We aimed to traverse Ålfotbreen, which is an ice cap, and then ascend Blånibba via Gjegnalundsbreen. We received valuable information from the Florø Turlag, but best of all was the advice to go in May with ski and the offer by Kjetil Tveranger to guide us. In the event the party consisted of one YRC member and Kjetil.

At our start point, Grøndalen, the river provided a magnificent waterfall and to avoid river crossings we used an alternative route which included two steps of moderate rock. When we joined the snow we fitted skins and mounted steadily up into a valley and up to Blåbrebu. After a rest we decided to continue over Ålfotbreen to Gjegnabu. We left at 4pm, which indicated Kjetil's confidence, and it took us almost ten hours including rests, but it never became really dark. The skiing was not really very difficult but the incompetence of the Briton made it seem so.

The next day was a straightforward route up Gjegnalundsbreen to Blånibba and then to Månyta in blazing sun. The Briton felt the strain from the day before but was inspired by the magnificent scenery. Three days of good weather had been forecast and as this was only the second day we felt secure for our return to Blåbrebu. It was a delightfully relaxed outing. We lunched perched like eagles at the top of a crag with fabulous snow and rock scenery in every direction. The final descent to Blåbrebu was beyond the Briton's ability to ski so, as on other occasions, he walked.

Our final day illustrated the fascination of the area. We agreed to climb Keipen which involved a descent of about 300m to get round a crag. We then found the river almost impassable and the route was abandoned because the river would be even higher later in the day. A very long detour to Keipen was possible but Saga was a shorter and easier alternative. Saga was very straightforward in the clear weather with a wonderful summit buried beneath a cornice. The other side of the mountain was truly precipitous. We returned, packed our gear and descended to our start point at Grøndalen.

Jostedalsbreen in summer (early July)

Jostedalsbreen is often referred to as the largest glacier in mainland Europe but it is like an ice cap with glaciers descending from it in all directions. Slingsby devoted a lot of time and effort to exploring this area, usually with local Norwegians. He made first ascents and did new routes across the ice cap; he also repeated routes not attempted for many years. He visited Lodalskåpa more than once and his wife made the first lady's ascent.

Two separate parties visited Jostedalsbreen in 1992 but one party of three did no more than traverse Lodalskåpa. Our other party was of seven Britons and occasionally one or two Norwegians. We approached Lodalskåpa from Jostedalen, which is unusual, and traversed from a camp at the head of Lodalsbreen. The route from there up Småttene was tortuous but safe and, after crossing a further crevassed area on the N side of the glacier, we followed a steep snow slope to the eastern summit. We had magnificent views from the snow slope but after the rock ridge to the main summit we were in cloud all the way down the normal route as far as Bohrsbreen. However, we found Ståleskardet with its recognisable windscoop, and the descent from here to the tents was interesting but straightforward.

We split the section from Fossheim to Bøyadalen into two by camping above Instebotnvatnet which reduced the journey time to Bøyadalen. We crossed four unnamed tops, just as Slingsby had, and enjoyed views into Kjøsnesfjorden. After reaching the main plateau a long curved route on breakable crust was followed to drop down to the normal Lundeskardet route at Kvitevardane. Even in clear weather we had to rely almost completely on compass and altimeter to cross this changing desert of snow. Once the normal route was found the descent to Bøyadalen presented no problems.

We left the Flatbrehytta at 4pm and climbed up to Flatbreen where we were surrounded by stunningly beautiful snow and ice scenery. Unusual snow conditions provided a snow cliff to surmount and, after contouring round upper Bøyabreen, a direct line was taken to the cairn (Snoadvarden). The journey was made harder by breakable crust but gave magnificent views of the whole Hurrangane range. After a long tea break at the hut, Kvannebakkbu, we descended the snow slope to Strupen and then on to Bevringsstølen.

When the cloud lifted sufficiently we left our camp at Høyset to start for Larsnibba and Geitaskjeret. We walked up Haugadalen and up into Jostebotn, crossing some distinctive moraine boulders, each about three metres in height. These gave way to heather, normal moraine and then we continued up the snow to Larsnibba summit. Despite the deteriorating weather we continued to Geitaskjeret which is also called Onsdagnibba and is not often visited.

We set off to ascend Fremstekåpa from Vetledalssaeter along the well marked track in Stordalen towards Erdalsbreen and continued up this glacier into low cloud accompanied by the crashes of ice avalanching off the nearby slopes. A compass guided us safely to the rocky ridge summit of Fremstekåpa but poor visibility robbed us of the anticipated impressive view of Tverrfjellet and Lodalskåpa. We then set off northwards onto Vetledalsbreen and the well marked route back to the hut.

Jotunheimen in summer (July and August)

This is the most popular mountain area in Norway with many of the highest mountains and plenty of facilities for walking. Slingsby was attracted back repeatedly and in one period of six days made six first ascents. Many YRC parties visited Jotunheimen, the main party being centred in Årdal and two members camping for five days at Spiterstulen. As in other areas help and companionship came from all the Norwegians that we met and it was particularly pleasing that Norwegians were involved in the only ascent of Store Skagastølstinden, that is Storen.

Our first party of three arrived at Årdal in the middle of July to meet a Norwegian friend, all with the intention of climbing Storen by traversing the mountain from Slingsbybreen to Bandet. We established a camp in Midtmaradalen but bad weather and future commitments reduced the party to one Briton and one Norwegian. When the weather cleared late in the day we walked up to Skagastølsbu on the Bandet and met two Norwegians also planning to climb Storen and who were familiar with the route. They guided us to the summit direct from Bandet and shared abseils down. With the limited visibility, rain and new snow, this probably made the difference between success and failure.

Our main party of six set up camp in Årdalstangen and ascended the two tops of Vestre Austanbotntind which is a short distance east of the road at Berdalsbandet. The route was simple, with minimal scrambling, but we met extensive boulder fields and greasy rock which required great care. When we looked at the more difficult ascent of the main summit in rain and low cloud we decided to return to the cars. The adverse weather, which was a feature of our stay, made us abandon an intended three-day trip in favour of a journey by car and boat to Torfinnsbu where we climbed the highest of the three summits of Torfinnstindane. The route took the most easterly gully with some short steep rock pitches and some snow. Whilst at Torfinnsbu we were lucky to meet Knut Lykken whose great grandfather climbed with Slingsby and who had many stories to tell.

Our party now divided: one group climbed Galdeberget from Eidsbugarden and the other group attempted Stølnostinden from Koldedalen. Both parties were hampered by low cloud but the route up Galdeberget was resolved by accurate compass work and presented no technical difficulties. We all went to Olavsbu from which one group climbed Mjølkedalspiggen whilst the other climbed Mjølkedalstind, both in cloudy and unfavourable conditions. Three of us then walked up to the hut in Stølsmaradalen and made an attempt on Midtmaradalsryggen but allowed the weather to beat us. The other three walked up to the hut at Vettismorki. We had all enjoyed the view of fabulous waterfalls along the valley to Vetti, cascading many hundreds of feet to join the river down Utladalen. The initial walk up to Stølnosi en route to Stølsnostinden was straightforward, but then again we found ourselves in dense mist. Our compass led us over a series of small snowfields to an ancient cairn covered in moss. Our altimeter setting, when checked at the campsite, led us to believe that we had reached the summit.

The departure of our main party signalled a day of good weather and the arrival of two members to camp at Spiterstulen. From then the weather varied from dull and wet to atrocious. It took two attempts before the conditions allowed them to climb Glittertinden. They had a most exhilarating day, with a close view of a golden eagle, and finally reached the summit in a blizzard.

Another pair driving home from Lyngen knocked off Glittertinden and Galdhøpiggen with great glee on successive days. Glittertinden, done from Grønbui via Glitterheim, provided the most excitement because the pair had no map or route description. The near complete whiteout and blizzard reduced the time spent checking that the summit had truly been reached but equally it reduced the risk of discovering that it was corniced! The weather continued wet for the ascent of Galdhøpiggen but they had a series of stunning views of the Jotunheimen peaks during a half-hour period near Keilhaus topp. Then the weather reverted to add more new snow to the existing layer, but this time the summit was positively identified. Their skilled descent by bumsliding made a suitable impression on ascending Norwegians.

Sunnmørsalpene in summer (July)

Of Sunnmørsalpene Slingsby said, they 'are bewitching and are like glorified Coolins of Skye' and 'during the eighties and nineties friends and I practically completed the mountain exploration.'[3]

Two pairs of members met at Sæbø and enjoyed good companionship with the Norwegians, and help from them in organising a helicopter ambulance to move an injured man when one pair slid about 300m down a glacier in full view of the Patchellhytta. Two of us went directly from England to Hjortedalen at the southern edge of Sunnmøre. The next day we walked up Blåbredalen with its long slabs of rock leading up to the snow and made our way to the summit at 1443m, traversed by Slingsby on the way to Storhornet. The pinnacled ridge to the next summit looked very forbidding so we descended to Indre Aksla and down to the camp. We then moved on to Sæbø to meet the other pair and ended up camping together at Ørsta. En route we left the cars, walked up Litledalen and climbed Dalagubben. We found this craggy mountain with its summit ridge straightforward, but much looser and more lichen covered than similar mountains in Scotland. This was one of the fine days, with breathtaking views.

Low cloud was a problem on Kolåstinden. After we had walked up to Kvanndalsskardet we could just distinguish the gap in the ridge which took us onto the main glacier, high on the E side of the mountain. We stayed on the snow following the rocky ridge and climbed a false summit before finding the way to the true summit barred by a huge bergschrund. We frightened ourselves on the moss-covered ridge before descending without reaching the main summit. We then transferred to Patchellhytta just above Øye which provides a comfortable centre for many mountains. The first day, in fine weather, we traversed round the W side of Brekketind, mostly on snow, in order to climb Brunstadhornet from the south. This route enabled us to look at Slogen,

Above Middle Atlas: Jbel bou Iblane from Jbel bou Naceur. (*Hamish Brown*) (p165)

Below Beni Smint with Jbel bou Iblane behind. (*Hamish Brown*) (p165)

53. Indian British Panch Chuli Expedition. Chris Bonington near the summit of Panch Chuli II, 6904m. (*Graham Little*) (p98)

54. The climbing team, from L: Muslim Contractor, Bhupesh Ashar, Wing Cdr Anil Srivastava, Stephen Venables, Chris Bonington, Harish Kapadia, Graham Little (behind), Monesh Devjani, Dick Renshaw, Vijay Kothari, Stephen Sustad, Victor Saunders. (*Graham Little*) (p98)

The traverse of Rajrambha, 6537m. Crossing Menaka summit.
(*Stephen Venables*) (p98)

Above
Caltha palustris himalayensis (marsh marigold)

Facing page, above
Panch Chuli V, 6437m, from the summit of Rajrambha

Facing page, below
Camp on the crossing to the Pyunshani valley.

(*Photos: Stephen Venables*) (p105)

59. *Above* East Greenland: Slangen Pass

60. *Below* P 1720. The ascent followed the mixed snow and rock ridge falling directly from the summit, centrally towards the camera.

   (*Photos: Jim Gregson*) (p136)

Above Looking across 16 September glacier from P 1720

Below Ulimaut in Sermiligaq fjord

(*Photos: Jim Gregson*) (p136)

63. *Asphodelus albus*
    (white asphodel)

64. *Orchis papilionacea*
    (pink butterfly orchid)

65. *Trollius europaeus*
    (globe-flower)

66. *Pulsatilla alpina*
    (alpine pasque-flower)

(*Photos: Teresa Farino*) (p206)

Brekketind and Smørskredtindane, all magnificent mountains with the pointed Slogen as the most notable.

The next day we divided. One pair left early to try for the two higher peaks of Smørskredtindane and the others left later and followed a straightforward route to the eastern summit of Slogen and then on to the main summit. The day started clear but with threatening cloud. Our early pair climbed the ever steepening glacier up to the saddle between the two highest peaks of Smørskredtindane. We descended the other side on poor snow, but the chosen climb proved harder and more continuous than expected so the route was abandoned. Whilst we sat eating, all the surrounding mountains disappeared as a rain storm struck. We decided our luck had run out and that we would have to descend via the saddle and glacier.

Where we had front-pointed up there was now wet sugary snow which looked as though it could avalanche, but it was a badly placed crampon which led to the accident. The belay pulled out. One of the pair who had now returned to the hut from Slogen reported: 'They seemed to fall for an age – two tiny black dots silhouetted against the snow – until they hit a rock band and were lost from sight.' A perfectly organised rescue ensued to take one of the fallen to hospital, whilst the other walked down to the hut with only bruises. Maybe our luck had not run out after all. All the Norwegians helped. They ran to the valley to call the helicopter, brought a blanket up the hillside and allowed us to use their telephone. No one could have done more or done it more pleasantly and unobtrusively.

Lofoten in summer (July/August)

The unique character and beauty of these islands has long been recognised by British mountaineers, who first discovered the attractions of Lofoten at the turn of the century. One of those early pioneers was Slingsby who made extended visits there in 1903 and 1904. He wrote: 'The aiguilles of Lofoten have an uncanny atmosphere about them in addition to their great beauty.'[4]

Our party was twelve strong but the weather was poor; there was rain every day, some of it extended and torrential. The journey by road from Bergen to Lofoten is about 1000 miles and was completed in 2½ days. We spent nearly all our time there at three centres. We started and finished camping near Svolvær and, in between, we camped on a wonderful beach at Buneset and just managed to find space for all of us to camp at Reknes.

Buneset was a short walk over a low pass from the head of Bunesfjorden. Despite the weather, four of us went to look at Bisplua. We abandoned the crumbling northern ridge going up from Vindstad, even though we believed Slingsby had found this route acceptable. We then found a route up a stream and scrambled to a col west of the summit where we climbed half a dozen rock pitches to the feather bed of moss on the small flat summit.

The second day was fine and clear nearly all day and we managed to get a lift by boat to the southern end of Forsfjorden where we divided into two groups. One group went west towards Hermannsdalstinden, fighting our way over boulder strewn slopes covered in thick carpets of sodden moss and, just to make things really interesting, dense birch scrub. We scrambled up onto Brynliskardtind and then onto Klokkaåttetinden. After a slight descent we overcame a steep brown slab by an airy arête onto the N ridge of Hermanns-dalstinden. The summit provided an excellent viewpoint of the stunning ridges on Breidtinden and Ertnhelltinden, which looked incredibly difficult and serious routes. Meanwhile, the other group headed for Munkan, ascending the wooden staircase and following a cairned route to the new hut on the west side of the mountain. The main peak is a pyramid of sound granite whose gentler sloping W ridge appeared to be the easiest route. The worst of the scrub-covered slabs were avoided and only about six short roped pitches were required to reach the summit.

We had four days camping at Reknes and a lot of rain. The weather decided that we only had one day's climbing and we all agreed to go up the Snøskard glacier and look at the W peak of Rulten. Two of the party descended to the west of the col and climbed up onto the ridge but found themselves in a complex tower system with hard climbing, poor visibility and rain. The climb was abandoned. We had repeated sightings of a pair of White Tailed Sea Eagles and felt our short exploration of Rulten was worthwhile if only for a closer view of these magnificent birds.

From the camp at Kabelvåg, we climbed Løva at the beginning of our stay in Lofoten and on our last full day we climbed Svolværgeita, the Goat, above Svolvær and jumped between the horns – a joyful finish!

Lyngsalpene in summer (July/August)

Slingsby wrote of 'the sharp peaked ranges and mysterious haunts of the frost giants about the Lyngen fjord, where nature has, apparently, developed her wildest and most eerie forms.'[5] When Slingsby and friends went to Lyngen the journey took eight days but, despite this, the friends made repeated visits to these mountains. They are still a long way from Bergen, over 1000 miles, but this did not deter our party of fourteen. Our contact with Norwegians was very limited but we were greatly impressed by the efficient way in which they mounted a search and rescue operation late on a Saturday.

On a dubious cloudy morning a group of four of us followed a route of steep scree, steep snow and the short loose SE ridge to the summit of Istind from Urda. A very satisfactory first outing. A similar cloudy morning the next day found us walking from Høgtun through the trees and up the moraine to Isskardbreen with the intention of climbing Trollvasstind and Store Isskartind from Slingsbyskardet. Five of us continued mounting the glacier into a beauti-ful snow bowl surrounded by rock peaks where we had a moment of sunshine. One pair climbed Trollvasstind which proved to be an awkward ascent with large amounts of loose rock and short vertical sections. A good view of Isskartind from Trollvasstind enabled this pair to by-pass a lesser summit and many of the difficulties and ascend Store Isskartind whose summit overhangs a spectacular cliff.

The other pair climbed a lesser summit of Isskartind and then descended and crossed Slingsbyskardet to climb Trollvasstind. During the descent a

boulder came down the mountain and knocked Roger Allen off the cliff onto
the inaccessible N side of the skardet. Shouts brought the whole party together
but brought no response from Roger. During the next few hours two heli-
copters, a rescue team from the Tromsø Alpine Club, the local doctor, and the
police who co-ordinated the operation all arrived. Roger was seen at about
2am and was reached at 2.30am. He had fallen a long way and had died in the
fall.

The next day was sunny but we were all too shocked to decide sensibly what
to do next and mostly we just wandered about aimlessly. There were for-
malities to complete with the police. It was a very edgy and peculiar sort of
day. The contacting of Sue Allen the next day seemed to release most of us
from the feeling that we should hang about any longer. A party of three set off
for North Cape and everyone else went for a walk. Two of us climbed
Kavringtind, south of Lyngseidet, and found Drooping Saxifrage, a plant
which our book did not place in Scandinavia. Soon a little more enthusiasm
for the mountains asserted itself and another ascent was made of Kavringtind
and we visited Koppangsbreen, SW of Lenangstind and climbed Goalbårri. A
solo journey was made of the tops round Gjerdelvvatnan (Kavringtind, Kval-
vikfjellet, Ruksesvargaisi and Rornestinden).

The final day seemed to typify so much of Norway in the summer of 1992.
The morning was remarkably wet so instead of attempting Store Fornestinden
we drove to Kippanger and tried a rather complex compass route through the
cloud and enormous crevasses on Koppangsbreen. However to our astonishment we eventually reached what might have been the correct col for climbing
Store Lenangstinden. Eventually we reached a summit with a small cairn but it
hardly seemed impressive enough to be the true summit. We had all reached
equilibrium wetness – water was running out of clothes and boots as fast as it
was arriving! After that everyone headed south by car.

Epilogue

Slingsby had an enthusiasm for many other places in Norway to which we
were unable to devote much time or where we achieved little. For instance, we
completely neglected Trollheimen because one of the allocated pair suffered a
head injury in a fall and we had no replacement. Other areas where we were
less than successful included Romsdalen, Kjerringøy, Sørfold and Dovrefjell.
Limited space precludes a detailed description of our activities in these areas.
Overall, the weather in Norway during the summer of 1992 was much worse
than usual and we also suffered the great sadness and trauma of two serious
accidents. However, I hope that this article has provided a taste of what was
achieved in the mountains with the help of our Norwegian friends.

The most important result of the project is the friendships that we have made.
A special relationship has developed between the YRC and the Årdal Turlag,
our first overseas kindred club, and we have been honoured with an invitation
to be represented on the management board of the Slingsby Institute, an
organisation founded to foster good relations between Norwegians and Britons
and to strengthen our mutual interest in the wonders of nature.

Participants in the Norsk Project

British

Ken Aldred	David Hick	Howard Papworth
Mike Allen	Howard Humphreys	Neil Pomfret
Roger Allen	Jason Humphreys	Roy Pomfret
John Barton	Raymond Ince	Peter Price
Alan Brown	Mike Kinder	Arthur Salmon
Kevin Brown	Cliff Large	Graham Salmon
Derek Bush	Alan Linford	John Schofield
Cliff Cobb	Angie Linford	David Smith
Dorothy Crowther	Paul Linford	Fiona & Richard Smith
Ian Crowther	Harvey Lomas	Helen Smith
John Devenport	Duncan Mackay	Mike Smith
Iain Gilmour	David Martindale	Derek Smithson
Marcia Godden	Pam Mayhew	John Snoad
Mike Godden	Ainsley Mayhew-Seers	John Sterland
Steve Goulden	John Medley	Sue Thompson
David Hall	Rory Newman	

Norwegian

Johnny Bruheim	Petter Arnt Løvdahl	Arve Tvedt
Steinar Bruheim	Jan Schwarzott	Kjetil Tveranger
Edvin Folven	Vidar Søyseth	Rune Valsvik
Rein Arne Golf	Johan Støyva	Biko, the dog

ACKNOWLEDGEMENTS

We would like to thank the following non-members for their valuable help with the Norsk Project: Erling Eggum of the Klingenberg Fjordhotel, Finn Hagen of Den Norsk Turistforening (DNT), Pat and Peter Lennon of Mountain and Wildlife Ventures, Hedi Lund, Petter Arnt Løvdahl of Årdal Turlag, Arild Meyer, Jan Schwarzott, John Snoad, Johan Støyva, Kjetil Tveranger of Florø Turlag, and Jocelin Winthrop Young.

REFERENCES

1 William Cecil Slingsby, *Norway: the northern playground*. D Douglas (Edinburgh), 1904.
2 Geoffrey Winthrop Young: Biographical Notice in *Norway: the northern playground* by W C Slingsby. Blackwell's Mountaineering Library, 1941.
3 William Cecil Slingsby, *Norway: the northern playground*. D Douglas (Edinburgh), 1904.
4 *Ibid*
5 *Ibid*

New Directions

ROB COLLISTER
Mountains and Running

I was near the top of Scafell, soaked to the skin and not warm. The showers of the previous hours had settled to a heavy, persistent rain which was cascading down the gully in little waterfalls. Although it was the end of May, my fingers were numb. My feet, in Walsh running shoes, were numb too, and skating about on the greasy rock. It was growing dark – there was perhaps half an hour to nightfall. I realised that this could not be Broad Stand but, on the other hand, I had no torch and there was not enough time to descend and find the right way. It had to be up.

I was 200ft above the screes at a bulging constriction. The only feasible route was out of the gully – more of a chimney by now – to the right. I made a long step across to straddle the gap, trusting my feet not at all on flat slippery ledges. Then I needed a handhold to pull myself across but nothing seemed quite positive enough for frozen fingers. Yet to retreat from here would not only be difficult but would mean benightment. I lurched across with a heave and a prayer and scrambled up into a grassy haven.

There was no going back now. But I quickly realised that the difficulties were far from over. With more than a hint of panic, I tried first a greasy slab on the right, then a steep corner on the left, liking the look of neither. The likelihood of a bivouac crossed my mind, but it did not bear contemplating. I was dressed in trackster bottoms, a T-shirt and a thin sweater, under a lightweight cag that ceased to be waterproof years ago. I had been running for 13 or 14 hours in a circuit of the lakeland fells. I had no food left in my bum-bag. I would be hypothermic in minutes, let alone hours, if I stopped moving.

Settling for the slab, I found myself poised on small holds, with little of relevance for my fingers and no faith at all in the studded soles of my shoes. One leg started to shake. I was conscious of gloomy space beneath me. I was frightened, and angry at getting myself into such a situation. Before my foot could be shaken off, I made the stretch upwards, right hand settling on a rounded hold just as my left foot shot off. The hold was not enough. Both knees scrabbled on the slab giving just enough purchase for the fingers of my left hand to claw into a tuft of grass. Heart thumping, blood racing, I hauled myself up.

No time to waste. Stumbling on into the gloaming I emerged onto the upper slopes of Scafell to meet the full blast of a gale. Quickly, I visited the summit and returned a few yards to where a small path dropped down the other side of the ridge. The map I had borrowed had been trimmed at the 2000ft contour and I had to assume that downwards would lead to Wasdale. Scree soon turned to grass, and even after I had lost the path I was able to continue running through the dark. Once, I nearly tripped over a startled fox. Eventually, I hit a stony track running beside the boundary wall of some woodland. Civilisation could not be far away. Finally, the dim glow of an interior light loomed up ahead and, with relief, I joined Alan and Joy in the warmth of their little car, where they had been waiting for some time. Every so often a violent gust would rock it alarmingly. The rain beat on the windows. Without regret, I called off my attempt on the Bob Graham round.

Fell running is what you make it. It can be just a branch of athletics; equally, it can be a form of mountaineering as rewarding as any other. For me, it provides a greater sense of personal freedom than either hill-walking or roped climbing, and it need not be lacking in adventure ... Walkers have always been a little scornful of runners for their cavalier treatment of the hills. You can't see much of your surroundings, they argue. And it is true, you don't notice much except the stones at your feet when you are grinding up to Bochlwyd or skipping from rock to rock over the Glyderau. But perception can be intensified by fatigue and views are all the more wonderful for the effort expended. Striding out over the turf of the northern Carneddau or bounding down the long ridge that leads from Moel Siabod to the Pen y Gwryd, I, for one, know a delight and an exuberance rarely felt at other times. Sights, sounds, sensations may be absorbed fleetingly, subliminally even, but they have a powerful effect and the bubbling sense of well-being that follows a mountain run goes beyond the merely physical. It is a gladness of spirit, never experienced running on a road, that grows out of the cloud song of skylarks, the casual acrobatics of a raven, the sparkle of raindrops on grass after a shower, the spongy softness of sphagnum underfoot, the rich glowing green of polytrichum moss in evening sunlight, or the sudden clap of wings as three terrified pigeons hurtle past, a peregrine in hot pursuit. All those individual strands that make up the texture of a mountain day are amplified by the effort and absorption of running. Much detail in the landscape fabric is missed by passing swiftly over it, but that which registers has an immediacy and impact unknown to the more sedate traveller. It is more akin to the experience of the climber who may notice the cluster of crystals in a pocket, the tiny fern sprouting from the back of a crevice, the flow-banding in the rock at his feet, but is rarely in a position to linger over them.

One of my favourite ways of enjoying the hills is to combine running with soloing relatively easy climbs. This introduces dramatic changes in pace and focus, while demanding even greater concentration. I well remember one outing of this type. It was during a grey, cold spell in October; perfect weather for running, chilly on the fingers for climbing. Starting later than intended on the Amphitheatre Buttress of Craig yr Ysfa, I ran by way of Carnedd Llewelyn and classic climbs on Tryfan, the Idwal Slabs and Glyder Fawr down into the Llanberis Pass. By the time I reached Cyrn Las the autumn day was drawing to a close. I had run many miles and climbed 2500ft of rock. All went well, however, until that point near the top of Main Wall where it becomes necessary to move left round an arête onto a steep wall overhanging a deep, dark gully. It must be one of the most exposed pitches in Wales. As I stepped round, my fingers reached that degree of cold when it is hard to tell whether they have a firm grip or not, when even large holds do not feel quite large or incut enough. For several minutes I was uncomfortably aware that there was not another soul in Cwm Glas, night was drawing in, there were hundreds of feet of air beneath me, and I did not relish down climbing what I had come up. Finally, I made the moves. Adrenalin propelled me up the rest of the climb and onto Crib y Ddysgl, where gravity took over and I jogged contentedly down the zigzags to Glaslyn. I was weary, but acutely conscious of my surroundings, so familiar and yet so strange: the silent, empty cwm, a yellow, rising moon reflected in the dark water of the lake, and Snowdon hulking hugely overhead. I slept well that night.

Of course, not every excursion has to be quite so strenuous, nor does it have to become an epic to be memorable. One of the attractions of both running and soloing is the amount you can do in a short space of time. It is possible, for example, to squeeze in a climb, or a mountain, or both, before breakfast . . . Early one summer's morning, when mist was rising from the edges of the Mymbyr lakes and the reflection of the Snowdon Horseshoe was marred only by the dimples of rising trout, I left the car at Pen y Pass and jogged sleepy-legged up to Lliwedd. A red sky in the west and a lurid yellow light from the rising sun were soon smothered by grey stratus, with a few sinister lenticulars hanging beneath like Zeppelins, that boded no good. No matter, I would be up and away before the weather broke.

There was no one about except a few indifferent sheep and a pair of noisy ravens. The grass was bright with specks of colour: yellow tormentil, blue milkwort, pink lousewort – strange names but much loved, and inseparably associated with summer in the hills. On the crag, bell heather was in bloom, the bilberries not yet ripe. The rock was dry after a long spell of fine weather and warm to the touch from the early sun. The climbing, nearly 1000ft of it, was a delicate delight, with sloping holds for the feet and pinch-grips for the fingers. It would be a nightmare in the wet. I referred to the guidebook once or twice, for lines on Lliwedd are not obvious and it is easy to climb into difficulties. But most of the time I simply followed holds well-worn by the nailed boots of previous generations. I felt myself the inheritor of Archer Thompson and Winthrop Young and thought of that day when Mallory dislodged a boulder near the top, setting off an avalanche that gave the route its name.

I emerged onto the summit to be startled by demonic shrieks and roars from Cwm y Llan far below. Then the penny dropped: shepherds were gathering the sheep for shearing. On Bwlch y Saethau, the Pass of the Arrows, where Arthur fought his last battle they say, a man was leaning on his crook, shouting to his dogs. I bade him good morning and received a perfunctory nod in return. I was not surprised. Welsh farmers, unlike their Lakeland counterparts, have never seen mountains as anything other than grazing land, and regard any other activity upon them with an attitude that varies from amused indifference to angry contempt. But then, both their language and their way of life are sore-pressed these days. Perhaps a defensive attitude is inevitable. I shrugged resignedly and ran on up the steep screes of the Watkin Path, not much faster than walking, probably, but good for legs and lungs, I tell myself. And so to the highest point in England and Wales where, as yet, all was quiet.

Way below, the water of Llydaw and Teryn and the distant Mymbyr lakes glinted in the grey-blue mistiness, enfolded by the arms of Siabod and the Glyderau. In the east, too, lakes were the only features to stand out from the enveloping haze – silver reflections up on the Moelwyns, around Manod, and, farthest of all, little Llyn Conwy set in the boggy heath of the Migneint. A one-legged herring-gull cocked its head hopefully but I had nothing to give it.

Over the airy crests of Crib y Ddysgl and Crib Goch I ran with care, making it a point of honour to balance along the knife-edge, then, stride lengthening, down the path and back to Pen y Pass. I glanced at my watch. It was exactly three hours since I had left the car. There was time for a quick cup of coffee in Capel Curig before starting work. Rain was in the air; the best of the day was over. But I did not mind. I had made the most of it and in my pocket was a keepsake – a small but perfect crystal from one of the stony ledges of Lliwedd.

MARK DIGGINS
A Flight of Fancy

Our intention, on that March morning, was to ski to the foot of the Aiguille Verte, climb the Couturier Couloir and, having reached the top, to 'take off' attached to the parachutes we had in our rucksacks. This form of transport for the descent had obvious attractions – no scary abseils, no jarred knees, and the convenience of 'floating' down to the valley base – easy! Why then, having wobbled, climbing boots on skis, to the foot of the climb, were we scared out of our minds? And why, as we approached the summit, were we getting more and more anxious, when normally anxiety levels decrease as one gets nearer to the top? The fact was, this was a gamble. Would we find an adequate take-off area? Would the wind be coming in the right direction? Or would we be blown backwards into oblivion? These questioning thoughts were in my mind as we bashed our way up the interminable couloir. The ice was hard and my mind was occupied. Half-way up we reached some unstable snow and detoured off to the right through the rocks, up narrow ice runnels, steeper but more interesting. Eventually we reached the top of the couloir and the angle relented. The climbing became tedious and my mind wandered to the events which had brought us to this situation.

I recalled, three or four years earlier, our first parapenting lessons. Our 'tutor' was an obsessed American sky diver who believed that you did not need to jump out of aeroplanes in order to fly, that you could take off on foot with a wind in your face, and that the chute could be made to come up above your head and fly like a kite. Then, as you advanced forward at a jogging pace, the canopy would assume a more rigid wing shape and develop lift, carrying you into the air. The lighter the wind, the more you had to run; and in a strong wind you might not need to run at all.

That was the theory, but for Paul Aubrey and me there was to be no gradual learning process. For our first lesson we were simply strapped into the harness and told what to hold on to as, with a fixed stare, we ran down the hill hoping that the bundle of rags dragging along behind us would assume a regular shape, float above our heads, and lift us off the ground. Steve, who must have been an 'adrenalin junkie', had provided some spicy obstacles: once airborn, ie five feet off the ground, we were asked to turn left to avoid a pine tree, change course again to avoid a hay rake and barn, and then land precisely in front of a house. Failure to do so would result in hitting the side of the house at about the ten foot mark. Paul executed his first flight amazingly well, miraculously (as it seemed to me) avoiding all obstacles. I have to admit that I declined this initial opportunity on account of my too fertile imagination. On his second flight, Paul twisted his ankle on take-off, his foot going down a rabbit hole.

Our next opportunity came some months later but we had, meanwhile, put much thought into how to learn more safely. We had spent days familiarising ourselves with the canopies by flying them over our heads like kites. The main controls are by lines which go from each hand to the back corner of the canopy. You steer to the left or right by pulling down with the left or right hand. By pulling both 'brakelines' together you can slow down your forward movement but your descent rate increases. I discovered that the canopy was remarkably sensitive.

It was now winter and we wore skis for our next attempts. We started on small snow-covered hills; skiing into the wind the chutes filled easily and take-offs and landing went smoothly – too smoothly for Steve, who decided that we now needed 'big air' experience. Paul and I smelt danger but we too were getting hooked on the adrenalin that paragliding gives. We took a cable-car to the top of a peak and searched around for a slope with a moderate angle and a slight breeze blowing up it. Unfortunately for us we were unable to find a perfect location, so Steve chose one that was 'second best'. This was a steep slope of about 45 to 50 degrees. Steve assured us that our increased speed would inflate the chutes more quickly. I sincerely hoped so. A further complication was that we had to take off quickly in order to clear the cable-car wires that lay in our flight path. If they could not be cleared a landing would have to be forced on avalanche debris. I felt quite nervous as I embedded my ski heels into the slope, climbed onto my skis, strapped myself in, took hold of the cords – and looked down the 1000ft or so to the bottom. I set off at a remarkable speed with my eyes half shut, and immediately the chute inflated, pulled at my harness and lifted me into the air. I cleared the cable-car wires with a few hundred feet to spare and landed comfortably on the frozen lake below. Paul was less fortunate; he had not been able to clear the wires but had landed unscathed in the avalanche debris.

Having survived our initiation into parapenting we spent the next few years consolidating our skills and introducing other climbing friends to the sport. It didn't all go smoothly and I can recall many injuries and 'landings' into the top of pine trees. On one occasion, when coming in to land, I veered to avoid an unseen telephone wire and unavoidably went crashing through a tree, ending up suspended and looking down into the astonished eyes of a large group of people who, until then, had been enjoying a peaceful barbecue. With their wide eyes and toasting forks they looked slightly menacing. I broke the ice by saying 'bonjour', which only increased their amusement and my own embarrassment. All this was a useful learning experience.

During this time Paul and I were strongly attracted to the mountain tops. We enjoyed the whole process: choosing the mountain, the climb up it and the flight back down. But the game gradually became more serious and the pressure increased to take off when it would have been more prudent to retreat on foot. As we approached the summit of the Aiguille Verte the gravity of the situation was all too apparent and questions regarding wind direction and strength and suitable take-off sites loomed large in our minds. We had checked the weather forecast: blue skies, a light wind from the south-west, all should have been perfect. However, as we climbed the summit ridge above 4000m, things were quite different. The wind was from the north-east and was blowing strong and cold. The summit failed to provide us with the usual elation; our minds were too much occupied with getting down. We had hoped to take off from a shoulder on the Dru side of the mountain, which would have been perfect with the wind from the south-west. Instead, we had a tail wind of about 20mph running straight down the ridge and making a take-off impossible. We decided to wait for an hour or so to see if the wind abated. The alternative to flying down was a cold bivouac and a descent down the Whymper couloir in the morning – not a pleasant prospect – and now it would be too dangerous from avalanche and stonefall.

We soon realised that the wind was not going to drop, so we would have to take off across it. We ascended to a levelling of the ridge and chose our take-off point. We had enough area to lay out the canopy on the southern side of the ridge while we ourselves stood on the northern side looking down the Nant Blanc face and into the void below. There was no room for a running take-off and no room for error. Two paces was all we had to the top of the 3000ft ice face. The wind was from the right. We talked at great length about what the wind might do to our canopies and we reckoned that, having pulled the chute up into the wind, the canopy would be twisted and slammed down to the left. We would then have to stand firm and pump the brake to bring it back up and, in a split second, make that enormous committing decision to go. Paul elected to go first and I would stand behind him roped up ready to grab hold of him if he lost control. We were prepared and outwardly in command of the situation, but inside my heart was pounding, my tongue was bloated in a dry mouth and I could hardly speak from nervousness.

Paul lifted the canopy into the air and it behaved as we expected – but it was moving really fast and as he pumped forcefully on the right brake the canopy came up above his head in an instant, and he turned and went! It all seemed to have happened in a flash and I could hear him whooping with relief somewhere down below. Suddenly I felt very lonely. I coiled the rope and put it in my sack; the wind seemed to get colder and my heart was pounding. I hoped that my canopy would behave in the same way that Paul's had – I did not dare to contemplate anything else. I was totally committed to jumping and the situation felt very scary. I tried to breathe slowly and move methodically as I strapped myself in. I checked that the chute was laid out correctly and that the lines were not twisted. Then, with a sharp intake of breath, I moved my arms and lifted the mouth of the canopy into the wind. It filled with a loud clap and pulled strongly to the left, almost unbalancing me. I released the left brake and pulled on the right, shouting at the canopy 'Come on, come on!' It came up above my head and I felt the upward pressure on my shoulder – I stepped and went, and in that instant saw the bottom of the face 3000ft below.

I whooped with relief and steared towards the Dru but now I was becoming aware of my cold hands and headed down to the valley. I circled above the sunny meadow in Les Praz and touched down quite close to Paul. We shook hands, aware of how much we had risked. The grass was warm and the early spring flowers were emerging. We lay there for a while feeling the warm sun while I waited for the hot aching in my fingers to subside. Then we went for a cup of tea and sat quietly contemplating the implications of what we had done. Yes, it could be a serious game, and one shouldn't allow it to take over. Since that memorable day in March 1989 I have had no desire to fly again.

Looking back

TREVOR BRAHAM

John Tyndall (1820–1893) and Belalp

(Plates 74, 75)

Belalp 2137m has a magnificent situation on the northern edge of the main alpine chain where it joins the Bernese alps. To the south, rising above the Rhone valley and Brig which can be clearly seen, there is a panorama of mountains, dominated by Monte Leone, situated to the east and west of the Simplon pass. To the north the Aletschhorn and Nesthorn are hidden behind rocky spurs which divide subsidiaries of the main Aletsch glacier, whilst to the north-east the ridge of the Eggishorn descends gently to the popular tourist areas of Bettmeralp, Riederalp and the Aletschwald. The great charm of Belalp is its relative isolation which has enabled it to preserve an atmosphere of unspoilt beauty so rarely found nowadays in an alpine resort. Once considered difficult of access, Belalp can today be reached by a motor road from Brig via Naters and Blatten, 1322m. At Blatten a cable-car transports summer visitors (and winter skiers) in 15 minutes to the top station at the western end of the alp. But a much more interesting approach from Blatten village is along narrow well-worn tracks through rich mostly conifer forest, climbing at first gently then more steeply before breaking out above the treeline to the edge of the alp. This is dotted with no more than a handful of dwellings locally populated in the summer but abandoned in winter. A single foot-track stretches across the alp from west to east providing a panoramic terrace facing south. At the far eastern end of the alp stands the only major building in the area, the Belalp Hotel, which seems to be poised directly above the massive final sweep of the Grosse Aletschgletscher.

Belalp Hotel, or rather a wooden inn containing 10–12 rooms, was built in 1858 by Leopold Bürcher-Anderledy. In 1861 Gervas Klingele, who was then operating three hotels in Brig, obtained a part interest in Belalp and by 1866 he became the sole proprietor of the hotel. Thereafter the large stone building as seen today was constructed.[1]

The hotel's most prosperous period occurred between 1870 and 1890, alongside the development of mountaineering in Switzerland. Over 80% of the summer visitors were English, and between June and September each year the hotel was filled to capacity; this despite the long 1500m climb from Brig on foot or by muleback, and for ladies in a sedan-chair carried by four porters. The outlines of a tennis court, laid out for the benefit of the hotel's English guests, can still be seen today! The Belalp Hotel was run by members of the Klingele family for over 100 years until the summer of 1968, when its proprietorship passed into the hands of the present owners, the family of Thérèse Jaeger-Eggel. Caesar Jaeger, son of Thérèse, writing to me recently, has hinted that the family are in discussion with a group of persons who are interested in acquiring the hotel for redevelopment and extension. If the inevitable should happen, I for one will be immensely thankful for the privilege of having been a guest at the hotel whilst it still breathed what seemed to me an atmosphere and charm not very different from that experienced by so many distinguished earlier visitors. Amongst these were A W Moore, F F Tuckett, Horace Walker, A A Reilly, C E Mathews, Miss Brevoort, W A B Coolidge, John Tyndall and many others, as entries in the Visitors' Book, commencing in 1861, amply illustrate.[2]

John Tyndall made his first acquaintance with Belalp on 13 August 1861, six days prior to his success in achieving the first ascent of the Weisshorn with the guide J J Bennen, and a year before his climb with Bennen and the brothers Carrel to the shoulder on the Italian ridge of the Matterhorn which is still referred to as Tyndall peak. The 'alpine wildness' of Belalp appealed strongly to Tyndall, and he wrote that he considered the view from there to be 'the most beautiful in the Alps'. Shortly after his marriage to Louisa, daughter of Lord Claude Hamilton, in July 1876, Tyndall received permission from the town council at Naters to construct a villa on the Lusgen meadow above Belalp. Although the price of the land was fixed at SFr 900, Tyndall donated altogether SFr 2512 to the school and other local causes.[3] The villa was ready for occupation in November 1877. It stands above the Belalp Hotel and the little chapel which dates from the same period. Although Tyndall built his 'London' home in the Surrey hills near Hindhead, he regarded the Villa Lusgen as his 'spiritual' home. Here he returned year after year to wander, to meditate, to work, and to entertain friends. The villa is regarded by some as ugly. It has never seemed to me that it fits wholly into the landscape, sitting there inexactly as some piece of foreign creation. Following his first visit in 1861 Tyndall visited Belalp every summer until 1893. In 1887 the Naters Town Council elected him to honorary citizenship, citing his kindness and loyalty to the people and the medical assistance that he regularly provided to the sick during a period of over 25 years. His last sojourn at the Villa Lusgen took place during September and October 1893, shortly prior to his death at Hindhead on 4 December 1893. His wife Louisa continued to visit the villa for several years, spending a few weeks there during the summer. She died in 1940 at the age of 95. In 1964 her nephew Sir Richard Proby sold the property to a Swiss buyer who still owns the villa today. It is rarely occupied. Its future conversion into a museum filled with Tyndall memorabilia would seem to me to provide the villa with more purpose.

Above the Villa Lusgen, where the alp rises to an eminence before falling gently to a rolling expanse that leads to the foot of the Sparrhorn ridge, stands an impressive granite stone, drawn from a nearby glacier, which was raised to John Tyndall's memory by his wife. The Communal authorities at Naters maintain the area, and have installed notices directing visitors to the memorial. The stone, simply engraved, commands a superb aspect in every direction and conveys a sense of loneliness and dignity. It is isolated from view until one is almost within its reach. The unveiling of the memorial took place on a

Sunday at the hour of sunset on 27 August 1911 in the presence of a large local company and invited guests including members of the Swiss Alpine Club which had elected Tyndall as their third Honorary Member. The ceremony was followed by a dinner at the Belalp Hotel and a fireworks display.

1993 marks the hundredth anniversary of John Tyndall's death. It would be nice to think of a small group from the AC gathering at the Belalp chapel and at the monument in remembrance of one of their former Honorary Members.

NOTES AND ACKNOWLEDGEMENTS

1 I am grateful to Barbara Dangar for passing on to me originals of the correspondence exchanged in the years 1947–48 between her husband and A Klingele, grandson of Gervas Klingele, about the history of the Belalp Hotel.

2 For details of the earliest Visitors' Book of the Belalp Hotel, see article by D F O Dangar 'Early Expeditions from Bel Alp', *AJ56*, 347, Nov 1948.

3 I acknowledge my thanks to the Communal Authorities in Naters for information about the Villa Lusgen, Tyndall's honorary citizenship of Naters and the Tyndall memorial, together with other details about Tyndall's connections with Switzerland based upon research carried out by Peter Rudolf Merz (1928–1975) of Visp and Dr Werner Sackmann of Basel.

T A H PEACOCKE

Five Times on the Matterhorn

My first attempt on the Matterhorn was in 1935. In two previous seasons it had been on the agenda, but on both occasions conditions had made it impossible. This summer I had been climbing with three friends, first at Saas Fee and then at Zermatt. We had some success at Saas, but very little was achieved at Zermatt owing to continuous bad weather. One morning we had ventured out to do the Matterhorn Couloir on the Riffelhorn in the teeth of a violent wind, sleet and storm, with icy water streaming down my sleeves and out at my boots! After this we were confined to the flesh-pots of the Monte Rosa Hotel. Staying at the Monte Rosa was very reasonable in those days. Full pension was 11 or 12 Swiss francs per day, with the pound worth 18 francs. Finally my three friends could stand the weather no longer and departed to North Wales.

As soon as they had gone the barometer started to rise. I had another week's holiday and no companions, so I engaged a young guide named Adrian Lagger; we joined forces with Dr N S Finzi, the celebrated radiologist, who had the redoubtable Franz Biner as guide. We did a traverse of the Ober Gabelhorn straight from Zermatt, starting at 1am. There was no Rothorn hut then, only the Trift Hotel which was exorbitant and only saved 1½ hours. I remember Finzi having some difficulty with the Grand Gendarme and saying 'Pull, Franz', whereupon Franz, a man of enormous strength, lifted the doctor bodily with one arm.

Two days later I decided to go for the Matterhorn with Adrian. We walked up to the Hörnli hut in four hours; there was no cable car in those days. The weather had been really hot in the valley but was cold at the hut; after all, the date was now 7 September. There was no guardian in the hut, just a young German climber who said he was going to do the climb alone – a piece of extreme foolishness. We got the fire going, cooked our usual soup and retired to bed. Next day it was extremely cold and we did not get off until 6am. The sunrise was perfect, but a strong NW wind was blowing. After climbing the little bit of steep rock just above the hut, we traversed on to the E face, zigzagging about up ribs and along couloirs. Here we were reasonably sheltered from the wind, but we met it in full force when we regained the E ridge. We soon reached the old hut, now a ruin, where we halted for some refreshment. We were being followed by the *Alleingänger* who had no idea how to find the way. We continued, keeping close to the E ridge, to the Moseley slab which gave us about 100ft of nice rough rock and so reached the Solvay hut at 9am, where we had a second breakfast, and the *Alleingänger* arrived. He had the cheek to offer my guide 15 francs to take him to the top! This without any reference to me. Adrian promptly refused. I was much relieved when he decided to stay in the hut, for he had been an anxiety to us on the way up.

We left the Solvay at 9.30 and, after climbing the upper Moseley slab, we dodged about on the E face until we reached the shoulder. Here we struck up a snow slope and then along the ridge where we met the full force of the gale. The snow took us to the final rock buttress, and here we found fixed ropes and chains; in the prevailing conditions this part would have been extremely difficult without them. We could see the Whymper couloir to the right where the 1865 accident occurred. Though less steep than the buttress, it was very smooth and lacking in holds. It looked a bad place.

Above the buttress, the angle eased considerably with mixed snow and rock. We reached the top at 11.45, five and three-quarter hours from the Hörnli. The view was perfect; however, the wind was so strong and the cold so intense that we only waited two minutes. My left hand in a glove was numb and had to have the circulation restored, accompanied by the usual agonising feeling which Mummery so aptly described 'as though your fingers were being slit with red-hot knives'.

The descent to the Solvay, where we arrived at 1.30, was uneventful. Here I offered to put the lone German on our rope, but he declined and started down with infinite slowness. We stayed in the hut for about an hour and had a good meal, a rest and enjoyed the superb views to the east. Then we set off down and soon caught up with the German. We told him to follow close behind so that he did not knock stones on to us. The rocks of the little rock-wall were now iced over, and we had to take a route more to the left. I said to Adrian that we should see the German down this part, but he disagreed and said he was sure he would be all right, so we went on to the hut. There we found several people manning a telescope and watching the antics of our *Alleingän-ger*, who could not climb down. He took out his rope and attempted an abseil, but he failed to fix the rope securely and it came off the knob! He fell backwards down the last bit. There was a gasp from the onlookers and we all hurried to the place. We carried him to the little hotel which is next to the hut, and telephoned for a doctor and a mule; he had, in fact, sprained his ankle and had to spend the night in the hotel and be taken down the next day. We were delayed for over an hour by this incident and did not get back to the Monte Rosa until after 8pm, where I received a tumultuous welcome and a most excellent dinner washed down with a good bottle of Munich beer.

My next ascent was in 1938 in a party of three with George Meade-King and David Hodgkinson. After a few days of bad weather, which foiled designs on the Zmutt ridge, the barometer was rising again, so we decided to make for the Hörnli hut and climb the Matterhorn by the ordinary way, as my two friends had not been up the mountain . We reached the hut at 4.30pm, to find six others there already and more on the way. The Hörnli was very small in those days and only held 20. I was thankful to get up at 3am, after a very poor night packed like sardines, in order to light the fire.

The morning of 24 August was fine and we got off at 4am. We were not the only aspirants to the summit; there were at least 20 others, but we were fortunately in the lead and clear of their stones! We reached the Solvay in three hours and halted for a second breakfast. Two guided parties now unfor-tunately passed us. The conditions above the Solvay were bad, with about a foot of fresh snow, and the wind was strong and cold, though not so severe as in 1935. The parties in front were very slow going up the fixed ropes on the ridge above the shoulder and held us up, but they would not let us through. We reached the top at 11am, three hours from the Solvay. The view was perfect, without a cloud; a pity we could not enjoy it, as it was much too cold to linger. However, we could see the great E ridge of the Dent d'Hérens which we planned to climb in two or three days' time, given fine weather.

We started down first, ahead of the two guided parties. At the top of the second long rope we met an oddly assorted ascending party: an old guide, a young girl and a young Swiss man. The girl was obviously exhausted and David went down the rope to the first platform to help her up. Unfortunately the rope joining David to George got entangled with the girl's rope, and the young man's rope became twisted round the piton holding the fixed rope. Added to all this, the first guided parties came down from the summit and rudely pushed past us; this meant that there were now four people on a platform four feet square! The girl had hysterics; she was shivering with cold and quite exhausted. There was a perfect cats' cradle of ropes. The first guide made no attempt to help the poor girl – I was furious with him, particularly as he had kept us waiting on the way up, and I dressed him down in Schweizer-deutsch. Everyone was talking at once, and no one understood a word the others said. George, amazingly serene as usual, kept perfectly calm. Then the second guided party arrived from the summit and also pushed past, making things even worse. Meanwhile I was getting colder and colder and more and more angry but eventually, having decided to unrope myself, I was able to disentangle the ropes. At last, after half an hour of chaos, we could continue down and the old guide started to drag the poor girl to the top. We got to the Hörnli hut at 6.15 and down to Zermatt at 8, where we had a warm welcome and an excellent dinner, washed down with a bottle of Bouvier.

My third attempt had to wait until the war was over. I had a great desire to climb the Zmutt ridge, and I did get the chance in 1947 with Gordon MacKay and A M Binnie. On 17 August we left the Schönbiel hut at 2.15am, the weather looked perfect, but there was a cloud on the summit of the Matterhorn. This approach to the Zmutt ridge from the Schönbiel, the tradi-tional way, is very tedious. The modern route from the Hörnli hut is much shorter. We first had to make a long descent and cross a wilderness of stones up the side of the small glacier leading to the little col where Mummery bivouacked on the first ascent. We then crossed more moraine to reach the couloir which runs up to the start of the snow ridge. This couloir gave us better rock which ran to a broad ledge. From this we made the mistake of climbing too far to the right, up steep rocks which led to the side of a hard ice arête. We then lost some time traversing further left to gain the snow ridge lower down. The time was 8.15 and we stopped for a second breakfast. Then, wearing crampons, we continued up the delicate icy crest of the ridge. The view on the left, of the Matterhorn glacier far below, was most impressive.

We reached the start of the gendarmes at 9.15. The rocks were not difficult, but it was slow going because Binnie was having difficulty in climbing carrying the rope in his hand. It took us two hours to cross the gendarmes, known as the Dents de Zmutt, and so reach the upper rocky ridge. The rocks, though steep, were well provided with good holds and we made reasonable progress, but higher up the arête steepened and became increasingly difficult owing to snow on the rocks and poor holds.

The position was becoming unpleasant. There were no belays and Binnie was experiencing greater and greater difficulty. We had to climb one at a time and Binnie frequently needed help. The last 200ft were a stern business. I managed to reach a small platform about a foot square, with no belay. I called to Binnie to come up, but he said 'I can't climb this, you will have to pull me'. I looked down many thousand feet to the Matterhorn glacier below. I pulled him to my little platform and told him to stand still while I finished the pitch. I climbed the snow-covered rocks with great care. A slip on my part and the whole party would have fallen 3000ft to the glacier. At last I reached the little shoulder and found a good hold. I have never said a more fervent 'thank God' than on this occasion. I now took in Binnie's rope and Gordon quickly joined us. The time was now 1.30.

We now climbed up more easily to the foot of the overhang where a traverse to the right is necessary. The correct way is up a little slabby couloir to reach another sloping ledge which leads back to the left to the upper part of the ridge. I did not dare to make this traverse as I could not have held the party should anyone slip. The Tiefenmatten face is a slabby place with no holds and demands absolute steadiness. I had no alternative but to go on up and up, hour after hour. Eventually we reached Carrel's Corridor, a broad ledge leading to the upper Zmutt ridge. At one point the ledge is broken by a 50ft drop. Here I said we must do an abseil, but Binnie said that he could not do this, so we lowered him down and soon abseiled down to him. This was the famous place where, on the first ascent from Italy in 1865, a few days after Whymper's successful ascent from the Swiss side, the Abbé Gorret lowered Carrel to reach the top while he unselfishly stayed behind to pull Carrel up again on his return.

From the foot of the abseil we continued easily along the corridor to reach the upper part of the ridge and then, after pleasant climbing, reached the summit at 4.45. We had climbed the Zmutt! But what a time we had taken – 14½ hours. Had I realised that Binnie would be so slow I would never have taken him up. To be fair to him, he was much out of practice because of the intervening war years, whereas I was very fit having been training the Lovat Scouts in mountaineering. Binnie was in fact a very steady and safe climber and I was probably needlessly apprehensive. On the summit I felt the strain and had to sample the contents of a certain flask. The weather was perfect, without a cloud in the sky. We were seen from Zermatt making tea on the top of the Matterhorn! After a brief snack we set off down expecting to reach Zermatt that night, but owing to the party's extreme slowness we had to spend the night in the Solvay hut. We had a frugal meal of the remains of our provisions before we turned in. The next morning we soon sped down to the Hörnli, and reached Zermatt at 12.45. We had a mild celebration in the evening and drank a bottle of Bouvier in honour of the Zmutt and to the memory of Mummery who made the first ascent.

My fourth ascent of the Matterhorn was two years later, in 1949. I had been able to persuade my climbing companion of pre-war days, David Hodgkinson, now married with a family, to join me. On 19 August there was a perfect morning, but with a strong wind high up, and we left for the Schönbiel to do the Zmutt. We intended to descend the Italian ridge, stay the night in the Italian hut and then do the great E ridge of the Dent d'Hérens; an ambitious programme. Next day the weather looked perfect and we were the first party away, at 2.30am. Having done this climb only two years before, I found the route quite easily. We only had a folding candle lantern which unfortunately went out and proved very difficult to relight owing to the wind. In the couloir beyond the little col the rock was loose and we could not avoid dislodging some stones. We warned the two guided parties below us to take shelter, but they called on us to stop. We were most reluctant to do this as we did not want to lose time, and we became the recipients of some rude remarks. We soon managed to cross over to more solid rock in the right fork of the couloir.

Two guided parties now overtook us, but we all kept close together and reached the start of the snow ridge at 6.30. Here we sampled the contents of our thermos, for the weather was cold. In 40 minutes we were at the Dents de Zmutt and moved quickly along these. As we were only two, and I had such an excellent companion, we made much better progress than last time. The arête beyond the Dents de Zmutt was surprisingly easy without the fresh snow which had hindered us so much in 1947. We reached the shoulder at 10 and after ascending another 200ft we traversed right. It is a nasty slabby place like the tiles on the roof of a house. There are no belays and no holds and with a drop of 3000ft below great care is necessary. About half-way across we found a little couloir leading up, and after about 100ft we traversed back and reached the upper part of the Zmutt ridge above the overhang known as the Zmuttnase. These traverses were quite a pleasure this time, with an absolutely dependable companion behind me.

We reached the top at 12.30, about four hours earlier than last time. It was a great moment, for David and I had planned to do the climb 14 years previously but had been prevented by the war. The weather was superb. We rested on the top for half an hour, drinking in the view and savouring this great moment before we started down the Italian ridge. We soon reached the first of the fixed ropes; the second led to the famous 'Jordan' rope ladder. This had recently been renovated and all 12 rungs were intact. The ladder took us to the third and fourth ropes and so to the Col Félicité, the start of Carrel's famous traverse across the Tiefenmatten face which leads to the upper part of the Zmutt ridge. We soon reached the Enjambée which gave no trouble and so to the Pic Tyndall, which is really a shoulder, where we arrived at 3pm and stopped to have some tea in order to satisfy our raging thirst. Renewing the descent, we reached the Crête du Coq and traversed below this on the Swiss side. This soon brought us to the Linceul, a small patch of névé. Here we made a serious mistake by following tracks in the dust and reached a hopeless-looking couloir.

We realised that we were too low and had to reascend by a long chimney to the ridge below the Crête du Coq. We left the ridge almost immediately by another fixed rope down the famous chimney immortalised in Whymper's *Scrambles*, and so bypassed the Great Tower and then, with two more fixed ropes, we reached the Italian hut at 7.30. David remarked 'I never wish to see another fixed rope. They are so inexpressibly vulgar!' If only we could have done some abseils.

We found the hut crammed full; its situation is very fine, but inside the babble was indescribable. That night will live long in my memory. We cooked ourselves some soup from melted snow. This was hard to get and needed a careful descent held on a rope. We were allotted two places on the upper sleeping bench, with a sheepskin as a mattress and a blanket and a half each, and we prepared for the night. The roof was low and supported with a beam so arranged that if we sat up suddenly our heads struck the beam. Occasionally my Italian neighbour would start up, hit his head against the beam with great violence, utter '*Sacramento!*' and then relapse again into semi-consciousness. The fug was almost intolerable and made sleep impossible. At 3am the guides, who were sleeping on the floor, got up and the first party set off soon afterwards. Later, while David and I were preparing a leisurely breakfast, Jean Pallisier, who seemed to be a sort of custodian of the hut and had climbed the Matterhorn about 140 times, arrived in a state of great excitement. He had been up to the top in one hour 35 minutes and down again in 35 minutes. This, he claimed, was a record! To me it seemed a travesty of mountaineering. He was so excited that he gave us the best part of a bottle of Chianti before dashing down to Breuil with the news.

After this rather exhausting interlude we finished our breakfast, drank some of the excellent Chianti and set off down the mountain. Our over-ambitious plan had been to do the E ridge of the Dent d'Hérens, but we were much too tired. Soon we reached the Col du Lion and looked down the Swiss side at the fearsome couloir that Mummery had scaled with Alexander Burgener. Then on down the Great Staircase, and back to Zermatt over the Furggjoch.

And so, finally, to 1952. My companion Donald Ross was very keen to do the Zmutt, but I feared that there was too much snow. So we decided on the ordinary way up the Matterhorn as Donald had not climbed the peak before and we were rather short of time. We went up to the Hörnli taking our 200ft line, as we hoped to descend the Zmutt. So, on 30 August 1952, I ascended the Matterhorn for the fifth time. We took 6½ hours for the ascent. I was very slow owing to pain in my left knee which I had injured the previous year in jumping over a bergschrund. The view from the summit was perfect – once again, there was not a cloud in the sky, but I was too tired to attempt the descent of the Zmutt. Poor Donald had a very dull day, I fear, though he was glad to have climbed the Matterhorn. Though I did not realise it at the time, this ascent proved to be my last.

As I write, some 40 years later, the standard of climbing by the younger generation has advanced beyond recognition. However, I do feel that some climbers take unwarrantable risks and do not have sufficient regard for the sanctity of human life. Mountaineering is an adventurous sport, but it is not a form of war.

Wildlife, Geography and History

Picos de Europa

(*Plates 63–66*)

The Cordillera Cantábrica, like the backbone of some great supine beast, runs along the north coast of Spain from the Pyrenees to the Portuguese border. Like a slipped disc, Picos de Europa is displaced to the northern, seaward side of the spine, although still linked intimately with it through the mountain pass of San Glorio. There are several legends concerning the origin of the name Picos de Europa, the most popular of which derives from medieval times. The glittering teeth of these mountains were supposedly the first sight of *terra firma* for land-starved European fishermen as they returned from trawling their nets in the northern seas.

Only 15km from the Costa Verde, Picos de Europa receives most of its weather from the Atlantic; the climate is cool and moist, the valleys lush and verdant, and mists occur so frequently that spring and autumn travellers may never see the tops of the mountains. In *bable*, the lilting dialect of the Asturian people, the gentle mist-like rain from the Atlantic that so regularly sweeps across this land is called *orbayu*, whilst *encainada* is the shepherds' name for the low-lying cloud that comes swirling over the mountain passes without warning.

Sheltered, north-facing corries in the peaks conceal permanent icefields or *cembas*, whilst even the valleys are mantled with snow for four or five months of the year. On the other hand, the climatic boundary between the Atlantic and the sunnier sub-Mediterranean passes through the south-eastern corner of Picos de Europa, and thus fauna and flora more typical of the rest of Spain also have their place here.

In contrast to the slates and shales of the Cordillera Cantábrica, Picos de Europa is a land of pale limestones, laid down in the warm seas of the Lower Carboniferous over 300 million years ago. Although far to the south of the Arctic ice-sheets, localised glacial activity during the Ice Ages created the typical frost-shattered topography of today, with its ancient hanging valleys and glacial cirque lakes. Huge circular hollows, known as *hoyos* or *jous*, are sunken into the mountain plateaux – lunar landscapes filled with shattered limestone rubble, relics of former Ice Ages.

Limestone is a soft but highly permeable rock which has little surface expression of water; almost all erosion takes place underground. Percolating ground waters and underground streams create huge caverns and galleries populated by stalagmites and stalactites. These can be entered from the outside world via sinks or swallow-holes in the limestone, technically known as *dolines*, some of which extend vertically for hundreds of metres: a speleologist's paradise. This *karst* topography, an eroded limestone landscape produced by percolating ground-water and underground streams, is particularly well-developed in Picos de Europa owing to the high level of rainfall. Almost every level shelf has been eroded along its constituent joints to form the characteristic *clints* (ridges) and *grikes* (clefts) of limestone pavement, with its typical flora of green spleenwort (*Asplenium viride*) and holly fern (*Polystichum lonchitis*).

Picos de Europa comprises three towering massifs, separated from one another by precipitous gorges through which flow the southernmost salmon rivers in Europe. Together they resemble a great bat, spread-eagled and facing the sea; the central massif forms the oval torso whilst the more slender, uplifted wings are represented by the western and eastern mountain ranges.

The westernmost boundary of Picos de Europa is the Desfiladero de los Beyos, a narrow ravine carved out by the Río Sella. The adjacent massif, Cornión, receives much of the precipitation brought into this land by depressions over the Atlantic: about the same amount of rainfall is deposited annually over the Highlands of Scotland. This *macizo occidental* (western massif) thus retains its verdant allure throughout even the driest of seasons, and although not boasting the highest or most striking peaks, is home to Peña Santa de Castilla, a distinctive crenellated summit, beloved by many who know these mountains well.

The central massif, known as Urrieles, is undoubtedly the most awe-inspiring, crowned by a number of peaks exceeding 2600m in height. John Ormsby, in the earliest description of these mountains in English, writes 'looking at Picos de Europa from any elevation, it would appear about as hopeless to go in search of the highest peak as it would to try to determine which is absolutely the tallest spine on the back of a hedgehog.' (*AJ*6, 67, 1872) Nevertheless, a brave attempt was made to do so, and Torre Cerredo, at 2648m, was deemed to be some six metres superior to Llambrión, although the absolute accuracy of these measurements is thought to be a little dubious today. Peña Vieja is also of considerable height, attaining some 2613m, but the jewel in the crown is indubitably Naranjo de Bulnes (2519m). This almost conical block of limestone, known to the local people as *Picu Urriellu*, is depicted in mountaineering legend as something of a Spanish 'Matterhorn', unclimbed until the beginning of the 20th century. It was conquered for the first time in 1904 by Pedro Pidal, Marquis of Villaviciosa, and his Valdeón-born companion Gregorio Pérez, otherwise known as 'el Cainejo'.

Urrieles is divided from Cornión by the most spectacular gorge in Picos de Europa: La Garganta del Cares, also described as 'The Divine Gorge'. This cleft in the living rock owes its existence to the tireless action of the Río Cares which, since time immemorial, has been carving a bed for itself between these two massifs. The walls are almost sheer, rising in places to over 2000m; these cliffs are a favourite haunt of that elusive bird the wallcreeper. If you look up you may see a group of griffon vultures drifting lazily across that narrow band of blue which represents the sky. From Caín in the south to Puente Poncebos at its northern end, la Garganta del Cares stretches for some 12km. This is one of the most famous walks in Picos de Europa, along a narrow mule-track that has been carved from the wall of the gorge high above the spray of the thundering river. You cross from side to side over fragile bridges and in some places are walking inside the mountain itself, along tunnels where the roar of the river is but an echo.

The gorges of Picos de Europa are so sheltered from climatic extremes that many of the trees and shrubs clinging precariously to the walls are those typically of the Mediterranean. Wild jasmine (*Jasminum fruticans*) and barberry (*Berberis vulgaris*) bloom amidst the glossy evergreen foliage of strawberry trees (*Arbutus unedo*) and Spanish laurel (*Laurus nobilis*), whilst the turpentine tree (*Pistacia terebinthus*), a close relative of the pistachio, spreads its leaves in the sunniest spots together with wild figs (*Ficus carica*), walnuts (*Juglans regia*) and olives (*Olea europaea* ssp. *sylvestris*).

Andara (or the *macizo oriental*) is the smallest and easternmost of the massifs of Picos de Europa. It is separated from Urrieles by the Río Duje, which joins the Cares at the Puente Poncebos, and from lesser mountains towards Santander by the Liébana valley, home of the Río Deva and eastern margin of Picos de Europa. Spring comes earlier to this valley and, as it lies in the rainshadow of the peaks of Urrieles, you can be assured of rather warmer and sunnier weather here. The Río Deva starts life, as do all of the main rivers of Picos de Europa, as a bubbling spring deep within the mountains, before wending its tortuous way eastwards, then northwards, and discharging into the Bay of Biscay. Its headwaters arise in the sheer natural amphitheatre formed by the mountains at Fuente Dé, an abbreviation of *Fuente Deva* or *Fuente de Eva*, meaning literally 'Fountain of Eve'.

Part of the journey of the Río Deva is through the Desfiladero de la Hermida, a third magnificent gorge. Despite the better climate of this part of Picos de Europa, one village in the gorge, the hamlet of La Hermida, perched on the western flank, is reputed to receive not a ray of sunlight for almost six months of the year. The peaks are less imposing in Andara, and are certainly less well-explored; the highest are Morra de Lechugales (2441m) and Pico Cortes (2370m).

Since the death of Franco, Spain has fragmented to form no less than 17 autonomous communities, each with its own regional government and a liberal ration of self-rule. Three of these autonomies are each responsible for a part of Picos de Europa: Asturias (formerly Oviedo) to the north, Cantabria (Santander) to the east, and Castilla-León (León) to the south-west. The meeting point of the three is at the 2570m summit of Pico Tesorero in the central massif.

Covadonga, in Asturias, the site of a shrine to Our Lady and the canonised San Pelayo, is one of the most-visited national monuments in Spain. In AD 722 a certain King Pelayo faced the Moorish invaders who had previously conquered almost all of the Iberian peninsula. The decisive battle was fought at Covadonga, when the supposed intercession of Our Lady caused an avalanche that crushed the Muslim forces, allowing Christianity to win the day. King Juan Carlos II has referred to Asturias, because of Covadonga, as ' . . . the primary and eternal source of the nation'.

In 1918 the Parque Nacional de la Montaña de Covadonga was created, covering almost the whole of the western massif. Together with Ordesa in the

Pyrenees it was the first National Park in Spain and is also one of the oldest in Europe. Since the *raison d'être* for its existence was originally purely historical and religious, it was not until fairly recently that the immense worth of the wildlife and scenery of Covadonga was realised. There has since been some attempt to moderate the effects of agricultural intensification and to preserve the beauty and diversity of the National Park, despite the problems associated with two million visitors every year.

The Cordillera Cantábrica is thought to be one of the earliest areas in Europe to be settled by Palaeolithic man; evidence of the existence of these people is to be found along the length and breadth of the Costa Verde. Altamira, close to Santillana del Mar, is the most famous of a series of caves depicting life-sized paintings of horses, deer, and other animals with which early man shared his world. A small cave lying at Buxu, a few kilometres east of Cangas de Onís, Asturias, is the nearest known locality to Picos de Europa which contains the marvellous works of these ancient artists.

By the end of the last glaciation, nomadic tribes of hunters and fishermen were scattered throughout Spain. The extensive deciduous woodlands of Picos de Europa were gradually cleared to provide grazing for the first domesticated animals, and for growing a few crops, as these Mesolithic and Neolithic peoples eventually opted for a more settled existence. Only fragments of the primeval forests persist here today, having been widely replaced by characteristic secondary grassland and heathland communities.

The pattern of land-use is much the same today. Where the river valleys widen out somewhat there may be a little level ground suitable for growing potatoes, maize or onions for family consumption. For the most part, however, the steep mountain slopes are clothed in haymeadows, naturally bounded by hedges and dry-stone walls. Above the meadows lie the rough grazing lands – known as *monte* – dominated by a seemingly endless variety of gorses, brooms and heathers. This habitat type can be equated with the *fridd* of the Welsh hills, here found largely above the natural tree-line, which lies at approximately 1300m in Picos de Europa.

Fragments of deciduous oak woodland persist in the wetter valleys, whilst evergreen species more typical of drier Mediterranean communities, such as holm oak, holly oak and cork oak, dominate the canopy where forests still exist in the Liébana valley. At high altitude stunted beechwoods, the natural climax woodland cover of much of the Cordillera Cantábrica, can still be found. Some of these forests are so inaccessible that they remain undisturbed by man and have been shaped only by natural forces.

Above the *monte*, little vegetation impinges on the purity of the pale, almost luminous, limestone except where glacial morainic deposits have collected in natural basins in the mountains. These sites, known as *vegas*, are roughly equivalent to the 'alms' of the Alps, and are utilised as summer grazing for the autochthonous herds of sheep, cattle and goats that form the basis of the economy in Picos de Europa.

If you look closely at the seemingly bare limestone you will see that in fact low-growing, tussock-forming plants nestle in every nook and cranny. At high altitudes you can find half a dozen species that are unknown outside these mountains; they are endemic to Picos de Europa. These include a small blue and white species of columbine (*Aquilegia discolor*), a houseleek (*Sempervivum cantabricum*), a milkwort (*Polygala edmundii*), and a low-growing toadflax (*Linaria faucicola*), among others. One of the more famous species which is found only in these mountains is the blue-leaved petrocoptis (*Petrocoptis glaucifolia*), wondered at by generations of botanists who have been fascinated by the sub-alpine flora of Picos de Europa.

Despite the notoriety of the high altitudes as a botanical paradise, my own idea of heaven is to be found in the gloriously colourful haymeadows. Managed in a traditional manner since they were first reclaimed from the primeval forest, these meadows represent some of the most floristically rich Atlantic grasslands in Europe. Some 50 species of orchid have been recorded here, including the evocatively named pink butterfly (*Orchis papilionacea*) (Plate 64), lizard (*Himantoglossum hircinum*), man (*Aceras anthropophorum*), woodcock (*Ophrys scolopax*), fly (*Ophrys insectifera*) and sawfly (*Ophrys tenthredinifera*) orchids, to name but a few. Dark, exotic tongue orchids (*Serapias* spp .), towering white asphodels (*Asphodelus albus*) (Plate 63) and Pyrenean lilies (*Lilium pyrenaicum*) decorate these meadows, whilst the montane grasslands are renowned for their pasque-flowers (*Pulsatilla rubra*, *P. alpina* (Plate 66) and *P. vernalis*), anemones (*Anemone pavoniana*), dog's-tooth violets (*Erythronium dens-canis*) and Pyrenean fritillaries (*Fritillaria pyrenaica*). At the edges of melting snowfields, the tiny Asturian jonquil (*Narcissus asturiensis*), and hoop-petticoat daffodil (*N. bulbocodium*) form yellow-studded sheets in the *vegas* in early summer.

For me, one of the most exciting discoveries concerning the haymeadows of Picos de Europa is that they are crammed with plants that are also native to Britain, but are seen so rarely there today: greater yellow rattle (*Rhinanthus serotinus*), round-headed leeks (*Allium sphaerocephalum*), martagon lilies (*Lilium martagon*), burnt-tip orchids (*Orchis ustulata*) and globe flowers (*Trollius europaeus*) (Plate 65) in an almost endless array.

As the climate is perpetually humid here, especially in the western valleys of Picos de Europa, no less than 28 species of fern have been recorded, whilst the moss and liverwort communities of these mountains are very similar to those of the Western Isles of Scotland, and of Ireland. Other plants found also in Ireland include large butterwort (*Pinguicula grandiflora*) and St Dabeoc's heath (*Daboecia cantabrica*).

The people of these mountains have medicinal uses for almost all the meadow flowers – mallow for bronchial complaints, chamomile for aiding digestion. Their herb-lore has been passed down from father to son, from mother to daughter for hundreds of years. Most villages also boast a small clutch of beehives, either traditional ones made out of hollow tree-trunks or cylinders of cork, or the more recognisable, modern variety, the flowers of the haymeadows providing an endless source of nectar: the raw material of delicious honey.

Other artisan crafts practised by the people of Picos de Europa include the preparation of fine cheeses of high gastronomic status: Cabrales, Picón, Gamonedo and Beyos. Cabrales is the most famous of these, hailing primarily from the region of the same name, in Asturias, while Picón, from the villages of Bejes and Tresviso, in Liébana, is very similar. Both cheeses are made from a mixture of cows', goats' and sheep's milk, the curd being strained through horsehair. The young cheeses are wrapped in plane or oak leaves and then taken to cool limestone caves high in the mountains for three months to a year to mature. Traditionally the preparation of these cheeses uses milk taken only from native breeds of animals. The sheep are of the *lacha* breed, the goats originate from the Pyrenees and the cattle are either *casinas* or *Asturianas de la montaña* – small, red animals from Asturias – or *tudanceas* – wide-horned, grey-roan animals from Cantabria. Both breeds are well adapted to the harsh winter climate and annual ascent and descent to the upland *vegas*.

Parts of these untamed mountains remained unseen and untrodden by man until the 1960s. They are indeed one of the last truly wild places in Europe. The Cordillera Cantábrica, in particular Picos de Europa, has been described as one of the few surviving areas in Europe where the original post-glacial mammalian fauna remains virtually intact. Wolves and bears still roam the primeval forests, both so isolated from the populations of Central Europe that they have evolved into separate Spanish races. Over 60 mammalian species are known to frequent the mountains and valleys of Picos de Europa: riches indeed. But the visiting naturalist, unfortunately, is unlikely to see many of them. Many of the small mammals are extremely secretive; some are nocturnal, some are just shy. Species such as the highly endangered Pyrenean desman, a large aquatic mole, for which the clear mountain rivers of Picos de Europa are an international stronghold, have declined more in the last 25 years than in all the previous centuries, owing for the most part to man's increasing interference with and destruction of the natural environment.

Anyone who ventures even a short way into the mountains will undoubtedly encounter the king of that realm: the chamois. Now present in quite large numbers, these gloriously agile creatures can be seen springing up almost vertical cliffs and balancing on the most inaccessible ledges. Wild boar forage for underground tubers in the deciduous woodlands, but are rather wary of intruders and you are lucky if you catch more than a glimpse. One of the easiest ways to see these magnificent wild pigs clearly is to delay visiting the area until the onset of cold weather in the autumn, when they come into the villages to forage for potatoes in the fields, doing considerable damage to the crops in the process.

Of the airborne representatives of the animal kingdom there are plenty. An enormous list of birds has been compiled for this area, most of them breeding, but pride of place must go to the raptors, or birds of prey. The rocky peaks are the favoured haunts of golden eagles and both griffon and Egyptian vultures, whilst short-toed and booted eagles soar in the thermals over the passes in search of their prey. Hen harriers quarter the rough heathland areas, goshawks and sparrowhawks patrol the woodlands and buzzards are ten-a-penny. Nesting on the rocky ledges in the heart of the peaks, kestrels swoop overhead and occasionally a peregrine will dive past, like a small, dark arrow.

But the most characteristic bird of the Cordillera Cantábrica must be the capercaillie. Again so isolated from the rest of the population that it has become a separate race, this bird differs from its Scottish relatives by living in deciduous, not coniferous woodlands. Its main haunts are the high altitude beech forests, where it is joined by a host of small birds not commonly associated with Spain: crested tits, pied flycatchers, tree pipits, nuthatches and treecreepers. Black woodpeckers, now increasingly scarce in Europe, as well as their great, middle and lesser-spotted cousins, are also most at home here, together with large numbers of green woodpeckers and wrynecks. Those who are night-birds themselves should be able to distinguish the voices of no less than six species of owl, as well as the distinctive whirring song of the nightjar.

The high peaks are favoured by a number of specialised montane birds, including snow finches, alpine accentors, rock thrushes and black redstarts, whilst huge flocks of choughs and alpine choughs wheel tirelessly overhead. A solitary raven may cross the valley below you and the song of skylarks will fill the air. For those who wish for a taste of something a little more exotic, however, bee-eaters, hoopoes and golden orioles are not uncommon in the southern and eastern reaches of Picos de Europa, and red-backed shrikes, now driven to extinction as a breeding bird in Britain, can be seen everywhere.

Many reptiles and amphibians live in Picos de Europa, some preferring wet habitats, some dry; some surviving only at high altitudes, some confined to the valleys. The alpine newt is a particularly interesting case, the whole Spanish population living in just a few glacial lakes, one of which is Lago de la Ercina at Covadonga. Similarly, the Aesculapian snake in Spain is confined to these mountains, and the viviparous lizard, despite being widespread in Europe, occurs only in the Pyrenees and the Cordillera Cantábrica in Iberia. Yet another example of such a restricted distribution is the Iberian rock lizard, now reduced to just four isolated Spanish populations; the Cantábrican specimens have probably evolved into a separate race.

When the cloud cover is low, or the *orbayu* is driving in from the Atlantic, you are likely to encounter large numbers of black and yellow fire sala-manders; despite their high colouring these creatures are totally harmless. As with many of the amphibians and reptiles of these mountains, however, the local people are highly suspicious of them, fearing that they house evil spirits.

The butterflies that occur in these mountains represent well over one-third of the entire European fauna. In addition there are many races which occur nowhere else in the world, and many threatened and endangered species. The hay meadows are alive with fritillaries and skippers, blues and coppers, whilst hairstreaks dance in the sun-dappled glades of the deciduous woodlands. Even the uplands have their own particular butterfly fauna, largely represented by a variety of ringlets.

The variety of wildlife present in Picos de Europa is apparently endless; the amount that you can experience in a fortnight in June only fractionally less so. The local people take pride in their history and their culture, their customs and their originality but they are always willing to extend their warmest hos-pitality to you. The sight of such mountains in any weather is enough to uplift the heart and delight the soul, but the utmost tranquillity of Picos de Europa is what draws me back time after time; that sense of being alone in the wilder-ness and at one with nature.

A M SNODGRASS

The Early History of the Alps

'After all,' he said, 'the Alps are inhabited and cultivated; they beget and rear living creatures.'

> *Hannibal's words to his troops, according to Livy.*[1]

And what looked like a wall turns out to be a world
    With measurements of its own
And a style of gossip.

> *W H Auden, 'Mountains'*[2]

Two quotations, 2000 years apart in date, express the same unchanging truth about the Alps: that for millennia past, they have been a populated landscape, housing a distinctive human culture with traits stronger and more persistent than the political boundaries which they have always transgressed. Hannibal's hesitant army and Auden's lowland tourist both needed to be reminded of this hidden but inhabited world. The history of the Alps is the history of how the horizons of this world, at first regional in scale, were gradually extended until the Alps formed an indispensable link in the communications of a whole continent, while still retaining their own character.

Much of the earlier evidence for this process is archaeological, and a few major discoveries can be seen as landmarks of change. A good place to start is with that remarkable event of September 1991: the discovery of the body of 'Similaun Man'. Here was a corpse, from some 5000 years ago, preserved in a rock crevice with his equipment, just as he had been in life. He wore protective clothing and boots of leather stuffed with straw or grass, and carried a bow and fourteen arrows, a flint-bladed knife and a copper axe (the finds which gave a provisional dating), kindling flints and what seems to have been a form of wooden carrying-frame.[3]

For Alpinists, the find has an interest of its own. The altitude at which the body was found is sensational enough – 3210m up at the head of the Niederjochferner which flows down towards Vent in the upper Ötztal. One detail, the apparent tattooing on his back, has led to speculation that he was a stranger in those parts. But there may be more significance in the exact location of the find – a little below the Hauslabjoch (3279m), a high but direct pass leading from the Ötztal to the Val di Senales (Schnalstal), now in Italy. This latter is a rare example of a valley lying on one side of the main Alpine watershed but only readily accessible, until modern times, from the other. The gorge at its foot debouches into the upper Adige valley but was impassable for the first few thousand years of the valley's occupation: the 'back door' from the Ötztal was almost the only way in and out. Writing in 1980, Ludwig Pauli made what turned out to be a prescient observation: 'The grazing rights, valid to this day, of the Schnalstal shepherds in the Ötztal, and the annual driving of sheep across the snow-covered passes in early summer and autumn, testify to the long-standing communications across today's national frontiers.'4 That 'Similaun Man' should have met his end near this very crossing convinces me that he had a connection with this local traffic, rather than coming from further afield. Why else should he have climbed so high when, for long-range travellers, there was a wide choice of lower passes? There are features of his equipment which suggest that, although under 30 years of age, he may have had the status of a 'holy man'. In that case, he could have climbed up there to meditate; but the choice of location strengthens the case for his having had a link with a nearby community.

Next, we leap forward in time to an Iron Age cemetery at Grächwil, just north-west of Bern. Here, an excavation in 1851 brought to light an ornate bronze water-jug, two feet high, which was soon recognised as being of Greek workmanship. More recent research has dated it to about 580 BC, and established that it was probably made at Taras (Taranto), a Greek colony in southern Italy. The find-spot on the Swiss plateau is low-lying, and it is not certain that it had been carried over the Alpine passes; an alternative route would have been by ship to Massalia (Marseilles), another Greek colony, and then up the Rhône and overland from the Lake of Geneva. Finds like this are explained by old-fashioned archaeologists as the result of what they vaguely call 'trade', but at this early date we have better evidence for the exchange of gifts, for diplomatic purposes, between one community and another. A chain of such transactions could bring a rare and valuable object like this all the way from the Mediterranean coast to its final resting-place in the grave of a local notable.

The next find, later in date and different in important ways, is that made in August 1962 at Erstfeld in Kanton Uri. Here some men were digging down to dislodge a large boulder on the mountain-slope when they came upon a cluster of four neck-torques and three bracelets, all of gold. This time the workmanship pointed to a place of manufacture far to the north, probably in the Rhineland; the date was about 400 BC and the context was not one of a burial. The best explanation (again, one that has no connection with 'trade') is that these were deposited as dedications to propitiate the gods of the mountain before crossing the pass, or to thank them afterwards. Such offerings were common in the Alps from prehistory to the Middle Ages. The best-documented series is from the neighbourhood of the Great St Bernard, where we even know the name of the pre-Roman deity, Poeninus, who presided over the crossing. He was later identified with Jupiter and is commemorated to this day by the name of the Pennine Alps.

Some centuries later again, but still perhaps pre-Roman, is a discovery made in 1954: a late Egyptian clay scarab-amulet, picked up near the Rojacher hut (2718m), above the Rauriser Tal which forms an alternative northern route to the Grossglockner. Another gold torque had earlier been found lower down on the same route. These can both probably be explained as pass-offerings, though the owner of the scarab may have lost it before he could dedicate it.

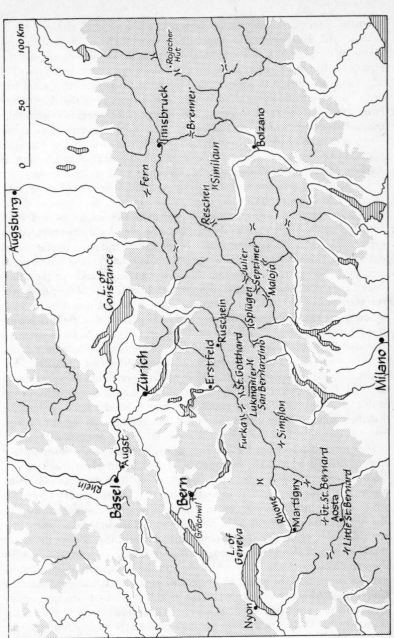

Principal Alpine passes used in antiquity, with sites of major archaeological finds

Finally, passing over the Roman period to which we shall return, we may consider the Ruschein hoard. Ruschein is above Ilanz in the Vorderrhein valley, at the point where a side-valley branches off south-west towards the remote Diesrut and Greina passes. Road works in 1904 uncovered a hoard of 123 coins, together with ear-rings and pieces of a necklace. The hoard had been buried intentionally, at some date just after 790 – the date of the latest coin – but the interesting thing is the geographical range of origin of the coins. There were pennies of Offa king of Mercia and Egcberth of Kent; but also a coin each of the caliphs al-Mahdi and Haroun-al-Rashid of Baghdad. Haroun, we know, once sent a delegation to Charlemagne in his court at Aachen, which provides a suggestive background for this exotic discovery.

This sequence of archaeological finds shows a progressive lengthening in the range of communications passing through the Alps. The Similaun find shows that, before 2000 BC, people were prepared to face strenuous and risky crossings of the highest passes in encompassing their local objectives. At an even earlier stage, the Neolithic settlement of Europe and the first adoption of agriculture, one school of archaeological thought holds that the first target of settlement had been the mountain-slopes at mid-height and not the valley floors. For a population living in such surroundings, the use of the passes over the main watershed would have been much less intimidating than for low-landers. The two finds from Grächwil and Erstfeld show that, by later prehistory, there were long-range north-south routes, extending as far as southern Italy and the lower Rhine, which could take an Alpine crossing in their stride. At this period, the scatter of objects on and around the passes is actually rather wider than in the ensuing Roman period, reflecting no doubt the wider choice available to single travellers, mounted or on foot, than to the more channelled traffic of the Roman Empire. Finally, the finds from the Rojacher hut and Ruschein suggest much longer routes still, running in a south-east to north-westerly direction, from the very cradles of civilisation to our own islands.

It is time to turn from the evidence of archaeology to the documentary history derived from texts, inscriptions, language and place-names, which begins to be available just before the advent of the Romans upon the Alpine scene. This evidence is enough to suggest that the century between 50 BC and AD 50 was the most significant era in the whole history of human settlement in the Alps. It brought the Alpine region, as never before and seldom since, into the orbit of a single political system. More permanently, it gave the wider world an insight into the inner geography of the Alps, and a set of names for the sub-divisions of the range which we still use today. Greek and Roman sources tell us that the name, 'the Alps', is based on a Celtic word meaning simply 'high mountain'. (The modern use of 'alp' to mean a pasture, especially a seasonal mountain pasture, dates only from the Middle Ages). But it was the Romans who, in the first century BC, distinguished the *Alpes Maritimae*, the *Alpes Cottiae* (from the name of Cottius, a friendly ruler in the strategically important region round the Mont-Genèvre pass), the *Alpes Graiae*, the *Alpes Poeninae*, the *Alpes Lepontinae*, the *Alpes Raetae*, the *Alpes Carnicae* and finally (their only concession to jingoism) the *Alpes Iuliae*. Within these sub-ranges, a very small number of massifs and a few individual peaks were picked out under the name *mons*. Monte Viso enjoyed this rare distinction because of its relative height, conspicuousness, and the fact that it was the source of the Po. *Mons Adula* or *Adulas* was similarly picked out as being the source of the Rhine: modern locations for it have varied between the St Gotthard area and the neighbourhood of the Rheinwaldhorn, according to whether the Vorderrhein or the Hinterrhein is thought more likely to have been the main branch in Roman eyes.

Another point which the historical evidence makes clear is that the native population, at least by the time that the Romans came into contact with it, was neither homogeneous nor static. Old-fashioned physical anthropology, with its round-headed 'Alpine race', used to suggest a different view, with underlying continuity of population from time immemorial. This theory will no longer stand up today. The Celtic-speaking Helvetii who, around 100 BC, occupied the Swiss plateau from the Rhine and Lake Constance to the Bernese Oberland and the north shore of the Lake of Geneva, were merely the largest of a constellation of Celtic tribes who between them held the Jura, the Valais, the Haute-Savoie, the Val d'Aosta and the Ticino. But Greek and Roman writers agree that the Helvetii, who had only arrived in the then recent past, had expelled another people, the Ligures, who were to find a lasting home further south, along the Italian Riviera. These Ligures had not belonged to the Celtic language-group; nor did the important confederation of the Raeti, who were now the eastern neighbours of the Helvetii in the Graubünden and Tirol. These examples are enough to show the mixed nature of the Alpine populations, and from this it follows that any distinctive features of those populations must have been environmentally, rather than genetically or racially, determined.

It was Julius Caesar's conquest of Gaul which led to the Roman involvement with this Alpine world. At Caesar's death, the Roman Empire was left with a very awkward northern frontier. It ran from the North Sea up the lower and middle course of the Rhine, only to turn sharply south-westwards from the neighbourhood of Basel, along the Jura, round the western end of the Lake of Geneva, and then some way further south again, before it turned eastward, roughly along the line of the Italian lakes. A huge unoccupied salient was thus formed, into which fell not only the whole of the Swiss and Austrian Alps, but also the Val d'Aosta, the Graian Alps on the Franco-Italian frontier, and a number of valleys further east on the Italian side of the Alpine watershed. No pass further north than the Mont-Genèvre offered a secure passage for the armies, from Roman territory to Roman territory.

Caesar himself, though clearly aware of this glaring defect, had no time to take more than preliminary steps to rectify it. He planted one colony at Noviodunum (Nyon), 25km beyond Geneva along the north shore of the lake, and planned another at the place later called Augusta Raurica (Augst, 10km east of Basel) which was founded immediately after his murder. More significant, though, was his treatment of the Helvetii, who had actually provoked his own conquest of Gaul by their mass inroad, deep into Burgundy, in 58 BC.

After their defeat, Caesar spared the survivors and sent them, to the number of 110,000 men, women and children, back to their homeland on the Swiss plateau, thus creating a subdued and relatively friendly buffer-state in the middle of the unoccupied salient. But the Helvetii did not control the Valais, a region of special concern to Caesar and to his successors, since it provided the northern approach to the Great St Bernard, which was to be the pivot of all Roman activity in the Alps for the next 500 years. Here Caesar attempted a more drastic measure, sending the Twelfth Legion by way of the Lake of Geneva to Martigny, in the autumn of 57 BC, with orders to build a fortification and winter there. The attempt failed: after seeing off one ferocious attack by the tribes of the upper Rhône valley, the Roman force had to withdraw before the winter. But due notice had been given to the peoples of the Alps.

A full generation of civil wars intervened before the Romans could turn their powers against the Alps once again. But this was one of the first problems addressed by Augustus once he was ensconced in power. The consul A. Terentius Varro Murena was sent against the Salassi, the tribe occupying the Val d'Aosta, in 25 BC. They had been troublesome in recent years, and they received no mercy: the valley was depopulated, 44,000 people sold into slavery, and the new colony of August Praetoria (Aosta) planted at the point where the routes diverge to the two St Bernard passes. The Little St Bernard was immediately opened as a short cut from Italy to Gaul, and a road for wheeled traffic built over it: but the main watershed of the Swiss and Austrian Alps had still to be breached.

In 15 BC the Romans embarked upon this major operation with extraordinary speed and finality. The task was entrusted to two princes of the Imperial family, Augustus' eventual successor Tiberius (then aged 27) and his younger brother Drusus. It took the form of a gigantic pincer-movement, completely encircling the central Alps. From the Adige valley, Drusus' forces advanced in a frontal attack on the powerful Raeti, the primary target of the campaign. Crossing the Reschenscheideck (and perhaps simultaneously the Brenner), the legions descended on the valley of the Inn, crossed to that of the Lech, probably by the Fernpass, and did not stop until they had reached the south bank of the Danube. Meanwhile they had joined hands with the forces of Tiberius, who had moved eastwards from Basel by way of the Lake of Constance. The entire territory of the Vindelici of southern Bavaria, as well as that of the Raeti, was annexed in a single summer and the Alps, which had acted as a barrier to Roman expansion for two centuries, had been secured in the space of a few months. The documentation of the campaign is thin – even more so than the later conquest of Britain, for example – but it does not seem that active fighting was involved in what are now central and western Switzerland. The Helvetii must have accepted the transition to direct Roman rule, and the tribes of the Valais, finding themselves surrounded in such depth, abandoned thoughts of resistance.

The organisation of the new territory under Augustus showed a fine disregard for what we might think of as the 'natural' Alpine frontiers. A new province of Raetia was set up to include not only the territory conquered by

Drusus, but also the Valais: an arrangement which only begins to make sense if the east-west route over the Oberalp and Furka passes was in full operation. The lands of the Helvetii and their neighbours in the Jura, on the other hand, were incorporated into Gallia Belgica. Any system which resulted in Belgium and the Bernese Oberland belonging in the same province, while Martigny came under the administration of the new provincial capital at Augsburg (Augusta Vindelicum), wears an odd look for modern eyes. But seen from Rome, it made more sense. Three key points in Augustus' new system were the three places which still bear his name in some form: Aosta on the left flank, Augst in the centre and Augsburg on the right. To serve their purpose, they had to be efficiently linked with each other and with Rome. Three Alpine crossings had to be opened up, to link the first and second of these places, and to link the second and the third to Rome. But the issues were bigger still, since beyond this triangle lay the whole of central and northern Gaul and the Rhine frontier. The strongest motive of all for the conquest of the Alps had been to shorten the lines of communication to these further regions, and potentially to a remoter objective – our own island.

It took time to upgrade the Alpine routes to the necessary standard. The evidence of milestones, coins and a few documents shows that the fulfilment of this task can be mostly credited to the Emperor Claudius (AD 41–54), and it was clearly linked to his successful invasion of Britain. So swiftly had the Alpine crossings become stepping-stones to objectives on a European scale. Claudius turned his attention first to the Great St Bernard, to which both the approaches were at last under Roman control. The main controversy here has been as to whether or not the Roman road for wheeled traffic ran all the way over the summit (2469m). For a long time, the experts' view was that it did. Now, however, the latest authority on Roman roads in Switzerland, Armon Planta, maintains that the approach roads to the north and south, which are well documented, were linked only by a stretch of mule-track over the highest ground.[5]

The Great St Bernard route was finished by AD 47; the tribes of the Valais were then detached from Raetia, given a favourable administrative status and a new capital at Martigny, and linked instead to the tribe of the Ceutrones in the Haute Savoie, presupposing access over one or more of the cols leading to Argentière. Already Claudius had turned his attention to the next most urgent undertaking, the road linking northern Italy to Augsburg, which was to bear his name as the Via Claudia, and which followed the route of the march of Drusus, the Emperor's own father, 60 years earlier. Here there was one intractable problem, which Roman engineers were only to solve a century or so later: the gorge of the river Isarco, just above Bolzano, which blocked the direct approach to the Brenner. The main arm of the Via Claudia took the detour westwards from Bolzano, over the Reschensheideck and down to Landeck in the Inn valley; but there was a variant route further east, which went from the Adriatic up the valley of the Piave to the eastern Dolomites, past the Lake of Misurina, and then westwards down the Pustertal which led to the foot of the Brenner.

Two of the essential links were now in place, on the left and right flanks; but it remained highly desirable to provide a direct route to the central area of the triangle, the region between Basel and the Lake of Constance. The modern motorist, when travelling north from the Italian Lakes, has half a dozen obvious alternative routes to choose from: the Simplon, the St Gotthard, the Lukmanier, the San Bernardino, the Splügen, and the Maloja/Julier route. Every one of these passes had already been in use in pre-Roman times, yet for the rapid passage of Roman armies, several were ineligible. Altitude on its own held few terrors, as the case of the Great St Bernard shows: the most serious obstacles for the Roman road-builders were to be found lower down, in the gorges that blocked the approaches to so many of the Swiss passes, as with the Brenner further east. The Simplon was barred by the Gondo gorge above Domodossola, the St Gotthard by the Schöllenen below Andermatt, the San Bernardino and the Splügen by the notorious defile of the Hinterrhein at the Via Mala. None of these barriers precluded the use of detours over the higher slopes, but these were unsuitable for large bodies of men and their baggage. This difficulty did not apply to the Lukmanier, the lowest of all the passes of the central Alps, and the neglect of this possibility for a traffic-road until medieval times is mysterious, but nevertheless a fact.

There remained the route over the Maloja and the Julier, along with its more direct and only slightly higher variant, the Septimer. This turned out to be the answer to the Romans' problem. In 1917 Douglas Freshfield wrote an article[6] in which he strongly upheld the claims of the Septimer as the primary Roman route, disparaging the claims of the Julier which he thought had been mainly used in conjunction with the Bernina. It is true that the Septimer shows substantial signs of Roman use, although these do not include (as had at first been thought) traces of an actual Roman road. But Freshfield's case has now been much weakened, owing to recent researches by Armon Planta.[7] He has examined the stretch of the Roman road at the ascent of the Maloja from the Val Bregaglia, not of course needed for an approach to the Septimer, and found that where the modern road makes the ascent in 22 curves, the Romans made do with two or at most three. He has also re-investigated the Julier, where even the casual traveller can hardly fail to notice the two separated halves of a single commemorative Roman column which once stood on the summit, along with a probable pass-sanctuary like the one of Jupiter Poeninus on the Great St Bernard. The northern descent from the Julier does encounter the defile of the Schinschlucht below Tiefencastel, but this is easily circumvented by way of Lenzerheide, with an easy descent to Chur. Here, at the point where all the crossings of the Graubünden Alps converge, was established the small outpost of Curia, later to be promoted to the status of a provincial capital when Raetia was divided into two separate provinces.

Thus was established the main framework of Roman communication through the Alps. Some of the passes involved secondary crossings too, such as the Jougne above Vallorbe in the Jura, which was the essential continuation of the Great St Bernard route north-westwards. Other passes were opened up further east, such as the Plöcken and the Radstädter Tauern, to provide access to a different part of the northern frontier. This first system was to undergo some later modification, notably through the conquest of the gorge above Bolzano, which gave the Brenner route that advantage in directness and modest altitude which it has retained ever since. The further conquests of the Emperor Trajan, which were held by the Empire from about AD 100 to 260, and the establishment of the separate provinces of Upper and Lower Germany, had the effect of taking the Alpine provinces temporarily out of the frontier zone. This led to demilitarisation and the blossoming of civil amenities. The lowlands witnessed the growth of fully-fledged Roman towns at Augst and at Avenches (Vaud), a spa at Baden (Kanton Aargau), and half a dozen smaller settlements whose names – Basilia, Eburodunum, Genua, Leusonna, Salodurum, Turicum – live on in the familiar forms of Basel, Yverdon, Geneva, Lausanne, Solothurn and Zurich. Splendid villas were built in Aargau and the other northern cantons, and one outlying example was excavated at Alpnach, where the road begins its climb from the Lake of Lucerne to the Brünig Pass.

But none of this Romanisation made much impact on the Alps proper. The distinctive Alpine economy and society, with its emphasis on pastoralism and dairy products, went far back into prehistory, and the Romans did little to change it. The mineral resources of the Alps were considerable but, for a power in control of a geographical area the size of the Roman Empire, far from unique. The majesty of the mountains drew only disparaging epithets – 'cruel', 'windy', 'wintry' – from the Roman poets; their people were noted only for their susceptibility to goitre. The lasting gift of Rome to the Alps was in the field of communications: the demonstration that, far from being impassable, the Alpine passes could be surmounted with sufficient speed and ease to become the optimal routes for trans-continental journeys. This is perhaps especially clear to an archaeologist whose work takes him on an annual overland drive to Greece and back. The Alps are where the variant routes, spreading out over widely-separated countries, all converge: only in this stretch does the same corner, the same Gasthaus, the same view suddenly return to prompt the memory of past years.

Before the curtain fell on antiquity, one final episode took place which has also left an indelible stamp on the Alps, this time in the field of language and place-names. Every Alpinist knows how the language and names change from French to German along the line across Switzerland that passes between the Val d'Anniviers and the Turtmanntal in the Valais Alps, between Sierre and Leuk in the Rhône valley, and then bends round in the Bernese Oberland so as to pass to the west of Gstaad, the Gastlosen and the Jaunpass. For much of its course, this line marks the high-water mark of the incursion of the Alamanni from central Germany. It was they who first drove the Romans back from the advance frontier of Trajan to the line of the Rhine; and who then, after two centuries of relative stability, crossed the Rhine in earnest in AD 455. They carried the Germanic language up to the Alpine watershed and, in the eastern Alps, even across it. The Western Empire was by now too weak to repel the interlopers; it formally recognised them and their territorial gains in its death-throes. Further west, Latin and its descendants survived; an isolated group of Latin-speakers also hung on in Raetia, between the Lake of Constance and the Engadin. Over the centuries, this pocket shrank ever southwards, but never quite disappeared; it lives on today in the Romansch of the higher Graubünden valleys.

There may be a few readers of the 1953 edition of the SMC Guide to the Northern Highlands who recall the story of the RAF aircraft which crashed in eastern Assynt in 1941, and how the searchers came on the wreckage of a crash from World War I which no one had sighted during the intervening 25 years. They would probably agree that it is hard to think of a spot in the Alps where such a course of events could occur. This is a populated landscape; one purpose of this article is to show for just how long that has been true.

REFERENCES

1 Livy xxi, 30, 7
2 W H Auden, 'Mountains' in *The Shield of Achilles*. London, 1955.
3 Many quite detailed accounts of this find have now appeared in the national press in this country and especially in Germany. Reports, late in 1992, that the find could be an elaborate hoax should be disregarded.
4 L Pauli, *Die Alpen in Frühzeit und Mittelalter*. Munich, 1980, p222.
5 A Planta, 'Zum römischen Weg über den Grossen St Bernhard' in *Helvetia Archaeologica* 10, 15–30, 1979.
6 D W Freshfield, 'The great passes of the Western and Central Alps' in *Geographical Journal* 49, 2–26, 1917.
7 A Planta, 'Die römische Julierroute' in *Helvetia Archaeologica* 7, 16–25, 1976; and 'Zum Römerweg zwischen Maloja and Sils' in *Helvetia Archaeologica* 10, 42–46, 1979.

One Hundred Years Ago

(*with extracts from the* Alpine Journal)

(Plates 67–70)

We have arrived at the middle of January, and the journey over the Julier Pass is still accomplished on wheels and has been so throughout the winter. At Zermatt the sky is cloudless and the weather is so mild that were it not for the snow we should imagine it was spring time. The road to and from the Riffel Alp is continually used, so that visitors can spend the day there. The only drawback is (and some people may consider it an advantage) that the railway from Visp is closed and so the journey must be made in the old way, either on foot or on mules to St Nicholas and from there by sleigh or carriage.

One of the visitors staying at Zermatt early in 1893 was Hermann Woolley who on 17 January, accompanied by Gabriel and Joseph Taugwalder, made the first winter ascent of the Rimpfischhorn. After climbing the WSW ridge, or Rimpfischwänge, the party was delayed for an hour below the final rocks by a strong wind but succeeded in reaching the summit where the view was perfect in every direction.

The splendid conditions in many parts of the Alps, enhanced by occasional snowfalls, continued throughout the winter months and well into April when a notable success was achieved by another member of the Alpine Club.

The exceptional weather this spring has rendered just possible an unusually early ascent of the Dent Blanche. On Tuesday, April 25, Mr. Owen G. Jones, with the guides Antoine Bovier and Pierre Gaspoz, and with porter Bovier fils, effected a safe ascent of the mountain by the south ridge.

The expedition lasted for nearly 36 hours, a quarter of this time being spent on the ridge itself, and included a bivouac at the Bricola Alp where the party enjoyed hot chocolate before returning to Evolène.

By the end of June, when an ascent of the Matterhorn had already been recorded and many Alpine regions were affected by a severe drought it was clear that excellent climbing conditions were in prospect.

The summer of 1893 will long be remembered as an extra-ordinarily favourable one for climbing. Week after week a clear sun was shining out of a cloudless sky, and the result was that more peaks were scaled than in any previous season since the gloriously fine year of the Queen's Jubilee.

As in the previous year a number of outstanding expeditions was completed in the Mont Blanc range and the Montenvers Hotel was crowded with visitors, amongst whom were some of the best amateur climbers of the day. One of the visitors was A F Mummery who with J N Collie, Geoffrey Hastings and W C Slingsby set out on 24 July to attempt 'the peak round the corner', the prominent aiguille which at one time had been described as the Aiguille de Blaitière derrière[1] and which despite many previous attempts was still unclimbed.

As all of the party were fresh from England their pace was miserably slow. One had a railway headache, another could not go uphill, whilst a third could not go down, and the fourth showed the greatest desire to add to his local geographical knowledge by making, about every half-hour, minute observations. These, it may be added, were at all times of greater value if made in a sitting posture.

On the following day although out of condition the party, led by Mummery, succeeded in forcing a route across the SW and E faces to reach the NE ridge and the summit of the peak now known as the Dent du Requin, the name proposed by Collie and adopted after the climb.

On 7 August Mummery and his companions completed another notable expedition by making the first traverse of the Aiguille du Plan. Starting from the Pèlerins glacier the party overcame numerous difficulties to reach the summit by way of the unclimbed W face, the col now known as the Col des Deux Aigles and the upper section of the N face, above the point at which Mummery, Slingsby and Ellis Carr had been forced to abandon their attempt to climb that face in the previous year.

After making the first ascent of the Requin the party had returned to the Montenvers where Mummery, as he later recalled,[2] was taught 'that in mountaineering, as in all the other varied affairs of life, "l'homme propose mais femme dispose."' The femme in question was Miss Lily Bristow who on 5 August, accompanied by Mummery and Slingsby, became the first lady to climb and to traverse the Aiguille du Grépon. The climb, during which Miss Bristow photographed Mummery leading the ascent of his eponymous crack, was immortalised by the famous comment[2]

It has frequently been noticed that all mountains appear doomed to pass through the three stages: An inaccessible peak – The most difficult ascent in the Alps – An easy day for a lady.

Later in the month Miss Bristow took part in other fine climbs including, on 24 August, an ascent of the SW, Italian ridge of the Matterhorn with Mummery, Collie and Hastings.

On 8 August G H Morse, J H Wicks and Claude Wilson completed the first traverse of the Grépon in the reverse direction, ascending the peak by way of the SSW ridge. Five days earlier this party had made another new ascent, reaching the summit of the Aiguille d'Argentière by climbing the SW face and the ESE ridge. Two smaller unclimbed peaks below the neighbouring Aiguille du Chardonnet were also ascended during the month: Aiguille Forbes on 2 August by J J Brigg, Eric Greenwood and Alfred Holmes with Jules and Omer Balleys; and Aiguille Adams Reilly on 23 August by Gustav Euringer with Alphonse Payot and Edouard Folliguet.

Other notable achievements were the fifth ascent of the Brenva ridge route on Mont Blanc by J P Farrar with Christian Klucker and Daniel Maquignaz on 26 July – a climb which, Farrar later recalled, 'involved the most continuously heavy step-cutting in hard steep ice I have ever seen' – and a remarkable feat, at the age of 52, by Paul Güssfeldt. Having been granted special permission 'in the interests of science' to cut short a journey with the Emperor William II Güssfeldt accompanied by Klucker and Emile Rey, two of the greatest guides of the period, and by César Ollier as porter reached the summit of Mont Blanc on 16 August by way of the Brenva glacier, the Aiguille Blanche de Peuterey and Mont Blanc de Courmayeur. The expedition, which lasted for 88 hours, necessitated two remote bivouacs and a dreadful night 'in the cabane of the Rochers Rouges, packed together with 12 workmen'.

Elsewhere in the Alps many other parties were able to take advantage of the favourable conditions. In the Dauphiné the E, summit ridge of the Meije was traversed on several occasions and on 12 August Louise and Marie Lacharrière, accompanied by Pierre Gaspard *père*, became the first ladies to complete this route. In the Pennine Alps on 10 September Carlo Restelli, with Mattias Zurbriggen and Ludwig Burgener, followed a difficult route on the E face of Monte Rosa to reach the summit of the Nordend. Starting from the Marinelli hut the party succeeded in climbing very steep rocks and exposed slopes between the famous couloir and the Brioschi route before joining that route on the ridge below the summit.

Further east two peaks in the Bregaglia group were climbed for the first time: the distinctive Ago di Sciora in the Sciora chain on 4 June by Anton von Rydzewsky with Klucker and Rey; and Punta Sant'Anna or Piz Badilet on 26 July by Count Francesco Lurani with a party which included Carlo Magnaghi and Giovanni Fiorelli. In the Dolomites on 11 August Gilberto Melzi, with Giuseppe Zecchini, reached the summit of Cimone della Pala by way of the unclimbed NW ridge, a route followed by the Dutch climber Jeanne Immink who on 12 September, accompanied by Walter Schulze and the guides Michele Bettega and Sepp Innerkofler, became the first lady to climb and to traverse this peak. On 26 August Ludwig Norman-Neruda, with Antonio Tavernaro, completed the first traverse of Sass Maor, having ascended the peak by a new route from the north.

The magnificent weather was particularly welcomed by Dr Jules Janssen, the astronomer, who was able to proceed with his ambitious scheme of building an observatory on the summit of Mont Blanc. The hut which then stood on the top of the Rochers Rouges had been erected to provide shelter for the workmen engaged in the project and by August some 15 tonnes of materials had been transported at considerable expense to the Petits Rochers Rouges, the rock outcrop 230m below the summit, under the supervision of Frédéric Payot.

> The structure is two storeys high, with a terrace. The rectangular base is about 33ft. long by 15ft. wide. A spiral staircase runs the height of the building, and unites the two storeys and the terrace, which is raised several feet and supports a platform intended for meteorological observations. The walls, windows, and doors are double. When everything was on the spot, the carpenters were sent to the top to put the building together. By a happy chance they had 15 days of absolutely calm weather, and by September 8 the observatory was in place – walls standing, floors laid, staircase up, windows in; all done, in short, but a part of the terrace. Impatient to see the new work, M. Janssen hastened to the summit and on September 11 reached the new building which, upon inspection, he found entirely satisfactory, with one exception. It was not as deeply buried in the snow as he had ordered.

After spending four nights in the observatory and carrying out his first tasks with the aid of a spectroscope Janssen was convinced that the resistance of the snow was sufficient to support the building but Edward Whymper, who during the night of 8–9 August had camped at the summit in perfect conditions, expressed his doubts.[3] 'It is not the liability of sinking *into* the snow, but the strong probability that any building erected on the top will sink *with* the snow, which gives rise to apprehensions about the stability and maintenance of M. Janssen's observatory.'

No such doubts were expressed over the location of another famous refuge which was inspected by a distinguished visitor.

> On the evening of August 15 her Majesty the Queen of Italy left Gressoney for the Punta Gnifetti, on the summit of which has been recently built the new observatory hut, 'Regina Margherita', constructed by the Italian Alpine Club.
>
> After a two days' stay at the Chalet de Stafel the royal party moved to the Capanna Linty[4] (3,100m.) in the neighbourhood of which a camp had been established. Thence the Queen started on the morning of the 18th, at 4.30 A.M., attended by her Excellency the Marchesa di Villamarina and by Prince Strozzi, and accompanied by Miss Villamarina and by Baron Peccoz.
>
> After climbing the rocks at the foot of the Gastrelet Glacier, and leaving Capanna Gnifetti to the left, her Majesty arrived at the Lys-Joch at 9.30 A.M., where she was met by Signor Gaudenzio

Sella and by Signor Vittorio Sella, who photographed the party. From this point the Queen walked very quickly to the foot of the Punta Gnifetti, which she reached exactly at 12 o'clock.

Her Majesty was received at the top of Punta Gnifetti by Signor Costantino Perazzi, Signor Gaudenzio Sella, and Signor F. Gonella, members of a special committee appointed by the Italian Alpine Club for the construction of the cabane. Signor Perazzi made a short speech, expressing admiration of the courage her Majesty displayed, and gratification at the great interest she always took in mountaineering and science. At 2 o'clock the committee took leave of the Queen, who, with her party, remained in the cabane for the night.

The inauguration of the new building on 3 and 4 September was celebrated in style by Luigi Vaccarone and Guido Rey who, with Zurbriggen, Burgener and Casimir Thérisod arrived at the end of the proceedings, having completed a new route to the Colle Gnifetti from the Marinelli hut. Other refuges which were completed by the end of the season having been constructed on or near the sites of earlier buildings included the Luigi Amedeo di Savoia hut on the Italian ridge of the Matterhorn and the Orny hut[5] below the Trient plateau.

In the Pyrenees the completion of a remarkable shelter required the use of dynamite. During the summer Count Henri Russell supervised the construction of *la Grotte du Paradis*, his seventh and last grotto a few metres below the Pique-Longue, the highest point of the Grand Vignemale. The grotto was dry and Russell celebrated by spending the night of 26–27 July at his new abode, alone with the mountain.

In the Caucasus exploration was continued by Woolley, J G Cockin, F W Newmarch and G A Solly who arrived in the central region without guides in July. Although bad weather and dangerous snow conditions frustrated their attempts to ascend the S, higher peak of Ushba (4710m) they reached a number of high passes and climbed to a considerable height on Tikhtengen (4610m) above the Tsanner glacier before being defeated on the W ridge.

In East Africa an important contribution to the exploration of Mount Kenya was made by the naturalist Dr J W Gregory. After arriving in the region as a member of an abortive expedition Gregory organised his own party and during the course of a remarkable journey succeeded in reaching the base of the peak with Fundi Mabruk, a Zanzibari porter, and in climbing to a height of about 4750m on a glacier below Point Lenana (4985m) which he named the Lewis glacier. Gregory also named other prominent features in the area including the Teleki valley, after the Hungarian explorer who had reached the head of that valley six years earlier.

Many successful expeditions were undertaken in other ranges. In the Hindu Kush region on 21 April the Hon C G Bruce joined forces with Francis Younghusband to climb a peak above the Chitral valley; in the Japanese Alps the Rev Walter Weston, who had already climbed Fujisan or Fujiyama and Yarigatake, ascended Okuhodakadake (3190m) on 25 August; and on 4 October W H Cozens-Hardy reached the summit of Durmitor (2522m), the highest peak in the Montenegro region. In Canada S E S Allen and W D Wilcox, after making unsuccessful attempts to scale Mount Victoria and Mount Temple from a camp beside Lake Louise, moved to the Selkirk range where they completed the first ascent of Eagle Peak (2854m), to the north of Uto Peak and Mount Sir Donald.

At home a number of new climbs was completed in the Lake District where, as in the Alps, exceptionally dry conditions were experienced. On 2 April Charles Hopkinson and W N Tribe made the first ascent of Scafell Pinnacle from Deep Ghyll, a fine achievement for the period. Other notable first ascents included Collier's Climb on Scafell by Joseph Collier and S B Winser, also on 2 April; Pier's Ghyll on Lingmell by Collier, Winser, H S W Jones and G Fairbairn on 29 April; and the Crowley Route on the Napes Needle by Aleister Crowley on 28 August. Sergeant Crag Gully in Langstrath was climbed on 6 September by O G Jones and J W Robinson and on 26 December Jones, who had been lying on the billiard table in the Wastwater Hotel 'thinking of the different kinds of nothing'[6] made the first ascent of Kern Knotts Chimney on Great Gable, accompanied by Robinson and W H Fowler.

An event which aroused considerable interest was the publication of the *Mountaineering* volume in the All-England Series, written by Claude Wilson and illustrated by Ellis Carr. Describing the book[7] as 'a practical guide for would-be climbers' Wilson explained in his introduction that

> mountaineering is one of the finest and healthiest exercises in the world, and, as such, it must command a continuous supply of recruits: the important point is that those who do enter, and will continue to enter, its lists, should understand the principles which alone make it a justifiable recreation.

As the end of the year approached, after a memorable climbing season, it was time to take stock.

> And now the giants of the Alps have all been climbed, and the mountaineer who wishes to break fresh ground must go further afield, or else must content himself with seeking out new and difficult ways to the summit in place of old and possibly easy ones. Still the possible permutations and combinations are practically inexhaustible, or at any rate present an infinite variety which may suffice for many generations.

It was also a time to look back. On 4 December the death occurred of John Tyndall, the great scientist and mountaineer whose name will always be associated with the Weisshorn and the early climbing history of the Matterhorn. There surely could be no finer tribute to any mountaineer than the recollection of Tyndall by C E Mathews.

> He loved the mountains with all his heart, and he made his mark in his day.

REFERENCES

1 J D Forbes, *Travels through the Alps of Savoy*. Edinburgh, Adam and Charles Black, 1843.
2 A F Mummery, *My Climbs in the Alps and Caucasus*. London, T Fisher Unwin, 1895.
3 Edward Whymper, 'The Alps Revisited', Part IV. *The Graphic* Vol L, No 1299, 467–470, 1894.
4 Located on a ridge near the Alta Luce plateau and now in ruins.
5 Replaced by a new building constructed in 1977 and now relocated on the slopes of the Dent de Vaulion (1483m), Jura region, Canton Vaud.
6 O G Jones, *Rock-Climbing in the English Lake District*. Keswick, G P Abraham and Sons, 1897.
7 Claude Wilson, MD, *Mountaineering*. London, George Bell & Sons, 1893.

. Queen Margherita of Italy on the Lysjoch, 18 August 1893.
(*Vittorio Sella*) (p223)

. Queen Margherita of Italy at the Margherita hut, 18 August 1893.
(*Vittorio Sella*) (p223)

69. Dent du Requin (*C Douglas Milner*) (p223)

. Kern Knotts Chimney, Great Gable.
(*G P Abraham & Sons Photos, Keswick*) (p223)

Above
3. Large crevasses on Island Peak. Baruntse's fluted ice in the background. (*Malcolm Rutherford*) (p170)

Facing page, above
1. Kackar Dag: Avucor valley. (*J G R Harding*) (p154)

Facing page, below
2. Refuge at Bulut Dag. (*J G R Harding*) (p154)

Above
74. Hotel Belalp and chapel seen from Villa Lusgen. (*Trevor Braham*) (p196)

Facing page
75. Tyndall memorial above Belalp.
(*Trevor Braham*) (p196)

76. Andy Fanshawe, 1963–1992
(*Alan Hinkes*) (p326)

77. Dudley Frederick Oliphant Dangar, 1902–1992 (p323)

Area Notes 1992

COMPILED BY ROY RUDDLE

LINDSAY GRIFFIN

The Alps 1992

Lindsay Griffin would like to thank Robert Durran, Graham Ettle, Mireille Lazarevitch, Michel Piola, Marko Prezelj, Simon Richardson, Franci Savenc, Slavko Svetičič and Blyth Wright for their help with these notes. He would welcome further information and new route descriptions for publication in these pages at: 2 Top Sling, Tregarth, Bangor, Gwynedd LL57 4RL.

THE WINTER SEASON

Long periods of cold but stable weather followed the heavy, pre-Christmas snowfall (2m in the valley) in the Mont Blanc massif and, although there was little extra snow for a period of seven to eight weeks, the prevailing, strong N and NE winds kept it fairly intact at lower altitudes. With the Midi téléphérique fully operational by early February, the Vallée Blanche quickly regained its popularity. More frequent snowfalls started to appear in March/April and it was thought that the avalanche risk would be quite high. In fact there were few slides and seemingly fewer incidents. The worst occurred late in the season and involved three well-respected ski-guides. Performing for a photographer in the vicinity of the Col du Plan they were windslab avalanched, swept into a crevasse and killed.

Ecrins Massif

Waterfall-ice enthusiasts will be pleased to hear that a new guide *Oisans aux six vallées*, which describes 250 icefalls in the region adjacent to the Ecrins, has been published at 120FF. the authors are local activists Francois Damilano and Godefrey Perroux.

Pic Sans Nom   Jean-Christophe Moulin made a solo (probably the first) winter ascent of the *Raie des Fesses* in a rapid time of three hours. This route, which follows the obvious narrow central couloir on the N face, was first climbed by Boivin, Diaferia and Vinnet-Fuasset in 1976 and thought at the time to be the hardest ice gully in the Alps (85°+).

Pelvoux   Moulin, this time roped with others, made the first winter ascent of the difficult ice gully originally climbed by Patrick Bérhault and, with Gilles Rivière, climbed a new gully on the **Trois Dent**, a subsidiary peak of the Pelvoux which already holds one of the most famous ice couloirs in the range – the *Couloir Chaud*. In the last couple of years the latter has collapsed due to the very hot summers and is no longer complete below half height. Crossing the Violettes glacier on the classic traverse of the Pelvoux has become an increasingly dangerous business in the summer months due to stone and ice fall.

Mont Blanc Massif

Mont Blanc   The first winter ascent of *Divine Providence* was achieved by Roberto Bressan, Saverio Occhi and Paolo Tamagnini, three young aspirant guides from Italy, from 5–7 January. The temperature was low throughout the ascent, but conditions on this E-facing wall were reasonable with early morning sunshine allowing the leader to climb in rock boots while the other two jumared (the whole ascent was made at a grade of A3 and 6b). Climbing in the dark they reached the top of the pillar during the night of the 7th. By now the cold was beginning to take its toll and Tamagnini was developing frostbite. The next day the party made a tricky descent of the W flank to the Col de Peuterey and so back to the Fourche. The route has now received around 15 ascents since its inception in 1984.

Mont Maudit – SE face of the SW shoulder (4361m)   Donatella Coppa, Gianni Lanza and Bill Ramella made the first winter ascent of the *East Spur* on 28–29 January. Surprisingly, it seems most likely that this was only the second ascent of the route first climbed 33 years ago by Bonatti, Ferrario and Oggioni!

Aiguille de Saussure   Complicated approaches ensure that, despite excellent granite, this aiguille is rarely climbed. The first winter ascent was made by Joshua Getter and Ivan Ghiradini over two days in February/March, via a new route which crosses the original Balmat/Mollier at half-height. The party apporoached via the N face of Mont Blanc du Tacul and climbed eight or nine pitches on the pillar at around V/V+ with a little A2. The route, named *Vacances d'Alpinistes*, has an overall grade of TD+/ED1.

Roi de Siam The traditional route on the SE face is the *Manet/Courcelle/Fontaine/Streng* (250m IV/V−), and a popular addition in more recent times is *Serenissime* (250m 6a) on the right side of the face. On 4 January the first winter ascent of the latter was made in four and a half hours by Coppa, Lanza and Ramella.

Grand Capucin On the 7–8 February, in 9 hours climbing time and with a bivouac close to the top, Jean-Christophe Lafaille made the first solo winter ascent of the *Directe des Capucins*, back-roping the 14 pitches. As much of the route involves wide cracks, in-situ protection is still rather sparse.

Trident du Tacul The very next day (9 February), Lafaille soloed *Weekend in Transylvania* on the SE face (200m 6b). This took him three hours and, as with the climb on the Capucin, he was favoured by dry conditions and relatively mild temperatures.

Grandes Jorasses A now highly tuned Lafaille set off from the Leschaux hut on 9 March for an attempt on a new direct route to the summit of Pt Croz. After climbing 250m of mixed ground on the left side of the spur and above the level of the Second Tower, his chosen line reached the crest via the right side of the great monolith (the obvious line up the left side had already been climbed in 1991 by Slavko Svetičič). This involved a number of pitches of hard aid climbing and, despite winter conditions, was not immune to stonefall. Unfortunately bad weather forced a retreat after four days. The first opportunity for a renewed acquaintance came on 23 April. Making much faster progress than previously, he was able to reach in a single day the site of his top bivouac and on the 24th climbed 12 further pitches on compact rock and icy smears to the Second Ice Field. The final 300m, completed the next day, involved sustained climbing on rock of a quality that left much to be desired! *Le Chemin des Étoiles* (1000m ED3) is mainly 5/6a, with a short section of 6b on the final pillar. Half the pitches involved aid and on these there were several sustained sections of A3. The true independence of this line is hard to gauge: once on the spur the route must, from time to time, correspond with the rarely climbed *Direct* by Keine and Werner in 1974. Earlier in the year, Marc Batard spent nine days establishing a new route up the right flank of the Walker Spur following a line of cracks and dièdres in the vague depression that lies between the *Cassin* and the icy runnels of the *Boivin route*. The main difficulties, on the right side of the Grey Tower, were on excellent granite (V+ and A2), but after his eighth bivouac, close to the Red Tower, Batard was forced to finish up the final 250m of the *Cassin*, as the rock on the flanks of the spur above this point becomes quite abysmal. Although an impressive solo performance, the route – *Le Colombe et L'Enfant* (29 December–6 January) – is unlikely to gather the crowds. The climbing of north-facing alpine rock in winter is far from popular and in this case impracticable during the summer due to heavy stonefall.

Col de l'Aiguille Verte Possibly the first winter ascent of the *Argentière side of the W gap* was made solo by Pierre Biedermann on 8 March (although a winter ascent was nearly achieved in 1972 by Sangnier who crossed the central spur high up to finish near the E gap). The route was first climbed in 1975 by Bettembourg, Cuenet, Charlet, Mangeot and Ghilini. It gives a classic medium grade ice climb with two steep sections of 65° and 75°, but is rather exposed to stonefall. There are fixed anchors for a rappel descent of the SW side.

Les Droites   The rather esoteric *Czech route*, (Semon/Slavik 1979 ED2 VI/VI+ A2) on the left flank of the *Couzy Spur*, received its first winter ascent in January by David Autheman, Marc Cotto and Fred Vimal.

Petit Dru   A team of Polish climbers have made the third winter ascent of the *French Directissima* on the W face. It is not known whether the Poles went to the summit or not, although their time of eight days, during early March, suggests that they probably did. Recently the climb has rejected the attempts of several talented rock climbers to produce a free super-route: the grade remains ED2 (6b A2).

Valais

Monte Rosa   Of all the great icy walls in the Alps, the E flank of this peak has dimensions that compare most favourably with those exhibited by many of the austere faces throughout the Himalaya. Approaching via the Macugnaga téléphérique, amenable conditions on the glacier allowed Bojan Pockar and Matjaz Jamnik to reach the foot of the face in six hours, at 7pm on 7 March. After the difficult overhanging wall of the rimaye they climbed unroped for four hours (500m 55°), up the ice slope to the left of the *Gardin route*, to reach the prominent spur clearly visible on this side of the face, where they bivouacked at 3600m. Next day they continued unroped for 200m (60°–80°) before seven difficult pitches through the rocky barrier at the top of the spur (one AO, two VI+ and the rest VI–/VI with icy runnels up to 85°) led to the ice slopes close to the *Cresta Signal*. Working up right in deteriorating weather they joined the 1931 *Lagarde/Davies route* and followed it to the top. After a night spent in the Margherita hut, the next day provided an eight hour epic as the climbers fought their way down featureless ground in blizzard conditions to the Alagna téléphérique. *No Pasaran* (1400m ED2) is thought to be one of the hardest and biggest mixed routes created in this region of the Alps during the last few winters.

Bernese Oberland

Eiger   On 9 March at 5.30am Catherine Destivelle began her attempt to be the first woman to solo the classic 1938 route. By 3pm she had reached the ramp where surprisingly dry conditions aided her progress. The Exit Cracks were reached at 7pm and climbed by headtorch. On short sections of the route she used a self-belaying technique, but in order to save time simply cut off the part of the rope in use and abandoned it, rather than descend to release the belay. Her judgment in this matter proved correct and she emerged from the final pitch trailing two five-metre tails! At 10.30pm, after a rapid 17 hours climbing, she arrived on the summit to be met by Jeff Lowe and a welcome sack full of bivvy gear.

Dolomites

Brenta Franco Corn and Mauro Fronza made the second winter ascent of the *Steinkoetter route* on the SW face of the **Campanile Caigo**, part of the **Cima Mandron**. This 400m grade VI was climbed on 5 January. Not content with this outing, they moved across to the S face the next day and repeated the other *Steinkoetter route*, this time making the first free ascent at VII (French 6b). Guido Bonvicini made the first solo winter ascent of the *Maestri route* on the **Corna Rossa** in one day, despite difficulties of VI/A3 and a 12m roof high on the face, and on the **Croz dell'Altissimo** Lia Celva and Giorgio Gionannini made the first winter ascent and second overall ascent of the 1983 *Accademici route* (650m VII). The often tried icefall known as the Principessa on the **Torrione di Vallesinella** finally succumbed to Renzo Springhetti and Fabio Stedile. There still seems to be considerable scope left for new water-ice climbs in this region of the Eastern Alps.

Pala On the SW face of the **Cimon della Pala**, Michele Cestari and Dario Sebastiani made the first winter and second overall ascent of the *Girasole Pillar* on 5 January. This 900m route, first climbed in 1986 by R and G Corona, is all free at grade VII.

Sorapiss Alfredo Pozza and Mauro Valmassoi made the second overall and the first winter ascent of the recent *Dall'Omo/Svaluto Moreolo/Valmassoi route* which takes the SW dièdre of the **Cima di Cacciagrande** (500m VI). This took place on 4 January. The same team also climbed a number of 250–330m icefalls in the same area (TD– and below).

Pelmo Later in January Pozza teamed up with the same Ferruccio Svaluto Moreolo to make the first winter ascent of the classic *SE Pillar* (Bellodis/Franceschi 1955 route) on Monte Pelmo. Although not sustained the pillar is 800m high with maximum difficulties of VI/VI+ and a 10m section of A1/2. It also has a descent which could be decidedly tricky in poor snow. The pair completed this route, which would take an average of 9 hours in summer, in a rapid 10½ hours.

Marmolada d'Ombretta *The Fish* had a probable second winter ascent by Slovenian climbers Janez Kesnar and Marko Prezelj. They broke trail to the foot of the face on 4 March and fixed the first 150m, retiring to a bivouac close to the Falier hut. The next day, in dry though cold conditions, they were able to reach the second big terrace by 9pm (last two pitches by head-torch). Despite nasty conditions in the exit chimneys only four hours were needed to reach the summit cableway. The climbers found the route almost completely equipped with pegs, negotiated the difficulties at VII and A3 and made the majority of the aid moves on skyhooks. They felt the possibilities for good nut/Friend placements were fairly rare but recommend carrying a selection of both!

Civetta Pozza then moved across to this area where on 12 March he made the first solo winter ascent of the classic *1938 Liebl/Schober route* on the steep and exposed E face of the **Pan di Zucchero**. On 18 March he made an impressive 'enchaînement' on the **Torre Venezia**. Starting with the classic

Andrich/Faè on the SW buttress (300m V+/VI), which he completed in 3½ hours, he turned his attention to the *Livanos route* (VI) on the same face, which took him 3 hours 45 minutes. Finally he dispatched the classic W face (Castiglioni/Khan 399m IV/IV+) in less than an hour. Perhaps the most impressive winter ascent of the season came from Marco Anghileri and Lorenzo Mazzoleni on the NW face of the **Cima su Alto**. From the 13–16 March they climbed *Marino Stenico* on the exposed Central Pillar. The main difficulties (VI+ and A4) occur on the top 450m of this 800m high wall and can be reached from the left via much easier ground. However, on this occasion the party climbed the route direct to make the second overall ascent (third of the top section). Their achievement is all the more impressive given the sunless aspect of this face. All the routes previously described in this Dolomites section have been on, more or less, S facing walls, where conditions can be almost summer-like during stable anticyclonic weather in the winter months.

THE SUMMER SEASON

Alpinists creating new routes during the summer of 1992 could be divided, quite distinctly, into two groups: (a) those climbing new rock routes which, more often than not, were equipped at the time with all the necessary bolts for a rapid free ascent by subsequent parties (these routes are, in the main, difficult and of very high quality and, despite opinions expressed in certain quarters, the lines followed by these routes are entirely independent), and (b) those putting up new lines on the big walls – generally faces that are already well known and prestigious. Some of these lines have been brilliant; others perhaps a little contrived. It is interesting that for the second year running, almost all the 'Great Faces' of the Alps have gathered a new route. On a more sombre note there were approximately 32 deaths (including missing persons) in the Mont Blanc massif, many associated with stonefall – most notably the great French alpinist and ENSA guide Alexis Long, who was responsible for scores of new routes on both rock and ice in the Western Alps, many in the company of Gabarrou. On a lighter note, two British alpinists discovered the remains of the Indian Airways 'Kangchenjunga' which crashed in 1966 and re-emerged from the glacier this August.

Vanoise

Lionel Daudet has made solo ascents of two rarely climbed routes on the Epena in fast times. On 27 August he climbed the *Voltolini/Rod route* (ED1 500m) and the following day the *Rod/Schneider route* (TD 800m). On the second route he passed several pegs, but there appeared to be none on the first. Later he climbed two routes on the **Aiguille de la Vanoise** – a spectacular blade of rock reached easily from Pralognon – in rapid times. On 18 September, using a back rope only on the very hardest sections, he soloed *Larmes du Soleil* (6c+) in 1½ hours and then followed this with an ascent of the classic *Desmaison route* (TD 300m) in 1 hour.

Mont Blanc Massif

Mont Blanc From 18–24 August Francois Damilano made a solo crossing of the Mont Blanc range, keeping more or less on the crest of the main NE–SW spine, from the Grands Montets to Les Contamines. Tricky spots were the exposed, loose and rarely crossed Arête des Rochassiers before the Triolet plateau; descending to the Col de Leschaux via, initially, the S ridge, then the W flank of the Eboulement; the initial snow crest of the classic NW ridge of the Aiguille de Leschaux, which had disappeared leaving smooth blank rock; and the summit of the Petites Jorasses, where he was forced to race down the SW flank in a violent storm to the haven of the Gervasutti hut. He lost a day, marooned by a blizzard in the Col de la Fourche hut, but next day climbed the Brenva Spur and crossed the summits of Mont Blanc, Bionnassay, Dômes de Miage and Aiguille de la Bérangère, to finish that night in Les Contamines. The whole venture was completely self-supported; he carried a modicum of food and fuel, 100m of 7mm rope plus plenty of nuts, slings, krabs etc for rappels, and a walkie-talkie through which he was able to receive weather updates.

A group of aspirant guides, led by Patrick Berhault and including Fred Vimal, climbed the W face of the **Aiguille Noire de Peuterey** (*Ratti-Vitale*), the SW face of the **Gugliermina** (*Gervasutti*) and the **Central Pillar of Frêney** (*classic route*) in one day – 25 August. On the **Red Pillar** warm conditions can make access across the upper Brouillard glacier almost suicidal and several prospective customers have been forced back before reaching the foot. Guy Muhlemann and Simon Richardson took perhaps the most logical start which begins just left of the foot of the pillar and climbs to the top of the pedestal in two pitches (6a then 5+). This avoids the stone-swept couloir of the original start. They continued to free climb the chimneys above, finding them dry and over graded (5+ and 6a would be more accurate) and completed the ascent to the summit of the Blanc, enjoying an early bivouac on the Brouillard ridge. Although they felt a fast party could reach the summit easily in a day (10–12 hours), the whole outing is still rather committing and fully deserves its ED1 grade.

On the **Grand Pilier d'Angle** *Divine Providence* was climbed several times over the summer and was given a *Direct Start* (250m 6c 6c obl) during an attempt by a party from the FFME (Fédération Française de la Montagne et de l'Escalade) led by Alexis Long. J-C Lafaille's 1991 route *Un Autre Monde* had its second ascent by Michel Fauquet and companion. Fauquet, who has now climbed both lines, confirmed that *Divine* is much the better route.

Aiguille Croux There was much activity during the summer on this fine rock peak close to the Monzino hut, with Romain Vogler continuing his exploration from the previous year. The rock is rather curious and compact, which no doubt accounts, in part, for its neglect over the years. Looking at the SE face, the new routes are, from left to right; *La Descente aux Envers* by Simone Badier and Vogler on 17 July. This is situated a little after the short descent (down ledges and steps) made when approaching from the hut. It is a short route (7a 6b obl), but one of the steepest in the range! *Entre les Gouttes* (80m 6b+ 6a obl) is only two pitches but a good introduction for those parties wishing to familiarise themselves with the type of rock found on the Croux. It was climbed by Badier and Vogler again on the 16 July. Further right, on the left side of the main face, Manlio Motto and Vogler put up the *Que cherches-toi Jean Marie?* (7 pitches 6c 6b obl) on 29–30 August. *Euroteam*, by the same two plus Gérard Long on 12 September, is an eight-pitch route (6c 6b obl) which cuts the classic *Hurzler-Ottoz* (1935) at the top of pitches three, four and seven. On the E face Motto with Guido Azzales and Gianni Predan created *Vuoto a Perdere*. This 13-pitch route (450m 7a/b with one point of aid 6c obl), which required the placement of 54 bolts, is very difficult to reach at the end of the season due to the chaotic nature of the Frêney glacier – access is aided by a fixed rope at the base of the SE spur, and the start of the route lies 100m to the right of it.

Mont Maudit   On the E face of the **Androsace Pillar**, just to the right of *Marin d'Eau Douce* Giovanni Bassanini and Rudy Buccella put up a new 200m route. *Il Volo di Icaro* is 7a and was climbed entirely with nuts for protection. Guy Muhlemann and Simon Richardson made the first free ascent of the pillar to the summit of Mont Maudit by climbing *Marin d'Eau Douce* until one pitch below the 7a+ crux, and then taking a dièdre out right to the crest, where they continued up *Maudit Blues* (see Topo 2) to the pillar top. From there they followed the original *Bertone-Zappelli* route to the Frontier Ridge (5+ and Scottish 3) and a bivouac just below the Pointe Androsace (ED2 6c 15 hours).

Mont Blanc du Tacul   Previously unreported is Graham Ettle and Blyth Wright's ascent of the *Central Pillar Direct* minus the *Tours Carrée and Rouge* (TD+). The lower buttress seems to have had very little traffic, but after the first pitch is of good quality. The starting point is nearer 3300m making the whole climb c950m (in fact the party started to the right which avoided current rimaye problems and potential serac fall – a rising traverse line regained the route on pitch 2). The crux pitch on the right side of the crest is probably 6a+. It appears that few parties follow the *Boccalatte Direct*, yet even the couloir was not easy and the last pitch below the junction with the *Gervasutti route* was wet, icy and about Scottish 4 (it does have a fixed rope on the top part). From here the distance to the summit is rather longer than suggested in the guide, being more like eight pitches to the foot of the final grey tower. On the Gervasutti Pillar the dog-leg shown after pitch 15 is a little confusing. The route does cross on to the right flank at this point but the crux follows and is probably British 5c if climbed free (though traditionally A1). Above, the chimney leads to grade III ramps. Ettle considers it important to stress that the ramps end at the distinct brèche and the 20m crack follows on from it.

Grand Capucin   On 18 July Bassanini, in the company of Pascal Gravante and Mario Ravello, climbed *De Fil en Aiguille* (Amstutz, Banderet and Vogler 1991 7a and A1) with only two points of aid on the fifth pitch. At a suggested grade of 8a/8a+ this fifth pitch is now the hardest on the 'Cap'.

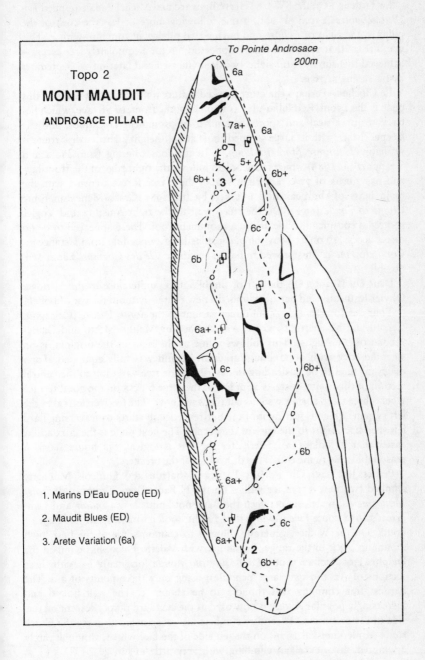

Topo 2
MONT MAUDIT
ANDROSACE PILLAR

To Pointe Androsace
200m

6a

7a+   6a

5+   6b+

6b+   **3**

6c

6b

6a+

6c   6b+

6b

1. Marins D'Eau Douce (ED)

6a+

2. Maudit Blues (ED)

6c

3. Arete Variation (6a)

6a+   **2**

1   6b+

Le Trident   On the SW face Hervé Bouvard and Michel Piola equipped *Les Untouchables* (250m 6b obl), a line following more or less the crest of the pillar to the right of *Eclipse* and having two pitches in common with it. This was a route that presented superb opportunities for a completely free ascent – achieved this summer, on sight, by Alain Ghersen and later on 16 September by Bassanini, at 7c+.

Le Clocher   Perhaps the most marked feature on the S facing walls of this peak is the 250m 'Red Pillar'. It has two faces; the front, or SE face, which lies back from vertical and sports a number of prominent cracklines, and the steeper E face with its large stepped roofs at half-height . The hardest route is probably *L'Empire State Building*, a tremendous offering from Piola and Strappazzon (1989) which more or less follows the right edge of the front face and has a crux of 7b/c. The right side of the E face forms a corner with the main mass of the peak and is taken by the 1985 Grassi/Meneghin route *Conflicto Finale* (6a+). On the steep wall to the right Amstutz and Vogler spotted a conspicuous line above a prominent roof. There appeared to be no direct access, so on 23 May the pair reached it by a pendule from a stance on *Conflicto Finale*. This proved to be the key to *Le Clé des Champs* (280m 6c+ 6b obl).

Dent Du Geant   On the left of the NW face, quite close to the N ridge, Olivier Ratheaux and partner climbed a new route – without the use of bolts!

Tour des Jorasses   A 250m direct variant to the *South Dièdre* (Calcagno, Cerruti and Machetto 1970 6a) was climbed by Manlio Motto and Gianni Predan on 15 August. This follows a line to the right of the original, is on splendid rock with a maximum grade of 6c and was fully equipped. Topo diagrams tend to be misleading in describing the free variation to the central section of this route. It starts 30m left of the large blocks on the good terrace where three steep corner systems cut the wall above. The free version takes the left system, which is just right of the buttress edge. It starts by traversing hard left then back right to the base of the corner. The next pitch is the crux and is easier that it looks (6a). Thereafter the line is logical. Six hours seems a reasonable time to the end of the difficulties at the brèche.

Petites Jorasses   On 15 July Patrick Gabarrou and Francois Marsigny climbed two new 550m ice gullies on the N Face. *Deux Temps* and *Trois Mouvements*, which lie between the Baumont-Smith NW *Couloir* and Gabarrou's 1991 route *Five Candles* to the right, took a total time of less than 15 hours. On the W face, generally thought to contain some of the best 'high mountain' rock in the range, Bassanini, with Valerio Folco, has climbed the Dalphin/Piola/Steiner route, *La Beauté du Monde* (originally 6a with three sections of A2 and two large pendules) using only three points of aid. The hardest free climbing was thought to be about 7c. The well bolted and increasingly popular *Anouk* is now used as the standard rappel descent on this side of the mountain. Adventure climbers are recommended to try the *Czech route* (Koller/Stejskal 1976) on the left side of the face which, although rarely attempted, gives excellent climbing with very little in-situ gear (TD 5+). It crosses the *Original route* before the latter reaches the snow patch and a number of parties climbing the *Original* now appear to take the *Czech* finish, which seems a better and quicker option. It is also worth noting that it is the long off-width crack below the old aided roof pitch that is VI and not the roof itself as shown in the guide.

Grandes Jorasses Three days after his climbs on the Petites Jorasses Gabarrou was back in the Leschaux hut, this time with Christian Appertet. Over the next three days the pair climbed a new direct route on the Pointe Marguerite, following the crest of the spur avoided on the right by the original *Couzy-Desmaison route*. With a very high freezing isotherm the party were almost constantly under the threat of falling rock and ice. They both took impressive falls and had an epic exit onto and escape down the W ridge in a ferocious lightning storm. The route contained some interesting mixed climbing, though main difficulties (5+ to 6b/c on rock) were found in a long overhanging dièdre above mid-height on the spur.

Aiguille du Tacul On this superb viewpoint Patrick Gabarrou and Francois Marsigny climbed a new route on the previously untouched triangular face, sandwiched between the NE ridge and Gabarrou's own 1978 route on the N face. The ascent, on 8 May, gave particularly thin mixed climbing (800m to the summit) and took the pair 7 hours.

An all-free ascent of the *Germain–Manfait route* on the W pillar was made by Robert Durran and partner. They thought it a reasonably good outing in a peaceful corner of the range, despite the lower part of the face having apparently received some rockfall damage. The climb was only 15 pitches, with the crux, the old A1/2 sections, going at an 'off-widthy' E2 5b/c.

Aiguille de Leschaux Durran and partner made an ascent of the rarely-climbed *Gogna-Rava Direct* on the NE face. However they stayed more in the line of the chimney-couloir and worked out left near the top. The result was a very serious HVS with some atrocious rock!

Aiguille de Talèfre Early in the season Durran also climbed the excellent *Gabarrou-Ponti Direct* on the NW face which he thought to be far superior to the *Swiss route* on the Courtes.

Aiguille des Pèlerins Starting just right of the *N Face Direct*(Dard/ Reppelin 1967) and about 100m left of *Nostradamus* (Piola/Sprungli 1980), Andy Parkin and Mark Twight produced *Beyond Good and Evil*. This 14-pitch route, climbed (after two previous attempts) on 21–22 April gives demanding mixed climbing on a sunless face. ED2 c600m 5+/A3 and sections of 90° ice.

Aiguille du Fou There was plenty of activity on the S face despite the inherent danger in access during hot summers. Bassanini (again) joined the small band of climbers to repeat the classic *American route* completely free (7b/c), and also made the very first on-sight free ascent of the Colas/Grenier 1988 route towards the left side of the face called *les Ailes du Désir* (originally 6b and A2, now 7c due to Ghersen in 1991). The Bellin/Boivin/Moioli route *Ballade au Clair de Lune* (ED3 6b and A3/4), which had its second ascent from Jean-Christophe Moulin last year, received three partial repetitions this season. All participants confirmed the fine quality and interesting nature of the route, but note that the amount of artificial climbing is not actually that great, much of the aid is in place and there are only four moves on skyhooks. Moulin returned this year with Marco Troussier to climb directly over the 7-shaped roof, cross the *American* next to the roof on the Diagonal Crack and, via a pendule, reach a line leading into *Ballade*, which they followed for one pitch before breaking out for an independent finish. *Les Visiteurs du Soir* has nine pitches (6b/c and A2) and was climbed on 18–19 July. On the same two days Jean-Francois Hagenmuller and Alexis Long were working on Un *Weekend à la Compagne*, which crosses the very compact and exquisite granite between the *American* and *Les Ailes du Désir*. This very sustained and difficult artificial route was completed on 25 August after 23 hours effective climbing time and was Long's last new route. It has four or five sections of A4 and will probably need two full days for a repeat ascent.

Bec d'Oiseau   Climbed free, the excellent SE pillar is probably French 6a.

Aiguille de l'M   The 1966 *Galbraith-McKeith route* on the NW face follows a rightward slanting crackline to the right of the *Couzy route*, finishing just left of a small summit sometimes referred to as the Pic d'Ecureuils. As a mixed free/aid route it has never been popular, but was included in the recent guide with a possible free ascent in mind. The latter was achieved by T Ball and G Ettle in July 1991. Although a little dirty in parts due to lack of traffic, the climb gave a very worthwhile outing and will, hopefully, now receive a little more attention. The '40m corner' on the third pitch is comparable to the Bat corner (Ben Nevis) and the crux – the original A2 pitch high on the route – is now a 5c (British) finger crack, which required some gardening. Overall, this 10-pitch route equates to British E2 5c and was completed in seven hours (see Topo 3).

Petit Dru   At 5pm on Easter Monday, Marc Batard began climbing the steep lower slabs of the W face. By hauling 75kg of equipment his object was certainly not a rapid ascent, but a mental and physical adventure of the highest order where he might, '... spend three weeks on a great Alpine wall in preparation for a demanding solo Himalayan project'. After a week, with nightly bivouacs in a hanging tent, he had reached a point halfway up the face, following a line just right of *Les Strapontins du Paradis*. There now followed a week of snow and strong winds, which made movement impossible but finally clear, cold weather returned and a somewhat weaker Batard was able to resume climbing. The crux lay in passing a huge band of overhangs that occur at about two-thirds height on the face and provided some worrying moments. Loose rock; some stonefall; and to add to the excitement he also managed to drop the outer shell of one of his plastic boots! His line joined *L'Esprit d'Escalier* and finally the original W face route. The summit was eventually reached on 8 May after a total of 19 days (despite this length of time the maximum difficulties were only 5+/6a and A1). However, with no real footwear for a dodgy, snowed-up descent and incipient frostbite apparent in one toe, he bivouacked for the last time and was evacuated the next day by helicopter. Another serious rockfall from high on the N face left the area around the base of the peak a virtual no-go area this summer. Large blocks travelled as far out from the W face as the Dru Rognon where they hit a bivouacking party, killing one member. The N face, traditionally considered reasonably safe from objective danger, has changed dramatically. Climbing

Topo 3
AIGUILLE DE L'M
NORTH WEST FACE
GALBRAITH/McKEITH ROUTE

Summit
Couloir
V
Couzy route
V+
III — Dirty Finger Crack
VII
Possible escape
Big ledge
VI-
Parallel dièdres
Old pegs — VI
Flake
Scree ledge — V+
Easy ledges
VII- — Overhang (40m corner)
VI
IV+
Plan de L'aiguille 2 hr

with a young alpinists course from the Fédération Française de la Montagne et de L'Escalade, the Directeur Technique National, 44-year-old Jeff Lemoine, a well-known and respected alpinist, was killed by a volley of stonefall.

Flammes de Pierre Ridge Exploration continues on the sunny walls of the S face, where there are, to date, eight routes between 100m and 350m – all sustained and with technical grades of 6b to 7a. On 23 July Badier and Vogler put up *Les Feux de la Rampe*, which takes the left side of the face below the chimney of *Flammes du Désir*. Vogler, this time with Motto, climbed *Les Pendules à l'Heure* (100m 7a 6b obl), which as the name suggests finishes, after three very fine and strenuous pitches, with a monster pendulum very much in Yosemite style! On Pt 3280m, which lies just in front of the **Pointe Michelle Micheline**, Denis Collangette, Mathieu Desprat, David Jongley, Eric Neves and Francois Pallandre have produced *Guère de Feu*. This is an excellent climb of 550m (6b+ 6a obl), completed over two days (9 and 19 July) and well equipped for a rappel descent.

L'Evêque – Pointe 3014m Starting up the first three pitches of *Monseigneur Lefèbre* Motto and Vogler then branched out right on to the crest of a fantastic rib of compact granite, finishing over the final roof of *L'Eminence Grise*. *Qui Cherche Trouve* is 250m (7a 6b obl).

Aiguille du Moine   On 18 August Vincent Banderet and Vogler completed *Mystique* (400m 6c+ 6b obl) on the E face. This was a route first begun in 1991 with R Cottet and C Ramirez and considered by the authors to be one of the finest rock climbs in the range! The initial pitches are quite strenuous and feature some sustained layback moves up the right side of a ragged flake. Above, a broad spur at a more reasonable angle is followed to the top. On the classic *E Face Direct*, Wright considers the crux on pitch 2 to be British E1 5b if the pegs in the main dièdre are followed and E1 5c if the thin crack out right is taken. Also on the *S Ridge Integral* he feels that the original grade V pitches should be reinstated in place of the IV+ in lines 8, 15 and 21 of the current guide book. He also notes that as the 'easy couloir' runs parallel to the ridge it is not possible to 'climb it to the ridge': the chimney and chockstone exit pitch occurs after c60m and is a good deal harder than IV!

Aiguille de la Varappe   On the SW face of this culminating point of the **Aiguille Dorées**, *Eole Danza per Noi* (Gravante/Piola 1990 380m TD+ 5+/6a) has certainly fulfilled the authors' claim. In the last two years it has rapidly become a modern classic; each day this summer saw numerous parties enjoying the varied climbing – sustained but at an accessible standard. The granite here is equal to the best found in the range (such as the **Grand Capucin**), which is why Piola returned, this time with Vincent Sprungli, to complete his explorations with two more routes. *Face au Large*, first started (and equipped) in 1990 by Piola, Desplan, Gravante and Monnet, begins at the same point as *Eole*. It then climbs compact slabs on the lower triangle, before reaching an unforgettable crack system passing to the left of the huge white roofs on the main face (380m 6c 6b+ obl). *La Chevauchée fantastique* (380m 6b+ 6a+ obl) climbs the left flank of the pillar before reaching the crest, which it then follows throughout. Good climbing ... but beware: this is the least equipped of any of the modern routes on the Aiguille.

Petit Clocher du Portalet   On the left side of the vertical E face, even further left than *Il a Sonné Douze* (Gravante, Monnet and Piola 1990 7a), Monnet and Piola have created *Rendez-vous avec la Lune*. This 200m 6c+ (6a obl) gives six excellent pitches despite the rock being a bit lichenous on pitches 3 and 5 and was climbed on 12 August. Muhlemann and Richardson climbed *Etat de Choc* on the N face. This is becoming one of the great classic alpine rock climbs from the 80s and, although very sustained and strenuous, taking a series of mainly smooth off-width cracks, the difficulty is rather overstated at VIII. The pair found the climbing to be around British E4 5c/6a and a double set of large Friends essential.

Grand Clocher du Portalet   The 400m high E face is a collection of large and very attractive slabby walls. They are clearly visible from the Petit Clocher or even from Praz de Fort, but access has always looked complicated despite a huge ledge that seems to cut right across the face. This summer Gérard Long, Olivier Roduit and, yes, that man again – Vogler, discovered a solution based on a disused route that originally formed a descent from the Petit Clocher. By following this and then a system of ledges across steep slopes (now cairned) they reached the face in 1½ hours and left their mark with a demanding outing – *La Face cachée de la Lune* (7b/c 6b obl).

Dalles du Plan de l'Arche These delightful series of slabs lie halfway along the path to the Orny hut. Set in a pleasantly 'rural' situation on the banks of a refreshing little stream, they offer plenty of scope for an entertaining interlude during the easy amble up to the hut. In the area where the established climbs *Dalle Inférieure* and *Mur Noire* lie, four more routes have been added. *Bisous Futés* is a two-pitch offering from Elisabeth Mercier and Michel Goy. It starts up the obvious diagonal crack to the left of *Dalle Inférieure* and is 5−/5. No equipment in place . . . yet. Monnet and Piola put up *La Grande Bleue* – a line very loosely based on a spur on the right side of the slabs containing *Mur Noir*. The rock is excellent and the pair felt confident to predict future classic status for this route (100m 6a 5+ obl). *Noir Ebène* (26m 6b) is a definite sports climb by the same pair and lies to the left of *Schtrumpf*. Later with Sprungli, Piola used the same belay points as *la Grande Bleue* to create a route which this time took the crest of the spur direct. *Le Pilier Azur* is 100m and 6c+ (6b obl). More details at the Orny hut.

Valais

Matterhorn Patrick Gabarrou has succeeded in completing one of his greatest projects – a new 'super directissima' on the N face. After three recent attempts he managed, together with Lionel Daudet, to force a line to the right of the 1981 Piola/Steiner *Directissima* on the Zmutt Nose. It was an extraordinary climb, reaching the summit of the Nose in an outrageous position. The route was named *Aux Amis Disparus* in memory of Gabarrou's many friendships terminated by mountain accidents. On 19 August Hans Kammerlander and Diego Wellig set out to climb up and down the four major ridges within 24 hours. Starting with an ascent of the Zmutt, they then descended the Hörnli, climbed the Furggen and descended the Lion in a record time of 23½ hours. In the process they accumulated a total height gain and loss of 8500m!

Bernese Oberland

Eiger On the N face, immediately to the right of the 1979 *Geneva Pillar*, Daniel Anker and Piola have climbed *Le Chant du Cygne*. Ascended in part on 29–30 July 1991 and completed on 17–18 July 1992, this 22-pitch climb follows the true crest of the pillar avoided by the 1979 route, finishing up the very steep rock on the left of *Spit Verdonesque Edenté*. Although all the bolts necessary for a free ascent are in place, this is a climb of traditional character where the main protection relies on the skillful usage of nuts and Friends. On the first 15 pitches the rock is very good, the standard is maintained at 5+/6a and escape is possible on to the *Geneva Pillar* at two points (common bivouac cave at the end of pitch 10). Above, the next five pitches form the crux, with the first three (6b+ to 6c+) on dubious rock. All this upper section has climbing of considerable exposure and the grade of this 900m route is ED3 (7a 6b+ obl).

Bregalia

At the time of writing there is no news on this year's new routes. However, as expected, the 1991 Swiss bolt route on the Badile, *Another day in Paradise*, had many ascents this year, including at least one ascent by a British party who thought the climbing 'brilliant' despite the lack of natural line.

Dolomites

Brenta   On the vast and complex NE wall of the **Cima Tosa**, Valentino Chini and Dario Sebastiani have climbed a new line between the great chimneys of the 1933 *Castiglioni–Detassis route* and the *Barbier route* to the left. *Acquario* is 750m and has individual pitch grades from V+ to VIII. The great chimneys mentioned above form, in their upper section, the left side of a huge pillar referred to as the Torre Gilberti, Here, Andrea Andreotti, Fabio Bertone, Diego Filippi and Marco Furlani have produced an 800m ED, *Il Volo dell'Aquila*, which is now the most direct line to the top of the pillar.

Sassolungo/Sella   On the E face of the main peak a previously unclimbed pillar succumbed to Bertoni and Furlani. The authors named the pillar the *Pilastro Paolina* and their 600m TD (VI) route *L'Ultimo dei Balkani*. On the steep compact walls to the right of the *Comici route* on **Il Salame**, Furlani and Ivo Rabanser have put up *Ipersalame* (500m VII A3). On the **Campanile di Val Montanaia** Mauro Corona and Alessandro Gogna have climbed a new grade VII on the spectacularly overhanging E wall. *Via del Novantesimo*, as the name suggests, was completed 90 years after the first ascent of the spire and lies between the old *Carlesso route* and the *Cetin-Dalla Porta Xydias*. Rather surprising was a new route at a very accessible grade on the popular Sella Towers. On the third tower Bruno Maccherini and Massimo Peci have created *I padri di Famiglia* – a 300m V+ on the NW pillar.

Marmolada   On the Ombretta the walls to the right of the *Ideale/Fish* area are cut at half-height by a huge terrace. Here the original route – the 1942 *Pisoni/Castiglioni* classic – weaves the easiest line up the face. Below the right-hand end of the terrace is a huge chimney-corner, which lies just to the left of the rounded buttress taken by the *Elfenbeinpfeiller route*. Following a line loosely based on the chimney and, higher, crossing the *Pisoni/Castiglioni* at two points, is *Savana* – a new route climbed solo in six hours by Slavko Svetičič on 3 August. The difficulties on this 750m wall are not sustained, though the crux, fairly low down on the route, is VII–. Also on the right-hand side of this wall is *Stone Path*, a 300m route put up on 21 August by Andreja, Franc Knez and Danilo Tic. It takes the crackline right of the two obvious parallel chimneys and is VI+. In September Knez and Svetičič were only able to climb on the S face of the Piz Serauta as the weather was too cold for bigger things. However, they were able to put up five new routes (see Topo 4). *Three Pitons and Four Roses* climbs to the summit on the walls to the right of the *Castiglioni route* (600m mainly IV and V with two consecutive pitches at around one-third height of VII+ and VII). *Joint*, a sort of directissima, which

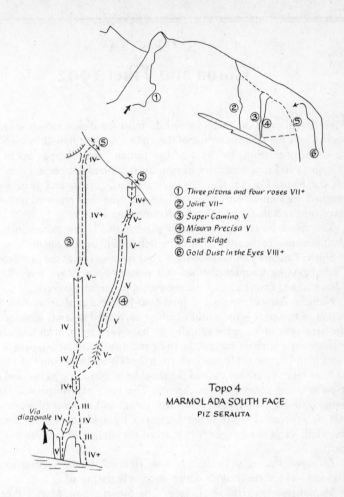

① Three pitons and four roses VII+
② Joint VII−
③ Super Camino V
④ Misura Precisa V
⑤ East Ridge
⑥ Gold Dust in the Eyes VIII+

Topo 4
MARMOLADA SOUTH FACE
PIZ SERAUTA

cuts through the ramp of the *Diagonal route* to finish near the top of the E ridge, was climbed in six hours on the 3rd. This 13 pitch route (*c*500m) is mainly V to VI+ with several easy sections and a crux, low down on the third pitch, of VII−. Near the start of the *Diagonal route* two adjacent lines *Super Camino* (350m V) and *Misura Precisa* (330m V) were romped up by the duo, climbing together, in 30 minutes each. Later the same day (6th), two Poles repeated *Super Camino*. Finally, on 9 September, they climbed *Gold Dust in the Eyes*, a demanding crackline in the yellow pillar on the far right (250m sustained at VI/VII with a crux of VIII+ 5 hours).

Tofana On the S face of the **Mezzo**, Alfredo Bertinelli and Massimo da Pozzo have climbed a hard new route which they named, with characteristic Italian brevity, *Agenti di Scorta dei Giudici Falcone e Borsellino* (IX− or French 7b). This 400m offering was climbed from the ground up and entirely free, despite nasty weather on the second day.

JÓZEF NYKA
China and Tibet 1992

Everest – Kangshung face   One of the most significant ascents in the spring season was the Chilean repeat of the 1988 US–Canadian–British route. The seven-member team, led by Rodrigo Jordán, used Sherpas up to 6450m (Camp 1) and supplementary oxygen for the summit attempt. From Camp 3 on the South Col Cristián Garcia Huidobro, Jordán and Juan S Montes reached the summit on 15 May. The expedition then removed 90% of their fixed rope and all camps and rubbish during the descent.

This fine achievement brings new prestige to Chilean mountaineering and their attention to the environment they left behind should equally be praised.

Shisha Pangma Central (8008m)   Four members from the Japanese Alpine Club Fukuoka Chapter climbed this summit on 6 May. Two, Toyobumi Miyazaki and Etsuroh Hino, did not use supplementary oxygen.

Namcha Barwa (7782m)   A joint Sino-Japanese expedition made the first ascent of this peak – the world's highest unclimbed separate mountain. Since the area opened 10 years ago all eyes have been on it, with Chinese teams attempting it without success. In 1990 and 1991 joint Sino-Japanese expeditions found a reasonable approach from the NW and an ascent line from the S. In November 1991 they crossed the shoulder of Naipun (7043m) and reached a point some 300m short of the top. The 1992 expedition was co-led by Sangju (China) and Tsuneo Shigehiro (Japan) and established six camps, the last at c7000m. Despite being hampered by unstable weather and heavy snowfall, 11 of the 12 members reached the summit on 30 October, in two parties.

Although the main summit is now climbed, there are two unclimbed 7000ers and several unclimbed high 6000ers in the massif.

Menlungtse (7181m) – SE face   The Slovene pair Marko Prezelj and Andrej Stremfelj, recipients of the 1991 Piolet d'Or, made two attempts in October. The first failed at 6400m because of bad weather, but the second, on 22–24 October, was successful. They climbed the face alpine style, with a bivvy at 6150m, to reach the Great Plateau at 3.30pm on 23 October and the virgin, main (eastern) summit three hours later. They described their 2000m ice route as very interesting, but dangerous in the lower part because of rock and ice fall (UIAA V). Menlungtse West (7023m) was climbed by Alan Hinkes and the late Andy Fanshawe on Bonington's 1988 expedition.

Before their ascent Prezelj and Stremfelj acclimatised on the neighbouring unnamed and unscaled Pt 6301m, which they climbed on 11–13 October (UIAA IV 45°–50° 700m 5 hours).

Broad Peak Central (8016m)   The first ascent of this peak from the Chinese side is included in the Pakistan area notes.

India 1992

Again a very active year, despite last year's earthquake and political uncertainties. The good news is some areas currently prohibited to foreigners, e.g. Milam valley (Kumaon), Nilkanth and Mana (Gangotri) and Kinnaur and Spiti (Himachal Pradesh) are likely to open up. Unfortunately peak fees are likely to start from $3000. Better check your budget; with the recent inflation in India things are more expensive than before. But like any difficult peak such mundane matters are not going to stop a mountaineer.

Sikkim

Chombu (6362m) A Japanese team led by Kenshiro Otaki was the first foreign expedition allowed to climb in North Sikkim for many decades (Kangchenjunga excepted). They reached a high point of 5900m on 29 October.

Kumaon – Garhwal – Gangotri

Indian British Panch Chuli Expedition 1992
Six Indian and six British mountaineers climbed in the Balati and Pyunshani valleys, east of Munsiary in the Pithoragarh District, U.P., in May and June 1992. This was the first time that Panch Chuli had been approached from the west by the Balati valley for 20 years. The expedition was the first to explore the Pyunshani valley.

Seven peaks were climbed over a period of forty days with altogether twelve team members reaching summits.

Panch Chuli II (6904m) was climbed by a new route – the W spur – and its SW ridge was climbed 19 years after the first ascent. The first ascent of **Panch Chuli V (6437m)**, a particularly challenging peak, and **Sahadev East (5750m)** were achieved. **Rajrambha (6537m)**, which has had one ascent from the north, was traversed by its E ridge over **Menaka** peak (6000m) and then down its W ridge and face in a five day alpine-style push. The Panchali glacier was explored and the southern valleys of the Bainti and Rula glaciers were observed.

Peaks climbed in the Pyunshani valley were **Draupadi (5250m)**, **Panchali Chuli (5220m)** and **Panch Chuli V (6437m)**, all first ascents. Vijay Kothari was air-lifted by helicopter from the glacier after surviving a fall. Stephen Venables miraculously survived an abseil anchor failure on Panch Chuli V, and after tense days a helicopter rescued him.

The expedition was led by Chris Bonington and Harish Kapadia. (Full details in articles 'Indian British Panch Chuli Expedition 1992' and 'Panch Chuli V' in this volume.)

Saraswati (6940m)   This peak lies on the Indo-Tibet border, rising from the Saraswati valley, above Badrinath. It is situated south of **Balbala (6416m)** near Mana pass and north of **Kamet**. It was climbed by an Indo-Japanese ladies expedition led by Inspector (Ms) Santosh Yadav and Mrs Reiko Teras-awa and the party named the peak after the river valley.

They approached from Badrinath along the Saraswati valley. Turning east on the Balbala glacier they reached the Schlagintweit pass (Schlagintweit had crossed from here to Tibet to approach Abi Gamin in 1855) and climbed the S ridge. No other party had reached the pass since.

Mana Northwest (7092m)   This is an unclimbed peak on the NW shoulder of **Mana**, leading to **Kamet**. A four-member team from Bombay, led by Arun P Samant, attempted it from the eastern approaches via the Purbi Kamet glacier, reaching 6900m.

Peak 6687m situated to the north was climbed by Suhas Kharde and Jagat Singh on 25 June. They established five camps up to 6450m.

Uja Tirche (6202m)   Bad weather and unseasonal heavy snowfall defeated a three-member team from Bombay, led by Vinay Hegde, on this peak in July.

Mana (7272m)   A 19-member Indian Army (Army Ordnance Corps) team from Secundrabad, led by Capt S P Malik, climbed this peak on 19 June. They approached from the Nagthuni glacier in the east and above Gupta Khal. The team was involved in an avalanche on 11 June and the injured members had to be evacuated. Earlier they climbed an unnamed 5730m peak ('Shakti Parbat') rising from Gupta Khal.

Kedardome (6831m)   An Indian team led by Sachin Karato climbed this peak on 2 June.

Thalay Sagar (6904m)   A seven-member British team established Base Camp on 10 May and climbed the spectacular S face on 6 June. Keith Milne (leader) and Tom Prentice reached the summit.

Rudugaira (5364m)   Susan Grimley, Tom Prentice and Gordon Scott, from the above expedition, climbed the N ridge.

Thalay Sagar   Hiroshi Kawasaki and Kimihiro Kumaga (Japan) attempted the W ridge. Camp 1 was placed at 5500m on 20 July, but the monsoon enhanced the danger of avalanche and they abandoned the attempt. Alfonso Vizan and Carlos Suarez (Spain) reached 6450m on the N face, descending due to avalanche conditions and the lack of a bivouac site.

Swargarohini I (6252m)   Nick Banks and Chris Smith made unsuccessful attempts on this peak from the north during May. A three man Spanish team, led by Jovier D Carrento, attempted the E ridge. They were beaten by bad weather and abandoned their attempt on 20 August.

Trisul (7120m)   Arthur B Ferguson, Robert Wade and Griff Smith (USA) attempted the W face, setting up Base Camp on 14 June and Advanced Base

Camp on 20 June. A long spell of bad weather prevented them from making much progress beyond this until July.

Panwali Dwar (6663m)   A Korean expedition failed on this peak due to bad weather and stove failure. The team, led by Her Tai Han, made their last camp (C3) at 6150m.

Satopanth (7075m)   Three Indian teams repeated the first ascent route (the NE ridge) – climbed by André Roch's team in 1947. The leaders were Prasad S Dhamal, Ms Chandraprabha Aitwal and Dr Salin Hu.

Chaukhamba I (7138m)   Col Amit C Roy (Corps of Signals, Indian Army) led a successful expedition from the north-east. Fifteen members reached the summit.

Bhagirathi III (6456m)   Seven Czechs, led by Dr Miroslav Coubal, attempted a new route on the W wall. Their high point was 5800m (5 September).

Draupadi-Ka-Danda (6038m)   An 11-member Japanese team climbed this peak in the Uttarkashi area. All members reached the summit in the period 10–16 August. Takamoto Nobuko (51) was killed in a rockfall near Bhuki while returning.

Pt 6193m (near the Bhagirathi group)   A Yugoslav expedition attempted the W face of this shapely peak on the Gangotri glacier. Januz Kejuot (leader), Maipin Kouoe and Ive Yeroz reached c6000m, but bad weather did not allow them to reach the summit.

Shivling (6543m)   An eight-member French team, led by J P Franchon, climbed the W ridge on 3 September.

Bharte Khunta (6578m)   An Indian team from Delhi reached 6450m on this peak. They approached from the Gangotri glacier and were led by R D Bhattacharjee.

Manda III (6529m)   Britons Ian Read, Andrew Cunningham, Richard Mansfield and Gary Murray climbed the SE face and the S ridge on 22 September.

Pt 6014m (near Manda)   A four-member British team attempted the E face. James McElwaire reached the summit solo on 18 September. They had earlier attempted Jogin III unsuccessfully.

Gangotri I (6672m)   Martin Moran's 13-member team were stopped at 6500m due to avalanche danger.

Yogeshwar (6678m)   Britons Steven Adderley, Malcolm Bass, Julian Clamp and Simon Yearsley made the second ascent, climbing the S face to the SE ridge.

Pt 6193m (Gangotri glacier)   A four-man Czech team led by Janez Kesnar failed on the W face.

Nilkanth (6596m)   In October Graham Little's four-man Scottish team reached 5600m on the SE ridge, the col between the third and fourth pinnacles. They gave up 'due to considerable commitment involved on the long, technical and dangerous climb'.

Maiktoli (6803m)   An inexperienced Indian team attempted this peak from the south. An avalanche killed four members at Advanced Base Camp.

Bhagirathi III (6454m)   Mark Gunlogson and Micha Miller climbed the Scottish route in 9 days from 23 September. It gave 30 pitches of granite and 500m of ice.

Nandabhannar (6236m), **Nandakhani (6029m)** and **Shallang Dhura (5678m)**   A Bombay team led by Divyesh Muni climbed these peaks around the Kumaon pass crossed by Ruttledge's porters in 1926.

Himachal Pradesh

M10 (5730m)   The 'Paramount Trekkers' expedition from Bombay, led by Dhiren Pania, climbed this peak rising above the Milang glacier. They had earlier attempted **Mulkilla (M4, 6517m)** and **M5 (6370)**. Both attempts were given up at about 5800m owing to crevasses and cornices.

Hanuman Tibba (5928m)   A three-member Japanese expedition led by Takashi Omosu failed to climb the W ridge.

CB51 (height not supplied)   A nine-member Italian team led by Giorgio Mallucci approached from the Samunder Tapu glacier and attempted the S ridge. The attempt was abandoned at 6100m after an avalanche.

CB14 (6078m)   A five-member Japanese team led by K Okano reached 5880m on 15 August. The NE ridge, which they were attempting, was too hard, with exposed ice.

Dharamsura (6446m)   A four-member Japanese team led by Zenkosuke Sakurazawa approached from Manikaran (Kulu) in July. Monsoon weather stopped them at about 5800m.

A five-member team, also from Japan, approached from the Bara Shigri glacier in Lahul. They climbed the SE ridge on 15 August. Jum Katori was the leader.

Pt 6225m (on the Bara Shigri glacier)   Christopher Cheesman, James Winspear and Richard Mason (UK) attempted this peak rising south of the Chandra river in Lahul. A serac collapsed on their route and the final summit attempt was stopped at 6000m.

Kishtwar – Zanskar – Ladakh

Tupendo I (5700m)   A British team met with an accident on this peak in the eastern Kishtwar. Jonathan Bamber was hit by a rock and broke his leg badly on 3 September. After two attempts a helicopter rescued him on 9 September. The seven-member team was led by David Mortimer and had at first intended to attempt Mardi Phabrang.

Matho Kangri I (6090m)   Seven members of this British expedition reached the summit in August. They were Michael Ratty (leader), John Shelly, Alan Rowland, Trevor Willing, Deepak Jhalani (liaison officer), Dorje Chatta and Phunchok Tanglas (high altitude porters).

Z3 (6270m)   A nine-member team led by Sergio Maturi climbed the NW ridge on 16 August.

Nun (7135m)   Four Italians led by Roberto Salavati attempted this peak in late August.

Kun (7086m)   A ten-member French expedition led by Albert Philippe climbed the peak by the E ridge.

Kang Yissay (6400m)   Carl Moore's seven-member American team climbed the N face on 15 September.

Eastern Karakoram

Mamostong Kangri (7516m)   This high peak continues to attract climbing teams. An Indian ladies team (all members of a pre-Everest expedition sponsored by the Indian Mountaineering Foundation – training for the 1993 Indo-Nepal Women's expedition to Everest) climbed the normal route from the Mamostong glacier. Fifteen climbers were successful in three groups. They left Delhi on 30 June, set up base camp on 24 July and all summited on 15 August.

Teram Kangri (7382m)   This high peak near the junction of the Teram Shehr and Siachen glaciers was climbed by an Indian Army team led by Col M S Gill.

BILL O'CONNOR

Nepal 1992

With contributions from Józef Nyka

A year of triumph and tragedy both on and off the mountains – 1992 was undoubtedly a 'horrible year'.

Dhaulagiri 1 – NE ridge A Russian expedition from Krasnoyarsk led jointly by Nikolai Smetanin and Vladimir Musyenko climbed the NE ridge (normal route). After establishing five camps along the route climbers Nikolai Zakharov, Peter Kuznetsov, Nikolai Smetanin, Valeri Kokhanov and Aleksei Gulyayev reached the summit from a camp at 7700m on 30 April. Having switched their objective from another route without permission, both leaders were punished by the Nepalese authorities for violating the rules. Neither will be allowed to climb in Nepal for the next five years.

Everest – South Col Sagamartha continues to attract the attention of expeditions from around the world. The large number of newly independent states will undoubtedly mean continued interest and income from the Baltic to Bosnia. I'm not so sure that the Sherpas will continue to accept titanium ice screws as part payment for their labours!

The Russians it seems are taking more than full advantage of their new found freedom. A Siberian expedition, sponsored by the Togliatti car factory, led by Vyachaslav Volkov and Ivan Dusharin controversially climbed the South Col route. Originally they had permission for the W ridge, but changed their objective to the South Col route despite their request to do so being turned down by the Nepalese authorities. Their first summit attempts on 2 and 4 May failed because of poor weather. However, conditions improved and four climbers reached the summit on 12 May. Two days later another four reached the summit. Some teams used supplementary oxygen. One of the summit climbers was Fyodor Konyukhov, a well-known Russian traveller and adventurer, but not a climber. It was his first time in high mountains! Once again the Nepalese responded to this violation of the rules by banning the eight climbers and the expedition leader from Nepal for five years.

On 15 May a Spanish expedition was also successful on Everest. They climbed the more difficult but safer 1981 American combination which links the Polish S Pillar with the upper part of the South Col route. TV cameraman Ramón Portilla and army officers Capt Francisco Gam and Major Alfonso Juez with two Sherpas reached the summit from Camp 4 (8000m) in ten hours using bottled air.

A Dutch expedition led by Ronald Naar reached the summit on 12 May. Naar and Edmond Öffner with Sherpas Nima Temba and Dawa Tashi reached the top from Camp 4 on the South Col. Ronald Naar has now joined the growing band who have climbed the highest summits on all seven continents.

Pierre Tardivel became the highest skier in the world – his 40th 'first'. On 27–28 September 1992 he skied down 3200 vertical metres from the South Summit (8760m).

Annapurna – S face   A Slovene expedition led by Tone Skarja hoped to repeat the British route. Having established their Base Camp on 29 September they made little progress owing to poor weather. A two-day long blizzard deposited 1½m of snow after they had established Camp 2 (5900m), but five days later they returned to the mountain, establishing a further camp at 6600m in appalling conditions. Progress was reduced to 100m a day. On 21 October Filip Bence and Iztok Tomazin reached a high point of 6700m. They made a further attempt at the Swiss route on the right-hand side of the S face.

Pierre Beghin died attempting the face. His partner Jean-Pierre Lafaille was given medical help by the Slovenians. Both expeditions left the mountain on 28 October.

Annapurna and K2 are the only 8000ers not to have been climbed by Slovene expeditions.

Cho Oyu – normal route   A six-member Slovene expedition climbed the mountain by the normal route on 21 September. Five climbers reached the summit. Conditions on the mountain were very cold and all members of the expedition had frostbitten hands and feet. The Slovene climbers did not use oxygen or Sherpas. The mountain was also climbed by Japanese, Italian and Spanish expeditions using oxygen and Sherpas.

Manaslu – normal route   A large international group led by Polish climber Krzysztof Wielicki climbed the mountain on 28 September by the normal route. The team, which included Polish climbers, Italians, Bulgarians and a Belgian, made a further attempt on 2 October. Using fixed ropes left by a Korean expedition, Polish climbers Dmowska and Sprutta with Vermeiren (Belgium) attempted to establish a third camp above 6600m. Caught out by darkness they attempted to reach a Canadian camp already in place. Miss Dmowska fell to her death from the fixed ropes before reaching the tent. The following day Vermeiren attempted to descend to Camp 2 but also fell, dying later from his injuries.

Ama Dablam   This most beautiful mountain continues to attract a lot of attention. Quick access (it is only a week from Lukla airstrip to Base Camp) means the S ridge attracts a large number of expeditions, both private and commercial. Sadly, it also accounts for many fatalities. Belgian climber Karen Van Dooren was killed on 26 October. Her body was not recovered.

Saipal (7031m) – NE spur   A party led by Chuck Evans explored remote NW Nepal and carried out a reconnaissance of the NE side of Saipal reaching 5700m on the NE spur.

Kathmandu Air Crash   Tragically, a PIA aircraft carrying a large number of British climbers and trekkers crashed in poor visibility on its approach to Kathmandu. Several members of the Alpine Club were amongst those killed – their obituaries appear in the In Memoriam section of this volume.

Trouble on the Trail   There were several reports of groups trekking into the Rolwaling being harassed by villagers, and at least one group was turned back. However, this does not appear to be a common occurrence and without full details it is hard to draw conclusions. Some incidents appear to have occurred close to the New Year festival and *chang* was mentioned in more than one account.

The Rising Cost of Climbing The really disturbing trend in Nepal is the rising cost of climbing. Everest in particular is fast becoming the preserve of the fabulously rich or well sponsored. Arguably it is a reaction to the growing number of commercial expeditions attempting 8000m peaks. With clients willing to pay a lot of money (£15,000 plus) to have a holiday on Everest and organisations willing to provide six-figure sponsorship (eg. British Telecom's sponsorship of a recent attempt on Makalu) mountains are big business for third world countries. But who can blame them when permits have been sold on for a big profit whilst expeditions have been known to charge 'loads of money' for others to use 'their' route through the Icefall. It seems that market forces are catching up with us and, true to Thatcherite principles, peak fees, like the Himalaya, are rising. The Nepalese along with Bhutan and China are cashing in on their assets and charging highly for the glory of climbing their highest, or highest unclimbed, mountains.

The downside of this is that it discourages small, lightweight expeditions that want to climb high mountains by difficult routes in good style. Sponsors and clients have more interest in success and risk free adventure than in style.

The Price of Adventure The price of adventure doesn't come cheap. Leo Dickenson made a dramatic film of the first balloon flight over Everest for Channel 4. Even so a peak fee still had to be paid – in this case twice. The air space on the Nepal side of the mountain cost a mere $2000 plus $2000 in trekking fees. The cost of the landing on the Tibetan side however really hurt, not just in terms of broken ribs. In this case the air space cost $100,000, the filming fee $110,000 and the transport out a further $55,000! On the ground the fee for Everest has also risen to $50,000 for up to five climbers. Extra climbers are charged $10,000 per head up to a maximum of seven. Surprisingly the peak fee for the N side comes cheaper, the Chinese charging $500 per head, but beware the land costs. Nepal is not yet the most expensive 'adventure playground'. The fee for Namcha Barwa (7782m) is said to have cost around $1,000,000, whilst it is rumoured that unclimbed Gangkar Puenzum (7541m) in Bhutan is even higher and there is no refund for failure!

PAUL NUNN
Pakistan 1992

K2 – Abruzzi ridge As usual several expeditions tried K2. A Swiss group of four men and Frenchwoman Chantal Mauduit reached 7000m during July in snowy conditions. Mauduit then joined a 17-member Russian–American expedition which prepared the route to Camp 4 at 8100m. Valeri Balyberdin (Russia) and Gennadi Kopieda (Ukraine) summited on 1 August, followed two days later by Mauduit and Aleksei Nikiforov. Mauduit had come to Pakistan after an earlier, unsuccessful, attempt on Everest and, with the death of Wanda Rutkiewicz, remains the sole female K2 climber alive.

Americans Ed Viesturs, Scott Fischer and Charley Mace ascended the Abruzzi ridge, reaching the summit on 16 August. Jonathan Pratt (UK) and Dan Mazur (USA) were unsuccessful, as was a New Zealand pair and a Mexican expedition, which abandoned its attempt after Adrian Benitez was killed descending in bad weather when an anchor failed. Ponce de Leon and Johan Lange (Sweden) from this party climbed the forepeak of Broad Peak on 31 July. Balyberdin and Viesturs are the sixth and seventh persons to climb the world's three highest peaks. These were the first ascents of the Abruzzi ridge since the numerous accidents and ascents in 1986. 79 people have succeeded on K2 to date.

Only one party attempted a route other than the Abruzzi. In July Polish climber Wojciech Kurtyka and the Swiss, Erhard Loretan returned to the unclimbed W face for the second time in three years, but were unable to make the alpine-style ascent planned owing to bad weather.

Broad Peak Seven expeditions made attempts from the Pakistan side. One attempt, by a group made up of people from several expeditions, was successful. The summiters were Scott McKee (USA), Dave Hambly (UK living in the USA), Spaniards Antonio Tapiador and Pedro Rodriguez, Catalan Eudwald Martinez and Romanian Constantin Lacatusu from a British commercial expedition. Roger Payne's British June-July expedition stopped around 7700m in deep and dangerous snow conditions.

Broad Peak Central (8016m) On the Chinese side, Catalan and Italian climbers made the most impressive first ascent of the year. Led by Jordi Magriña, they were accompanied by Kurt Diemberger who entered this little visited area with Julie Tullis, as part of an Italian expedition, in 1983. In 1991 he had been at the Festival of Onions in Tarragona and mentioned to the mayor that he knew a mountain which had some of the finest roots at its foot. This helped local climbers get sponsorship for a reconnaissance of the N Gasherbrum glacier in autumn 1991, which identified a route and climbed to 6500m.

In summer 1992 Kurt Diemberger returned to the Shaksgam with the Catalans and on 4 August Oscar Cadiach, Lluis Rafols, Enric Dalmau and

Italian Alberto Soncini reached the central summit of Broad Peak via the E face by the route explored in 1991. Diemberger thus fostered an ascent suggested in mid-1980s' explorations here, and helped open the process of climbing on the huge, remote N and E faces of the central 8000m Karakoram peaks, which began with the Japanese first ascent of the N ridge of K2 in 1982. (Full details in article 'Beyond Broad Peak: A Journey of Discovery' in this volume.)

Gasherbrum 1   A Polish commercial expedition led by Krystof Wielicki failed in June in poor conditions, when a windslab avalanche killed Italian Paulo Bernascone. Three expeditions were unsuccessful on the *Messner route* and a Japanese expedition failed on the *Slovene route*. Another Japanese expedition, led by Eiho Ohtani, attempted the Japanese couloir on the N face, but switched to the W ridge after trouble with deep snow. They gave up on 22 August after reaching 7000m. Their liaison officer, Nazir Sabir, returned to the route with high altitude porters Rajab Shab and Mehrban Shah and succeeded between 24–26 August. This was Sabir's fourth 8000m peak.

Gasherbrum 2   The normal route was climbed by several teams.

Trango Tower   Americans Greg Child and Mark Wilford climbed an extremely difficult rock route. They fixed rope on the lower section to a bivvy at 5700m, then made a push for the summit. A huge slab of rock, reported as 200m by 60m by 10m, detached itself from only 50m to their right and created an earthquake-like experience. The top was reached late on 23 August. On the **Great Trango Tower** John Middendorf and Xavier Bongard did a new route near the *Nowegian route*.

Skilbrum (7360m)   A Japanese team, led by Tadakiyo Sakahara and booked on Gasherbrum 2, were delayed in Karachi when gas cylinders hidden in baggage exploded during unloading. Two weeks delay led them to attempt an unclimbed subsidiary peak on the W ridge, at the head of the Biange (Younghusband) glacier. Three members climbed this subsidiary peak S and left of the main peak, but failed in their attempt on the main summit.

Latok 1   Catherine Destivelle and Jeff Lowe tried the N ridge. A first attempt in mid-July ended when Lowe suffered a knee problem. A second in August was stopped by bad weather after six bivouacs. The ridge was threatened by huge snow mushrooms suspended over sections of the climbing and the pair made a 'reasonable but dire' decision to abandon the climb. This was probably doubly disappointing to Lowe who was involved in the epic first attempt in 1976.

On the same route a New Zealand/British party of Carol McDermott, Dave Wills, Andy McFarland and Andy MacNae reached 5900m on two occasions, but no further.

Latok 2   Ted Howard (British) led an attempt on the much attempted, unclimbed NW ridge. Though less steep than Latok 1, it compensates in length with still unknown difficulties in the last 500m. A camp was established on the Latok col at 5900m in mid-August, but bad weather and wind curtailed attempts on 23 August, ironically just before a few settled days.

Early in the morning of 3 August Tony Riley and Paul Nunn found sparse remains, clothing and equipment of Don Morrison, who was killed on the

Latok glacier in a crevasse fall in 1977. Morrison's remains were about a mile from the area where he fell in a crevasse and were removed to Base Camp, examined by Dr Peter Jackson and interred under his memorial cairn opposite Pamshe peak, of which he made the first ascent with Ted Howard in 1975. Asghar Ali, the expedition liaison officer and a guide, went back early to inform relatives.

During this expedition the viewpoint peak (**Pt 5208m**) S of the Baintha Lukpar glacier, first reported climbed by the Italians in 1977, was repeated by Colin Farnsworth and Tony Riley and the same pair ascended the crooked rock pinnacle (**Pt 5250m**) towards the S end of the Biafo-Baitha Lukpar divide – almost certainly a first ascent, involving exposed rock climbing on the summit section.

On the Biafo glacier British climbers Andy Cave, Dave Heseldon, Paul Jenkinson and Neil McAdie tried another steep rock line on the W Biafo wall in August, but gave up after prolonged bad weather.

Fiyag (King's Peak, 5550m) The 1400m N face was soloed from the Passu glacier by Jonathan Preston (UK), while his partner, Roy Ruddle, was ill. It gave climbing up to Scottish 4 (TD overall). The peak is incorrectly marked as 5640m on some maps. Preston also soloed the S face of **Pt 5550m** (adjacent to Needle Peak, 6090m), climbing a gully direct to the summit (Alpine D).

It is also understood that a second attempt on **Crown Peak** on the Choktoi/Nobande Sobande glacier divide was unsuccessful late in the season and that one climber was killed.

Many other smaller groups from Britain were active in Pakistan, mostly on smaller peaks, and one had permission to attempt the huge E ridge of **Masherbrum**, but news is not available of their outcomes.

Nanga Parbat – Kinshofer route Six out of ten expeditions succeeded, including three Koreans, five Basques and two Poles on 1 July and two Czechs on 4 July. Pete Long led a five-person alpine-style attempt which did not succeed.

The Rupal face A French winter venture is reported to have been defeated by bad weather and high winds.

Nanga Parbat via the Mazeno Ridge
Doug Scott writes:
The W ridge of Nanga Parbat is about eight miles long from the Mazeno Pass. It is the longest ridge on any of the 8000m peaks, and remains unclimbed. Although Nanga Parbat is a very popular mountain, there has been surprisingly little activity on this major feature. In July 1992 we planned to climb the Mazeno Ridge in three stages. After acclimatisation, phase two involved climbing the Hans Schell route on the S side of Nanga Parbat, to 6900m (Camp 4). On 17 August, whilst descending the steep, loose rock between Camp 2 and Camp 1, a massive rock avalanche roared down. Serge Efimov and I found shelter with the rocks skimming over our helmets and sack. Sean Smith was turned upside down on the belay by the abseil 50m higher. Valeri Perchine, who was about to make the abseil, was swept down when a rock hit him in the chest. Sean sustained bruised ribs, a crushed toe and a smashed

helmet, but was otherwise OK. He climbed down with what was left of the abseil rope. Valeri stopped 100m down in a shallow depression on the steep face: he was lucky not to go another 1500m. As it was, he suffered broken ribs, a cracked pelvis and lacerations to the hands and face. It took two days to get him down to Base Camp.

Meanwhile, Alan Hinkes, Ang Phurba and Nga Temba had survived another huge rock fall the day before, after placing a food and fuel dump at 7000m. Alan decided to go home, a decision influenced as much by the death of two close friends earlier in the year as from his own near-miss. Sean went off to Gilgit for a medical check and Valeri remained at Base Camp to recover there over the next few weeks.

The remaining four members of the expedition went around towards the Mazeno Pass. After two days walking from Base Camp, we arrived to camp at 4800m amongst the moraine of the Mazeno glacier, some 3km SSE of the Mazeno Gap. Early the next morning Ang Phurba, Nga Temba, Serge Efimov and I set off to climb the ridge which goes N to Pt 6880, the first of the seven Mazeno summits, as marked on the 1936 German map of the area. We were carrying, on average, 25kg rucksacks, with enough food and gear to sustain us over an estimated eight days up and down, up the Mazeno Ridge to the summit of Nanga Parbat, and a descent down the Schell route. We moved together over the glacier and climbed roped up 45–50 degree ice slopes. After 12 hours' climbing, we arrived at a suitable camp site on the crest of the NS ridge, at about 5850m. We spent 26 August climbing around and over the pinnacles of the ridge, with some difficulty (TD) to camp at about 6400m. On 27 August we climbed up on ice and snow to Pt 6650 and then over the first of the Mazeno summits, Pt 6880. We continued E along the ridge, over Pt 6825, to camp on a windswept saddle, to the east. On 28 August we climbed up to Pt 6970, which was as far as we got.

The night before had been extremely windy: the Sherpas hadn't slept too well and Ang Phurba was definitely worried about the descent. He had been in the big rock fall with Alan and actually caught a rock on his chin; he was still somewhat demoralised from that and counselled a retreat. There was no way we could split the party and so we went into retreat, retracing our steps to Pt 6880 and continuing W and down towards the Mazeno Pass. We descended the steep, broken ground directly above the col and bivouacked at about 5750m. On 29 August we descended the last of the loose and dangerous rocks to the Mazeno Pass at 5358m, and eventually reached Base Camp, just before dark, after a 20km walk. It had been a good seven-day outing, climbing over new ground, including three of the seven Mazeno peaks, and seeing first-hand that this Mazeno Ridge, the W ridge of Nanga Parbat, could be the most elegant and safest way to the summit. However, the most difficult of these summits have yet to be crossed.

After collecting, burning and burying 45 sacks of rubbish from around Base Camp with the help of local children, we packed up. On 1 September we walked out to the road-head where Ibrahim, our excellent liaison officer, had the jeeps ready to take us to Gilgit.

Paul Nunn continues:
Following the steep rise in fees from Nepal, and discussions at the International Tourism Conference in Islamabad in early November, peak fees were raised substantially and a system charging extra for additional members beyond five was introduced for 1994 onwards.

Peak height	Royalty ($US)	Additional fee per member over five ($US)
K2	9000	1000
8000+	7500	700
7501–8000	3000	300
7001–7500	2000	200
6000–7000	1200	150

Peak fees are never welcome to mountaineers, and these will be no exception. They are not so extreme as the Nepali fees and the Pakistan Government maintains traditions of order in giving permissions, which reduces uncertainty for visiting mountaineers. Unfortunately, increased peak fees generally benefit central government and have almost no impact upon the environment.

At the practical level, it should be noted that many parties are using the Gondoro La as an approach or return route from the Upper Baltoro/ Concordia area. Though it takes a relatively short time it remains reasonably serious, with risk of stonefall on the Hushe side. It may also be as expensive as the other way now that the jeep road to Askole shortens the journey to a day from Skardu, weather and conditions permitting.

The road is not a forgone conclusion. Ted Howard's party found it broken by a landslide before Dusso in late July, entailing a two or three hour delay. Up the Braldu past Chokpoing, opposite the notorious slopes of the old walk-in, their five jeeps passed safely. As some of the climbers walked behind, the road split under their feet and a 10m section disappeared into the river. It was several weeks before restoration and the road is unlikely ever to be entirely safe.

North America and Iceland 1992

With contributions from H Adams Carter and Doug Scott

Alaska

McKinley (6193m)   The weather proved very severe and there were a larger than normal number of fatalities. One of these was Mugs Stump, one of America's foremost climbers, who had made some extremely difficult ascents with incredible modesty (eg the 2500m W face of Mount Tyree in Antarctica 1989). He met his death when tons of snow gave way on the edge of a crevasse, on the S buttress of Mount McKinley.

McKinley   A Korean team led by Sun Oh climbed a new route on the S face, between the *American Direct* and the *Japanese Direct*.

Foraker (5303m)   Tom Walter, Ritt Kellogg and Colby Coombs attempted the third ascent of the *Pink Panther* on the E face. High on the route they were overwhelmed by an avalanche and Walter and Kellog were killed instantly. Coombs lay unconscious for hours before taking equipment from his dead friends' packs and, over a period of six days, descending alone to the McKinley Base Camp. As well as breaking an ankle he injured a shoulder and his neck.

Huntingdon   Clay Wadman and Bruce Miller made a new route on the W face, to the left of Jay Smith's and Paul Teare's, which they rated as 5.10, A4. The ice was vertical in many places.

Mt Brooks   Randy Waitman and friends made a new route on the W ridge.

Stellar   Robert Wesson, Bob Jacobs and Gil Anderson climbed the N ridge having landed on the N glacier.

Canada

Proboscis (Cirque of the Unclimbables)   Paul Piana and Todd Skinner (climbers) and Galen Rowell (cameraman) climbed a new and extraordinarily difficult new route to the left of the only other route on the face.

Mt Logan   A joint expedition, using Global Positioning System equipment, measured the peak's height to be 5939m ± 3m. An Italian expedition led by Claudio Kerschbaumer tried a variation west of the *Humming Bird Ridge* between 14–23 May. They were rescued by helicopter at 4700m.

St Elias   John Bauman, Dave McGivern and Leo Americus attempted a winter ascent of the *Abruzzi route* from 4–23 March. Heavy snowfall forced a retreat from 3350m.

Mt Kennedy   Mike Fischesser, Bill Proudman, Diana McAdams, Joe Lackey and Nej Mulla attempted the E ridge from 28 April to 10 May. They failed because of bad weather and deep snow.

Northern Icefields Traverse   David Williams, Betsy Fletcher, Peter Stone and Markus Kellerhals traversed the northern border of the St Elias Icefields from the Donjeck river to McArthy, Alaska (9 May to 14 June).

Mt Steele   The same team climbed the E ridge.

Mt Manitoba   Five members of a team led by Peter Aitchison reached the summit from the Prairie glacier.

Baffin Island

John Turk and Conrad Anker travelled to the San Ford Fiord in NE Baffin Island. The ice breakup was later than it had been for years and this complicated their approach. They travelled for three days on snow mobiles and spent four more dragging their kayaks over pack-ice and across open leads of water. Eventually they reached Yosemite-like grade V and VI granite walls, which rose vertically from the water to 1500m. They made two ascents and then raced against the winter, emerging at Clyde with some difficulty through ice and freezing sea-water on 13 August.

Iceland Rock

Doug Scott writes:
In the south of Iceland and to the east of Skaftafell there is, at Borgarhafnarfjall, a 120m basalt crag known as Fallastakkanof. It is only one hour above the main road and can be seen sticking up like giant organ pipes. The rock is mainly good, it dries quickly and is a good place to visit from the excellent campsite at Skaftafell, should bad weather be passing over the high mountains to the north.

Snaevarr Gudmundsson and I established two routes here, one in 1985 (5c, 5c, 5b) more or less straight up the middle, and the other at Easter 1992 (5c, 6a, 5b). This route starts up the cracks just right of the prominent detached pillars and left of our 1985 route. The third pitch is common to both routes. A usual rack of wires and Friends will suffice, but add an extra large Friend.

DAVID SHARMAN

South America and Antarctica 1992

There has been a large increase in the number of ascents in Patagonia, and a compensatory decrease in activity in Peru. The relatively settled economic and political situations in Chile and Argentina compared with the unrest in Peru have undoubtedly contributed to this. Another factor may have been the reports of unusually unreliable snow conditions in Peru. No significant activity has been reported from Ecuador.

I am indebted to Marcelo Scanu, Duncan Thomas, Gerhard Feichtenschlager, Franci Savenc for invaluable help in compiling these notes.

Peru – Cordilleras Blanca and Huayhuash

The cholera epidemic appears to have burnt itself out and was never really a problem in the mountain regions anyway. In Lima a series of bomb attacks were aimed at the rich suburbs, but in the area around the Cordilleras Blanca and Huayhuash public notaries and businesses were the preferred targets rather than tourists. Later reports from Huaraz (January 1993) say that this level of violence has reduced. Despite all this there were three times as many commercial trekking/climbing groups in 1992 as opposed to 1991. However there were reduced numbers of private parties.

The weather was generally poor with frequent midday snowfall down to 4000m. This hampered activity on harder lines, as did the effects of the deglaciation which have reduced a number of icefields to 'falling granite boulders'. The pattern of wet/dry seasons appears to be shifting, with no snow at all during the normal wet months of December to March 1992. Repeats of popular routes were made and three harder lines:

Artesonraju (6025m) The second and third ascents of the 1979 route on the SW face were made by Argentines Teodoro Plaza, Tony Rodriguez, Marcos Frischknecht and Guy Costa with Australian Duncan Thomas and a Slovenian team. They confirm the difficulties as 800m, 50°–80° ice.

Santa Cruz (6259m) An attempt to climb the 1948 Swiss route was abandoned because the icefields have disappeared.

Huantsan Norte (6113m) Two attempts on the SW ridge were abandoned after continuous midday snowfall.

Bolivia

Huanacuni Eastward (5500m) Ade Miller led a six-member team from Southampton University MC. On 10 July they made the first British ascent of Huanacuni Eastward (5500m).

Argentina and Chile

Many international expeditions have headed for Patagonia where there has been a resurgence of new big wall activity. Local climbers have been similarly busy, mainly in the northern Argentine provinces of San Juan, Mendoza and La Rioja but also taking their fair share of Patagonian routes and visiting Peru.

Argentine Province of Mendoza

Cerro Cuerno (Horcones) (5462m) The locals Daniel Pizarro and Horacio Cuneti climbed a new route on this in January via a steep icefall and technical ground.

Aconcagua (6954m) Thierry Spichiger, Michel Vincent, and Jean-Paul Virnat took three days to climb the *Paragot route* on the S face combining it with the *Messner finish* on the 27 December 1991.The Frenchman Frederic Vallet then followed them up in 19 hours. An American couple meanwhile climbed this, the N variant of the normal, and the *Polish route*.

Patagonia – Northern Ice cap

Cerro San Valentin (3910m) The fifth ascent of this remote mountain was made by the SE ridge. An Argentinian party consisting of Edgar Krautner, Matias Kurtscheidt, Tomas Nunez, and Martin Schopflocher travelled by boat to Laguna San Rafael where they met with a Chilean party led by Claudio Galvez. After hauling sledges for 65km they climbed the ridge and summited in bad weather on 22 January 1992.

Southern Ice cap Traverses

An international expedition composed of Alberto del Castillo, Marcos Couch, Gabriel Ruiz, Alexandre Portela, and Jose Tamayo flew from Coihaque in Chile to Caleta Torte. They then went by boat to Golfo Calen and traversed the ice cap between 14 April and 4 May 1992, finishing at El Chalten in Argentina after 160km. A Spanish pair, Joaquin Colorado and Fabrizio Scanarino, skied a 100km route via Paso Marconi and Paso del Viento.

Fitzroy and Cerro Torre Groups

Fitzroy (3405m) The Swiss trio of Michael Pitelka, Kaspar Ochsner, and Ruth Baldinger climbed *El Corazon* on the E wall between the *Ferrari/Meles '76 route* of the E pillar and the *Yugoslav route* of the Devil's Dihedral. They began on 13 December 1991 and reached the summit on 20 February 1992 (1400m 5.10 A4/45)

Fitzroy   The *Argentine route* was climbed by Teo Plaza and a Spaniard on 24 January 1992.

Aguja Poincenot (3002m)   Argentines Maximo Schneider and Oscar Pandolfi climbed the *Whillans route* on 29 January 1992, as did Ramiro Calvo, Teo Plaza and two Brazilians.

Aguja Poincenot   Americans Steve Gerberding and Jay Smith climbed the SW face by a route called *Judgment Day* (VI 5.11 A1) to summit on 28 January 1992. This is reported to be a well protected route which may follow the Argentine line in the upper part.

Aguja Guillamet (2579m)   This was soloed by the Argentine Horacio Bresba before a pair of women from Buenos Aires, Patricia Malatesta and Marcela Antonucci, made the first all-female ascent. It was also climbed by Martin Greche and Pablo de la Fueste on 20 February 1992.

Aiguille de Saint-Exupery (2680m)   The *'87 route* on the S arête was repeated in 24 hours by Jon Lazkano and S de la Cruz on 10 December 1991 (ED 700m), reporting good snow and superb rock.

Aguja de l'S (2335m)   The second ascent of the *Austrian route* was made by Argentines Bernado Roil, Damian Llabres, and Hernan del Ri on 26 March 1992. This takes the E dihedral then the NE buttress (V 55° ice).

Cerro Torre (3102m)   Jon Krauker and Don Cauthorn made the fourth ascent of the *'74 Ferrari route* on the W face in a very fast time from 13 to 15 January 1992. The *Maestri route* was repeated by three parties.

Cerro El Mocho (1953m)   This summit forms the final peak thrusting from Cerro Torre's Compressor Arête. With easy access it has seven routes on its flanks, and Jay Smith and Steve Gerberding climbed another route on the S face called *Back to Front*. After fixing the bottom five pitches they climbed the top four on 2 January 1992 (VI/5.10/A4).

Cerro El Mocho   Between the S and E pillars is an ice couloir which rarely comes into condition. This was first climbed in 1986 by Italians and was repeated by Giorgio Passino, Patrick Gabarrou and François Marsigny.

Aguja Bifida Norte (2394m, the highest (N) top)   The Italians Casimiro Ferrari, Corrado Valsecchi, and Manuele Panzori climbed a route on the ESE buttress. Austrians Toni Ponholzer and Tommy Bonipace climbed another new route between Ferraris and Luthi's on the SE face before going on to climb the **Pefil del Indio** and the **Cuatro Dedos**.

Paine Group

Cerro Catedral (2200m)   Two expeditions based in French valley climbed routes on the splendid E face of this peak. The Americans John Catto, Charlie Fowler, Peter Gallagher and Messagre Kewdel climbed the logical central zone over 14 days with a final 5 day push to give *La Escoba de Dios* (VI 5.10 A4), summiting on 26 January 1992. Further to the left the Italian team of Paolo Fanton, Fabio Leoni, Mario Manica, and Danny Zampicoli created the originally named *Il Volo del Condor* (ED+ 850m VII- A3), summiting on 2

February 1992. This takes the steepest line up the pillar forming the left side of the face, and they report scope for many more lines.

Torre Sur del Paine (2500m)   The French pair of Vincent Sprungli and Michel Piola were particularly active this year. On the 19 January they began equipping a line up the centre of the 900m E face, to the right of the 1985 attempt by the US/SA trio. After fixing the lower 500m they went for it and created *Dans l'Oeil du Cyclone* (900m ED+ French 6b A4) reaching the summit on 28 February 1992.

Torre Central del Paine (2454m)   The 1200m E face saw two lines in the 91/92 period. Britons Paul Pritchard, Sean Smith, Simon Yates and Noel Crane created the uncompromising line of *El Regalo de Mowana* on 25 January 1992 after 25 days of climbing. The line takes the centre of the face and uses no bolts (1200m ABO- 5.10 A4). Further to the left *La Ballena de los Vientos* takes the E flank of the S pillar. Sebastian de la Cruz, Erik Brand, Steve Hayward, Jose Tamayo and John Lazkano climbed this in 20 days to finish on 24 November 1991. The line frees mediocre rock in the lower and upper parts and is entirely artificial in the centre section (1000m ED+ French 6a/b A3).

Torre Norte del Paine (2260m)   On 14 January 1992 Piola and Sprungli climbed *La Ultima Esperanza* on the E face in one day using very little aid and report that it may go free in good conditions (French 6c A2 600m TD+). Two other parties made ascents of the normal route on the S arête. An Italian team completed the ascent of the left summit, which was probably unclimbed.

Evelio Echevarría writes:
In recent years the popularity of the Parque Nacional Torres del Paine has increased, but so have its ecological problems. Appeals and regulations seem to produce meagre results. In 1990, 110 Latin American students cleaned Aconcagua spotless from top to bottom. In 1991 the Italian climber Mario Manica removed all the refuse lying at the base of the Torres del Paine.

Stronger solutions are now being sought and Latin American national park experts are watching with interest an Argentinian experiment. Authorities of the Parque Aconcagua have raised the entry fee from US$12 to US$80 per visitor and rangers now give you a plastic bag with the instruction to bring down all your refuse. This unpleasant policy has met with great success. Will the Chileans follow the Argentinian example?

Antarctica

Mount Vinson (5271m)   Doug Scott, Sharu Prabhu and Roger Mear led six clients to the summit of Mount Vinson on 7 December 1992.

Mount Shinn   Two of Doug Scott's clients, Andre Hedger and Sundeep Dhillon, climbed Mount Shinn.

DOUG SCOTT

Central Asia 1992

The Fansky Mountains

On 13 June Rick and Alison Allen, Sharu Prabhu and I arrived at Moscow airport. Serge Efimov from Ekaterinburg was there to meet us and take us to the Fansky mountains. Three days later, after sightseeing in Samarkand, we drove all day by truck and jeep, along good roads, and finally a rough track, up into the mountains and a Base Camp at the road-head, and just north of the Alaudin Lake. Just across from Base Camp there was a temporary summer settlement, now occupied by Tadzhiki nomads, pasturing their goats, sheep and cows, on grass which had only recently emerged from the spring snows. We spent the following day setting up camp and a sauna, resting up and bouldering on the excellent limestone blocks on the valley floor. The following day, very unfit, we took 4½ hours to walk by the incredibly clear water of the lakes, and through scented juniper forests to the Alaudin Pass (3730m). There were many more lakes in the valley on the other side.

After spending a day rock climbing three pitch routes on the lower cliffs across from Base Camp, we marched up, over green pasture and forest, to camp in the valley below the moraine. The next day we climbed up in bad weather to camp at 4020m on glacier moraine below the peak Zamok (5070m).

On the 22nd we left camp and walked up the Zamok glacier, steepening into a couloir which we climbed, and after a long traverse to the north, reached the SE ridge. After a total of five hours' scrambling and walking we reached the summit of Zamok (the Castle). These high mountain peaks have a flavour all of their own. A touch of Hunza in the valleys and the feel of Austrian limestone mountains in the higher regions. Although they do not reach much over 17,000ft, there are a lot of them, a veritable jumble of impressive rock faces, alpine ridges rising up out of deep wooded valleys. The late and plentiful snow certainly gave the area a distinctive alpine flavour. In summer, one can imagine them dry to rock and scree. We left the summit and made our way all the way back to Base Camp. We spent the 23rd resting up and bouldering.

On the 24th we left Base Camp to attempt the highest peak in the Fansky mountains, Tchimtarga (5482m). We camped at 4000m just above the Mutne Lake. It had been a long 10-hour day and didn't finish until we had passed under the Kaznob Pass, turning west onto the glacier, which eventually leads up to the Tchimtarga Pass between Tchimtarga and Energy Peak.

On the 25th we packed our glacier camp and moved up towards the rocks. Serge, Sharu and I teamed up together, while Rick set off ahead with Valeri in the lead. Valeri Perchine was one of Russia's finest rock climbers and currently helps train young rock climbers for competitions. The deep covering of snow made difficult rock climbing even harder. Eventually, we arrived at a good bivvy ledge on the rocks of the E ridge at 5000m, where we spent the night in Serge's five-man tunnel tent, cooking on a lightweight pressure cooker he had designed himself. Serge is a nuclear physicist but seems to spend most of his time planning expeditions and climbing in the Himalaya. He was on the first ascent of the SW pillar route of Everest and also recently climbed Kangchenjunga. He led the first ascent of the E ridge of Cho Oyu on which Valeri reached the summit.

On the 26th we climbed the E ridge. After many hard pitches (grade 5) we stopped some 50m below the summit. The morning of the 27th dawned brilliantly but with huge cloud banks to the north. We roamed across several summits, including the highest, and then made a long descent down the N ridge to a pass, and then abseiled down in waist-deep snow, and over cliffs threatened by avalanche, into a gorge. We glissaded on our backsides and then walked a mile down towards Mutne Lake. That same evening, as the weather broke, we staggered into Base Camp, very satisfied from having made this four-day climb. It seemed to Rick, Sharu and me to be quite hard, certainly TD+ with all the spring snow. Serge and Valeri were, like all guides, very fit, good movers over mixed terrain and climbed well up steep rock – we were glad to have them direct operations and lead most of the route.

Rick went off and re-climbed Zamok peak with Alison, who by then was much fitter and acclimatised. On 30 June we packed up and left Base Camp for Samarkand. Two days later we arrived back in Moscow and caught the plane to London. It was an excellent trip and a great place to have visited. Serge organised everything superbly, helped by his friends from the Urals.

Our initial fears of food shortages proved groundless as there were plentiful supplies in Samarkand markets, and fresh milk and bread were available from the local Tadzhiki. Valentina, the cook, produced excellent food down at Base Camp.

On the hill it was interesting to slip into the communal approach to mountaineering favoured by the Russians. It worked well all five of us in Serge's tent, cooking on the one stove and pressure cooker. There is a weight advantage and the group can more easily keep in touch with each other's feelings regarding the progress of the climb. Later in the year the same system proved effective on Nanga Parbat, where Serge and Valeri joined our mainly British expedition to the Rupal side and the Mazeno Ridge (see page 259).

Summary Doug Scott, Rick and Alison Allen, Serge Efimov from Ekaterinburg, and Sharu Prabhu Sherpa climbed in the Fansky Mountains of Tadzhikistan in June/July 1992. They climbed: **Zamok (5070m) via the SE ridge** and **Tchimtarga (5482m)**, the highest peak in the Fansky range, **via the E ridge, descending down the N ridge** (TD+).

Pamir

Tadzhikistan   A British party arranged a joint trip, with friends from Minsk, to the Moscvina glacier Base Camp (4200m).

Pik Korzhenevskaya (7105m) was climbed by the normal route.

Pik KGB (c5600m) – NE face   A new route was climbed by Tony Park and Dave Wilkinson (D/TD).

Pik Kirova (6372m) – N face   Phil Thornhill soloed a probably new route.

Eastern Tadzhikistan   A team from Imperial College London, led by Phil Wickens, visited the remote Abdukagur valley area and made five British first ascents:

Pik Malish (5430m) – SE ridge

Pik Kovshovich (5850m) – NW face

Pik Tanymas (5998m) – W ridge

Pik St Exupery (6063m) – SW ridge

Paris Commune (6354m) – NE ridge

They also formed the first collection of mosses, lichens and diatoms of the area for the Natural History Museum.

Mongolian Altai

Huithen (4356m) – S face   Lindsay Griffin, Julian Freeman-Attwood and Ed Webster reached the summit of the unclimbed S face of Huithen, Mongolia's highest peak. They also made 23 ascents of peaks and lesser summits in the Tabun Bogdo area. (See article 'Mongolian Escape' in this volume.)

Huithen (4356m) – N ridge   Steve Berry and party climbed the mountain from the north.

Eastern Caucasus

The Snegovoy and Bogosskiy ranges in the west of Dagestan received their first visit by British climbers in late summer 1992. A joint British/Ukraine expedition, led by Paul Knott and Nick Drobotenko, made ascents of: **Diklos (4285m) via the S ridge, Addalashukhgelmeer (4151m)** and **Addala East (4025m).** (See article 'Mountains of Dagestan' in this volume.)

Urals

Narodnaya (1885m)   Though of modest height, this is the highest peak in the Urals. It was ascended by Marion Elmes and Alan Martley.

ANDREW WIELOCHOWSKI
East Africa – Recent Activity

Despite recent recessions in Europe and the United States, political unrest in Kenya, rising prices in Tanzania and Aids in Uganda, the East African mountains continue to attract thousands of visitors each year. Most continue their pilgrimages up the 'normal routes' as a result of which facilities are very stretched during the peak holiday periods (especially December).

Rwenzori

A welcome development is that the Rwenzori are now a national park, slowing the gradual encroachment of human activity up the valleys. Entrance fees at present are very reasonable and all the services provided are much more efficient than in the past. No advance arrangements need be made prior to your arrival in Kasese. Just visit the offices of Rwenzori Mountain Services and in a few hours you will be ready to go. Large new huts at Nyabitaba, Bigo, Elena glacier and Kabamba have taken the pressure off the old huts and limited campsites. Unfortunately the bogs, with their magnificent flora, are being churned up by the increased numbers of visitors. The solid bridge placed just below the confluence of the Bujuku and Mubuku rivers has removed a very hazardous crossing and opened up the mountains for a greater period of the year – in the past this river crossing has occasionally stopped progress altogether. A wood causeway has been placed across the upper Bigo Bog; it is about 300m long, very straight and at present very visible from above. Some say this is visually more offensive than a 20 metre wide band of mud but it is certainly more pleasant to walk on. As usual the classic routes to the main summits are frequently repeated but there appears to be very little new route activity.

Kenya

As independent new lines are almost non-existent on Mount Kenya's main summits, attention has turned to eliminates on the minor summits. A notable addition was the ascent of the almost overhanging W face of Point John (4883m) in January 1992 by Pat Littlejohn and John Mothersele in nine hours. The route is 11 pitches long (just over 300m) and involves sustained, superb climbing, using natural protection throughout. Two of the pitches are graded 6a but despite the surroundings the route itself involves mainly in-balance climbing following good crack systems. The overall grade given was

E4. In December 1992 good snow conditions permitted the ascent of *Christmas Buttress* a line of fine icy corners 50m left of Point John Couloir (Andrew Wielochowski and Chris Mockett, Scottish Grade 4, six pitches).

Park fees on Mount Kenya have gone up yet again and the normal visitor must expect to pay about £12 for every day spent in the park. However, the new warden, Bongo Woodley, is very favourably inclined towards visiting climbers and he has negotiated a special climbers' park entry rate of about £7 per day.

Poi, in northern Kenya, has again been visited. Littlejohn and Mothersele repeated the *East Face route*, eliminating the short aid pitch at 5c, and climbing the following 100m directly upwards at 5b (E3 overall).

The same pair visited some of the minor outcrops in the Nairobi area and confirmed the high quality of the new route activities at Lukenya and Embaribal where Iain Allen and other local climbers are putting up hard new face routes, mainly on clean, high quality rock. Most of these new routes require bolts for protection. Visiting climbers are recommended to visit these two locations and, if time permits, the even more spectacular cliffs of Hell's Gate and Kitchwa Tembo in Tsavo National Park. On these big game park cliffs it is possible to climb and game watch simultaneously.

Kilimanjaro

The prohibitively high entry fees to the more remote areas of Kilimanjaro (more than £35 per day) have deterred climbers from visiting the mountain. The much cheaper and less interesting Marangu route is still as popular as ever and the huts continue to be overcrowded in the December–January holiday period. Sadly, the amount of litter in the remote areas is growing and some of the campsites are becoming unpleasant. It is hoped that a few percent of the entry fees collected by the Kilimanjaro National Park could be directed towards keeping these exceptionally beautiful places clean.

There is a growing tendency noted amongst local climbers for the short November/December rains to linger until January. This means that snow and ice routes can often be in excellent condition in December. In January 1993 the lower sections of the Breach Wall were very well snow-clad and routes such as the *Messner Direct* and the *East End route* (John Temple and Tony Charlton) were in very fine condition. Under good snow cover the *East End route* appears to offer a particularly fine way onto the Balletto icefield (four pitches of Scottish Grade 4). This could then be followed for about three pitches to the upper sections of the Heim glacier, the lower half of which, in recent years, has become very unpleasant at times.

ADRIAN DRAGOS DEFTA

Mountaineering in Romania

The Romanian Carpathians, though relatively recent geologically, form part of the great Alpine chain. With their moderate altitude and ease of access, they offer picturesque landscapes, and abundance of flora and forests, and there is plenty of accommodation for visitors. They also offer fine rock climbing, snow and ice climbing and all kinds of classic mountaineering.

Although the Carpathians were visited from time immemorial by shepherds, the first recorded climb was in 1839 when A I Vaillant and the prelate Angelescu reached the summit of Omu peak (2505m). From 1921 onwards, the Bucegi massif was explored by the Titeica brothers who made the first map of the area. In 1935 Niculae Baticu made the first ascent of the N face of Galbenele (UIAA grade IV). This was the start of Carpathian rock climbing, but it was not until 1955 that the biggest wall, Paretele Vaii Albe, was climbed, by Alexandru Floricioiu, Roland Welkens and Norbert Hiemesch. Their route *Blue Crack* (*Fisura Albastra*), which covers the hardest section of the wall, is probably the best-known alpine route in Romania (see topo on p274).

The Romanian Alpine Club

In 1934 the Romanian Alpine Club was founded on similar lines to western alpine clubs. It built several refuges and chalets and organised climbing courses. After the Second World War the many changes in Romania adversely affected the normal development of climbing. In 1948 the Romanian Alpine Club was dissolved and replaced by the Federation of Mountaineering and Tourism. Competitions took the place of traditional climbing and few mountaineers had the opportunity to climb abroad, in the Caucasus or Altai or Pamir or in the Western Alps. Nevertheless some fine mountaineers emerged, including Emilian Cristea, Taina Dutzescu, Emil Coliban and Nicolae Cojan.

After the revolution of December 1989 the Romanian Alpine Club was restarted and its activities resumed with enthusiasm; some of its older members who had joined before the war made an essential contribution. But the Club still faces hardships of every kind, including shortage of printing technology, loss of funds, lack of accommodation, and so on. Few of its members have had the opportunity to climb in other areas and an important activity of the Club is the development of overseas contacts and co-operation with western alpine organisations. A very special relationship is developing with the Alpine Club through exchange of publications and reciprocal visits, and the National Officer of the British Mountaineering Council, Roger Payne, has given the Club generous help with making links all over the world and in helping us to acquire quality mountain equipment.

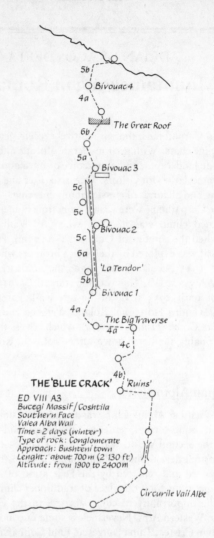

THE 'BLUE CRACK'

ED VIII A3
Bucegi Massif / Coshtila
Southern Face
Valea Alba Wall
Time = 2 days (winter)
Type of rock: Conglomerate
Approach: Bushteni town
Lenght: about 700 m (2 130 ft)
Altitude: from 1900 to 2400 m

The Romanian Alpine Club is planning to build more mountain refuges and to look after the climbing areas ecologically; also to establish a Romanian Association of Mountain Guides. We would like to organise an international meeting between climbers of many countries, on the western model. These plans will be difficult to bring about owing to lack of funds and a strong sponsor, but we would very much welcome visits by British climbers to show them the lesser known and very good climbing opportunities in Romania.

The Bucegi massif

Among the Carpathian mountains the Bucegi massif is considered the most important climbing area in Romania. It has long and steep rock faces, a large and spectacular tableland at around 2200m, and many varied routes. Of special importance is Mount Coshtila (2490m) with its four big walls: Valea Alba Wall, Eagles Wall, Coshtila Wall and Galbenele N face.

The approach to Coshtila starts from Bushteni, a town about 80 miles north of Bucharest. The main alpine refuge is the 'Coshtila', built in 1938 by the Romanian Alpine Club. Many routes can be climbed from this refuge, including:

Eagles Wall (nearest to Busteni), 300m high: *Innominata* 6b, *Stone Butterfly* 6b, *Policandrul* 6b, *Mult-Dorita Crack* 6b.

Valea Alba Wall, c1000m, with some long routes: *Diedrul Pupezi* 6b, *Blue Crack* 6b (see topo diagram), *Speranza Superroute* 6b, *Red Crack* 6b which is one of the most spectacular routes. These routes provide true alpine mixed climbing in winter.

Bucegi massif is the birthplace of Romanian mountaineering because of its good geographical position between Bucharest and Brashow. There are plenty of cable cars, chalets and hotels, and opportunities for skiing and caving.

Romanian Carpathians

1	Bucegi	10	Retezat Massif
2	Kingstone (Piatra Craiului)	11	Cerna Valley
3	Postavarul	12	Banat Massif
4	Greatstone (Piatra Mare)	13	Western Mountains
5	Tchewcash	14	Gutyi
6	Virghish Gorges	15	Rarau Massif
7	Fagarash Massif	16	Tcheahlau Massif
8	Shureanu	17	Bicaz Gorges
9	Buila Vinturaritza		

Mount Everest Foundation
Expedition Reports 1991–92

SUMMARISED BY EDWARD PECK

All the expeditions summarised below received the approval of the Mount Everest Foundation. MEF approval, in most cases accompanied by a grant, is generally an important first step in seeking assistance, financial or otherwise, from firms or other organisations. The MEF itself does not normally offer sponsorship.

The expeditions briefly described in the following notes took place between June 1991 and September 1992. The notes were compiled from reports received up to 1 December 1992. Copies of the full reports are lodged in the Alpine Club Library and in the Archives of the Royal Geographical Society and may be consulted in those places.

The Americas and the Arctic

91/17 *Leeds Baffin Island Expedition* (June–July 1991)

This five-member team succeeded in a first ascent of the S face of Mt Bilbo, and attempted new routes on Mt Adluk and Mt Breideblik in the Auyuittuq National Park area of Baffin Island.

91/36 *Bristol University Rio Paute Headwaters Expedition*
(July–August 1991)

This mixed team (6 British, 5 Ecuadorean), working in co-ordination with the East Anglian Ecuador Cloud Forest Expedition (see 92/6), set out to study aspects of the cloud forest and aquatic ecosystems of the Pulpito valley, headwaters of the Rio Paute in Southern Ecuador, camping at 2300m–2400m. Projects included fog drip, fish ecology, amphibians, plant fungi and macro-invertebrates.

92/6 *East Anglian Ecuador Cloud Forest Expedition*
(October 1991–May 1992)

This joint scientific team (5 British, 7 Ecuadorean) investigated interaction between cloud forest ecology and peasant farmers in two areas of South Ecuador: the Pulpito valley (Prov. Canar) and Ingapucara (Prov. Azuny) between 2500m and 3000m.

92/9 *Torres del Paine* (December 1991–January 1992)

Two of this four-member team succeeded in a new route (600m of A2/A3 and some A4) on the Central Pillar of the Torres del Paine. They named the route *El Regalo de Mowana* (the Gift of the Tehuelche God).

92/15 *Scottish Stauning Alps Expedition* (May 1992)

This seven-member party succeeded in their objective of the first complete ski traverse of the Stauning Alps (NE Greenland) from Nordvestfjord in the south to Kap Petersen in the north, making at least one first ascent en route.

92/21 *Scottish Bersaerkertinde Expedition* (July 1992)

This four-man team's objectives, the N face of Bersaerkertinde and the NE face of Attilaborgen were foiled by deep soft snow and fast-running rivers.

92/23 *Southampton University Bolivian Expedition* (June–August 1992)

The initial aim of this six-member team, to climb Huanacuni (5789m) by a new route, was abandoned; but they made first British ascents of Huanacuni Eastward (5500m) and of six or seven other peaks over 5000m in this area.

92/27 *Parrots in Peril, Ecuador* (March–July 1992)

This team (4 British, 4 Ecuadorean) achieved their aim of surveying various sites up to 3200m in the Podocarpus National Park to assess the threat to three species of parrot, and also to assess the environmental impact of gold-mining and colonists on the Park.

92//28 *British East Greenland Expedition* (July–August 1992)

This party of nine succeeded in identifying and climbing Wager's Cathedral Peak (2600m) and some subsidiary peaks in the Lindberg and Lemon ranges of the Kangerdlugssuaq basin of East Greenland. They also sledged from the Lindbergs to the coast, visited Wager's 1936 food dump and did some botanical fieldwork. (See article 'Lindbergs and Lemons' in this volume.)

92/29 *British Kahiltna South* (April–May 1992)

This two-man team succeeded, at their third attempt in making the first ascent of Peak 9070 (ft) from the N side in the area south of Mount Hunter.

Himalaya

91/11 *Saga Himalayan Expedition to Jaonli* (September–November 1991)

This six-member team (five over 60) attempted the unclimbed E side of Jaonli (6632m). Two climbers reached 21,000ft on the S ridge, turning back at a point where the earthquake on the night of October 19/20 had made a huge cleft, overlooked by unstable ice blocks, across the ridge.

91/14 *New Zealand Alpine Club Kulu Centennial* (August–October 1991)

This 18-member party had as its objectives Papsura (6451m), Devachan (6187m) and Sentinel (5939m) at the head of the Tos Nullah. Devachan and Sentinel (by W ridge) were climbed but the attempt on Papsura was abandoned when one climber fell to his death.

91/15A *British Winter Himlung Expedition* (November–December 1991)

This six-member party aimed to make the first British ascent of Himlung (Annapurna Group) by the S ridge. Time and weather frustrated their attempt at about 6000m on this impressive route.

91/20 *Chamlang 1991* (September–October 1991)

Four climbers of the six-member team made a successful first British ascent of Chamlang from the Hongu valley by the long and interesting S ridge. (See article 'Big Bird Flapping Wings' in this volume.)

91/22 *British Langtang Lirung SE Ridge* (October–November 1991)

Despite careful acclimatisation on Naya Kanga and other peaks, this four-man team, who found themselves competing, alpine style, for the SE ridge of Langtang Lirung with a fully equipped Japanese expedition, retreated owing to intestinal troubles and bad weather conditions.

91/39 *Kusum Kangguru* (October–November 1991)

Two of the three climbing members of the party succeeded in the first ascent of the S ridge of Kusum Kangguru (6369m), having approached the mountain up the Kusum Khola. (See *AJ97*, pp22–26) This ascent was shortlisted for the 1992 Piolet d'Or award.

91/45 *Cerro Kishtwar* (September–October 1991)

Two groups of the six-member party nearly made the first ascent of Cerro Kishtwar (6220m) by two routes on the NW face, but retreated 100m from the summit.

92/3 *British Saipal Expedition* (April–May 1991)

This six-member party did not succeed in their main objective of climbing Saipal (NW Nepal) by a new route from the east, but they did carry out a first reconnaissance of the NE side of Saipal, reaching 5700m on the NE spur, and also travelled through the little known region of Humla.

92/4 *Thalay Sagar Expedition* (April–June 1992)

Two members of this seven-member party succeeded in climbing Thalay Sagar (6904m) by a new route from the south – the first British ascent and seventh overall. Others in the party climbed Rudugaira (5364m) and made new routes on unnamed pinnacles up to 5700m. (See article 'Thalay Sagar' in this volume)

92/5 *Swargarohini 1992* (May 1992)

This two-man team made two serious attempts on the N face of Swargarohini (believed unclimbed, though an Indian party reached 200ft below the summit in 1990) but were defeated by unsettled weather conditions and heavy snowfall.

92/11 *Indian British Panch Chuli Expedition* (May–June 1992)

Six Indian and six British climbers succeeded in climbing peaks in the Panch Chuli massif, approaching it from the west. Panch Chuli II (6904m) was climbed by W spur (1st ascent) and SW ridge (2nd ascent). The party also achieved first ascents of Sahadev East (5750m), Panch Chuli V (6437m), Panchali Chuli (5220m) and Draupadi (5250m), while a second ascent of Rajrambha (6537m) led to its traverse via the E ridge and the first ascent of Menaka Peak (6000m). (See articles 'Indian British Panch Chuli Expedition 1992' and 'Panch Chuli V' in this volume.) The ascent of Panch Chuli V was shortlisted for the 1992 Piolet d'Or award.

92/20 *New Zealand Cholatse* (September–October 1992)

Three climbers in one group and one solo climber succeeded in the first ascent of Cholatse (6440m) by the rib on the W face.

92/22 *Exercise Ultimate Challenge Ama Dablam* (April–May 1992)

Two of the nine climbers from the three Services succeeded in reaching the summit of Ama Dablam (6856m) by the SE ridge (normal route), being the 99th and 100th persons to do so.

92/25 *British Expedition to Eastern Kishtwar* (August–September 1992)

This six-member climbing team achieved their third objective of a second ascent of Tupendo II (5600m) by the S ridge, but serious injury involved retreat below the summit of Tupendo I (5700m). Their major objective, Mardi Phabrang (6060m), was abandoned.

92/35 *North Wales Annapurna I South Face*

Tragically, all four members of the team died en route to Nepal in the Kathmandu air crash on 27 September 1992.

92/41 *British Hagshu North Face* (September 1992)

These three climbers repeated their 1989 attempt on the N face of Hagshu (6300m) but again were foiled by bad weather, at about 5550m.

92/43 *British Garhwal Expedition* (September–October 1992)

This five-member party succeeded in the first ascent of Manda III (6529m) and attempted the N ridge of Point 5550m.

Karakoram

91/18 *Great Karakoram Expedition (Ultar)* (August–September 1991)

This strong six-member team set out to make the first ascent of Ultar I (7388m), an unclimbed peak overlooking the Hunza valley. Attempts via the S ridge and the SE face failed when a broken crampon and a broken ice hammer enforced a difficult and dangerous retreat. (See *AJ97*, pp49–54)

91/19 *British Masherbrum II Expedition* (August–September 1991)

This 14-member team succeeded in the first British ascent of Masherbrum II (*c*7200m) from the Bolux glacier by the SE ridge.

92/23 *British Masherbrum Expedition* (August–September 1991)

Of nine climbers only four acclimatised properly and of these only two reached Camp 4A (6500m) on Masherbrum (7821m), retreating owing to bad storm conditions.

91/24 *British Gasherbrum II* (May–July 1991)

This 8-member team (2 British) undertook to climb Gasherbrum II (7772m), alpine style, and very nearly succeeded, but were defeated by incessant bad weather and strong winds.

91/82 *Sheffield Batura Expedition* (July–September 1991)

This six-member party made a first ascent of Peak 5300m, south of Shani peak. After three attempts, they reached a point 100m short of their main objective, the unnamed 5973m peak in N Batura. Two trekked out up the Hispar and down the Biafo glaciers in 10 days.

92/1 *Sokha Brakk* (July–September 1992)

This three-member party climbed Piper's Peak (5495m) and made two unsuccessful attempts (reaching 5250m) on the NW face of Point 5956m (west of the Biafo glacier) named by them Sokha (after the Sokha glacier) Brakk (peak).

92/12 *Scottish Nanga Parbat Expedition* (June–July 1992)

This five-member team attempted an ascent of Nanga Parbat by the Mummery Rib on the Diamir face. They abandoned the Mummery Rib in favour of the Kinshofer route, reaching 7200m before health problems forced a retreat on 9 June.

92/13 *Broad Peak Traverse* (June–July 1992)

Early monsoon conditions with severe avalanche risk frustrated this strong six-member team from achieving their objective of climbing the SW face of Broad Peak (8047m). Three attempts at the summit were abandoned at 7650m. A successful solar lighting system was installed at Skardu under Prince Sadruddin Aga Khan's Rural Support Programme.

92/18 *British Latok II* (July–September 1992)

This eight-member party's objective of the first ascent of the W ridge of Latok II was foiled by bad weather at 20,000ft, after three attempts.

92/33 *Gemini Karakoram* (August–September 1992)

One man of this climbing pair made solo first ascents of Point 5550m (Passu glacier) by the S face ice couloir, and of the N face and NW ridge of Fiyag (5550m) (also known as Badshani or King's Peak).

92/34 *Shani North Face Expedition* (August–September 1992)

This two-member team climbed Sentinel (5300m) but bad weather and illness prevented them from achieving their objective of a first ascent of the N face of Shani Peak (5880m) in the Naltar valley.

92/39 *British Biafo Glacier Expedition* (July–August 1992)

This three-man party succeeded in their objectives of an ascent (probably not the first) of Mango Brakk (17,500ft) and the first ascent, by the SE face, of Gama Sokha Limbu.

92/45 *Matho Kangri Expedition* (July–August 1992)

This four-member team achieved their objective of a first British ascent of Matho Kangri (6230m) but by the W ridge and not, as originally intended, by the N face.

92/48 *British West Biafo Wall Expedition* (July–August 1992)

Plans by this team of four to climb the sub-6000m walls between the Sokha La and the Hispar La at the head of the Biafo glacier were frustrated by bad weather and rock falls.

Central Asia and the Far East

92/44 *Imperial College Pamir Expedition* (July–August 1992)

This team visited the remote Abdukagur valley area of Eastern Tadzhikistan and made five British first ascents of mountains from 5400m to 6350m. They also made a unique collection of mosses, lichens and diatoms from this virtually unknown area.

92/10 *Mongolian Altai 70 Years Expedition* (July–August 1992)

Three climbers reached the summit of Mount Huithen (officially 4356m, on the map 4374m), the highest mountain in Mongolia, by its N ridge.

92/51 *China Caves Project, Sichuan* (Summer 1992)

This party made preliminary investigations of this fine series of karst cave systems in the Xingwen National Park in South Sichuan. They also carried out geological fieldwork on the limestone karst of West and Central Tibet.

92/52 *Caves of Thunder, Irian Jaya, Indonesia* (July–September 1992)

This nine-member team which met with daunting administrative difficulties, achieved their objective of exploring and surveying 'the world's largest underground river' on their second visit. They accurately located the cave entrance by Global Positioning System and witnessed, at considerable risk, 'the third biggest chamber in the world fill to the roof in the most spectacular flood ever'.

Book Reviews 1992–93

The Ascent of Everest
John Hunt
First published in 1953
A new edition with a Foreword by John Hunt
Hodder & Stoughton, 1993, pp280, pb, £12.99

The 1953 British Expedition to Mount Everest and the First Ascent by Sherpa Tenzing Norgay and Edmund Hillary on 29 May 1953 placed mountaineering once again firmly in the public eye at the time of the Coronation, with, it seemed, the ultimate achievement of the highest summit in the world. John Hunt's book, first published in 1953, was a classic of the era, inspiring many of us (I was 9 at the time) to take part in exploration and climbing. In a review in this 40th anniversary year I can do little more than salute the achievement, the planning and the drive which made the ascent successful.

In literary terms, this is a factual account of a great endeavour. The reader can actually understand how the expedition took place, its neo-military structure, how the ascent so nearly failed as it ground slowly up the Lhotse Face. The post-modern expedition book draws in more emotion, more controversy and more vignettes of the curious personalities involved in mountaineering. To have done so in 1953, and with this great success, would perhaps have belittled the achievement, and now 40 years on would make it seem more dated. It is still a good read.

Hodders, with a loyal and distinguished track record in mountaineering literature, have produced an admirable, affordable paperback, highlighting one of the most memorable of all summit photographs on the cover – I wonder how often Ed Hillary kicks himself for not making sure he had one of himself on top too.

It is worth recording something more: the royalties from 1953 went towards the setting up of the Mount Everest Foundation. That generous tradition continues with this edition, and there are not many expeditions which continue, four decades later, to support mountaineering.

John Hunt has written a fitting historic foreword, and Ed Hillary a postscript recalling sadly the junk, cost and commercialisation of Everest – and his own efforts to help Nepal and the Sherpas who have given so much to us.

Hodders have also published a leather-bound presentation volume, limited to 500 copies, signed by all living members of the 1953 team. It is expected that this will be sold out by the time this review is printed; any enquiries to the Alpine Club.

Charles Clarke

Alfred Gregory's Everest
Alfred Gregory
With a Foreword by Jan Morris
Constable, 1993, pp180, black & white photographs, £16.96

Each major Everest expedition gives the world a few selected images that remain in the collective memory. The Americans gave us their stunning shot of the West Ridge soaring up into the clouds. Captain Noel is probably remembered best for his photograph of Mallory and Irvine setting off on their fateful climb. Fifty-one years later Doug Scott immortalised Dougal Haston on the summit, glowing with palpable pride in the last rays of sunshine.

The drama of 1953 has been summarised over the years in a few oft-published shots of the Icefall, the famous photo of Bourdillon and Evans slumped in exhaustion after their extraordinary push to the South Summit and back, the picture of Hillary and Tenzing on the South-East Ridge below Camp IX, Hillary's shot of footsteps on the final ridge and, of course, the classic ikon of Tenzing on the summit. But, for every published expedition photograph, there are always a hundred negatives or transparencies that languish unseen in filing cabinets. For Alf Gregory, the official photographer in 1953, the 40th anniversary is the perfect excuse to bring some of those unseen photographs to light, using them to complement some of the images we all know so well.

Gregory chose to make his personal record in monochrome. Despite the fact that some of the pictures have been converted from colour, the quality is superb. Amidst the current plethora of glitzy colour mountain photography, it makes a refreshing change to see a whole book of black & white prints, produced with loving care by a master of the darkroom, and well reproduced by Constable. The negatives and transparencies only came into Gregory's possession recently. Some of them suffered in the past at Printing House, but the odd blob and scratch does not matter here; in fact they add to the feeling that this is a very valuable historical document.

The photographer makes it quite clear in his introduction that the book is not only a historical document but also very much a personal record of the expedition and of his love for Nepal. He writes with huge enthusiasm about the thrill of being invited by Shipton to join the 1952 Cho Oyu expedition and given the opportunity to roam freely over Sola Khumbu during what now seems a lost age of innocence. The photo of his first sight of Everest, from Rolwaling, captures all that magical sense of unlimited space and opportunity; similarly, his delicately radiant images of Kathmandu and Bhaktapur, devoid of video shops and Coca-Cola signs, give us modern tourists a glimpse of what we have missed.

The 1953 leadership change is glossed over in Gregory's introduction. By deliberately avoiding controversy, he seems to be saying that this nostalgic celebration of a great event is not the place for opening up old wounds. In fact he writes with warmth and generosity about all his companions in 1953. Where a modern climber might complain at having to turn back 350m from the top, Gregory thanks fate for letting him get that high, on that memorable afternoon 40 years ago, when he, George Lowe and Ang Nyima left Hillary and Tenzing poised for their summit bid.

During that afternoon of 28 May, Gregory was shooting colour film. Here he has converted the shots to black & white, using high contrast to isolate Hillary and Tenzing, dark figures in a white wilderness, as they emerge from the depths of the Western Cwm. Close-ups include detailed studies of Lowe changing film and Ang Nyima adjusting his oxygen set – both taken bare-handed at 8350m. These are two of the pictures that have not been published before. There are many others, like the shot of two Sherpas striding dynamically onto the South Col, doing a heroic final sprint for the camera at the end of their long slog up the Lhotse Face. Two pages later, by contrast, we see Da·Namgyal, obviously exhausted after his climb with John Hunt, sprawl-led on the bleak scree of the South Col.

There are other interesting details, like the wonderfully dated shots of Sherpas strapping 10-point crampons to bendy leather boots topped with puttees, and a close-up of the special high-altitude boots that now look like bizarre galoshes; but as official photographer in 1953 Gregory had also to capture the monumental scale of the mountain. No one since has really superseded his shots of the South Col, which evoke all the chilling bleakness of that desolate spot. Likewise his pictures of the Western Cwm use tiny human figures to convey the immensity of the place; and the prints are beautifully made, with figures silhouetted against a white background that retains just enough detail to give form and texture to the snow.

Alfred Gregory's Everest is a picture book. Apart from the introduction and a foreword by Jan Morris, the only text is a running commentary of brief captions. The designer at Constable has chosen a simple, classic typeface and used a lot of clean white paper to give the pictures plenty of space to speak for themselves. My only criticism is that the publishers did not have the nerve to go for a black & white dust jacket. The dim colour picture they have used, printed from a poor duplicate transparency, is, for all its misty nostalgia, a poor advertisement for the images inside, which recall a great adventure with sparkling vitality.

Stephen Venables

Coronation Everest
Jan Morris
Boxtree, pp128, £6.99 pb

Newspapermen and mountaineers operate in different worlds. Reporters have
their deadlines and hunger for the hard, swift-moving facts of a story. Climbers enjoy the isolation of a seemingly eccentric sport, pursued at a snail's pace
far from the nearest telephone or FAX machine. 'Because it's there' will hardly
satisfy the journalist with 1000 words to write and a news editor back in
London drumming his fingers. As they lurk at base camp worrying about what
to put in the next cleft stick heading for civilisation, expedition correspondents will inevitably be thrown back upon their powers of invention or skill at
describing the various ways in which paint can dry.

In 1953 James Morris tackled these problems with great panache. He had
never been on a big mountain when *The Times* dispatched him to Everest to
file reports of the British attempt led by Colonel John Hunt. Unlike Boot of the
Beast, who was similarly plunged into a deep end, Morris succeeded brilliantly
in sending back reports of great humour and atmosphere culminating in a
scoop to end all scoops – news of the conquest of the world's highest
mountain released several days after the event on the morning of the Queen's
coronation.

This was as much a problem of logistics for Morris as it was for Colonel
Hunt in getting his chaps to the summit. But as cipherer, negotiator and
author of elegant dispatches, James Morris – 'a very parfait gentle journalist'
as one expedition member described him – triumphed. A telegram which read
'Snow conditions bad stop advanced base abandoned yesterday stop awaiting
improvement' was decoded in Printing House Square, we know not how, as
'Summit of Everest reached on 29 May by Hillary and Tenzing'. The closely
guarded preparation proved wise, for the message was intercepted and rival
papers reported that the expedition had failed.

Coronation Everest, by James Morris, is reprinted for a greatly changed
world to mark the 40th anniversary of that first ascent. The young gentleman
from *The Times* has become a woman, the leading travel writer of her time,
and Everest has changed hardly less. Much of the enigma which wreathed the
summit 40 years ago has gone; lost in the trample of hundreds of feet across its
top and upon every face and flank; lost to litter and tourism and the satellite
links that bounce immediate words and pictures from the very summit.
Coronation Everest gives a backward glance to a different and more romantic
age, when Britain was proudly monarchist and climbing Everest reflected high
achievement in every sense. What Jan Morris thinks about those Everest days
reflects in her foreword to the new edition and rereading the book does jolt a
memory of Everest as the closest platform to eternal space and an age when
news travelled at a measured pace by hand of runner.

Ronald Faux

Himalayan Climber
A Lifetime's Quest to the World's Greater Ranges
Doug Scott
Diadem Books, 1992, pp192, £19.99

The author, an old friend, will not misunderstand that I, one of his many admirers, should have entertained inner misgivings when accepting Geoffrey Templeman's invitation to review this book for the *Alpine Journal*. It appeared to be just another 'coffee table' volume, embellished with the superb quality of mountain photography which we now take for granted, with illustrations of dramatic moves on hard routes with which many of us are familiar. But for this invitation, I might well have skipped through the photographs and placed the book alongside a row of other works of similar size and quality of production. After all, I have known about Doug Scott's great achievements and did not expect to be further enlightened about his record.

But those reservations were misplaced. This is the Odyssey of a man who has made mountains a way of life. He has climbed just about everywhere in the world, not only (as the sub-title of the book implies) in the higher ranges, but on mountains and crags, small as well as great. Unlike many books in this format, the eye should not be mesmerised by the marvellous pictures; the text must be read. For through it the reader can discern not only the high quality of the climbs, but something of the philosophy and nature of a man dedicated to his mountaincraft in a degree which is rare even among other leading professionals.

Scott's quest has taken him to ranges in every continent except South America. The list of the summits he has climbed, many of them as first ascents, and the standards of the routes by which he and his companions have chosen to climb them, are best appreciated by his peers in the fraternity of mountaineers. Climbers use the word 'commitment' to describe a determination to press on upwards, sometimes in the face of almost superhuman difficulties and almost beyond the limits of endurance. Doug has often committed himself in that sense. As an example of sheer persistence, it would be hard to better the eleven bivouacs his party endured on the East Pillar of Shivling; or the six nights he spent, with other companions, above 8000m during a traverse of Makalu.

He maintains that when, in such adversity, a decision has been made to continue the climb, fear and anxiety tend to be dispelled, 'creating space for an inner peace'; the handicap of tension is removed from the action. As regards fear, he echoes the experience of others among us mountaineers; when death has appeared inevitable 'I registered only curiosity ...'

But Doug Scott is not foolhardy. Decisions to carry on have been made after a sober appraisal of the experience, stamina and skill of himself and his fellow climbers. He has turned back when his judgement dictated accordingly. I fancy that he shares with me memories of such 'failures' which are as satisfying as his many successes. Doug has demonstrated commitment, too, by returning again and again to certain great peaks which seem to have had, for him, a magnetic attraction: Everest, K2, Chamlang, Makalu. The latter mountain, he tells us, 'had such a hold on me that I was to go there four times in all'.

Nor were the highest mountains the only lure; he has paid no less than six visits to Iceland.

Whether it be because of or despite his exceptional achievements, the author is essentially a person of great humility. He admits that, after climbing Everest with Dougal Haston by its SW face and surviving unscathed a night in a snow hollow on the summit ridge: 'I thought I was invincible, could do anything. I was far too arrogant.' He avers that this mood may have had some bearing on the accident he suffered, and the eight days' ordeal, with both his legs broken, on his descent from the Ogre. Mountains, he writes, have helped to strip him 'of my sense of self-importance'.

It requires more than he has revealed through his writing to identify Scott as the caring person he is; for he tells little about himself, and even less about his climbing partners in this autobiography. Yet there is some hint of it in his references to local mountain people, and in his allusion to a great sadness in his personal life. He is also a man of firm principles. Sensitivity and principle may account for the very few expeditions during which there was a lack of harmony among the team.

'What does it mean, and why do I do it?', he asks in his Postscript. 'At its finest moments climbing allows me to step out of ordinary existence into something extraordinary . . .', 'to come alive in an environment where every step of the way is more difficult than the last . . .', 'not knowing where it will end – maybe on the summit and, if not, then as long as it is at the limit of endurance, that will have been enough to satisfy the soul and liberate the spirit . . .'

These may seem random unconnected thoughts which come to Doug's mind at the end of the book. They provide, at least, part of the answer to what lies behind his compelling urge to climb.

John Hunt

(Editor's Note: The *Alpine Journal* does not usually publish more than one review of each book. However, in the case of *K2: The 1939 Tragedy* and of *Sea, Ice and Rock*, two reviews have been included in order to reflect different shades of opinion.)

K2: The 1939 Tragedy
Andrew J Kauffman and William L Putnam
The Mountaineers/Diadem Books, 1992, pp224, £14.99

This was an expedition which not only ended with the deaths of one member and three Sherpas, but resulted in extensive controversy and recrimination when the survivors returned to the United States. The authors' thesis is that Wiessner was a great climber but an inadequate organiser; and that the blame he received, which was later transferred unfairly to Jack Durrance (whose diary, released after Wiessner's death, is used extensively in this account), was only partially merited. The tragedy was also caused by a whole chain of adverse circumstances.

Wiessner, of German origin, who had climbed in Europe, America and the Himalaya, was better qualified to lead a Himalayan expedition than most American climbers of the period. The rest of the team were comparatively inexperienced. The group were on the mountain for nearly three months, using the Abruzzi Ridge route. Very soon it became obvious that Wiessner intended to lead from the front and, although he appointed a deputy, there was no proper organisation at Base Camp. In all, nine camps were set up, with Wiessner and Dudley Wolfe, and Sherpa Pasang Dawa Lama, forming the assault party and everyone else employed as load carriers. Wolfe, who had helped to finance the expedition, was an energetic man but no climber. He appeared to treat Wiessner as his personal guide.

Wiessner himself, with Pasang Lama, reached a point about 250m below the summit. When the lead party, which had been held up by several periods of bad weather, dropped down a couple of camps to replenish supplies for a further attempt, they were shocked to find that the tents had been stripped. On the way down Wolfe fell, taking Pasang Lama with him. Wiessner managed to hold them, but Pasang Lama was badly hurt. Wolfe insisted on staying at Camp 7 – he was afraid he would lose acclimatisation if he descended! Two days later Wiessner and Pasang Lama reached Base having found all the other camps stripped.

Meanwhile, the porters had arrived for the walk out, two expedition members had gone home and the others, having seen no sign of life on the mountain for several days, had allowed the Sherpas to go up to remove equipment. In a rescue bid, four Sherpas, including the sirdar Pasang Kikuli, ascended to Camp 6 from which three continued to Camp 7 to bring Wolfe down. They found him lying in his own excrement, unwilling to leave his tent. They descended to Camp 6 for the night, and next day the same three went back up. Neither they nor Wolfe were seen again.

The book is notable on two counts: first because this American expedition is not so well known here as its importance merits, and secondly because it describes in detail how mountains were climbed before the age of the jumar. The account starts well, with good build-up and ever increasing tension as the tragic climax approaches. But it is difficult to understand how, even as long ago as 1939, any expedition could have been organised so ineptly. The authors tend to overplay their hand in their cumulative listing of problems: no radio, a divided party, no knowledge of the effects of the 'death zone', Sherpas with no command of English . . . The reiteration of these and other errors of judgement makes ultimately for tedium. However, the book is an important one, well written, and most of it extremely readable.

Livia Gollancz

Ed Webster writes:
Young climbers browsing the bookshelves might well wonder why a new title, K2, The 1939 Tragedy, would chronicle a Himalayan expedition over 50 years old. But interest in the ill-fated 1939 American attempt on K2 lives on for several reasons. The expedition's controversial and driven leader, Fritz Wiessner, was one of the century's finest mountaineers and rock climbers. On

July 19, 1939, with Pasang Lama, Wiessner came tantalisingly close – within 800ft – of making the first ascent of K2. He spearheaded the climb in modern style, using neither bottled oxygen nor radios. At a time when no 8000m peak had been scaled, Wiessner's near success foretold the future of mountaineering.

Yet the 1939 attempt on K2 ended in heroic, bitter tragedy. An American climber, Dudley Wolfe, and three Sherpas who went to his rescue, Pasang Kikuli, Pasang Kitar, and Phinsoo, all perished. The circumstances that precipitated the disaster were, as the American counsel in Srinigar who later interviewed Wiessner and Jack Durrance put it, 'of a very complicated nature'.

Briefly, following two separate unsuccessful summit attempts, Wiessner and Lama descended from Camp XI to Camp VIII, where Wolfe was in support. When all three descended to camp VII at 24,700ft to retrieve additional supplies, they found the camp stripped: the tents were open and filled with snow, the reserve sleeping-bags and mattresses were gone, and food was scattered in the snow.

While Wolfe waited alone at Camp VII the next day, Wiessner and Lama continued down. In succession, they discovered that every camp on the mountain had been evacuated. More dead than alive, Fritz and Lama stumbled into basecamp where they met the rest of the team, who thought they had died in an avalanche. Wolfe was now stranded, alone, at Camp VII, where he died.

In *K2: The 1939 Tragedy*, the authors have attempted to 'lay down as accurately as possible the events of the 1939 American Karakorum Expedition to K2 and to dispel misconceptions which have grown over the years', and have promised to tell 'the full story of the ill-fated Wiessner expedition'. Intriguing and commendable goals, but are they achieved? Do the authors maintain their objectivity and even-handedness when appraising the roles, actions, and responsibilities of each member of the 1939 team?

Unfortunately, they do not. Kauffman and Putnam have indeed clarified several sections of the expedition's tangled story by revealing Jack Durrance's diary entries, but the book, in general, portrays Fritz Wiessner as a blunt, headstrong, uncommunicative egomaniac, while making every effort to characterise Jack Durrance as a humanistic, caring individual, who did the very best he was capable of.

It is worth mentioning that Kauffman and Putnam initially began this project as a biography of Wiessner, and sent him various chapters to review. Wiessner was so incensed by the material that he flatly refused to help them further. Consequently, the pair abandoned the biography project, and the present book contains none of Wiessner's photographs, nor any direct diary quotations, save a few passages from a typed copy he loaned them early on.

The book is extremely well written and beautifully illustrated with crisp black-and-white photographs from Durrance and Chappel Cranmer's personal collections. Throughout the book, however, Kauffman and Putnam, old-school mountaineers themselves, judge Wiessner within the context of conservative 1930s standards. But should a person or mountaineer be viewed solely within the context and confines of the era he lived in? Seen through the eyes of climbers today, Wiessner was not rash, but rather a determined leader, decades ahead of his time.

The true legacy of the 1939 American Karakorum Expedition to K2 is that Fritz Wiessner and Pasang Lama came within feet of rewriting the history of mountaineering. Annapurna, the first 8000m peak climbed, wasn't ascended until 1950 by the French, who used radios and oxygen (though not on their summit climb); Everest was scaled in 1953 by a large British team who also used both oxygen and radios. Wiessner was one of the first Himalayan mountaineers to consciously limit his use of technology in order to maintain the mountain's challenge.

Wiessner predated Chris Bonington's approach by 30 years, leading from the front where the action was, and not from the safety of the rear. Fundamental to this style of leadership, however, is that the team members below the leader must follow his orders, execute their tasks on the mountain, and fully support the summit team. This sense of duty is even more vital when radios do not provide instant communication between camps.

Tragically, in 1939, Wiessner's orders were not followed. Several members were injured and forced to descend, and personal duty and common sense did not prevail. The clearing of camps was begun before the summit team had safely quit the mountain. In hindsight, Wiessner's downfall was that he went to K2 with a generally unqualified team whose members exercised poor judgement and showed little personal initiative, especially when Wiessner wasn't directly supervising them. Wiessner later said that had he been partnered by Paul Petzoldt in 1939, he felt he would certainly have reached the summit.

The revelatory 'new information' promised by the authors consists of quotations, opinions, and information gleaned from Jack Durrance's long-withheld personal diary. Following the expedition, Durrance maintained a 50-year silence on the controversy. He finally broke it in 1989 when he loaned the authors his diary. Durrance's diary entries make for fascinating reading, are intelligently and sensitively written, and give great insight into the inner workings of a 1930s Himalayan expedition.

Although as leader of the expedition Wiessner was initially blamed for Wolfe's and the Sherpas' deaths, in later years blame shifted to Durrance, who, Wiessner claimed, ordered the removal of the sleeping-bags and mattresses. Regarding the early evacuation of the camps, *K2: The 1939 Tragedy* tells us that Jack Durrance, recuperating at Camp II on July 17, was asked in a note by Eaton Cromwell, the team's deputy leader, at basecamp, to 'salvage all the tents and sleeping-bags you can, we have ample food'. 'At Camp II, therefore,' write the authors, 'Jack had simply done his tasks as the agent for his superior. So one might rightly inquire as to whether Jack merited blame for stripping the mid-mountain camps.'

Unfortunately, the authors do not fully examine the related, crucial issue: Durrance decided to evacuate not only Camp II, but sent two Sherpas up to evacuate Camp IV, a decision that sent dire events in motion. Stripping Camp IV, the strategically most important, well-stocked, mid-mountain camp, had fatal consequences. While Sherpas Pasang Kikuli and Dawa were removing the gear from this camp, they met two other Sherpas, Tse Tendrup and Pasang Kitar – who were supposed to be supporting the summit team – descending from above. Kikuli, the expedition's sirdar, immediately ordered them back up – but the damage had been done. When two days later Tendrup and Kitar came to believe that the lead climbers had died in an avalanche, having seen that the lower camps were being dismantled, they decided to save the expensive sleeping-bags and mattresses and stripped Camps VI and VII.

Four days earlier, on July 13, Jack Durrance had made yet another such decision – yet Putnam and Kauffman gloss over this point too. Heading to Camp VII, Durrance had begun suffering from the altitude and decided to descend. Wiessner ordered that Durrance should descend to Camp VI, rest until he felt better, and ascend for a summit attempt if he improved. Nonetheless, he was to remain high on the mountain with Pasang Kikuli to help supervise the Sherpas and the transport of loads. Unfortunately, Durrance's health worsened. He descended all the way to Camp II, insisting that both Dawa, his personal Sherpa, and Pasang Kikuli accompany him, thus removing the last remaining figure of authority who could oversee the Sherpas above. According to Wiessner, Kikuli strongly protested, stating later that 'Doctor Sahib', Durrance, had taken him away from his job.

Rather than cite Durrance's two decisions, Putnam and Kauffman argue that the most causative factor in the tragedy was Wiessner's decision to 'leave' Dudley Wolfe at Camp VII (at 24,700ft) during their descent on July 22nd. Wiessner has said that Dudley Wolfe himself requested to stay behind; there seemed no reason for him to descend since Wiessner was only intending to go to Camp VI, pick up supplies, and return the next day to rejoin Wolfe and launch another summit bid. When Wiessner and Lama discovered the stripped camps below, they realised that there was no way they could climb back up to Wolfe; they had left their only sleeping-bag with Wolfe, and the pair had already endured one forced bivouac the previous night.

The authors claim Wiessner should have expected trouble below when he first stumbled onto the ruins of Camp VII. This is easy to say in hindsight, but who could have honestly predicted the dismantling of nearly an entire support and safety system, five camps in all?

What is most disturbing about *K2: The 1939 Tragedy* are the numerous jabs made at Wiessner – insinuations that seem to reflect more personal bias than fact. Fortunately for history, there was one more member of the 1939 K2 expedition, an impartial observer who also put his impressions down on paper. He was the expedition's interpreter, the Indian schoolteacher, Chandra Pandit, who was questioned by past AAC President Lawrence Coveney in the 1960s. Kauffman and Putnam presumably did not know about Pandit's testimony – he is not quoted in their book – however, he gives a quite a different and damning picture of the American climbers and their British transport officer at basecamp regarding the early evacuation of the camps. His testimony clearly supports Wiessner's term for the evacuations: the sabotage.

Kauffman and Putnam have presented Jack Durrance's side of the story in *K2: The 1939 Tragedy*, but the book will not be the last word about this controversial expedition – the crowning triumph of Wiessner's climbing career, and the enduring tragedy which haunted every member of the expedition for the rest of their lives.

Ed Webster

Ed Webster climbed with Fritz Wiessner twice before Wiessner's death in 1988. Ed has been working on his biography since 1983, interviewed him extensively on the subject of the K2 climb, and has read most of Wiessner's personal papers on the subject. This review first appeared in the American magazine CLIMBING and is reproduced by kind permission of the Editor and the author.

Sea, Ice and Rock
Chris Bonington & Robin Knox-Johnston
Hodder & Stoughton, 1992, pp192, £15.99

Sea, Ice and Rock is a mountaineering adventure narrative of a sailing-cum-climbing expedition to the Kangerdlugssuaq area of the East Coast of Greenland in 1991. It is designed for a general readership, and has all the strengths and weaknesses that implies.

There is no doubting Chris's ability to tell a good story. He really is easy to read, though the style is now a bit too predictable, a bit too secure. Knox-Johnston is just as effective, and it all rattles along very nicely, with large type and plenty of good photographs. It has not been well sub-edited, but for a good read that hardly matters. It's an enjoyable yarn, even if the enjoyment doesn't come cheap – two to three hours' reading for £15.99 seems steep, given that this is not a reference book or something one is likely to reread.

For a mountaineering audience the interest is really in the sub-text, for in relating Chris's attempt to make the first ascent of the Cathedral, the highest point of the Lemon mountains on the north shore of Kangerdlugssuaq, the book records an interesting case of misjudgement. The expedition's crucial mistake was too tight a schedule and, as a result, the climbing party of Chris, Jim Lowther and Knox-Johnston had no time for a proper reconnaissance and found themselves on the wrong mountain. This turned out to be very hard, perhaps harder than anything else in the range, and a lack of gear – spare ropes, for example, to leave for retreat – hampered attempts to climb it. Unstable weather was another problem. Meanwhile the 'right' mountain – the mountain which is both the highest in the area and was named Cathedral by Wager in the 1930s – was found by the first ascensionists in 1992 to be relatively straightforward.

The climbing narrative is made interesting by the involvement of Knox-Johnston, whose job was to get the party to and from Greenland in his 32ft ketch *Suhaili*, but who had hardly done any climbing before. Chris has never denied that he is not the most patient of men and is not really cut out to encourage novices up mountains. His writing on this is diplomatic but, as on most other things, it proves disarmingly honest if one reads it carefully enough. Prior to the climb it is essential to teach Robin a few basics; so 'we trailed over to the foot of a gully still in the shade on the other side of the cirque'. That verb says it all really.

The outcome is predictable, and just the sort of thing about which Bonington writes well: an explosion of frustration halfway up the climb when it becomes clear that things are not going as he had hoped. This doesn't quite tally with Knox-Johnston's claim in the last paragraph of the book that 'we had been together for nearly two months and there had never once been a cross word between any of us,' but it is much more interesting. They retreat, and on a second attempt (which still doesn't take them to the summit) proceed *sans* Knox-Johnston.

This leaves the sailing part of the adventure, which is Tilmanesque and immediately appealing. However, it is clear that Chris didn't really take to ocean sailing. In fact neither Bonington nor Knox-Johnston really seems to have taken to the other's sport. Knox-Johnston writes revealingly and honestly of the way his mind is forever on his boat even in the midst of the climbing, while the problem for Chris seems to have been that during the voyage he felt like a passenger. He also felt seasick, and one finds it hard to believe that on the return journey, which included several storms and sounds pretty miserable, he wasn't sorely tempted to jump ship. The outward journey was a different matter, as there was an undeniably glorious reward awaiting: the whole experience of approaching the Greenland coast slowly by sea. That must be absolutely magical, and it is the one part of the expedition that anyone who has only been in to Greenland by plane must envy.

Phil Bartlett

Lindsay Griffin writes:
The plan was simple, and were it not for the obligatory film crew even Tilman would have approved. The master mariner would introduce Bonington to the delights of ocean travel, and in return the mountaineer would help Knox-Johnston reach a lofty summit. A challenging programme was quickly agreed. The team would sail from Britain to the Arctic waters of Greenland aboard Knox-Johnston's 32-foot ketch *Suhaili*. There, in the limited time that pack-ice would allow a safe anchorage during the summer, they would quickly despatch an attractive unclimbed peak called the Cathedral and sail home. As a mere whipper-snapper, my first expedition had taken me to Greenland and, coincidentally, to climb a mountain called the Cathedral. With the realisation that there were 'other Cathedrals in the lives of men', my interest in this duo's travels through unexplored terrain was immediately aroused. The whole story is told in fractionally over 100 pages (it's true, modern narratives really are getting slimmer!), and whilst this is an extremely well produced book with some stunning colour plates, it falls short of being a truly great read.

To my mind the text is somewhat let down by the chapters from Knox-Johnston. I am convinced that the voyage to the East Coast and the final penetration of the ice-choked Kangerdlugssuaq fjord, must have been in many ways every bit as serious and exciting as the subsequent attempts on the mountain. Unfortunately this does not come across and I don't believe that it is simply because I am unable to relate as easily to the chapters on sailing.

Contrast these with the central part of the book. Time ashore for Bonington, Knox-Johnston and the third team member, Jim Lowther, is by necessity very limited. It is certainly not long enough to allow a thorough reconnaissance, and the team attempt a crenellated rocky peak which they believe to be Cathedral, the highest point in the Lemon mountains, on the basis that the only available map marks it at this location. It turns out to be hard, very hard in fact, and with Knox-Johnston, if you will excuse the pun, well out of his depth the team decide to retreat.

With just a day or two left, Bonington and Lowther leave for a second attempt, and the next 28 hours are vividly described by Bonington, writing at his best. The drama, the anxiety, the air of commitment when making two diagonal rappels into a deep chasm in order to bypass a pinnacle, the tricky climbing on poor rock, the eventual failure, the analysis of their mistakes – it's all riveting stuff. Climbing back out of the abyss in the hours of dusk and after a long hard day, Bonington battles with a steep and difficult iced-up crack. The atmosphere is tense: Lowther and myself are willing him to succeed and we both breathe a hearty sigh of relief when he does so.

The hefty glossary of climbing and sailing terminology show that this book has been written for the public at large. However, for the more serious scholar, whether mariner or mountaineer, a wealth of information is to be found in the excellent appendices: these document the history of both sailing and climbing expeditions to this and neighbouring regions of the East Coast.

Despite failing on the mountain, one feels that this has been a successful and most harmonious expedition to an area of great potential. Anyone planning a trip to Greenland's icy mountains would do well to include this book in their list of background reading.

Lindsay Griffin

The Water People
Joe Simpson
Jonathan Cape, 1992, 239pp, £13.99

The novel tells the story of Chris, quiet and observant, and Jimmy, wild, egocentric and a bit touched, and their Himalayan expedition. Jimmy has strange ideas which Chris ridicules – ideas of eastern mysticism and the water people. It is a story of states of mind; and you can read it both ways: from Chris's point of view, or you may choose, for the duration of the novel, to believe in the water people.

I think it was a film director who once said he wanted to start his next film with a volcano erupting, and work up to a climax. Simpson opens with the volcano, and certainly ends with a stupendous climax. To put the mountaineering analogy, the novel opens with foothills and finishes up in mountains. But in between there are the plains, where the narrative is less compelling, though the images and smells of the subcontinent are vivid enough. About half way through I found myself wondering if Simpson had used this first novel to unload some of his observations and travel diaries – it somehow has that feel to it (the unexplained translocation from India to Hunza and from Hindi to Urdu, for example). This is foreign travel seen through intelligent eyes, but not always pushing the story along. I asked Simpson about this, and he said that I was wrong; the 'plains' were background scenery, necessary for understanding the story.

This book is interesting, a good read throughout, and in places absolutely compulsive. I look forward to Joe Simpson's next novel with enthusiasm.

A V Saunders

The Darkness Beckons:
The History and Development of Cave Diving
Martyn Farr
Diadem Books, 1992, pp280, £22

Now that the whole surface of our dwindling natural world is subjected to the prying eye of the satellite, the field for genuine exploration has changed. Mountains still offer the occasional uninvestigated detail but for exploration on a grand scale, the future must lie on the ocean bed and under the earth's surface. Deep sea diving is an increasingly challenging and expensive technological pursuit; speleology was traditionally a low-tech sport but as far back as the last century cavers realised that 'sumps' – submerged sections of passage beneath the water table – were a tantalising hindrance to exploration. Cave-diving took up the challenge of these sumps, eventually using artificial breathing equipment to cover long distances underwater.

Martyn Farr is one of the world's foremost cave-diving pioneers and this magnificent new book, produced to Diadem's usual thorough standard, is a reference work for experts. But it is also a book to excite and amaze the layman. Many of the photographs (reproduced here in copious quantity and quality) induced in this reviewer feelings of claustrophobic terror. However, the book also makes one look beyond the terror and palpable danger of what many consider the most perilous sport of all, to a magical secret world. Take, for instance, Farr's description of exploring Somerset's famous Wookey Hole: 'I pushed my hand through the gap and a tantalising vision appeared. Beyond the squeeze bright blue water led the eye over speckled sandbanks down into a small, but continuing, passage.'

That was 60 metres below water level! Subsequent explorations revealed that this particular passage was in fact a dead end; but Wookey Hole was nevertheless a landmark in British deep diving. Normal compressed air is only safe to minus 40 metres. Below that the problems of nitrogen absorption and the associated 'bends' dictate special gas mixes and elaborate decompression procedures. Cave diving has only developed through the inventive use of increasingly complex technology and, as Bill Stone observes in his lucid foreword, the cave divers who survive are those who master the technology and the safety rules with meticulous dedication. Compared to the rather haphazard nature of mountaineering, cave diving seems rigorously disciplined.

Farr repeatedly stresses the technical thoroughness of his sport, but he does not attempt to hide the dangers. All the horrific deaths are here to read, but they are explained coolly and objectively. While most of us would never have the mental control to cope with those dangers, we can admire the calm skill of the experts who do.

The book traces the history of the sport from the first explorations in southern France and in the cold murky sumps of the British Isles to exciting recent developments all over the world. It is a fascinating story about using increasingly sophisticated equipment to make and break spectacular records; but it is also the story of brave pioneers fired by a burning ambition to see round the next corner. Cave diving, like mountaineering, seems to be more than a mere sport: it is a romantic journey into the unknown.

Stephen Venables

The State of the World's Mountains. A Global Report
Ed Peter B Stone
Zed Books, 1992, pp291 + xx, npq

Mountain World in Danger
Climate Change in the Forests and Mountains of Europe
Sten Nilsson & David Pitt
Earthscan Publications, 1991, pp196 + xi, £8.95

Both these books address the fundamental environment and development threats facing montane areas in Europe and the rest of the world today. Both have been written to raise awareness and stimulate international action – particularly *The State of the World's Mountains*, which was compiled expressly for the UNCED 'Earth Summit', held in Rio de Janiero in June 1992. But although both the texts have their *raison d'être* in advocacy (Stone's book even acknowledges that 'the political goals outweigh the scientific'), the quality of the collated data and its analysis (by a wide range of mountain specialists, including a number of Alpine Club members) can hardly be faulted.

This is especially the case with Peter Stone's fine volume, which was initiated by the Swiss-based group, Mountain Agenda. The authors state that the report was compiled and published in only one year using multiple authors from five different continents (including Antarctica!), and that the coverage was therefore felt to be inadequate. This *caveat* is disingenuous, to say the least: the book is probably the best single volume available on the issue. Moreover, it is well structured and readable, alternating commendable brevity where required with deeper and thought-provoking analysis in the individual case study regions.

The book is divided into ten main sections, which firstly overview the subject and then step into individual chapter overviews on major mountain areas including Africa, the Alps, the Himalaya, 'Mountains North and South' (a hotch-potch of 'lesser' regions, including *inter alia* China, Baffin Island and

our own Cairngorms), the Andes, the former Soviet Union and the Appalachians, before ending with two chapters on mountain protected areas and
climate change.

Stone *et al* are not afraid to search for and postulate answers to difficult
questions, such as why mountains have been so low on the environmental
agenda compared to other 'sexier' topics such as tropical forests, regional and
global air pollution threats, etc. This, they contend (convincingly) , is because
of their geopolitical isolation and disenfranchised constituencies – away from
the main decision-making centres in the lowlands. However, in one case study
(the Alps) it is suggested that the most recent image of the mountains – as a
'disaster region' – has been conversely promoted by a city-based media corps
distanced from the mountains, both geographically *and* intellectually.

Here and there, small points such as this, and others relating to the real or
imagined 'fragility' of montane ecosystems, or the need for *better-planned*
hydro-electric power schemes utilising baseload nuclear power (rather than no
such schemes), suggest rather 'light green' tendencies on the part of some of
the authors, especially with regard to their occasionally narrow view of
'conservationists' and their 'alarmist' views. Two chapters (the Andes and the
Appalachians) also seem rather anomalous, being overly academic and not
really addressing the core development issues underlying the other case studies
and the book itself. But these are small points which hardly detract from what
is a truly *magnum opus*, which – with widespread circulation – deserves to put
mountains high on the environmental agenda way into the 21st century.

This was also the aim of Professors Nilsson and Pitt's smaller volume,
Mountain World in Danger, which addresses itself to the considerable socio-
economic consequences that large-scale atmospheric warming would have on
the world's cryosphere regions, with a particular emphasis on the forests and
mountains of Europe. Here, despite the carefully measured tones of the
scientist, the threats of climate change to montane areas are clearly
emphasised – suggesting that change could be much more rapid in these
regions where fewer buffering mechanisms exist (a point also made in Stone's
book).

Obviously this book, with its narrower remit, is more for the specialist or
committed reader whose appetite may have been whetted by the Stone
volume. It is unfortunately rather less digestible than the former book –
probably owing to its report-style format and rather monotonous layout.
Nevertheless, its scope (within the subject itself) is very wide ranging and
commendably pro-active; together with the excellently summarised appendices, *Mountain World in Danger* maps out a much needed radical agenda for
the urgent protection of our mountains. Nilsson and Pitt (in common with
Stone *et al*) are also careful to emphasise that although high-level political
action should be the overall focus, resulting policy cannot be developed in
isolation from the ways and wishes of indigenous mountain people and their
culture.

Andrew Tickle

Classic Climbs in the Caucasus
80 selected climbs in the Elbruz and Bezingi regions
of the Svanetian range
Friedrich Bender
Diadem, 1992, pp318, £14.99

At last! A British guide to the Caucasus. Actually it's a translation (with a few minor amendments) of Bender's German guide. The author has in fact produced a comprehensive set of fully detailed guides to this range and must be the ideal man to produce a 'selected climbs' guide of this type.

The dissolving of the USSR and associated red tape has, of course, greatly eased access to this superb range, and Western interest is rapidly being rekindled. This guide will doubtless do much to boost popularity still more. It selects 80 of the finest routes of all grades and all areas of the range. Some of these, such as the Bezingi, have not been visited by British mountaineers for many years. The style of presentation is modern – a far cry from the tattered absorbent pages of all the other guides to the Caucasus that I have seen. A durable plastic cover sporting the classic shot of Ushba is enhanced by 27 magnificent colour photographs inside. An extensive series of black and white photographs, maps and diagrams complete the picture and provide a very useful and readable guide. The 58 pages of background information give an excellent 'feel' for the area and are well worth reading.

The one feature that I do find rather irritating is that the diagrams are clearly taken from Bender's comprehensive guides and are peppered with route numbers that bear no relation to the text. This is initially rather confusing but the quality of the diagrams is good and I can't pretend that this is anything other than a minor quibble. In fact it could be argued that the extra information provides a useful supplement to the detailed descriptions. Either way, it does not affect what is a well presented, readable and, most important of all, inspirational guide. If you are even mildly interested in visiting the area ... buy it!

Mick Fowler

The Alpine 4000m Peaks by the Classic Routes
A guide for mountaineers by Richard Goedeke
Diadem Books, 1991, pp240, £12.99

Eastern Alps. The Classic Routes on the Highest Peaks
A guide for mountaineers by Dieter Seibert
Diadem Books, 1992, pp176, £12.99

These well produced plastic-covered paperbacks have been published in an identical format. Yet they differ markedly in their content, in the way they have been initially written, and in the way they have subsequently been reproduced.

Goedeke is an established alpinist with new routes to his credit. He is also a member of the West German Green Party and his concern for the mountain environment is a recurring theme throughout the text. He concentrates on describing the normal routes to the summits of the great alpine peaks, but also draws attention to a number of other classic lines on the mountain, irrespective of difficulty. Not being a collector of 4000m peaks, prior to reading this book I debated its usefulness – all the relevant information was already available, albeit in eight different works. However, I was in for a surprise. The text is both interesting and entertaining, the information seems well up to date, and route descriptions appear to complement rather than duplicate those in existing English guides, some of which are now more than ten years old.

Seibert concentrates on the normal routes up the major glacier peaks of a dozen different areas (around 50 peaks in total), from the Cima di Rosso in the west to the Hohe Dachstein of Eastern Austria. Apart from the latter, all the peaks are well over 3000m and within the scope of any experienced glacier traveller. If possible, a traverse is described and, on occasion, a detour on the descent to pick off a neighbouring peak. Each route is accompanied by a map (though they missed out Disgrazia!) which I found less cluttered and more pleasing to the eye than those in Goedeke. Descriptions are brief – as you might expect for a glacier walk followed by a snow arête. Goedeke includes paragraphs on the 'dangers and pleasures' of each route. Many of the 'pleasure' paragraphs are flowery and romantic, as one might expect, but I especially liked his appraisal of the Breithorn: 'after climbing this ordinary route any other ascent will be especially enjoyable'!

In both books the photographic reproduction is excellent. Coloured images are bound together, monochromes are inserted into the text. All show detail clearly and many are inspiring. On a large number of Seibert's lesser known peaks the potential for much harder ice or mixed climbing, on attractive ridges or faces, is obvious. However, most of these shots are either taken in spring, after fresh and heavy snowfall, or in the summers of yesteryear. Readers expecting this sort of scenery in mid-August will be in for a disappointment.

A personal criticism, and one about which others might disagree, concerns the way these books have been translated. In general, it is probably an advantage to preserve the original feel of the text, even if this results in a flow of words which, although unambiguous, sound unnatural to the English reader. This works relatively well with Goedeke, mainly I suspect owing to an interesting and often entertaining original. However, in Seibert I found the prose hard going, sometimes unclear, and not helped by several sentences 50 to 60 words long without a single punctuation mark! On the routes of Seibert's that I knew (not that many I'm embarrassed to say) I found two basic directional errors, one well-outdated description and a few statistical mistakes. This unfortunately makes me a little suspicious of the overall accuracy in the rest of the text. Where the two books overlap there are a couple of discrepancies, and I found myself agreeing with Goedeke in each case.

Seibert is a dry and in some ways unimaginative read – quite the opposite to Goedeke – and there was little except the brilliant photographs that inspired me to get out there. Despite these drawbacks it is an invaluable work. It draws attention to peaks hardly known to most British climbers and in a number of cases not covered by any guidebook in the English language. We are indeed thankful to Diadem for being sympathetic to the widening interest in climbing.

Lindsay Griffin

Antarctica. Both Heaven and Hell
Reinhold Messner
Translated from the German by Jill Neate
Crowood Press, 1991, pp384, £19.95

Over a period of 13 weeks in the winter of 1989/90, Reinhold Messner turned from his mountain conquests to Antarctica, completing a journey of 2800kms, on foot, pulling sledges. He crossed from the edge of the continent across the Thiel Mountains to the South Pole, and then on to McMurdo Sound on the Ross Sea; a magnificent achievement. His companion on this journey was Arved Fuchs, a German adventurer who had crossed the Greenland ice cap with dog sledges, paddled round Cape Horn in a one-man canoe in winter, and marched to the North Pole earlier in 1989 – a companion, you would think, to equal Messner in effort and endeavour. But, as a business journalist quoted in the book says: 'Even his friends have their problems with Reinhold. The South Tyrolean is an ego-maniac. Preferably, he does everything himself because only he satisfies his demands for perfection.'

Thus, even though there were, apparently, no quarrels on the actual trip, the disputes and acrimony started immediately afterwards, and in my view this spoils the book. Writing about daily exertions in the wastes of Antarctica needs to be a little inspired to hold the reader's attention, but when page after page is filled with complaints about how slow Fuchs is, how he doesn't smile, and so on, I found myself skipping many pages and concentrating on the historical sections which are interlaced with the story.

At nearly 400 pages the book is too long, but the actual diary of the trip is interesting, and the chapters on environmental problems and the Chronical of Antarctica Expeditions are very useful.

Geof Templeman

The Turquoise Mountain. Brian Blessed on Everest
Brian Blessed
Additional material by John-Paul Davidson
Bloomsbury, 1991, pp218 + 6, £14.99

Anyone who saw the TV film of Brian Blessed on Everest will know what to expect from this book: a larger-than-life, ebullient, theatrical character who writes in exactly the same way as he talks on TV. And yet Blessed's joy in being among the mountains, his interest in climbing and his enthusiasm in following in Mallory's footsteps are self-evident throughout. Anyone less like Mallory in character and appearance it would be hard to imagine: the slender, introverted, serious Mallory, as opposed to the robust, extrovert and uproarious Blessed. The tweed jacket, pipe and pith helmet don't fool anyone.

One difference from the TV version is that Blessed is naturally the star of the film, with others rarely seen, whereas in the book his film crew, led by director John-Paul Davidson, play important roles, as do his climbing mentors David Breashears and Jeff Long. The over-the-top style does get a little wearing at times, but it is a fascinating book, well worth reading. The author's sheer enthusiasm comes through well. He never falters, even when told by a Chinese liaison officer, 'You is Mallory! ... Ha, ha, ha, ha! ... You big, fat Engliss gentleman, who will not go higher than Base Camp.' Blessed smiled, touched his hat, thought of him as a four-eyed pillock, and moved courteously on. Moved on, in fact, to 25,400ft on the North Ridge. A great effort. He's going back in 1993.

Geof Templeman

High Altitude Medicine
Edited by G Ueda, J T Reeves, M Sekiguchi
Shinshu University Press, Japan, 1992, pp546, npq

This volume is the Proceedings of the Fourth International Symposium on High Altitude Medicine, held at Shinshu University in 1991. The papers deal with all aspects of oxygen lack and cold and cover recent research on these subjects in both man and animals. It starts with two review articles. The first deals with co-operative work between scientists of Shinshu University and those of the High Altitude Medical Research Centre at Xining in China during an expedition to the Amne Machin range of North-East Tibet. The second comes from Jack Reeves of the University of Colorado and his co-workers in the US, and deals with the sympathetic systems (flight and fright). This evaluates the important effect this system has on the heart and peripheral blood vessels in equating oxygen supply with demand.

One of the later sections deals with the rupture, due to oxygen lack, of the small blood vessels of the lung as a possible cause of high-altitude pulmonary oedema. A great deal of work is going on to elucidate the cause of this mysterious illness and our member Professor John West of the University of California, San Diego, is playing a leading part in this research.

The scope of this volume is wide, and it ends with an unusual paper on the chemical composition of perfumes used in Japanese and Tibetan religious ceremonies.

This is an important volume in the growing amount of work published on the medical hazards of mountains and though primarily for medical scientists, this type of information should be available in any comprehensive mountain library.

Michael Ward

Operation Everest II. 1985
Charles S Houston, Allen Cymerman, John R Sutton
*US Army Research Institute of Environmental Medicine,
Natick, Massachusetts, 1991*

Hypoxia and Mountain Medicine
John R Sutton, Geoffrey Coates, Charles S Houston
Queen City Printers Inc, Burlington, Vermont, 1992

A Colour Atlas of Mountain Medicine
J Vallotton, F Dubas
Wolfe Publishing Ltd, 1991

The 'first ascent' of Everest in a decompression chamber was made on 30 July 1946 at Pensacola Air Base, Florida, by two volunteers, after 30 days' gradual acclimatisation. They remained 'on the summit' for 21 minutes and exercised on a stationary bicycle. Neither used supplementary oxygen. This experiment, Operation Everest I, was masterminded by our Honorary Member Professor C S Houston, then a flight-surgeon in the American Air Force, and Richard Riley, a distinguished respiratory physiologist. It showed, for the first time, that man could acclimatise to the altitude of the top of Everest, but not that he could get there by his own unaided efforts. It was to be another seven years before the summit of Everest was reached using supplementary oxygen and 32 years before it was climbed without its help.

Operation Everest I was the first serious attempt after the Second World War to understand the main problem of Everest, that of hypoxia. It was a landmark experiment of great importance in the fields of aviation, mountaineering and medicine and well known to Sir Bryan Mathews, Dr Griffith Pugh and others who, for 15 months prior to the departure of the 1953 Everest expedition, worked on and solved the high-altitude problem.

Operation Everest II 1985 is an account of both Operation Everest I in 1946 and its follow-up, Operation Everest II, in 1985. Masterminded again by C S Houston with Alan Cymerman and John Sutton, Operation Everest II was carried out at the US Army Research Institute of Environmental Medicine at Natick, Massachusetts and many well known physicians and physiologists were involved. After a general account of each experiment much of this volume is given up to the scientific papers that stemmed from this experiment and every aspect of altitude physiology is covered.

Operation Everest II was the counterpart of the American Medical Research expedition to Everest in 1981, led by our member John West. Whilst it is possible to carry out sophisticated work in a decompression chamber, it is not possible to mimic field conditions. Each investigation complements the other. Each is expensive, as a decompression chamber has to be manned by technicians 24 hours a day. Both groups of work are much admired and have made many important contributions.

Hypoxia and Mountain Medicine is the seventh in the series of monographs which detail the proceedings of the hypoxia meetings held every two years. Again, these were the brainchild of C S Houston and started at Yosemite in 1975, following meetings at Plas y Brenin and the Middlesex Hospital the same year. These have burgeoned and become an important stimulus for research worldwide. The papers in this volume reflect that wide-ranging interest, with contributions on liver transplantation, oxygen lack in air crews, as well as many other aspects of medicine. For the mountaineer about to go to the Himalaya, the article on 'Pre-Acclimatisation in the Hypobaric Chamber' should be required reading. An important new theory with supporting evidence of the cause of high-altitude pulmonary oedema is put forward by John West. This volume and the meeting in 1991 were dedicated to Herman Rahn, an American respiratory physiologist whose depth and breadth of knowledge helped to lay much of the groundwork for our modern understanding of the oxygen transport system. The next meeting, in 1993, will be dedicated, very appropriately, to Dr Griffith Pugh whose work between 1951 and 1953 contributed so much to the first ascent of Everest.

A Colour Atlas of Mountain Medicine is an important addition to the considerable number of articles and text books which have been written about the medical problems of those who ski, climb and trek in the mountains. Their increasing numbers are mirrored by the many disorders of cold, exercise and altitude which they suffer. This book shows in stark pictures and detail how serious these disorders can be, and how difficult are the many rescue techniques required.

Over a million casualties occur in the mountains every year and there are about 100,000 air rescues, with 60% being by helicopter, whose pilots show amazing skill and bravery. New mountain sports present new hazards and new rescue methods. A striking amount of information is provided by each of the contributors who come mainly from the mountain countries of Europe, and there are articles on avalanches and lightning strikes, as well as on cave, crevasse and helicopter rescue. The photographs may upset some readers, but they do emphasise that mountain rescue, and accident and emergency medicine and surgery, is highly skilled, very professional, and efficient. It is also very dangerous. Many rescuers are both mountain guides and medically qualified. Mountain rescue is not an occupation for the amateur character-builder.

Michael Ward

Journal of Wilderness Medicine 1992 (Vol 3)
Edited by Paul Auerbach (US) and Oswald Oelz (Europe)
Chapman and Hall Medical, London
Four issues per year, subscription rates vary

The Wilderness Medical Society was founded in the United States in 1983 to provide knowledge of medical conditions encountered in the wild places of the world. In five years it grew to 2000 members including many medical scientists from different specialities. During this period a Newsletter kept members informed but in 1990 this was considered insufficient and the *Journal of Wilderness Medicine* was started. Published four times a year, it has now doubled in size, which emphasises both its need and popularity. It has two regular editors: Paul Auerbach in the United States, whose field is underwater medicine, and Oswald Oelz in Europe, whose field is mountain medicine. The editorial board comes from all continents.

The *Journal* publishes original work and clinical reports on cold and heat, on high altitude and diving, on the effect of hazardous plants, animals, reptiles and insects, both on land and in the sea. There are accounts of search and rescue, legal matters, and the field management of illness and injury, as well as natural disasters. The effects of global warming on the changing pattern of disease and many other matters related to the wilderness are also discussed.

So far, a high percentage of the articles have been related to mountains and all concerned with the health of trekkers and climbers will benefit from a glance at the pages of this journal.

Michael Ward

John Muir. The Eight Wilderness Discovery Books
Introduction by Terry Gifford
Diadem Books/The Mountaineers, 1992, pp1030, £16.99

Diadem have followed up their Tilman and Shipton volumes with the biggest compendium yet: over 1000 pages of John Muir's eight complete, unabridged books on the American wilderness. It seems amazing that you can actually get eight books into one, albeit very hefty, volume, but modern papers and printing make this possible. At just over £2 per book, this has to be the bargain of the year. So, once again, all praise to Diadem for producing this book, and to Terry Gifford for the idea.

It is probable that very few of today's climbers in Britain have read any of Muir's books, since only two of them, *The Mountains of California* and *My First Summer in the Sierra*, have previously been published over here. Even though John Muir originally came from Scotland, his name will largely be known here through the recently formed John Muir Trust. In America, however, his name is a household word wherever wilderness questions arise, and his books are continuously in print. It was after the Civil War that Muir decided to go to South America from his home farm in Wisconsin, intending to walk to the Gulf of Mexico. On the way he found the Yosemite valley and stayed there for six years, entranced by the beauty of the scenery and the flora and fauna. So began his obsession with the wilderness and its preservation. He visited many parts of the world, from Alaska and the Himalaya, to South America, Africa and his native Scotland. In 1892 he was instrumental in founding the Sierra Club, and became its first president.

The eight books published here range from journals and diaries, to guidebooks and autobiographical writings. All are worth reading – probably not at one sitting! They are as relevant now as they were at the beginning of the century.

Geof Templeman

Flammes de Pierre
Anne Sauvy
Diadem, 1991, pp176, hb £12.99, pb £8.99

These short stories, translated from the French, have the very smell of Alpine climbing about them. They are so knowing – about the climbing itself, about the physical arena around Mont Blanc, but most tellingly about the culture of motivations, emotions, reputations and bullshit that we would all recognise within any climbing community. Diadem is to be congratulated for holding up to us this witty and superbly polished mirror from Chamonix.

Readers of the *Alpine Journal* will be familiar with Anne Sauvy's carefully crafted surprises, but the range of these 16 stories may come as a further surprise. The liberation of grief, for example, in 'Montenvers', or the inner questioning of 'The Penance', complement the satire of 'The Star' in which the author of *The Sky on the End of my Ice-Axe, Festive Summits* and *Voluptuous Faces,* with lectures, films and advertising, eventually 'made a significant contribution to France's balance of payments deficit'.

The quality of translation deserves special recognition. Much of the humour derives from an intimate knowledge of the British climbing scene, and one suspects the contribution here of John Wilkinson ('maintaining a slightly scruffy but clean image'), Anne Sauvy's husband. For example, as a professional name for The Star, 'Rock Hardy would have sounded like parody'. Translation at this level of detail is expensive and time-consuming. In fact, giving us this collection prevented the author from writing more in French for 18 months. But already this book is having an influence upon our own writers of climbing stories and it will be one of those books that will be reread and retold in homes and in huts for a generation.

Terry Gifford

Last Days
John Roskelley
Hodder & Stoughton, 1992, ppviii + 212, £19.95

Roskelley's previous book *Nanda Devi: The Tragic Expedition* was a one-sided account written long after the event; I had not particularly enjoyed it. So I approached *Last Days* with no great enthusiasm, particularly as the dust jacket states 'A World-famous Climber Challenges the Himalaya . . .'. In fact, I enjoyed the book immensely. It is in two parts: a two-man ascent of the NE face of Tawoche, and an alpine-style attempt on the SE ridge of Menlungtse. The photo of the NE face of Tawoche, towering over Pheriche in Sola Khumbu, shows the difficulty of the undertaking – 'straight up' doesn't do it justice by a long way!

Roskelley first attempted Tawoche in 1984 with Bridwell and Sakashita, but prudently retreated in the face of continuous stonefall. So it had to be a winter ascent. In February 1984 Roskelley was once more back on the face, this time with Jeff Lowe, but after only one day he had to retreat when he knew he had cerebral oedema. After waiting a week, they started up again. This time, high on the face, it was Lowe who got sick, with nausea and dehydration. As Lowe had a history of bouts of oedema, this was worrying; but they pressed on, through storm and rockfall, to make the summit after eight days on the face. A nightmare descent followed.

The following year Roskelley teamed up with Jim Wickwire, Greg Child and Jeff Duenwald for the SE ridge of Menlungtse. Much of this account is taken up with the approach through Tibet, relations with their Chinese interpreter and liaison officer, their Tibetan yak herders, and highlights such as seeing a snow leopard. When the climb actually began, after several days of storms, Wickwire announced he was leaving: home ties were pulling, his heart was not in it, and he felt too old for the climb. The other three continued, but with Duenwald expressing doubts about his fitness. After further storms forced a return to Base Camp, Duenwald found himself too weak to continue. Roskelley and Child carried on, but eventually further snowstorms and a wildly unstable ridge meant final retreat.

One can imagine that, in earlier years, Roskelley would have had withering contempt for companions who gave up on a climb, but time, age and family ties have mellowed him. Leaving Menlungtse his thoughts were that this had been his last expedition – until he saw the E face of Gaurisankar on the walk out. If his book on that is as good as this one, it will be very well worth reading.

Geof Templeman

Tyrants and Mountains. A Reckless Life
Denis Hills
John Murray, 1992, ppx + 262, £19.95

Never Judge a Man by His Umbrella
Nicholas Elliott
Michael Russell, reprint 1992, ppvi + 202, £14.95

Two excellent recent autobiographies have in common the fact that they both contain a little mountaineering and are great fun to read; but they are about two very different characters.

Denis Hills will be remembered by most people as the man arrested and sentenced to death by Idi Amin in Uganda, after writing a book which had been less than respectful about the dictator and his regime. Yet Africa remained one of his great loves, together with Germany, Poland and Turkey. After an early interest in Germany while at Oxford, he lived there in the early days of Hitler's rise to power, moving to Poland in 1936. Escaping in 1939, he made his way to Egypt via Romania, ending up as a liaison officer with the Polish forces and taking part in the battle for Monte Cassino. He later played a major part in rescuing Ukranians and others from being sent back to certain death in the Soviet Union. From the 1950s onwards, Hills held numerous teaching jobs in Germany, Turkey and Africa, never staying in one place for long and living in caravans and the houses of friends and acquaintances.

The mountaineering adventures described include ski-touring in the Alps, an ascent of Mt Ararat, and various trips in Turkish Kurdistan. He also climbed in the Virunga chain of volcanoes in western Uganda. But the main interest in Hills's book is the tale of his restless, ever-travelling life, always wanting to be where other people were glad not to be, and returning time and again to places from whence he had only recently been thrown out. No wonder those in authority generally groaned when he reappeared. This sort of life naturally wrecks marriages and now, in his 80s, he has apparently ended up in a bedsit in Twickenham. While he hasn't the deep intensity of Wilfred Thesiger nor the literary skills of Patrick Leigh Fermor, he runs them a very close second in interest.

Nicholas Elliott has led a very different life. Like Denis Hills, however, his work has taken him to many countries, and he has been involved in diplomatic work in the Hague, Turkey, Switzerland, Vienna and the Lebanon amongst others; there are cameo chapters on the Cicero spy case, and on his personal involvement with Kim Philby. But it is the early chapters of the book which will most interest Alpine Club members, for they concern his father, Sir Claude Elliott, former Provost of Eton and, of course, President of the Alpine Club from 1950 to 1953 at the time when preparations for the 1953 Everest expedition were under way. The author gives an amusing and affectionate portrait of Sir Claude, and includes several pages on the problems that faced the Everest Committee prior to the change of leadership from Shipton to Hunt.

Like Denis Hills, Nicholas Elliott is an enthusiastic skier, but, despite taking part in Winthrop Young's famous house-parties at Pen-y-Pass, he never took to climbing. These gatherings left fond memories with many famous climbers, but the author dreaded the visits. The discomfort was remarkable and the sanitary facilities totally inadequate. To one who 'did not enjoy climbing ... hated the cold, couldn't sing, and could hardly be on an intellectual level with the rest of the company', the experience must have put him off for life!

Only a small part of this book is about climbing, but don't let that put you off. It is well written and immensely enjoyable.

Geof Templeman

Turner in the Alps
The journey through France and Switzerland in 1802
David Hill
George Philip, 1992, pp176, £19.99

In July 1802, Turner set out on a three month tour through the Alps which took him to Geneva and Lucerne, Mont Blanc, the Val d'Aosta, the Bernese Oberland and the St Gotthard Pass. There were comparatively few alpine travellers at that time and, with the war with France only recently over, a journey like this was no small undertaking. In the course of his travels Turner made nearly 400 sketches, which resulted in more than 50 major pictures. Although he returned to the Alps several times when in his sixties, it was this excursion in 1802 which resulted in his greatest alpine paintings.

For anyone interested in Turner, the Romantic Era, the Alps, or all three, David Hill has produced a gem of a book. It is richly illustrated with colour reproductions of both sketches and finished paintings, as well as colour photographs depicting present day scenes which the author took whilst following the same route. Turner's journey and activities are described in detail, with added extracts from Murray and writers such as Byron, Shelley and Ruskin. This is a well produced and fascinating book.

Geof Templeman

Second Ascent. The Story of Hugh Herr
Alison Osius
Stackpole Books, Harrisburg PA, 1991, pp236, $19.95

The Merry-Go-Round of My Life. An Adventurer's Diary
Richard Hechtel
Vantage Press, New York, 1991, ppxiv + 220, $13.95

These two climbing lives (a biography and an autobiography) from the United States are very different in style and content. The subject of Alison Osius's book, Hugh Herr, is a young climber who was in the forefront of American rock climbing in the late '70s and early '80s when, in 1982, he and a companion were lost in a winter storm on Mount Washington. They battled for three days before being rescued, but the end result was the loss of both of Herr's lower legs through frostbite and the death of one of the rescuers. The book tells the story of his readjustment to 'normal life', and eventual return to high-grade climbing with artificial legs. It is a pity that this remarkable story is told in an over-adulatory style which grates after a while (to this reviewer at least!), with the few pictures being chosen mainly for sensational effect. It is also almost impossible to refer back to any particular point or episode, as there is neither an index nor chapter headings.

Richard Hechtel's autobiography is similar in that it, too, lacks an index and has few pictures, but there the similarities end. Hechtel is now approaching 80, and this charming little book tells his life story simply and with a touch of naivety. It splits neatly into two halves; his life in Germany up to 1958, and, after that, in the United States where he became an American citizen. His early climbing days were spent in areas such as the Berchtesgärt Alps and Wettersteingebirge, before moving into the Western Alps just before the war. His greatest achievement here was a solo ascent of the Peuterey Ridge in 35 hours in 1937. Having survived the war as a scientist in the aeronautical industry, he carried on with many hard climbs, notably the first ascent of the integral Peuterey Ridge in 1953. His activities after moving to America have included an ascent of Mt McKinley and climbs in the Himalaya, Africa, Ecuador and Bolivia, as well as walking the Pacific Crest Trail. The last photo shows him leading a route at Joshua Tree in 1987. The book is slightly unusual in having each chapter split into sections, each a page or so in length, headed 'About the pleasures of a porter', 'A restless night', 'On to the summit', and so on, but is nevertheless a delightful read.

Geof Templeman

Joe Dodge. One New Hampshire Institution
William Lowell Putnam
Phoenix Publishing, Canaan, New Hampshire, 1986
ppxiv + 162, $16.00

Place Names of the Canadian Alps
William L Putnam, Glen W Boles & Roger W Laurilla
Footprint, Revelstoke, British Columbia, 1990
ppxviii + 384, $22.95

The Worst Weather on Earth
A History of the Mount Washington Observatory
William Lowell Putnam
Mount Washington Observatory/American Alpine Club, 1991
ppxxii + 266, npq

Green Cognac. The Education of a Mountain Fighter
William Lowell Putnam
AAC Press, New York, 1991, pp14 + 242, npq

The above four books have all been produced comparatively recently by our member Bill Putnam; quite an achievement. The titles are mostly self-explanatory, but British readers should note that Joe Dodge, a New Hampshire institution as the sub-title indicates, was the best known inhabitant of the White Mountains, being huts manager for the Appalachian Mountain Club and founder of the Mount Washington Observatory, whose history is detailed in another of these volumes. *Green Cognac* is the story of the US Army's 10th Mountain Division, 1940–45, which fought in the Apennines in Italy in the Second World War, and of which Putnam was a member. Finally, in these brief notes, the book on the Canadian Alps is an alphabetical listing of every mountain with the derivation of their names, and includes some stunning colour photos. It is an impressive work of research.

Geof Templeman

The Climbers' Club Journal 1992
Edited by Smiler Cuthbertson

I am always pleased to receive the latest volume of the *Climbers' Club Journal*, and this one, under its new editor, is packed with good things: 36 articles in 136 pages, interesting photos, many in colour, with a further 30-odd pages of very readable reviews, obits and area notes. The scope of the articles is wide – from a little-known crag in the Rhinogs to the Karakoram, from Eurocrags to Dowbergill Passage. This is a satisfying, varied read, showing a thriving club.

Geof Templeman

Uganda Before Amin
Our family life in Uganda, 1949–1963
Anna Osmaston
Henry Osmaston, Bristol, 1991, ppvi + 88, pb, £6.95

Anna and Henry Osmaston sailed for Uganda in 1949 when he took up an appointment as an assistant curator of forests. They were to spend the next 14 years there in various locations, mostly 'up country', leaving after independence when thoughts of a future career and children's schooling made a change necessary. Anna Osmaston gives a vivid picture of family life in Uganda in the peaceful days before Amin. Their lives – and friendships – with their native servants, the trials and tribulations of bringing up children in the distant stations, the problems with the local fauna, and the joys of being able to go on impromptu safari are all well described and brought to life. A considerable part of the book is devoted to climbing forays in the Ruwenzori, the Virunga volcanoes, Elgon and the rocky hills of Acholi.

Obtainable from West Col Productions, Goring, Reading, Berks, RG8 9AA

Trekking in Tibet. A Traveller's Guide
Gary McCue
Cordee, 1991, pp304, £10.99

There have been a number of excellent Himalayan trekking guides in recent years by American authors, such as Stephen Bezruchka's *A Guide to Trekking in Nepal* and Hugh Swift's *Trekking in Pakistan and India*. Gary McCue's *Tibet* joins this group. The guide is in three main sections. The first deals generally with trekking in the country, the language, health problems, etc; the second major section details treks in five main areas – Lhasa, Shigatse, Everest, Shishapangma and Mt Kailas; the final section deals with natural history, the people and their culture. From the list of areas, it will be seen that the majority of treks detailed are in central Tibet, with Mt Kailas being the outlier, but these are the areas of most interest to the adventurous trekker. This is a very detailed and worthwhile addition to the literature of Tibet.

Mount McKinley. The Conquest of Denali
Bradford Washburn and David Roberts
Harry N Abrams, New York, 1991, pp206, npq

Washburn and Roberts have, between them, produced a glorious book on Mount KcKinley. Whilst they share the writing, the majority of the photographs are by Brad Washburn and are, as one would expect, superb. Most are black and white, but with two sets of colour interspersed. There is a lot of excellent reading here, as McKinley has a fascinating history. The authors share the chapters on the early attempts, then Washburn goes solo up to the first ascent. Roberts takes over for the 'Age of Washburn', and then Washburn finishes off on the extreme climbs of later years. The history of Denali has been told before, but this well written text, coupled with superb photographs, make this a book to treasure.

Sherpas. The Brave Mountaineers
Padma Sastry
Himalayan Mountaineering Institute, Darjeeling, 1991, pp76, npq

This is the first of two booklets on Sherpas by the HMI. Twelve Sherpas are featured, starting with Tenzing Norgay and including both older ones, such as Pasang Puthar, and younger, still active ones, like Dorjee Lhatoo and N D Sherpa, the HMI being a common link between many of them. The life story of each is recounted, together with details of the expeditions of which they have been members.

Walking Britain's Skyline. 45 Classic Routes
Tony Greenbank
Crowood Press, 1992, pp224, £18.95

There are numerous books on the market giving suggested hill-walking routes, many, as this one, linking a number of hills to give 'skyline' routes. Many, also as this one, are of large format with excellent colour photographs. Few, if any, however, have route descriptions like this one. The author set out to cover his 45 routes and take his photographs during 1991, and obviously had a whale of a time. You will find few detailed path directions here, but a fund of personal anecdotes, thoughts and general gossip which make for diverting reading. Not, as the author says, a book to take on the hill, but one to enjoy in the armchair, recalling memories of old favourites, or thinking of planning one or two of the more unusual ones included.

Escape to the Dales
45 walks in and around the Yorkshire Dales
Bob Allen
Michael Joseph, 1992, pp208, £13.99

Bob Allen's first two books, on the High and Lower Fells of Lakeland respectively, have been highly acclaimed and popular, and this volume continues in similar style and format. We are only given 45 walks in the Dales, as against the original 100 in the Lakes, the type is larger, and there are more small photos in place of the almost exclusively whole-page plates in the original Pic book, but there is still a good mix of information and personal experience, as before, with the excellent photographs expected from this author. The choice of routes is good and includes the Howgills and other marginal areas as well.

The Southern Highlands
D J Bennet
Scottish Mountaineering Trust, 1991, ppx + 214, £16.95

The SMC continues its excellent series of district guidebooks with this latest guide to the Southern Highlands, covering the area from Glasgow in the south to Loch Rannoch in the north, and from Oban in the west to Perth in the east. There is little to say about this guide that has not already been said about others in the new series; the descriptions and maps are good and the illustrations excellent. Covering some of the most popular Scottish mountains – the Arrochar Alps, Ben Lomond, Ben Lui, Ben Lawers – it is bound to be a sell-out.

A Munroist's Log
Irvine Butterfield & Jack Baines
Ernest Press, 1992, pp238, £9.95

The sub-title of this book really says it all, – 'Being a log in which to record ascents of those mountains in an extended list of 3000ft summits in the British Isles'. Each page is therefore divided into two for two separate mountains; after giving the name and height, you fill in the details for date, height, distance, weather, companions and 'Route and Notes'. Many people will enjoy having this hard-back book in which to look back on their memories, but it is a pity that there is only room for one ascent per peak. In other words, it caters for the real 'tick-it-off' Munro logger who never goes back a second time. But you can always stick extra pages in! The short section of colour photos is excellent.

The Alps (1986)
The Himalayas (1987)
The Karakoram (1990)
Photographs by H Fujita
Gyosei, Tokyo. Each volume pp96, 35cmx47cm, £70
(Obtainable from Han-Shan Tang Ltd, 717 Fulham Road, London, SW6 5UL.
Postage £9.50 per copy.)

These three volumes have been available for some time, but it is worth drawing attention to them here as copies are now in the AC library. The first thing that strikes you is their size: 35cms by 47cms is big. Not only are they coffee table books; if you put legs on them you could use them as coffee tables! As always with such books, there is the practical problem of storage, any conventional bookshelf being useless. They are more like works of art, with each double-page spread needing to be looked at from a distance – and many of the photographs are certainly worth looking at. The detail on most of the plates, and the quality of reproduction, is superb. You could almost plan a route, step by step, on some of the Himalayan peaks depicted. For my money, the earliest book, *The Alps*, is the finest, especially where Dolomite peaks soar over alpine flower meadows, but you have to admire Fujita's perseverance in sitting out bad conditions to capture many of his Himalayan and Karakoram peaks.

Geof Templeman

The following books have also been received by the Alpine Club Library during 1992:

Walking in the Dolomites. Gillian Price. Cicerone Press, 1991, pp96, £3.99

Modern Alpine Climbing. Equipment & Techniques. Pit Schubert, translated by George Steele & M Vápeníková. Cicerone Press, 1991 pp176, £5.95

The Handbook of Alpine Climbing. John Barry. Crowood Press, 1991, pp208, pb, £14.95

L R Wager. A Life 1904–1965. Compiled by Jane Hargreaves. Privately printed, 1991, pp142

Selected Alpine Climbs in the Canadian Rockies. Sean Dougherty. Rocky Mountain Books, 1991, pp320, £11.95

The Climbing Guide to Scotland. Tom Prentice. Crowood Press, 1992, pp206, £13.99

The Bernese Alps, Switzerland. A Walking Guide. Kev Reynolds. Cicerone Press, 1992, pp240, £9.95

Glen Coe. Rock and Ice Climbs, including Glen Etive & Ardgour. K V Crocket, R Anderson, D Cuthbertson. Ed by R D Everett. SMC, 1992, pp382 + x, npq

Bibliography of East African Mountains. Rheker, Taiti & Winiger. Institute of Geography, University of Berne, Switzerland, 1989, pp66 + vi, npq

Summits for All. 100 Easy Mountains for Walkers (The French Alps). Edouard Prevost, trans Jill Neate. Cordee, 1992, pp224 + viii, £8.95

The Southern Uplands. K. M. Andrew. SMT, 1992, pp182 + x, £16.95

From the Pennines to the Highlands. A Walking Route through the Scottish Borders. Hamish Brown, Lochar, 1992, pp230, £7.99

Les Alpes Vues du Ciel. Bernard Pierre & Pascal Kober, with photographs by Loic-Jahan . Editions Bias, 1991, pp128, npq

To the Top of the World. Alpine Challenges in the Himalaya and Karakoram. Reinhold Messner, trans Jill Neate. Crowood Press, 1992, pp256, £16.95

North of England Rock Climbs. Stewart Wilson. Cordee, 1992, pp382, £12.95

Walking in Ticino, Switzerland. Kev Reynolds. Cicerone Press, 1992, pp176, £9.99

Buttermere & Eastern Crags. R Graham, A David & T Price. Fell & Rock CC, 1992, pp366, npq

Hard Rock. Great British Rock Climbs. Compiled by Ken Wilson. Diadem Books, pp236 + xx, £19.99

The High Sierra. Peaks, Passes and Trails. R J Secor. The Mountaineers/ Cordee, 1992, pp368, $19.95

Wainwright's Favourite Lakeland Mountains. A Wainwright. Photos by Derry Brabbs. Michael Joseph, 1992, pp216 + viii, £16.99

Wainwright in the Valleys of Lakeland. A Wainwright. Photos by Derry Brabbs. Michael Joseph, 1992, pp216 + viii, £17.99

Bosigran and the North Coast. Des Hannigan. Climbers' Club 1991, pp246, £10.95

Gower & South-East Wales. Ed Alun Richardson. South Wales Mountaineering Club (1991), pp366 + xviii, £13.25

Froggatt. Peak Rock Climbs – 5th Series, Vol 3, Eastern Gritstone. Vol compiler Keith Sharples. BMC, 1991, pp388, £13.95

Ski Safe. A Safety Manual for all Ski Sports. Scottish National Ski Council. Cordee, 1991, pp94, £3.95

Avon and Cheddar. Martin Crocker. Climbers' Club, 1992, pp468, £14.95

Eduard Imhof (1895–1986). Ein Leben mit Landkarten. Viola Imhof. Verein für wirtschaftshistoriches Studien Meilen, 1990, pb, npq

Geodesy, Geophysics and Geology of the Upper Shaksgam Valley (North-East Karakoram) and South Sinkiang. Ardito Desio, *et al.* Consiglio Nazionale delle Richerche, Milano, 1991, pp202 + viii, npq

NOTE

I very much regret that reviews of **The Climbers** by Chris Bonington (BBC Books/Hodder & Stoughton, £16.55) and **My Vertical World** by the late Jerzy Kukuczka (Hodder & Stoughton £16.99) were received too late for inclusion but will appear in the next volume; my apologies to the author and the publishers.

Geof Templeman

In Memoriam

COMPILED BY GEOFFREY TEMPLEMAN

The Alpine Club Obituary		Year of Election
Dudley Frederick Oliphant Dangar		1931 (Hon 1969)
Anna Roelfsema	LAC	1938 (Hon 1970)
James Pringle Hope Hirst		1949
George McLaggan McGillivray		1962
Henry Norman Fairfield		1945
Andrew Fanshawe	ACG	1987
Tom Luis Sancha		1990
Arnold Alfred Galloway		1934
Sir William McEwan Younger		1927
Charles Eric Arnison		1943
Joyce Lancaster-Jones	LAC	1946
John Bryden Harrison		1938
Charles Selby Tilly		1944
Victor Wilkinson Dix		1940
Philip Mitchell	Asp	1992
John Bernard Meldrum		1922 (Hon 1985)
Cedric Roger Allen		1965
Mark Gambrell Miller	ACG	1989
William Leggatt Robinson		1977
Christopher Percival Baskin Briggs		1986
Theodore Nicholson		1960
John Martin Kretschmer		1957

The In Memorian list is, regrettably, a long one again this year, the Club having lost 22 members. Whilst the majority survived to a good age – in the case of John Meldrum a very good age – there were a few tragic cases where so much was still to be achieved, and one thinks especially of Andy Fanshawe, Philip Mitchell and Mark Miller.

In a number of cases, deaths occurred too late in the previous year for obituaries to be prepared, and I am therefore pleased to be able to include tributes to John Longland, Michael Vyvyan and Stuart Hutchinson, all of whom died in 1991. I am also happy to include an appreciation of Wanda Rutkiewicz who, whilst not an AC member, was well known to many of us.

John Henderson Longland 1936–1991

John Longland's death from a brain tumour at the age of 55 on 24 December 1991 was the more poignant for the contrast between his latter life dogged by ill-health and adversity and the exceptional achievements of his early years. As the elder son of an illustrious father, John might have succumbed to the psychological handicaps sometimes attributed to that relationship. Jack and John shared many mountain adventures together but John's achievements were entirely his own and he remained quintessentially his own man. His character was complex, combining the combativeness of an alpine pugilist with an incisive intellectualism and artistic bent. He could be abrasively caustic and this, compounded by an iconoclastic insouciance, sometimes created *mauvais pas* which more guileful men might have avoided. But those who knew him admired his courage, leadership and imperturbability. More particularly we loved him for his humour, exuberance and easy gift of friendship.

Born on 21 May 1936, John was educated at the Dragon School (of fond memory) and Oundle before going up to Jesus College, Cambridge in October 1954. In this traditional and unhurried atmosphere, the Cambridge University Mountaineering Club fermented with growing confidence. Led by a line of distinguished presidents – Brasher, Smith, Band, Chorley, Sutton, Langmuir and Downes – it had become the vogue to emulate Brown and Whillans and have a go at modern alpine routes. The Club's success was reflected in its membership. In 1951 this stood at 57. Six years later, when John succeeded Bob Downes as president in 1957, it had risen to 170 – a record to that date.

John arrived on this scene as a *wunderkind* with an impeccable climbing lineage. Unconcerned with age or reputation, he already knew and was known to everyone in the climbing world. His first roped climb had been at six. At eleven he was doing routes on Lliwedd with Alf Bridge and David Cox. As an 18-year-old still to do National Service he exuded competence and confidence; was a Climbers' Club member and had twice explored Iceland in 1953 and 1954 – in the latter year with a party of five other school leavers sponsored by the National Research Council to survey Thorisjokull's glaciers.

For climbing novitiates such as myself, *the* event of the CUMC Helyg meet in December 1954 was Longland's pre-dawn prologue on that first wintry morning – a dip in the Nant Yr Ogof when he literally broke the ice. Bumptious perhaps but not braggadoccio for John was ever an addict of the mountain plunge at all seasons. That first novice meet he led with tact, skill and patience for he was always a sympathetic mentor happy to climb with anyone. His mountaineering credo was stated in 'The New Order' (*CUMCJ* 1956) in which he exhorted the young to 'find respect and gratitude for the history and traditions which surround this cliff (Lliwedd) for they are closely interwoven with us linking our predecessors and ourselves – the ways of the mountaineer'.

At Cambridge, John had a voracious climbing appetite. In the two years 1954 to 1955 alone, he recorded over 300 climbs in Britain from Bosigran to Ben Nevis with over 50 different companions. But he was first and foremost a mountaineer who combined an elegant and economical climbing technique with the explorer's curiosity. For many undergraduates, two years of National Service had tapped springs of adventure in what was still a relatively untravelled world. The 1950s were, par excellence, the age of the university expedition. Of these, the Cambridge Pumasillo expedition 1957, led jointly by John and Simon Clarke (his CUMC successor president) was one of the most ambitious of its time. What distinguished the Cambridge Pumasillo from the 1954 Cambridge Rakaposhi and 1957 Oxford Haramosh expeditions was that Pumasillo, with an average age of 21, had no elder statesmen on board. At 20,300ft in the Cordillera Vilcambamba, Pumasillo was reckoned to be the highest virgin peak outside Asia. It had resisted several previous attempts – including that of the 1956 British Huagaruncho expedition. Its ascent by the Cambridge party was an exceptional achievement – lightly recorded in John's cable to the expedition's patron John Hunt 'All up, all down, all well. Pumasillo'.

With Pumasillo climbed, John had reached a summit of personal achievement at 21. In that same year he was elected to the Alpine Club. But while other members of the expedition returned home, John had fallen to the lure of South America and was to stay on in Peru for another two years. At Cambridge he had read Natural Sciences intending to become a doctor. Now he turned to freelance journalism with the *Andean Times*, taught English and, with his gift of tongues, became fluent in Spanish.

In 1958 John undertook a second Andean expedition to the Cordillera Blanca. His star was still in the ascendant on returning to England in 1959 when he became Senior Under Officer at Mons. During his National Service with the Royal Corps of Signals he spent much time training men in Norway. He might have stayed a soldier but instead joined Lever Brothers for whom he worked from 1962 to 1978 including six years spent in Bogota, Columbia. But his golden climbing years had been in the 1950s. Although he remained active on British crags and made an exceptional contribution to the Climbers' Club as assistant secretary, secretary, treasurer and vice-president (eventually, to become like his father, an honorary member) he effectively denied himself the presidency. In 1974 he had been appointed head of Lever Brothers Public Relations Planning but by 1978 he had left the company. Three years later his marriage was dissolved. At a time which should have seen the consolidation of a career and domestic fulfilment, he was left with neither.

John was still only 40 when in 1976 he embarked upon what proved to be his last alpine season with Charles Clarke, Peter Mould and me. He had not climbed in the Alps for some years and on the first day huffed and puffed his way up to the Vittorio Emanuele II hut. But he was always one to upset the odds and soon enough had rolled back the years. Whether on the complete Paradiso traverse or the 34-hour imbroglio on the Chardonnet, John was our imperturbable anchorman. His innate mountaineering ability, athleticism, clear-headedness and humour made him the ideal companion and this a hugely enjoyable holiday.

John's latter years were marred by ill-health and vicissitudes but his last job at the Wildfowl Trust, Slimbridge from 1985 to 1988 satisfied his love of conservation and the outdoor life and gave further scope for his literary talents. As editor of *Wildfowl World* he transformed a pedestrian black and white periodical to a modern colour magazine with 60,000 subscribers.

When John telephoned me on 20 November 1991 I had not seen him for a while. With characteristic robustness he announced that he had a brain tumour and that radiotherapy had left him with 'recalcitrant trousers around a recently acquired two inch gap'. But he was determined to attend the 1991 Alpine Club Dinner and we planned a CUMC reunion table with the Morgans, Peacocks and Stones. Sadly, this never took place. John was too ill to travel to London and three weeks later, on Christmas Eve, he died within the bosom of his family at Bakewell. John was devoted to his two children Jack and Bridget, and beloved of his family. He leaves a host of friends with memories of a warm, multi-talented man who experienced set-backs in both his professional and domestic life that would have broken lesser spirits. He had been an outstanding mountaineer who never lost his zest or sense of humour and retained to the end a courage, dignity and life force that those who knew him will never forget.

J G R Harding

John Michael Kenneth Vyvyan 1907–1991

Michael Vyvyan came from the Cornish family who lived at Trelawarren on the southern shore of the Helford estuary. The house is a mixture of 17th century restraint and Strawberry Hill flamboyance, nestling in twisting creeks and ancient oak woods. 'How did my ancestors get all this? Well, they were pirates and politicians mainly and then became respectable.'

While he was at school at Uppingham, Michael started climbing with A E Foot, that stalwart teacher-cum-alpinist who started many young mountaineers on their path. Michael also did some good routes with guides and became a fine all-round mountaineer. He was never in a hurry, unfussed, witty and with a steady ambition to climb big mountains.

In 1931 he joined the Diplomatic Service and was in Moscow during much of the 1930s. In 1937 he was a great encouragement to us on our Caucasus trip and would have joined us if it had been possible. Moscow was a depressing place in that decade for those who kept their eyes and ears open. Three things dislodged Michael from the diplomatic ladder: his appreciation of the realities behind the communist façade and consequent disagreement with our British tendency, by the 30s, to tolerate and be soft with Stalin; his yearning to get to the high untrodden mountains of Central Asia; and the War.

In 1938 Michael resigned from the Foreign Service and was elected to a fellowship at Trinity College Cambridge to teach modern history. During that summer he and Paul Secord made the first serious reconnaissance of Rakaposhi. That year there were only four climbing expeditions in the Karakoram – one American and three British. Michael's account in *AJ51* (1939) of their exploration of the Rakaposhi–Disteghil Sar group is a period piece and suggests something of his tenacity and powerful topographic grasp. They climbed the NW peak, 22,500ft – 'an easy and unexacting route ... had opened itself to us'! Perhaps, but they covered a great deal of ground during a period of exceptionally fine weather.

On the outbreak of war Michael joined the army as a rifleman and was then commissioned in the Black Watch. Subsequently he served in the SAS and Commandos. After a three-year secondment back to the Foreign Office in 1944, he returned to Trinity where he remained almost until his death.

Michael was a somewhat 19th century character, combining wide scholarship, a capacity for friendship with all ages, and romantic enthusiasms. I remember a camp fire in the valley below the Bernina peaks, by the Silser See. There were ten of us, from 15-year-olds upwards. The fire was burning low and Michael stoked the conversation: Central Asia, Nietzsche (who had died on the other side of our lake), food (Michael was a good cook), communism, climbs in the Lake District, commandos, electing college Heads and the Austro-Hungarian empire. Some of those teenagers still remember that evening.

Robin Hodgkin

Stuart John Grant Hutchinson 1926–1991

Stuart Hutchinson, who died on 3 October 1991, was born in Leatherhead but had family connections with Grantown-on-Spey which led him to explore the Cairngorms from the age of ten. His school encouraged him, so he developed a strong sense of independence in the mountains at an early age. After school he started at university but broke away to volunteer for the armed forces and as a young officer went to the near and middle east. He managed to arrange to have some of his training in North Wales.

On returning to civilian life he became very active with the Midland Association of Mountaineers as well as taking up caving, pot-holing and white water canoeing (which nearly cost him his life). Much later he took up small boat sailing; then, when nearing 60, skiing and, even later, ski moun-taineering. He climbed regularly in the Alps and throughout the UK, including visits to the sandstone outcrops in Kent, and Pembroke, Devon and Lundy. He made one visit to the Rockies and trekked up Kilimanjaro and Mount Kenya. He often expressed regret that his life was too full to join in our Club activities. He served on the BMC management committee at the time when he was also president of the MAM.

In his private life he was active in the solid fuel industry which led him to take a leading part in establishing a new livery company, the Worshipful Company of Fuellers.

On the Kenya trek in 1989 something seemed amiss because he allowed a porter to carry his 'light' day sack. Skiing at Wengen and climbing at Fort William in early 1991 were clearly a trial and he did not survive the operation which had become inevitable.

All who knew Stuart Hutchinson will remember his unique sense of time: he really had to be persuaded to return home before darkness or a calamity followed. On Mt Edith Cavell he was quite happy to sit not far below the summit to watch the sun go down, despite anxious companions some five hours below and the prospect of an unplanned bivouac.

Let Geoffrey Winthrop Young's words end this tribute:

> I have not lost the magic of long days;
> I live them, dream them still;
> Still am I master of the starry ways
> And freeman of the hill.
> Shattered my glass ere half the sands were run,
> I hold the heights, I hold the heights I won.

F R Robinson

Wanda Rutkiewicz 1943–1992

In May 1992 Poland and the international mountaineering community lost one of their most outstanding climbers: Wanda Rutkiewicz. She had been taking part in a Polish-Mexican expedition attempting the N face of Kangchenjunga. Wanda was last seen at 8300m, about 250m from the summit, on 12 May by Carlos Carsolio. She never returned.

Wanda Rutkiewicz was born in Lithuania on 4 February 1943. In 1946 the family returned to Poland and lived in Wroclaw and then in Warsaw. Wanda gained a degree in Science and Engineering and worked at the Institute of Mathematical Machines in Warsaw. At an early age she discovered her passion for the mountains. First she climbed on local rocks and then in the High Tatras where she did some extraordinary and extreme routes in both summer and winter. These, together with her natural ability, gave her the skills and toughness required for the superb and difficult climbs she was to achieve all over the world: in the Alps, Norway, the Pamirs, the Hindu Kush, the Andes, Patagonia, Tibet, Yosemite and, most of all, in the Karakoram and the Himalaya.

I had the good fortune of knowing Wanda from the days of her early climbs in the Polish Tatras. We used to meet at the Warsaw High Mountaineering Club and on climbs in the Tatras, particularly in winter; we became good friends. I could already see her tremendous potential ability. As a person she was a softly-spoken beautiful woman with the expressive eyes of an explorer, and very elegant. In the mountains she was strong-willed and determined, and had tremendous physical and mental endurance. She overcame bouts of pneumonia and anaemia and, after several leg operations, managed to walk 300km on crutches while leading a Polish women's expedition to K2. Though she sometimes climbed in mixed parties, she was particularly involved in women's mountaineering. She believed that women should take up the challenge, make their own decisions and take full responsibility for themselves.

Wanda's main attributes were extreme powers of endurance, intelligence, determination, ambition, and passion for the mountains. Those were the characteristics which made her such a brilliant Himalayan climber. Her achievements were legendary: in 1975, with Alison Chadwick and a Polish team, she made the first ascent of Gasherbrum III (7952m), then the world's highest unclimbed mountain; in 1978 she became the third woman and the first Polish and European woman to climb Mount Everest; and in 1986 she was the first woman to climb K2. Over 17 years she made 22 expeditions to the Himalaya and Karakoram, and perhaps her most phenomenal achievement was to be the only woman to have climbed eight out of the fourteen 8000m peaks. As a Himalayan mountaineer she had no equal among women and few among men.

Wanda was married and divorced twice; she had no children. Her commitment to her beloved mountains was total. Her professional and private life was always linked to the mountains. Full of optimism and energy, she could never retire from climbing even though she lost nearly 30 climbing friends on the mountains.

A very creative person, Wanda made several mountain films; the best known were 'Tango Aconcagua' and 'Snow Women'. She also wrote well and gave countless slide shows and lectures both at home and abroad. She often came to the Buxton Conference and always stayed with us in London. How I treasure the memory of those visits and how much it saddens me that there will be no more of them.

On 28 February 1991 Wanda Rutkiewicz officially announced her intention of climbing all fourteen of the 8000m peaks, calling it 'A caravan to dreams'. She wanted to attempt each 8000m summit having already acclimatised on the previous one, so that her body would function well at high altitude in a continuous process of acclimatisation. She believed it would then be possible to climb the rest of the 8000m peaks in a relatively short time. But her dreams were cut short tragically on Kangchenjunga when she was reported missing on 13 May 1992. The following summary of Wanda Rutkiewicz's most important climbs is a record of her achievement.

1967   East Face of Aiguille du Grépon (3482m) – first women's team ascent.
1968   East Pillar of Trollryggen in Norway – first women's team ascent.
1970   Peak Lenin (7134m) in the Pamirs.
1972   Noshaq (7480m) – first Polish women's ascent.
1973   North Pillar of the Eiger (3970m) by Messner's route – first women's team ascent and second overall.
1975   First ascent of Gasherbrum III (7952m).
1978   North Face of the Matterhorn (4477m) – first women's team ascent in winter.
1978   Everest (8848m) – first Polish and European women's ascent and third women's ascent.
1979   East Face of Grand Capucin (3838m) by Bonatti's route – first women's team ascent.
1985   Aconcagua (6960m) – South Face in alpine style.
1985   Nanga Parbat (8125m) by Diamir Face – first women's team ascent.
1986   K2 (8611m) – first female ascent.
1987   Shishapangma (8046m).

1989   Gasherbrum II (8035m) women's team ascent.
1990   Gasherbrum I (8068m) – first women's team ascent.
1991   Cho Oyu (8201m) – summit reached solo.
1991   Annapurna (8091m) – first woman to climb the British route on the
       South Face. Summit reached alone.

Wanda's family have suffered a tragic loss; the Polish and international
mountaineering community have lost the greatest ever female Himalayan
climber; I shall remember Wanda Rutkiewicz and miss her with much sadness
as my good and reliable friend.

Ingeborga Doubrawa-Cochlin

Dudley Frederick Oliphant Dangar 1902–1992

Fred Dangar was born at Wimbledon on 19 September 1902. He was educated at Rugby School and at Jesus College Cambridge. Before he was twenty,
whilst still living with his parents at Frensham House in Surrey, his lifelong
interest in the Alps began with a visit in the summer of 1922 to the area
around Chamonix and Finhaut. This was the first of over 30 visits extending
into the early 1960s to the mountains of Switzerland France and Austria. He
was initiated into alpine climbing by C H Wybergh, a member of the AC, and
a former schoolmaster at his preparatory school, Lambrook Berks, with
whom each year between 1923–1927 he climbed in the Bernese Oberland,
Arolla and the French and Austrian Alps. He was elected to the Club in 1931
having been proposed by Claude Elliott and seconded by C H Wybergh. Fred
climbed in the then traditional way with a guide, enjoying the contentment of
the amateur on the uncrowded mountains of that period without being driven
by any ambition to achieve feats of daring. His climbs between 1929–1936
included the Grand Combin, Matterhorn, Monte Rosa, Zinal Rothorn, Aguil-
les Rouges d'Arolla, Petite Dent de Vesivi, Gspaltenhorn and Wetterhorn, as
well as ascents in the Pyrenees and in the Gross Glockner group. He developed
a special interest in Switzerland, getting to know practically every corner of
the country, and acquiring during the course of numerous later journeys
accompanied by his wife an amazing depth of knowledge about the valleys
and the people of the upper mountain regions.

During the Second World War, having failed to pass his medical test for
active service, he served on the general staff reaching the rank of captain and
was posted at Dorchester where he acted as quartermaster.

Fred Dangar settled in Devon in 1946 and not long after he became more
closely associated with the Club's activities. His major contribution to the AC
was as Honorary Assistant Editor, together with Tom Blakeney, of the *Alpine
Journal* from 1953–1974. His capacity for meticulous research and accuracy
for detail, as well as his scholastic knowledge of alpine history and literature,
ideally suited him for work in which he excelled and which he enjoyed. His
many contributions to the AJ include vivid sketches of several of the earliest
Alpine ascents, details from the Fuhrerbuchs of famous guides, and (with Tom

Blakeney) a defence of Whymper's role on the Matterhorn ascent in 1865. In addition, unspoilt areas such as Belalp and Arolla, for which he had a special affection, were made the subject of delightful articles. Besides this he was responsible for the annual Alpine Notes section, and for the production of two consolidated indexes for the AJ covering the years 1927–1968 (Vols 39–73). His election to Honorary Membership in 1969 was a recognition of the value of his work. He was a member of the Swiss and Austrian Alpine Clubs and cultivated friendships with leading international climbers, his knowledge of French and German facilitating easier personal contact with many.

Apart from his archives on the European alps, Fred Dangar built up a valuable series of classified records dealing with the greater ranges. In 1960 after the first 21 volumes of the *Himalayan Journal* had appeared the H.C. felt that the time was ripe for preparation of an index. I approached Fred hesitatingly about whether he would agree to take on this additional task and was delighted when he agreed to do so. He subsequently produced two consolidated indexes for the *Himalayan Journal* covering the years 1929–1978, (Vols 1–35) and he was elected to Honorary Membership of the Himalayan Club in 1964.

I have reason to be personally grateful to him. When Fred and his wife Barbara attended the Swiss Alpine Club Centenary celebrations in 1963 they were seated at the luncheon table opposite the young daughter and son of the then president of the SAC Basel Section, and subsequently became good friends of the family. I met that daughter a few years later at their house in Dittisham and we were married not long after.

Fred Dangar was essentially to use a now unfashionable word a gentleman of the type that has become increasingly rare today, with personal qualities that combined modesty, humility, and a strong sense of family and moral values. He was utterly reliable in whatever he undertook, and would never accept anything second-rate from himself or from others. When we last met four months before he died I found that he had lost none of the fervour with which he enjoyed discussing mountain events and people, about which he retained an amazing memory.

His marriage in 1932 to Barbara (née Massie) resulted in a perfect partnership and long years of happiness. In September 1992 Fred would have celebrated his 90th birthday and in November of the same year he and Barbara would have celebrated their diamond wedding. To Barbara, their son Richard and daughter Rosemary, and to their grandchildren and two great grandchildren we offer our deepest sympathy.

Trevor Braham

Anna Roelfsema 1909–1992

Anna Roelfsema, Holland's most prominent woman climber, died in August 1992. She started to climb at the age of 15 and, with her brother Johan, was one of the first guideless climbers in Holland at a time when climbing without a guide was criticised by the *Dutch Alpine Journal*. Nevertheless, Anna and Johan (whose portrait is in the Alpine Museum in Zermatt) climbed many mountains together, amongst others the Breithorn Younggrat.

Working as a physiotherapist in a Hague hospital, Anna only had a fortnight's holiday, which she always spent in the Alps. She usually went to Zermatt, where she did the classic climbs including the Zmutt and Furggengrat on the Matterhorn. To her great grief, her brother – having joined the Resistance – was shot in 1943. After the war, Anna returned to Zermatt and climbed with the well-known guides Knubel, Bernhard Biner and, later, with Bennie and Gottlieb Perren. Her climbs included the Zinal Rothorn E face and the Obergabelhorn S face. In 1969 she climbed the Riffelhorn with Tenzing Norgay.

In 1968, when she was on the Titlis in Engelberg with a group of top women climbers, *inter alia* Nea Morin, Esme Speakman and Eileen Healey, they founded, there and then, the 'Rendez-vous Hautes Montagnes' (RHM) in an attempt to open the climbers' world more to women. They also wished to seek contact with women climbers behind the Iron Curtain and invite them to the 'Free Alps'. This resulted in 24 years of meetings on rock and on ice with old and new friends, in different countries, including the former Yugoslavia, Czechoslovakia and Bulgaria. Anna never missed a meeting.

Although she also climbed in the Dolomites, Wales, Scotland and France (Mont Blanc at the age of 61), Zermatt was her 'home' – usually as a guest of Hotel Monte Rosa. The Seilers, the Biner family, Pickelschmied Taugwalder, they were all close friends of hers. In 1969, after 33 years, she returned to the Breithorn, this time to climb the N face.

In various countries and in more than one generation, Anna had a large circle of friends, and she cherished them. The Bishop of Leicester and his wife (Cicely Williams), who spent their summers in Zermatt, invited her to their home. She was a warm-hearted person, full of interest in the climbing of the younger generation, who visited her and told her of their experiences. Her favourite saying was: 'The mountains give you so much happiness.'

Bernina de Mol van Otterloo

Henry Norman Fairfield 1905–1992

Harry Fairfield was a member of an informal group of friends who climbed in the Lake District and North Wales in the 1930s. I had the good fortune to join them during two periods of furlough from India, in 1933 and 1935; indeed, I have to thank Harry and his friends, as well as Edwin ('G') Kempson, for introducing me – an Alpine climber – to British rock in those far-off years.

The group consisted of A W (Bill) Osborne, Stewart Mitchell, Donald Murray, Norman Slack, Harry Fairfield and one 'Brian', who features in my climbing diary but whom I cannot now recall. I find that (the late) Jock Harrison, who survived a terrible ordeal on Masherbrum in 1938, joined us at one stage.

The climbs themselves are of no special account today. They included *Eagle's Nest Direct, Jones* from Deep Ghyll, *Moss Ghyll Grooves* and sundry routes on the Napes, Pillar, Serjeant's Crag and Pike's Crag in the Lakes, as well as climbs of a comparable standard in Snowdonia. What did matter was the friendship which the climbing created within our group: we were young, enthusiastic and enjoyed one another's company enormously.

Harry was very much a part of these episodes which, though brief, I treasure in my memory of him today.

John Hunt

Andy Fanshawe 1963–1992

Andy Fanshawe was killed in a fall while climbing Eagle Ridge, Lochnagar, in the Cairngorms on 14 March. He was 28 years old. One of Britain's most outstanding mountaineers, he was universally respected and liked in the climbing community for his immense enthusiasm and essential kindness.

Born in Helsby, Cheshire, Andy was introduced to the hills at an early age by his parents who were keen walkers. He was an active member of Wilmslow Grammar School's climbing and walking club, visiting the gritstone edges of Derbyshire and Cheshire from the age of 15. He was confronted with tragedy early in his climbing career when a schoolmaster, taking him and other youngsters up Sharp Edge on Blencathra in the Lake District in snow conditions, slipped and fell to his death. But Andy's enthusiasm for climbing was not diminished. In 1980 he climbed his first extreme, characteristically going straight in at E2 on *Vector* at Tremadog, falling off three times on the awkward crux on the top pitch, before finally climbing it.

In 1981 he entered the Royal School of Mines in London, studying geology. His enthusiasm for climbing was unabated with weekend forays to Scotland. His organisational ability was shown by his becoming secretary and then vice president of the Imperial College Mountaineering Club. At this time he led his first expedition, going to Ecuador to make the first ascent of the West Ridge of El Obispo (5319m), the first solo ascent of Monja Grande (5160m) and the second ascent of Fraille Occidental (5050m), with an ascent of Chimborazo and a quick dash down to Peru with Mark Dickson to climb Huascaran, with two packets of biscuits and two tins of sardines for rations – they were so broke.

After university Andy worked for a short time in mining engineering in South Africa and then for RTZ Oil and Gas in Britain, but a life in and around climbing was becoming increasingly important to him. He had his first full season in the Alps in 1985, starting in the Dolomites with the *Preuss Crack* and *Yellow Edge* and then moving on to the Oberland to make an attempt on the *North Face Direct* of the Gspaltenhorn. He was washed off it by a violent storm but returned a few days later to climb the *North Face Direct* of the Grosshorn. He finished the season in Chamonix, forming a partnership with John Taylor and climbing the South West Pillar of the Dru and the *North Ridge Direct* on the Droites.

Andy then embarked on his most challenging project yet – an expedition to make the first traverse, alpine-style, of the magnificent twin-peaked Chogolisa (7654m) in the Karakoram. It was an ambitious venture for a first Himalayan trip but the team were determined and well organised, and they received the Nick Estcourt Memorial Award. The climb was successful, a particularly bold ascent in the best style by the five participants.

On his return to Britain Andy became National Officer of the British Mountaineering Council. His enthusiasm and openness enabled him to relate effectively to the young climbers, the older members of the climbing fraternity who sat on the committees, and officials of various government departments; he cheerfully cut through red tape and made things happen. He hosted a series of successful visits by foreign climbers and an international jamboree for young climbers from all over the world.

During this period he was caught in an avalanche when on the way down from the summit of Ben Nevis in bad weather. His partner and best friend, John Taylor, was killed and he was severely injured. Within four months he was climbing hard once again, leading rock routes of E5 standard for the first time.

In 1988 I had the good fortune to get to know him well when he came on an expedition I led to Menlungtse in Tibet. Together with Alan Hinkes he made the first ascent of the West Peak – another bold and determined piece of climbing. The following year he led an expedition to Makalu. Although heavy snows forced them to abandon their attempt to make a complete traverse of the mountain, he made the first ascent of Peak 4 (6720m) with Ulric Jessop – a push of three days' hard technical climbing up its S ridge.

Andy left the BMC in 1990 and was appointed fund raising director for the Barrow Hospital Scanner Appeal. He approached the task with characteristic energy and helped raise £1.5m. In that year he married Caroline Jerran and moved to the Eden valley in Cumbria. Although he went two years without a Himalayan expedition, he made lightning forays to the Alps in the winters of 1990 and 1991, climbing the North Face of the Eiger and the Croz Spur of the Grandes Jorasses with Ulric Jessop. His first book, *Coming Through* (1990), describes his three expeditions. He was full of plans for the future, working on an ambitious book describing the 40 best alpine-style climbs in the Himalaya and planning an alpine-style ascent of the N ridge of K2.

Andy was a brilliant and forceful climber, a talented writer and an excellent organiser. Above all, he was a person whose enthusiasm, warmth and essential kindness had earned universal affection and respect. He will be sorely missed by everyone who had the privilege of knowing him.

Chris Bonington

Alan Hinkes writes:
Andy burst into the British climbing scene as BMC National Officer, having just boldly traversed Chogolisa with a group of friends. He had an irrepressible drive and enthusiasm. I remember him with the Polish climbers in Scotland in 1987. He turned up with giant catering tins of beefburgers and

sausages and tucked into the contents with relish not even bothering to reheat them. The Poles opted for Fort William's fish and chips! Andy and I quickly formed a friendship, often inexplicably addressing each other by our surnames. On Menlungtse we teamed up and climbed the W face of the West Peak, complementing each other and working together in harmony. There is no doubt that Andy was a brave and talented climber – a shooting star that flashed through the mountaineering firmament, never to be forgotten.

Tom Luis Sancha 1947–1992

Tom joined the Alpine Club in 1990, proposed by his father, Luis, who has been a member since 1957. Tom and I met that summer in Pontresina on an AC meet and did two climbs together. Thereafter we only saw each other three times. Our friendship promised so much more than it achieved and therein, for me, lies the sadness of his death at the age of 44.

Tom had a thoroughbred AC pedigree through both his father and his maternal grandfather, T G Longstaff. Eric Shipton had also been a family friend and he, Tom and Luis made a traverse of the central section of the Cuillin Ridge during the winter of 1967/68.

Tom made his first trip to the Alps when he was six and subsequently climbed the Sparrhorn in the Oberland aged nine. He continued his apprenticeship during his teens with his father, in both the Patagonian and Chilean Andes during the time that the family home was in Argentina. While at Cambridge he led two expeditions to Ecuador, in 1967 and 1969, making ascents of Cotocachi, Illiniza, Carihuairazo, Cayambe, Cotopaxi and Chimborazo.

During the next 15 years or so Tom was heavily involved in his work but managed several mountain trips as diverse as cross-country skiing in northern Sweden to soloing Mount Rainier. He also skied the *haute route* and climbed the Matterhorn. He made a three generation ascent of the Wildspitze with Luis, aged 70, and his children Emily, 12, and William, 10.

Tom had been a whizz at computer systems and became something of a legend within his field. In 1977 he founded Cambridge Interactive Systems which was so successful that, eight years later, he sold it and 'retired'. Shortly before he became ill he underwrote a canoeing expedition for both able-bodied and physically handicapped young people to Iceland.

Then, in 1987, the cruellest of blows, he was struck down by a brain tumour. For two years he fought with incredible courage, supported by his wife Sally, to overcome this crippling handicap, undergoing major brain surgery and radio therapy. Despite this, in 1989 he enrolled at Plas y Brenin on an alpine climbing course and, later, a sea cliff course. In 1990 having, as it were, re-learnt to climb, he joined the Alpine Club. In the spring of that year he and a friend, Wendy Smith, visited the mountains of Jordan and made an ascent of Jebel Rum.

A few months later my wife and I met Tom in the Alps. He spoke rather slowly and deliberately, clearly affected by his brain surgery, and was wonderfully open and honest about his tumour. He and I, with my wife Carol and Daphne Pritchard, formed a bit of a foursome and used to eat together in camp. He was a stimulating, delightful companion. Together he and I climbed the ordinary route of Piz Morteratsch and the East Pillar on the N face of Piz Palu. He was a solid, middle grade sort of alpine climber, which was remarkable for a man who had been as ill as he had,

In the autumn of 1990 he went on his third climbing trip of the year and, with Mark Miller and Wendy Smith, made an ascent of Ramdung Go in the Rolwaling Himal of Nepal. Wendy writes: 'Tom was very fit and went strongly. He was suffering from headaches which he thought was altitude but we now know this to have been the beginning of his second brain tumour.' Not long afterwards the second tumour developed yet somehow, despite almost weekly seizures, he managed a final climb of Cader Idris in November 1991, walking slowly on his right side and using ski poles.

In spite of further surgery and chemotherapy, Tom never lost his composure and sense of humour. In his last days, at home with Sally and his family, he fed himself almost up to his final hours, and only thought of those around him. My own sense of loss has more to do with what might have been rather than what was, for the time we spent together was little enough, though precious, memorable and rewarding.

The final words should come from an old friend, Thomas Forster, who spoke movingly in Churchill College chapel on 14 April 1992: 'To me Tom was the magical older brother I never had – fabulously successful, rich, gifted, worldly, knowledgeable, funny, generous, bossy and endlessly entertaining. Although he was stubborn and often thought to be arrogant he was completely free from personal vanity. He was a total realist. He never grew bitter and impatient over his dysphasia when people tried to prompt him with words to finish his sentences. He had great natural courtesy. Finally, he was a wonderful friend and *always* such fun to be with.'

Mike Binnie

Charles Eric Arnison 1901–1992

Eric Arnison was for many years head of his family firm of solicitors, with offices in Penrith, Cumberland. He was Clerk to the Magistrates at the West Ward courts of Shap and Hackthorpe, and Secretary-Treasurer of the town's Chamber of Commerce and Trade, posts which he occupied for 23 and 33 years respectively.

Eric was educated at Penrith Queen Elizabeth Grammar School and at St Bees where he became head of School House. In 1920 he entered into Articles and served the normal five years' clerkship with his father. After qualifying in 1926 he worked for a short period in London before returning to the family firm in Penrith and subsequently becoming a partner.

His proximity to the main climbs in the Lake District gave him the opportunity to become a keen rock climber. In 1930 he joined the company of local climbers, and his first climbs were *Main Wall* on Gimmer and most of the routes on Scout Crag. They used to meet at Keswick, Langdale or Coniston and 'tick off the climbs in the old Red Guidebook'. Eric relates in his memoirs how he climbed with the legendary George Bower, and knew the Abraham brothers, Dr Wakefield and Geoffrey Winthrop Young. The memoirs record his very full professional and sporting life and give an insight into his character.

Eric received his introduction to the Alps in 1932 when he visited St Gervais and walked round the Mont Blanc massif. He organised several trips to the Alps for his local climbing companions; in 1937 they all went to Chamonix where they 'knocked off 15 major peaks in 12 days'. During the war years Eric served in the Home Guard while on secondment to the Board of Trade. After the war he was soon back in the Alps 'sometimes with A B Hargreaves, Malcolm Milne, Hill Porter and Ewan Banner Mendus'. On this expedition he considered the Matterhorn to have been 'the plum' of several ascents, including the Nadelhorn, the traverse of the Rimfischorn, the Aiguille de la Tsa and the Douves Blanches.

Eric was elected to the Alpine Club in 1943, proposed by P J H Unna and seconded by E Anderson. He declared in his memoirs: 'It is about the only club where you are elected on merit and not by just signing a form and paying a sub.' He returned often to the Alps and, being an adept skier, he visited all the popular Swiss and French resorts and completed the *haute route* three times in either direction.

As Chairman of the British Mountaineering Council's Lakes Committee one of Eric's duties was to check aspiring guides for their certificates. He relates, in his habitual unassuming manner: 'It was a way of having a top climb, often above my standard.' He was also a member of the Keswick Mountain Rescue team. Eric occupied numerous other posts during his long life, including the presidency of the Fell and Rock Climbing Club, as well as of the Ski Club of Great Britain and the Lake District Ski Club. He was a director of the Ullswater Outward Bound School. His foreign exploits included an ascent of Mount Kenya in only 12 hours at the age of 68, and Mts Kosciusko and Ras Dashan in Ethiopia at the ages of 72 and 73 respectively.

On a more personal note, I would add that I cannot imagine my own boyhood without 'Uncle Eric', as I have always known him, and I will for ever be grateful for the generous part he played in my formative years. Our respective families passed several long summer holidays together both in Cornwall and in Scotland, in some of the wildest parts of the Western Highlands north of Ullapool. We often met too for climbing and fishing expeditions in the Lake District where both our families lived. Indeed, I am certain that it was thanks to Uncle Eric's experience, foresight and attention to detail that we, eager and carefree youths, did not meet with trouble on our many adventures. Although happily oblivious at the time, these holidays took us through an outdoor schooling with exhilaration, while Uncle Eric had the patience and the art to transmit, without our realising it, certain of his own talents, not least his knowledge and understanding of nature, which complemented our academic education. For all that I am grateful, and will not forget Uncle Eric.

Charles Eric Arnison died peacefully on 11 March 1992. Sadly, his wife Jean died in 1982. He is survived by a daughter and two sons. The Club, and all of us who knew this gentleman of great character, mourn his loss and extend our deep sympathy to his family.

Tony Joyce

Tom Price writes:
Eric Arnison was a spare and active man, enjoying vigorous health for most of his life and blessed with a sanguine and matter-of-fact disposition. He joined the Alpine Club in 1943 and was also a long-standing member, and one time president, of the Fell and Rock Climbing Club. Educated at St Bees School, he spent most of his working life as a solicitor in his native Penrith and was a highly esteemed and well-loved citizen of that town. His interests and enthusiasms were many and included rugby, shooting, fishing, natural history, travel, potholing, skiing and, above all, mountaineering. He climbed in Britain, the Alps, Africa, Australia and North America. Though he liked conviviality and good living, in the mountains he was a hardy traveller and even in old age accepted spartan conditions in huts and camps, as, for example, when he made an arduous journey in the highlands of Abyssinia at the age of 73. At 68 he was the oldest man to have climbed Mount Kenya. For all his adventures on crags and mountains, he was a devoted family man. He was a good friend, unsentimental but quick to offer practical help in time of need. At his memorial service, a very large crowd paid tribute to the passing of a fine and generous spirit.

John Bryden Harrison 1908–1992

Jock Harrison was always good to be with: quiet humour, quiet courage and, seemingly, no concern about himself. By the late 1930s he was an outstanding Indian Army officer and an experienced Himalayan mountaineer. He knew Indian flowers and birds. He was a fluent Urdu speaker and his unflapping friendliness was completely colour blind. His Punjabi troops nicknamed him 'Harree Singh' and his fame as a warrior and athlete lived on long after his early retirement.

Graham Brown and I met up with him in 1938 on our way to join James Waller's expedition to explore and, perhaps, to climb Masherbrum (7821m). Young Jimmy Roberts was to join us at Srinagar. Three weeks later, the heavily goitred Balti elders who greeted us at the head of the Hushe valley said we were the first climbers to come there since the Workmans. Even in 1938 there were only two or three other parties in the Karakoram, notably Charlie Houston on K2. They too had a hard time.

One evening in 1985 Jock was reminiscing about his parents and his early days. Where, I asked him, had his almost Kiplingesque enjoyment of India and his love of adventure come from? 'I was there as a child,' he told me, 'Simla, mainly. My father was an up-from-the-ranks officer. Then I went to a minor public school, Dean Close, where there was a marvellous Christian schoolmaster called Hedley Warr; he was a tremendous influence. He took us fell-walking in the Lake District.' At Sandhurst Jock's athletic prowess began to show, with a blue for high jump and hockey; and he was a King's Indian Cadet. In 1928 he returned to India and the 8th Punjab regiment. There were camping holidays in Kashmir and some more serious climbing – with James Waller to Nun Kun. On another expediton, in the Kangchenjunga massif, Jock remembered meeting several notable mountaineers: Marco Pallis who would never wear a topee because it symbolised the Raj, the ICS Resident from Gangtok who would never take his off for the same reason, and Freddie Chapman who scarcely ever wore a hat at all. Jock himself, like Marco, favoured a floppy Terai.

I asked him whether he served on the North West Frontier. 'Oh yes,' he said, 'the best times were the operations against the Fakir of Ipi in 1935 and '36. It was the real thing; but a pretty phoney war nevertheless. When I tried to leave a booby trap – a hand grenade and a trip – I was told to go back and remove it. Unsporting.'

Then came our serious and nearly fatal expedition to Masherbrum which had never been explored or attempted before. We pioneered the route which led the Americans to their success in 1960. Jock and I attempted the summit from a high camp and were turned back by bad weather. The story is told in James Waller's *The Everlasting Hills* (1939). Inevitably, we had Nanga Parbat 1936 and 1937 very much in mind. But it wasn't an ice avalanche which hit us during a night of gales; just a massive snow slide. We burrowed out into the pre-dawn, swirling darkness, managed to salvage boots and an axe, and then spent 24 hours in a blizzard trying to get down. Jock, being the stronger more experienced climber, took the axe and was anchor man, which was the main reason why his fingers were more severely frostbitten than mine. We spent a night in a crevasse but next day the welcome, fickle sun was shining. It was a long limp down and home to Srinagar. Jock, unable to walk or ride, was carried on a litter. In the army hospital and on the voyage home Jock began to realise that an active military career was over. But what a career it could have been!

Back in the Millbank military hospital Jock was finally patched up and was able to be active again. In 1939 he married Mary Webb, one of his nurses, a New Zealander. There followed 20 years of happy family life, mainly in New Zealand, but she died in 1959; in 1961 Jock married a second time. During the war he served as a staff officer in Ceylon. Then, for some years, he worked on the reorganisation of the New Zealand Army and retired as Colonel and OBE. He then became Military Secretary and Controller to Lord Cobham, the Governor General. His final job, during the sixties, was as bursar-administrator to the newly founded Cobham Outward Bound School.

He and Janet retired to live near Stroud, in a house with a steep garden and distant views. In his maturity and old age Jock lost some of his youthfully sharp Christian vision; though it had never shown on his sleeve. It changed into a gentler reverence for the good and the beautiful; and there was much of that around in the life that he remembered.

Robin Hodgkin

Victor Wilkinson Dix 1899–1992

Victor Dix, who died in June aged 93, was the former Professor of Surgery at London University and was an expert in the surgery of urinary stones and cancer of the bladder. Born on 24 May 1899 in Dorset, he was educated at Newcastle Grammar School before joining the Royal Flying Corps in the First World War, ending up as a flying instructor. After the war he went up to Trinity College, Cambridge, and then entered the London Hospital Medical College in 1921, qualifying in 1923 and becoming MRCP and FRCS in 1926.

During a spell in Berlin in the mid-thirties he learnt the new method of intravenous urography and brought this back to England, quickly building up a reputation in the treatment of hydronephrosis. At the outbreak of war he carried out emergency surgery during the Blitz, his house and private clinic being destroyed by bombing. He then joined the RAMC, serving in Egypt as a surgeon in a general hospital, before being posted to the Far East as a consultant surgeon to South-East Asia Land Forces.

It was in 1947 that he was appointed Professor of Surgery at the London Hospital, retiring in 1964. He was a founder member of the British Association of Urological Surgeons, becoming president in 1962.

A marvellous technical surgeon, he was quick yet unhurried and all operations looked easy in his hands. His breadth of knowledge enabled him to follow the Everest story with an understanding of both the altitude and climbing difficulties. I was very fortunate to have spent my formative years as a surgeon on his unit.

Tall, strikingly handsome and impeccably dressed, Victor Dix had many interests: photography, opera, Australian stamps (on which he was an authority) and, of course, mountaineering. He joined the Alpine Club in 1940 after several seasons climbing classic routes in the Alps, both with and without guides.

Michael Ward

C Philip Mitchell 1962–1992

Philip, who became an Aspirant Member early in 1992, died in an accident on 29 May while leading the *Regil Variant* on the NW ridge of Naranjo de Bulnes in Picos de Europa, northern Spain, with Duncan Ridley, who survived.

Born in Erith, Kent, on 12 August 1962 and brought up in Sidcup, Carshalton and Guildford, he worked in the video archives of the BBC. He was introduced to climbing about four years ago and soon relished his time on rock and in the mountains. He particularly loved the sea cliffs of Cornwall but most of all appreciated higher mountains and would set off for climbs with a beaming grin and unmitigated enthusiasm.

He had been on trips to the French Alps, Morocco and Corsica and was a recipient of the North London Climbing Club's SWAT award (Serious Weekend Ascent Team) when he climbed and descended the Italian Ridge of the Matterhorn with Duncan Hornby over a long weekend from London in 1991.

Philip's other passions in life were horse riding and Lindy Jive, a dance discipline which he performed with great expertise to the sounds of the 40s and 50s, particularly to his favourite artists Louis Jordan and Jackie Wilson.

Phil possessed an instantly amiable personality and is sadly missed by his numerous friends, particularly members of the AC, North London and Rockhopper Mountaineering Clubs, London Swing Society and the BBC. We send our condolences to his family.

Charles Clarke and John Godowski

John Bernard Meldrum 1885–1992

JB, as he had always been known to me and to other mountaineers, died in September 1992 at the age of 107. He spent his working life, when not on the hills, as an engineer in his father's firm in Manchester which made destructors specially designed for the disposal of unwanted used currency, a process which is ironic when one knew how careful JB was of his own considerable resources. He was, unsurprisingly, the oldest member of the Institute of Electrical Engineers. It was his interest in all aspects of mountains and mountaineering for which he will be best remembered. He joined the Alpine Club in 1922 and was delighted to have been elected an honorary life member on his 100th birthday. He was also a member of the Fell and Rock and Rucksack Clubs.

From the many stories one has heard he was an engaging eccentric with a sense of values firmly rooted in Victorian attitudes. He only started skiing when he was 65 but within a few years was skiing in the top classes and was always the 'last off the hill'. He remained a bachelor until he was 90, and it was only marriage which forced him to buy his first house: until then he had always led a somewhat nomadic life, taking his touring caravan for long visits to the Western Highlands in the summer, and over-wintering in his permanent caravan in Dorset.

Although he was never at the leading edge of mountaineering advances, he was never happier than when exploring and pioneering in remote mountain regions. He climbed in the Caucasus and the Alps between the wars and his last major trip was to the Atlas with Bentley Beetham when they were both over 70.

In his 20s JB was climbing with some of the leading lights of his day including George Bower, Fred Piggot, Bentley Beetham and Howard Somervell. In 1913 he made the second ascent of Central Buttress on Scafell. He was always particularly fond of Western Scotland and in this area appropriate memorials would be his first ascents of the Coire Mhic Fhearchair Buttress on Beinn Eighe and the Pinnacle Ridge on Garbh Bheinn of Ardgour. Together with my children Robin and Juliet, we have enjoyed following some of the routes he pioneered in the Lake District: without exception they demonstrate a quality of remoteness which half a century has not diminished.

JB was not a regular contributor to journals, but in 1921 he wrote about one of his early Alpine seasons based at Chamonix and Zermatt. With

Beetham, Bower and Somervell, he climbed the Chardonnet, Charmoz, and Midi and then from Zermatt, the Matterhorn traverse, the Wellenkuppe and the Dent Blanche.

He achieved national fame just after his 100th birthday when, as Britain's oldest car driver, he was involved in a minor accident; he was required to take a driving test. When questioned by the media, he made the typically pragmatic response that it might be simpler to find a new young wife to drive him about. After the death of his wife, Gladys Hurst, in 1982, he continued to live near Bournemouth where he retained an interest in mountains until he finally went into hospital for his last few weeks.

There will be few who have recollections of JB in the mountains but, like his family, the Club will reflect with sadness on the passing of a climber whose contribution to mountaineering in general has been considerable. His death marks the passage of mountaineering history as surely as the cairns of the Lakeland fells mark the passage of earlier generations.

Kim Meldrum

Cedric Roger Allen 1934–1992

Whilst descending a ridge on Trollvasstind in the Lyngsalpene of Norway, Roger was struck by a huge rock; he had no escape route open to him, and plunged 2000ft to an untimely death. Although a very experienced and careful climber he had suffered more than his share of bad luck and this was his third serious accident in the mountains. Now the mountains have extracted their settlement for the 40 years in which he enjoyed the experiences, the friendships and the fulfilment of climbing amongst them.

Born in Leeds in 1934, Roger graduated in Physical Chemistry at the University of Leeds and later gained a doctorate for his research. In 1960 he took on a lectureship at the University of Dundee to be near to the great Scottish mountains. He retired from the University in 1991.

Roger had wide-ranging interests, a sharp mind and a wry disarming wit; he could speak with knowledge and conviction on a host of subjects and was just good to be with. As president of the University Bell Club, he enjoyed the mind-stretching forum for the discussion of science and philosophy. His regular attendance at the University Chaplaincy concerts helped to fulfil his keen interest in music.

It was the mountains, however, that were to become perhaps the principal driving force in his life. He had the good fortune to have a wife who was his equal on the hills. Those of us who walked and climbed with him will know that he was never the man for a soft option; he would make his plans and would carry his companions along with him, always stretching his own and their capabilities. His knowledge and experience of the Scottish mountains were almost legendary and he must have climbed most of the Munros several times over, but I do not remember him counting them. On a day out with Roger one could be certain to take in that extra top at the end of a long hard day.

He had been an active member of the Yorkshire Ramblers' Club since 1953, joining the committee briefly, and was secretary in 1956/57. He enjoyed the respect and affection of that Club and was elected vice president for 1987/89. He became a life member in 1988. The Alps had a special attraction for Roger and over the past 40 years, he had climbed in most of the centres to a good standard, with many exciting and satisfying expeditions to his credit. He joined the Alpine Club in 1965 but was rarely in a position to attend meetings, living so far north. He was, nevertheless, very proud of his membership of the Club.

Roger would never have enjoyed growing old and being unable to get out on the hills and mountains. Perhaps he would have chosen to have ended his days in the mountains he loved, but at a much later date for sure. He leaves his widow Sue, two sons and a daughter, and, with his friends and companions on the hills, very many happy memories.

David Smith

Mark Gambrell Miller 1961–1992

The tragic and untimely death of Mark Miller in the PIA Airbus which crashed as it approached Kathmandu airport at the end of September 1992 has deprived British mountaineering of one of its most talented and prolific sons.

As a pupil of Wellingborough School in Northamptonshire and then at Denstone College, Staffordshire, Mark distinguished himself as an athlete, swimming for Northamptonshire County and playing rugby for the Kettering Colts. Whilst at Sheffield Polytechnic in the early 1980s he made the most of the city's proximity to the Peak District's many gritstone and limestone outcrops, soon becoming known for his characteristically bold routes on gritsone slabs, to which he gave typically imaginative and memorable names (*Science Friction*, E4 6a, on Froggatt Edge, and *Sex Dwarf*, E3 6b, on Millstone Edge, for example). His keenness and effervescent enthusiasm for the outdoors in general and climbing in particular was inspirational, instilling his companions with new-found confidence to climb at the limits of their technical ability.

These qualities became tempered with a deep respect for and understanding of the larger mountain environment as he became increasingly interested in alpinism. The classic apprenticeship followed, with long stays in Chamonix producing a rich crop of climbs, mostly made with his fellow Sheffield-based climber Sean Smith. These years of prolific alpine activity saw Miller making the first British ascent of the Hidden Pillar of Frêney, the second ascents of the *Gabarrou-Silvey route* on the Pic Sans Nom and the *direct route* on the N face of the Leschaux, and early ascents of the *Croz Spur Direct* and the N faces of the Pèlerins and Mönch in winter. All were characterised by their seriousness and technical difficulty. One winter was spent job-sharing as a dustman in Chamonix. The Alpine Binmen, as this group and their associates became affectionately known, were notorious for their poverty and simple love of the mountains.

In the mid-1980s the Binmen went east. After a very successful spring season in Peru, Miller's first Himalayan expedition was to the Kishtwar in India in the summer of 1984, and from then on the great mountain ranges of Asia consumed most of his energy. Doug Scott invited him to Pakistan in 1985, an expedition during which Miller climbed Diran, his first 7000m peak. Attempts on Rakaposhi (7788m) and Nanga Parbat (8125m) were abandoned owing to sickness amongst the team, but the infectious spirit of those mountains and the simple, hardy folk that live amongst them captivated Miller, and his life became a passionate crusade of expedition mountaineering from then onwards.

In the tradition of British mountaineers since the very first explorers ventured forth to the Alps over a century ago, Mark Miller's love of the mountains was a multi-faceted gem. His expeditions took him to some of the most spectacular places on earth in search of a match for his incredible strength, stamina and climbing skills (Makalu, Shivling and Masherbrum, for example), whilst his insatiable curiosity and love of the wilderness took him on exploratory expeditions (Hushe and Aling in Pakistan, 1989) and treks throughout the Himalaya with his beloved girlfriend Cath Speakman.

In 1990, with Andy Broom, he founded the mountaineering and adventure travel company 'Out There Trekking' (OTT), and this venture provided him with the perfect outlet for his boundless energies. He had found his vocation at last. His wealth of experience and affable nature stood him in good stead, and those of us who shared his life came to think of him as a survivor. Leading his first commercial expedition to Peak Lenin in the Pamirs in the summer of 1990, Miller deemed one of the regular campsites to be in a particularly dangerous spot and elected to pitch his group's camp in a safer place. During that very night a terrific avalanche swept the other camp away completely, killing over 40 climbers in the worst single accident in the history of mountaineering. Throughout the night Miller and his party searched through the debris and helped rescue two frostbitten survivors.

Mark Miller lived his life with the throttle fully open – whether on an 8000m peak in the Himalaya, on the crags of his beloved Peak District, mountain-biking in the Lake District, DIY-ing at home, or raving into the early hours at clubs or parties. For all who knew and loved him there is now a vast and strange emptiness which tears and time may heal.

Jonathan Tinker and Steve Razzetti

William Leggatt Robinson 1902–1992

Robin Robinson began climbing in Britain in 1921, enthusiastically and methodically, words which characterise everything he undertook. In 1937 Dr Tom Longstaff encouraged him to take to high mountaineering. This led to his first, guided, alpine climbs in 1939, when his ascents included Mont Blanc,

Aiguille du Tacul and Aiguille de l'M. During those pre-war years, because of his abiding interest in Italian art, literature and music, he also learned the Italian language. Thus the war found him in Himachal Pradesh in charge of two thousand Italian prisoners of war. His recounting of their stories was inexhaustible.

He went mostly to Italian mountains after the war in alternate years. (In the non-climbing years he and his wife travelled extensively in Europe, 'avid for culture' he would say laughingly, especially Romanesque churches.) Between 1947 and 1962 he climbed Adamello, Presanella, Grivola, Gran Paradiso and Monte Rosa (Punta Gnifetti) as well as Wildspitze and the Breithorn, always with guides, in addition to much exploration of the Val d'Aosta and the Dolomites by himself.

Then in 1973 he started again with a guided crossing of the Nuovo Weisstor pass from Macugnaga to Gornergrat with my wife and me. He said we had inspired him to a new lease of life. In truth, of course, it was he who had inspired us. Four years later we made an easy ascent of Cevedale together.

Robin's election to the Alpine Club in 1978, largely for his long experience and continuing enthusiasm, was a source of deep satisfaction. He responded by giving what assistance he could, such as preparing indices for volumes of the Alpine Journal, helping with its editing and translating and reviewing Italian books.

For eight of the next ten seasons we spent part of our mountain holidays together. In 1978, alone on the Sentiero Roma above Val Masino, he fell while cutting steps on hard snow between the Gianetti and Allievi huts and was slightly injured. After a laborious descent to San Martino he was taken to hospital to be patched up. That experience did not put him off.

1980 saw the conclusion of his lengthy exploration of all the side valleys of the Val d'Aosta. In 1981, in the woods above St Barthelemy, north of Nus, we chanced to meet a forester, one of his prisoners of war nearly 40 years earlier. In the Graian Alps in 1984 we embarked on a walk south from Ceresole Reale across the top of the Stura valleys, but had underestimated the difficulty of the terrain. Our first night was spent in exquisite discomfort in a cowherd's stone shelter. The three quarter-bottles of champagne I was carrying helped to atone for the hardship, but we abandoned that exploration the following day. Snowstorms had frustrated our attempts on Ortles in 1978 and Pyramide Vincent in 1982, and in 1985 we failed to climb Monte Viso from the Quintino Sella Hut. That was our last expedition together. Robin's last was based on Terme di Valdieri (Alpi Marittime) in 1987, his eighty-fifth year. His 'annual reports' – discursive, informative, amusing and reflective – were a delight to read. I treasure my copies.

Robin's last visit to the Club, appropriately, was for the Italian evening in November 1991. He died on 11 October 1992 after a short illness, five days after his 90th birthday, barely four months after his wife's death. He was a generous and considerate friend, ever the gentleman.

Alan Harris

Christopher Percival Baskin Briggs 1913–1992

Chris Briggs always remained an unmistakable Yorkshireman despite the fact that he lived in North Wales for the last 45 years of his life. His arrival at Pen-y-Gwryd in 1947 marked the beginning of a new epoch in the already long and varied history of that hotel. Somehow he and his wife Jo created an atmosphere quite different from that of any other hotel in Wales or anywhere else (except possibly the Old Dungeon Ghyll in Langdale), and this special character was largely a reflection of his own personality.

The move to Wales was a bold one. He had previously been an industrial chemist and had no experience whatever of hotel management. In 1947 petrol rationing was still in force, and for two or three years the hotel was seldom overcrowded. Chris could even do some rock climbing in his spare time. In the evenings the smoke room at P-y-G was the obvious meeting place for climbers, who were often non-resident but were very welcome to stay on until long after closing time. Soon, however, the demands of actually running the hotel became enough to occupy Chris's time very fully, all the more so because of the special problems created by its exposure to gales and driving rain and its liability to being cut off from civilisation for days at a time in the winter months.

For a good many years Pen-y-Gwryd was the official Mountain Rescue Post for accidents in a large part of Snowdonia. Later this job was taken over by professional organisations based elsewhere; but originally Chris Briggs and any volunteers who happened to be in the hotel would turn out as soon as an accident was reported, whatever the hour of day or night. Such rescues often involved working in storm or blizzard conditions, and over the years they saved many lives. Chris's organisation and leadership of this work was recognised, some people thought inadequately, when he was awarded the BEM.

In his younger days, Chris Briggs's views on most matters, including colour, were decidedly reactionary. So far as Pen-y-Gwryd was concerned, anyone whose skin was even faintly off-white was quickly shown the door, if indeed he ever got inside it. These views were put under severe strain, and had to be actually modified a bit, in 1953, when the news came through that Everest had been climbed. For there was no doubt that Sherpas had played a great part in the expedition's success and that one of them had even got to the top. Henceforward Sherpas were made more than welcome at P-y-G under some unwritten new rule; and in fact this was only the thin end of the wedge, for within a few years Indians too were climbing Everest and were being received at the hotel with similar hospitality if they visited England. Not surprisingly this hospitality soon began to be reciprocated, and the wheel came full circle when Chris and Jo Briggs began to find themselves paying regular visits to Darjeeling or Nepal, generally as guests of the Indian Mountaineering Foundation. In the hotel itself there are many relics which bear witness to Pen-y-Gwryd's close association with the 1953 expedition, the members of which foregathered there annually for many years at the appropriate weekend at the end of May.

Yet although by its situation and many of its associations Pen-y-Gwryd was very much a mountain hotel, it was far from being a hotel primarily for climbers. Climbing was never the main topic of conversation in the evenings, and most of the residents were there to enjoy the mountain walking, not in order to climb the rocks. A high proportion of the guests revisited the hotel year after year, and many of them, from many different walks of life, became personal friends of the family. In his heyday, which lasted the best part of 40 years, Chris seemed to need no sleep. Armed with his modest half-pint silver tankard, he would be in the smoke-room, usually standing against the wall, from the end of dinner until the last guest went to bed in the small hours. Yet he would be up and about, apparently as fresh as a daisy, long before the gong sounded for breakfast.

A regular feature in Chris and Jo's calendar was an annual fortnight's visit to southern Spain, which was responsible for the exceptional quality of their sherry. For many years, too, Chris had a fortnight's skiing holiday, always at Kitzbühel. But, so far as sport was concerned, his main addiction was to salmon fishing and, in particular, to fishing a stretch of water on the river Lledr. In the salmon season he would disappear there for as much of the day as he could spare. He was also a devotee of rugby football. Quite a number of people have occasion to remember the England–Wales international fixture whenever it was at Twickenham; the Briggs family would be dispensing hospitality in the West Car Park from some hours before the kick-off, and the larder and cellar of P-y-G seemed to have been half-emptied for the purpose.

These notes may seem to have been almost as much about Pen-y-Gwryd as about Christopher Briggs. If so, the reason appears in the first paragraph – namely that what P-y-G stood for reflected what Chris himself stood for: such things as friendship and the straightforward enjoyment of life, which were always so important to him. He was a much liked and much respected figure in North Wales, and it was a remarkable tribute to him when, some 25 years ago, such an undisguised son of Yorkshire was chosen to serve as High Sheriff of the very Welsh county of Caernarfon.

David Cox

Theodore Nicholson 1906–1992

After ten cruelly frustrating months following a severe stroke, Theo Nicholson lost a courageously fought battle for recovery on 28 October 1992. Sadly, it has to be acknowledged that all too many of those who shared in the strenuous days he loved so well are no longer with us; those who *can* remember are grateful indeed for their rich store of memories.

Thinking of his mountain days, one would surely best describe Theo Nicholson as the complete all-rounder. His record – on foot and on ski – ranged over at least ten countries, from Scotland and Norway to the South Island of New Zealand. His ski mountaineering began at Adelboden in 1928 with E C Tuke. It was to take him back to Switzerland often, to Austria and to Norway, where spring glacier-touring was his very special delight.

The war saw his skill and experience put to notably good use: volunteering for the 5th Scots Guards (Finnish Ski Battalion) in 1940; instructing in Commando mountain warfare at Braemar and on the rocks of North Wales; in the Canadian Rockies with the Lovat Scouts – training in the Columbia Icefields, Watchtower Valley and Maligne Lake areas; finally in Greece, with Mount Olympus a recurring attraction.

In addition to his membership of the Alpine Ski Club, Theo was a member of the Alpine Club, an honorary life member of the Lake District Ski Club and, since 1948, a member of the Scottish Mountaineering Club. In Scotland he took immense pleasure in doing all the Munros and, for strenuously good measure, much more besides. Striving to match his pace on the hill, or watching the grace with which he would execute a telemark, was almost as thrilling as to witness his high-speed swoop from Carn Ban into Glen Feshie after a meticulously planned winter crossing of the Cairngorms.

Theo would have liked mention made of these many mountain days. Yet there is so much more besides to remember. From as far back as 1926, when he was a special constable during the general strike, public service took up much of his time: assistant county commissioner for scouts; honorary liaison officer for Duke of Edinburgh awards; after the war, characteristically, taking a sympathetic, practical part in ex-service work.

An expert in woodlands and timber, he found more than ordinary satisfaction in his lifelong business career with Southerns, the timber merchants, with whom he was latterly chairman and joint managing director. Business aside, he took endless delight in walks in the Delamere Forest and, more particularly, in his own private woodland near his Kelsall, Cheshire, home.

As a close friend on and off the hills for nearly 50 years, I found that Theo was unfailingly the best of companions, always interested, always interesting, immensely good fun, never content with anything but the highest standards. This year, 1993, would have seen his diamond wedding. To Thelma, unselfish sharer of those near-sixty years, and to their children Elizabeth, David and John, and to their grandchildren, I offer these words of sympathy: wholly sincere, wholly inadequate.

Campbell R Steven

Alpine Club Notes

OFFICERS AND COMMITTEE FOR 1993

PRESIDENT	M H Westmacott
VICE PRESIDENTS	D K Scott
	S M W Venables
HONORARY SECRETARY	Dr M J Esten
HONORARY TREASURER......................	J M C Evans
HONORARY LIBRARIAN......................	D J Lovatt
HONORARY EDITOR............................	Mrs J Merz
COMMITTEE: ELECTIVE Members	M W Fletcher
	D W Hamilton
	L A Hughes
	J R Mellor
	R F Morgan
	Rear-Adm M G Rutherford CBE
	D J Temple
	Miss J A Turner
	S A Jones
EXTRA COMMITTEE MEMBERS...........	G D Hughes
	R Lawford
ACG CO-OPTED MEMBERS	R F Allen
	A C M MacNae

OFFICE BEARERS

LIBRARIAN EMERITUS	R Lawford
HONORARY ARCHIVIST......................	Miss L Gollancz
HONORARY ASSISTANT ARCHIVIST ...	Miss M Darvall
HONORARY KEEPER OF THE CLUB'S PICTURES...	D J Lovatt
HONORARY KEEPER OF THE CLUB'S MONUMENTS	D J Lovatt
HONORARY KEEPER OF THE CLUB'S ARTEFACTS...	R Lawford
CHAIRMAN OF THE FINANCE COMMITTEE...	R F Morgan
CHAIRMAN OF THE HOUSE COMMITTEE...	Rear-Adm M G Rutherford CBE

GENERAL MEETINGS OF THE ALPINE CLUB 1992

14 January	John Cleare, *Recent Random Travels of a Peripatetic Photographer*
11 February	John Town, *Altai Range from Both Sides*
10 March	Andy Perkins and Brendan Murphy, *Cerro Kishtwar – Seventeen Days on a Himalayan Wall*
21 March	North Wales Meet and General Meeting Lindsay Griffin, *Last Mountain on the Bone Trail*
14 April	Stephen Venables, *Ascent of Kusum Kangguru*
12 May	Andy Cave, *Extreme Alpinism*
15 September	Chris Bonington and Stephen Venables, *East of Nanda Devi: The Indian British Panch Chuli Expedition*
26 September	Lakes Meet and General Meeting Luke Hughes, *Travels in Greenland*
13 October	Kurt Diemberger, *Into the Unknown: the Secret Side of Broad Peak*
3 November	Italian Evening: *The Matterhorn and Neighbouring Mountains*

10 November	Phil Bartlett, *Greenland: a Wilderness Saga*
14 November	General Meeting and Symposium at Plas y Brenin, *Return to the Alps*
4 December	Annual General Meeting Valedictory Address by the President, Lt Col H R A Streather OBE
8 December	Special Meetings: André Roch, Film of the Swiss 1952 Everest Expedition
22 December	Special Christmas Meeting: Tim McCartney Snape, *From the Outback to Gasherbrum IV*

The Annual Dinner 1992 was held on 5 December at the Basil Street Hotel. The Chief Guest was André Roch and the Toast to the Guests was proposed by John Hunt and Stephen Venables.

CLIMBING MEETINGS 1992

22–23 February	ACG Winter Meet, Glencoe
20–22 March	North Wales Meet and General Meeting
25 July–15 August	Joint Meet with Climbers' Club and ABMSAC based at the Glacier d'Argentière campsite
25–27 September	Lakes Meet and General Meeting

THE ALPINE CLUB LIBRARY 1992

The library is now fully organised in the Charlotte Road premises, thanks to sterling work by Pat Johnson and Bob Lawford, assisted by others from time to time. The archives are in good order under the care of Livia Gollancz and Margaret Darvall. Since the move to Charlotte Road the number of visitors has more than doubled, but is still substantially less than it was at 74 South Audley Street. Enquiries by letter and telephone are, however, at record levels and the demands on the Himalayan Index continue to increase.

The Alpine Club Library Appeal, launched in 1991, was, at the time of writing, some £70,000 short of its £250,000 target. Alpine Club members had contributed £165,000 – a splendid effort not matched by outside donors in spite of the many approaches made by members of the Appeal Sub-Committee under the Earl of Limerick. Further fund-raising will be necessary if we are to maintain a high standard of service and, in particular, if we are to produce a badly-needed new catalogue. For current income we continue to benefit substantially from gifts and legacies of books, which are sold unless needed for filling gaps or as useful duplicates.

Mrs Johnson has resigned after 15 years as Librarian. All users of the library have appreciated the care with which she has always dealt with their requests, and will miss her. The present excellent state of the collection is testimony to her devoted work over the years. We wish her all the best for the future. We welcome Mrs Margaret Ecclestone as Pat Johnson's successor.

During my time as chairman, what has impressed me most is the amazing amount of effort put in by those principally concerned – both those already mentioned and Peter Ledeboer, Anne Andrews, Jerry Lovatt, and successive Honorary Treasurers and Archivists. Without them, there would be chaos. With them, we have a library of which we can be very proud.

Michael Westmacott

THE BOARDMAN TASKER MEMORIAL AWARD FOR MOUNTAIN LITERATURE

The tenth award ceremony was held at the Alpine Club on 15 October 1992. The judges were Ronnie Wathen (Chairman), Livia Gollancz and Terry Gifford. The winner was *In Monte Viso's Horizon* by Will McLewin (The Ernest Press). Shortlisted were *Flammes de Pierre* by Anne Sauvy (Diadem Books) which was runner-up, *Spirit of the Age* by Pat Ament (Adventure's Meaning Press, Nebraska), *My Vertical World* by the late Jerzy Kukuczka (Hodder & Stoughton), and *The Water People* by Joe Simpson (Jonathan Cape). As a result of intensive fund raising, the prize money was raised to £2000.

INDIAN MOUNTAINEERING FOUNDATION GOLD MEDAL

The IMF Gold Medal was awarded in 1993 to our member Harish Kapadia, Editor of the *Himalayan Journal* and co-leader of the Indian British Panch Chuli Expedition 1992, for services to mountaineering. Congratulations Harish!

PIOLET D'OR 1992

The Golden Iceaxe award for 1992, inaugurated in 1991 and judged by the Groupe de Haute Montagne, was won by Michel Piola and Vincent Sprungli for their first ascent of the E face of the South Tower of Paine, *Dans l'Oeil du Cyclone* (900m 6b A4). Also nominated for the award were Dick Renshaw and Stephen Venables for their first ascent of the S ridge of Kusum Kangguru in November 1991; Dick Renshaw, Victor Saunders, Stephen Sustad and Stephen Venables for their first ascent of Panch Chuli V; Mark Twight and Andy Parkin for *Beyond Good and Evil* on the Pèlerins (600m ED2 5+/A3); Chantal Mauduit for her ascent of K2 by the Abruzzi Spur – the only living woman to have reached the summit; Catherine Destivelle for the first female winter solo ascent of the N face of the Eiger; Francois Damilano and Thierry Renault for high grade icefall climbs; and Oscar Cadiach, Enric Dalmau, Lluis Rafols and Alberto Soncini for their first ascent of the E face of Broad Peak Central.

ALPINE CLUB SYMPOSIUM 1992: RETURN TO THE ALPS

The Symposium took place at Plas y Brenin on Saturday 15 November and, as usual, what promised to be a tiny audience blossomed at the last minute to fill the auditorium; over 120 attended. The themes of the meeting were first to remind us of our heritage and secondly to emphasise that the Alps are still the playground of Europe and very well worthwhile today.

Early British Alpine Exploration and the Formation of the Alpine Club
In his opening talk **Jerry Lovatt** focused on the early history of Mont Blanc including the first British ascent (the fourth overall) in 1787 and the ascent by Albert Smith in 1851, which had a significant effect on the popularisation of mountaineering in Britain. Key climbs and personalities prior to the formation of the Alpine Club in 1857 were identified. Finally, the major players of the Golden Age were introduced, culminating in Whymper's ascent of the Matterhorn in 1865. The talk was richly illustrated almost entirely with slides of contemporary material from the Alpine Club Library and Jerry's own collection.

Bregaglia and Bernina
Lindsay Griffin reminded us of the pleasures of the Italian Alps and enticed us with slides of Mello (a rock paradise) and the classics of Disgrazia, Piz Bernina and many smaller climbs. He emphasised the great changes in the terrain and pointed out the inadequacy of many of the older guidebook descriptions. Owing to the hot and dryish summers during the last seven years, ice routes in both areas should only be attempted in the late spring or very early summer.

Some Classic Four Thousanders
Will McLewin, whose book *In Monte Viso's Horizon* (The Ernest Press) won the 1992 Boardman Tasker Memorial Award, concentrated on four contrasting routes: the SW flank of the Gross Grünhorn, the NNE face of the Lenzspitze, the N ridge of the Weisshorn and the Diable Arête of Mont Blanc du Tacul. He urged us to climb mountains with an awareness of their character, to climb *with* instead of *on* the mountain and to make climbing an act of communication rather than conquest.

Some Hard Routes in the Mont Blanc Massif
Andy MacNae took the audience up several hard climbs including the *Czech Route* on the Petites Jorasses, the *Crétier Direct* on Mont Maudit and the *Bonatti-Gobbi* on the Eckphiler (Grand Pilier d'Angle). He described a dramatic accident on the Eckphiler in which he was severely frostbitten. Andy also mentioned the changes in the Alps during the last decade, particularly increased stonefall on certain routes.

The Brandler Hasse and the Croz Spur in Winter
Andy Cave continued in the modern idom with a striking account of the 25 pitch first British free ascent of the *Brandler Hasse* on the Cima Grande, which

Andy climbed with Paul Jenkinson in the summer of 1991. This was followed by his description of a bold, fast and successful ascent of the *Croz Spur* of the Grande Jorasses which he had done in March 1992 with Dave Hesledon.

The Dauphiné
John Brailsford is a veteran mountain guide with a detailed knowledge of the Dauphiné which is probably unsurpassed. With the help of excellent photographs and topos, John demonstrated the glacial changes that have taken place in his new homeland and the wealth of classic alpine and rock routes in this area.

The 1992 Symposium was organised by **Charles Clarke** and **Sheila Harrison.**
Charles Clarke

HYPOXIA '93 – THE EIGHTH INTERNATIONAL HYPOXIA SYMPOSIUM
Chateau Lake Louise, Alberta, 9–13 February 1993

To mark the 40th anniversary of the first ascent of Everest, Hypoxia '93 was dedicated to Dr Griffith Pugh, whose pioneering scientific work made the ascent possible. Four speakers paid tribute to his contribution: Charles Houston, Jim Milledge, John West and myself. The Symposium, a biennial event, attracted many speakers and a large audience from North America, Europe, Asia and Australasia. The programme covered a wide range of subjects including mountain medicine, the central and autonomic nervous systems, comparative physiology and the clinical physiology of hypoxia.
Michael Ward

UIAA IN KATHMANDU

Much of the work of the International Union of Alpine Associations (UIAA) is done through its specialist Commissions. That concerned with the mountain environment is the Mountain Protection Commission which met in Kathmandu in May 1992. I attended the meeting in place of Alan Blackshaw who, as Chairman of the Mountaineering Commission, had been specially invited but who was recovering from an operation. I was also wearing my Bhutan hat (or *Doh!*), since Bhutan was the only Himalayan country unable to send a representative.

The main item on the agenda was a paper entitled 'Target programme – avoiding waste and litter'. Many problems and potential solutions were discussed and resulted in the adoption of a recommended programme for member associations. Some of the important factors revealed by the discussions were that most mountaineers and trekkers take more equipment and packaging than is strictly necessary, and that too little non-disposable waste is carried out; there are too few facilities for waste disposal at designated campsites and other locations and, where they exist, most are inadequate; there is no on-going system or regular funding for the clean-up of the worst 'junk yards'; and no host countries have yet earmarked specific portions of peak and trekking fees for environmentally related activities.

This narrow focus on the most visible aspects tends to obscure the fact that the greatest threat to the Himalayan environment comes from degradation and unmanaged exploitation of forest and pasture resources – a process which mountaineers and trekkers contribute to rather than cause. To help redress the balance, the Chairman of the recently formed Himalayan Environment Trust, Captain Kholi (who was also representing the Indian Mountaineering Foundation), described the work of the Trust, patrons of which include a number of the world's leading mountaineers. Its first action had been to agree and seek widespread adoption of an environmental code of conduct. The MPC endorsed and adopted the code.

To help implement the code it was proposed that a Himalayan Mountaineering Network be established to keep host country mountaineering associations, ministries of tourism, and associations of trekking agencies informed about relevant new ideas and developments. It was thought that the International Centre for Integrated Mountain Development, based in Kathmandu, would be a suitable partner in building up a computer database for such a network. As a follow-up to the Kathmandu meeting, the BMC convened a meeting of tour operators, mountain guide associations and others in May 1993 at the RGS to promote the use of the code.

Peter Mould

THE ALPS THROUGH THE LOOKING GLASS

Unfortunately two of the coloured illustrations for our article *Wordsworth and the Alps* in the last Alpine Journal (*AJ97*, 203–209, 1992/93), Francis Towne's watercolour *Glaciere taken from Montanvert* (Plate 66) and Turner's painting *The Pass of St Gothard* (Plate 70), appeared in reverse as mirror images. The reversal of Towne's view from the Montanvert was particularly unfortunate as we were comparing it with similar views of the Mer de Glace, two of which were illustrated on a page facing the Towne.

We had suggested that in the larger studio version of Towne's view, also exhibited at Grasmere, he had made a concession to the Picturesque by introducing a foreground in which there are two figures with their backs to the scene, and that perhaps one of them was viewing the prospect, framed as a picture, in his reflecting landscape glass. Towne himself would never have used a so-called 'Claude Glass' to help him to compose a picture; but they were widely used at the time by travellers and artists in search of the Picturesque, notably by Thomas Gray in the Lake District. So we can console ourselves for seeing the familiar view from the Montanvert the wrong way round by realising that it is how it would have appeared in a 'Claude' or 'Gray's Glass'.

Janet Adam Smith and Peter Bicknell

Contributors

GEORGE BAND was the youngest member of the 1953 Everest team. He subsequently made the first ascent (with Joe Brown) of Kangchenjunga, and climbed in Peru and the Caucasus. In 1985 he climbed the Old Man of Hoy; in 1991 Ngum Tang Gang III (5640m) in Bhutan. AC President 1987–89.

PHILIP BARTLETT lives in West Yorkshire. He prefers exploratory mountaineering to rock climbing as he gets older and his arms get weaker. In 1992 he explored the Lemon mountains in East Greenland.

CHRIS BONINGTON CBE crowned his distinguished career in 1985 by reaching the summit of Everest at the age of 50. He continues climbing and writing at undiminished pace. His latest book *Sea, Ice and Rock* was published in 1992.

TREVOR BRAHAM is a company director. He has been on 14 expeditions to the Himalaya, Karakoram and Hindu Kush. He wrote *Himalayan Odyssey* and was Editor of the *Himalayan Journal* 1958–60 and of *Chronique Himalayenne* (SAC) 1976–86.

HAMISH BROWN is a travel writer based in Scotland, when not wandering worldwide or making extended visits to Morocco. His latest book *From the Pennines to the Highlands. A Walking Route through the Scottish Borders* was published in 1992.

ROB COLLISTER is a mountain guide, happily married with three children, who lives in North Wales. He regards himself as 'one of Fortune's favoured few' (in Churchill's phrase) who can earn a living doing what they love.

DAVID COX is a retired Oxford don. He climbed regularly in the UK and the Alps between 1954 and 1958 and was on Machapuchare (Nepal) in 1957. AJ Editor 1962–67, President 1970–72.

ADRIAN DRAGOS DEFTA has climbed in the Carpathians, the Caucasus, the Pyrenees, N Wales and Yorkshire. He has worked towards the successful revival of the Romanian Alpine Club and is a member of the BMC. He is currently studying in Britain.

KURT DIEMBERGER, whose climbing career spans over 30 years, made first ascents of two 8000ers: Broad Peak (1957) and Dhaulagiri (1960). He is an acclaimed mountain photographer and film-maker and has written two volumes of autobiography. His latest book *The Endless Knot* was published in 1989.

MARK DIGGINS has been a mountain guide for 11 years, mostly working at the International School of Mountaineering at Leysin, Switzerland. He is currently Training Officer to the British Association of Mountain Guides. He has climbed in N and S America, Africa and the Himalaya.

MAL DUFF was born in 1953 in the foothills of Mount Kenya. He has been a professional mountaineer since 1981 and has been on 24 expeditions to the greater ranges. He is married and lives occasionally in Scotland.

EVELIO ECHEVARRÍA was born in Santiago, Chile, and teaches Hispanic Literature at Colorado State University. He has climbed in North and South America, and has contributed numerous articles to Andean, North American and European journals.

CHARLES EVANS is a neurosurgeon who was Deputy Leader on Everest in 1953; with Tom Bourdillon, he made the first ascent of the South Summit. He was also on Cho Oyu in 1952, on Kangchenjunga, as leader, in 1955 and explored widely in Central Nepal and the Everest region.

TERESA FARINO is a British ecologist with an Honours degree in Botany and Zoology and a Masters degree in Conservation. She has been living in Picos de Europa for the past six years while working as a freelance journalist and photographer.

ALFRED GREGORY, FBIPP, Hon FRPS, was the official photographer on the 1953 Everest expedition and helped place the highest camp at 27,900ft. He now runs a highly successful travel company. His book of photographs *Alfred Gregory's Everest* was published in 1993.

JIM GREGSON is a teacher of Art. He has climbed in the Alps almost every year since 1972, and in recent years has taken up Nordic-style ski touring and ski mountaineering.

LINDSAY GRIFFIN, after a lengthy alpine apprenticeship, has concentrated on remote ascents in the greater ranges, including 42 Himalayan peaks. He intends to continue until increasing age, unfitness, accidents and a long-suffering wife call a halt to these activities.

J G R HARDING is a solicitor, but was formerly in the Colonial Service in South Arabia. He has climbed extensively in Europe, Asia, Africa and Australia.

SIR EDMUND HILLARY, ONZ, KBE, beekeeper, climber, author, lecturer. First to reach the summit of Mt Everest with Sherpa Tenzing on May 29th 1953. First to take vehicles overland to the South Pole in January 1958. Builder of schools and hospitals for the Sherpas and enthusiastic environmentalist. Honorary Member 1983.

RUPERT HOARE works as a geophysicist for LASMO and spends nearly all his holidays mountaineering or ski touring. He is currently based in Jakarta where the volcanoes of Java provide a poor substitute for the snowy peaks of the Alps.

LUKE HUGHES is a furniture designer with limited annual holiday – hence a lively interest in lightweight trips to East Greenland. Other ascents include the N face of the Eiger and to within 300m of the summit of Everest.

JOHN HUNT (Lord Hunt of Llanfair Waterdine) has had a highly distinguished career in the army, the public service and as a mountaineer. He led the 1953 Everest expedition, and his classic *The Ascent of Everest* was reissued with a newly-written Prologue in 1993.

HARISH KAPADIA is a cloth merchant by profession. He has climbed and trekked in the Himalaya since 1960, with ascents up to 6800m. He is Honorary Editor of the *Himalayan Journal* and compiler of the *HC Newsletter*. In 1993 he was awarded the IMF's Gold Medal.

PAUL KNOTT started climbing at Bath University. He has climbed in the Alps, the Altai, the Tien Shan and the Caucasus and plans to return to the intriguing countries of the former Soviet Union.

GEORGE LOWE OBE is a teacher who climbed with Ed Hillary in New Zealand, and subsequently in the Garhwal, on Cho Oyu, on Everest in 1953, on Makalu, and on the 3-year Trans-Antarctic expedition. He is Chairman of Hillary's Himalayan Trust in the UK.

KEITH MILNE is a geologist and has been on expeditions to Peru and the Himalaya to climb new routes. He has also climbed in Britain, USA (including Yosemite), Australia, New Zealand and the Alps.

Since Everest **JAN MORRIS** has published some 30 books, including works on Wales, Venice, Oxford, Manhattan, Sydney, Hong Kong and the British Empire, besides two autobiographical volumes and a novel. She lives in Wales and is an honorary fellow of the University College of Wales.

HAMISH NICOL, a Warwickshire GP, has been climbing for over 40 years in Great Britain, the Alps, Kenya and New Zealand. He advocated the admission of women to the Climbers' Club during his presidency – a victory for common sense.

PAUL NUNN PhD lectures in economic history at Sheffield. He has climbed for 30 years in the Alps, Caucasus and Baffin Island and taken part in 13 Himalayan expeditions. His book *At the Sharp End* was published in 1988. AC Vice President 1989–90.

BILL O'CONNOR, writer and photographer, has 28 Alpine seasons and 19 expeditions to the Nepal Himalaya under his harness. He currently runs his own adventure travel company and his books include *The Trekking Peaks of Nepal* and *Adventure Travel Nepal*.

T A H PEACOCKE, now 85, started climbing in 1929 with the OUMC. During the Second World War he trained Lovat Scouts as mountain troops, in Britain, in Canada, and finally in the Apennines. In 1968 he climbed Mount Cook.

SIR EDWARD PECK GCMG was in the Diplomatic Service until 1975 and climbed in the Alps, Turkey, Kulu, Borneo and E Africa. Since retirement he has trekked in Nepal and Bhutan and has climbed the Paine Grande in Patagonia by a new route.

ANDREW POLLARD is a junior children's physician in Birmingham. He made the first British ascent of Jaonli, 6632m, in 1988 and of Chamlang, 7319m, in 1991. He is deputy leader and research co-ordinator for the 1994 British Everest Medical expedition.

GRIFFITH PUGH is a medically qualified physiologist. After seven Alpine seasons, he joined Shipton's 1952 Cho Oyu expedition to investigate the use of supplementary oxygen for mountaineering and other high altitude problems. He extended this work on Everest in 1953. Honorary Member 1978.

ANDRÉ ROCH of Geneva skied and climbed in the Alps, Greenland, Himalaya, Canada and USA. For 30 years he worked at the Swiss Institute for Snow Research and is an expert on avalanche protection. He has written 13 books, hundreds of articles, and paints in his spare time. Honorary Member 1979.

ROY RUDDLE works as a software engineer and finds that third world bureaucracy is sometimes too frustrating to enjoy. His favourite high mountain area is Alaska, where it is possible to arrange everything in advance by telephone and pay by credit card. Asst Editor from 1992.

C A RUSSELL, who formerly worked with a City bank, devotes much of his time to mountaineering and related activities. He has climbed in many regions of the Alps, in the Pyrenees, East Africa, North America and the Himalaya.

MALCOLM RUTHERFORD (Rear-Admiral M G Rutherford RN CBE) is president of the Royal Navy and Royal Marines mountaineering club. He started climbing on Scottish winter classics as a Gordonstoun schoolboy, graduating to the Alps, Andes, and Himalaya, often with his wife Fleur.

DOUG SCOTT is one of the world's leading high-altitude and big-wall climbers who has pioneered new routes on many of the world's most difficult mountains. His book *Himalayan Climber*, published in 1992, is a record of a remarkable climbing career. AC Vice President 1992–93.

DAVID SHARMAN is an engineer in the oil and gas industry. He has climbed in North and South America as well as in the Alps.

DEREK A SMITHSON has spent most of his life working in the iron and steel-making industry. He has climbed or skied in the European Alps, Nova Scotia, South Africa, northern Sweden and Norway. He was president of the Yorkshire Ramblers' Club during its centenary year 1992.

A M SNODGRASS is Professor of Classical Archaeology at Cambridge and author of several books on Greek archaeology. His climbing career began in Scotland under the tuition of Edwin Kempson. After completing the 'Munros', he turned to serious Alpinism in the 1970s.

TONY STREATHER (Lt Col H R A Streather OBE) started mountaineering on Tirich Mir while serving in Pakistan. Later he climbed on K2, Haramosh, Malubiting, and Everest in 1976. When he reached the summit of Kangchenjunga in 1955 he became the first person to have climbed two 25,000ft peaks. AC President 1990–92.

GEOFFREY TEMPLEMAN, a retired chartered surveyor, has greatly enjoyed being an Assistant Editor of the AJ for the past 17 years. A love of mountain literature is coupled with excursions into the hills which are becoming less and less energetic.

WALT UNSWORTH is editorial director of Cicerone Press and former editor of *Climber* magazine. He has written numerous books on mountaineering including *Everest*, widely regarded as the definitive history of the mountain, which won the ITAS prize for mountain literature at the Trento Festival 1992.

STEPHEN VENABLES, besides enjoying several careers, all poorly paid, since leaving Oxford in 1975, has continued to ski and climb in the Alps, Andes, Africa and South Georgia. He has made 12 expeditions to the Himalaya, written three books and climbed Everest. AC Vice President 1993.

MICHAEL WARD CBE MD FRCS was Medical Officer on Everest in 1953. He is a consultant surgeon who has combined exploration in Nepal, Bhutan, Kun Lun and Tibet with high altitude research. He was made an Honorary Member of the Alpine Club in 1992.

MICHAEL WESTMACOTT was a member of the Everest team in 1953 and has since climbed in every continent except the Antarctic. On retirement from Shell International he set up the AC's Himalayan Index. Hon Secretary 1967–71, Vice-President 1977–78, AC President from 1993.

TED WHALLEY is a research chemist who works for the National Research Council of Canada. His extensive climbing experience includes many first ascents on Baffin Island and Ellesmere Island. He was President of the ACC 1980–84.

ANDREW WIELOCHOWSKI is a past instructor for the Joint Services, with first ascents in Scotland, the Alps, Himalaya, Norway and East Africa. Publications include a guidebook to East Africa, where he has climbed and explored extensively; he currently guides there.

CHARLES WYLIE was a Gurkha officer from 1939 to 1960 and Military Attaché in Kathmandu from 1961–64. He was organising secretary of the 1953 Everest expedition and was responsible for the Sherpa team. In 1957 he took part in Jimmy Roberts' expedition to Machapuchare.

NOTES FOR CONTRIBUTORS

The *Alpine Journal* records all aspects of mountains and mountaineering, including expeditions, adventure, art, literature, geography, history, geology, medicine, ethics and the mountain environment.

Articles Contributions in English are invited. Their length should not exceed 3000 words without prior approval of the Editor. **Articles should not have been published in substantially the same form by any other publication.** Authors are not paid for articles published, but they receive a complimentary copy of the issue of the *Alpine Journal* in which their article appears. Contributions should be sent to the Hon Editor, Mrs J Merz, 14 Whitefield Close, Putney, London SW15 3SS. Authors are asked to keep a copy.

Typescript Articles should be typed on A4 paper, in double spacing allowing a broad left hand margin, and on one side of the paper only. The Editor reserves the right to edit or shorten articles at her discretion.

References Details of other publications referred to in the text should be listed at the end of the article, and not as footnotes. They should include name and initials of author(s), title of book, place and date of publication, and publisher. For journal articles give author, title of article, volume number, first and last page of article, and year.

Maps These should be well researched, accurate, and finished ready for printing. They should show the most important place-names mentioned in the text. It is the authors' responsibility to get their maps redrawn if necessary. This can be arranged through the Editor, if required.

Photographs Only top quality photographs will be accepted. Prints (any size) should be black and white with glossy finish and with the author's name, in pencil, on the reverse side. Colour transparencies, in 35mm format or larger, should be originals (not copies).

Captions These should be listed on a separate sheet and should give title, author and approximate date when the photograph was taken.

Copyright It is the author's responsibility to obtain copyright clearance, to pay any fees involved, and to ensure that acknowledgements are in the form required by the copyright owner.

Summaries A brief summary should be included with all 'expedition' articles.

Biographies Authors are asked to provide a short biography, in not more than 40 words, listing the most noteworthy items in their climbing career and anything else they wish to mention.

Deadline Copy must reach the Editor by 1 January of the year of publication.

Index

1993 Vol 98